History of the
American Privateers

History of the American Privateers
The United States and the War of 1812 at Sea

George Coggeshall

History of the American Privateers
The United States and the War of 1812 at Sea
by George Coggeshall

First published under the title
History of the American Privateers

Leonaur is an imprint
of Oakpast Ltd

Copyright in this form © 2009 Oakpast Ltd

ISBN: 978-1-84677-782-0 (hardcover)
ISBN: 978-1-84677-781-3 (softcover)

http://www.leonaur.com

Publisher's Notes

In the interests of authenticity, the spellings, grammar and place names used have been retained from the original editions.

The opinions of the authors represent a view of events in which he was a participant related from his own perspective, as such the text is relevant as an historical document.

The views expressed in this book are not necessarily those of the publisher.

Contents

Preface	9
Message of the President	12
The Committee on Foreign Relations,	21
By the President of the United States of America	36
Tardy Justice	39
Introduction	40
Preparation for War	49
Captures and Prizes	80
Conflict with the English	112
A Coup de Main	141
Captain Shaler's Escape	172
Voyage to France	200
A Narrow Escape	241
Compelled to Leave the Channel	274
Great Meeting of Merchants	308
Captain Boyle's Cruise	339
Arrival at Fayal	373
Historical Facts and Reminiscences	398
Treaty of Peace	430
Appendix	441

GEORGE COGGESHALL

TO THE BRAVE AMERICANS WHO
SERVED THEIR COUNTRY IN PRIVATEERS
AND LETTERS-OF-MARQUE IN THE WAR
WITH ENGLAND, IN THE YEARS
1812, '13, AND '14.
THIS WORK IS RESPECTFULLY AND
AFFECTIONATELY DEDICATED
BY THE AUTHOR.

Preface

Although far advanced on the voyage of life, and sensible of the magnitude of the work he has undertaken, yet the author of this volume felt that his duty was unperformed while the *History of the American Privateers and Letters-of-Marque* remained unwritten.

High places in the temple of fame have been justly awarded to very many; who, in the national employment, have achieved exploits not more brilliant, displayed courage not more daring, seamanship not more masterly, coolness in danger not more remarkable than abound in the records of the private armed service.

But the brave and patriotic men who adorned that service, instead of being awarded a proud niche in that temple, have encountered neglect, and even obloquy. No testimonials of national gratitude have rewarded their blood-bought victories, and their invaluable services in crippling the resources of the common enemy. But their motives have been assailed, and cupidity and a desire for booty imputed to them as the impulses which led to their bold achievements.

It has been the object of the author to vindicate their characters, as well as to record their triumphs. If he fails to prove that their purposes were elevated and patriotic, and that they were most efficient in weakening the arm of our powerful and inveterate adversary, he has failed to do justice to his theme, and to the truth of history. He could have wished that the subject had fallen into abler hands; but he can, at least, bring to it fidelity of statement, and knowledge derived from his personal intimacy and frequent communication, both at home and abroad, with many of the commanders of privateers and letters-of-marque, during the war, and since.

He has been aided much in his collection of facts by information received from the captains and officers of the United States Navy, especially from Commodores Hull and Stewart, as well as from other intelligent gentlemen who bore an active part in the great conflict between the two nations. He has also found in many of the newspapers and other periodicals of 1812, 1813, and 1814, valuable official and statistical documents, especially in the excellent and accurate *Register of Mr. Niles*, published at Baltimore. Many of the facts recorded in these pages will also be found verified by Cooper's *History of the United States Navy*.

The author, himself, commanded, during the war, two letters-of-marque, the schooners *David Porter* and *Leo*, and at this late day, recollects almost all the important incidents of the war as distinctly as though they had occurred within the last two years.

It has been the author's aim to give the name of every privateer and letter-of-marque which sailed from our ports during the war, and he believes that he has done so, though a few may have been employed of which he finds no record.

He has also endeavoured to give the names of the commanders of each vessel, but probably has not succeeded in every instance, as the captains were sometimes changed during cruises, or were killed in action, and succeeded by others, and in many instances promoted to other vessels.

Many prizes were destroyed at sea, and many a gallant "brush" with an enemy of superior force occurred, of which no official record was made; but which, had it been in the national service, would have entitled those who conducted it to promotion and fame.

The author has also endeavoured, in his introduction, to show the justice of the war on our part, and to prove that it was waged purely in obedience to the great law of nations, as well as nature—self-defence.

England had virtually warred on our commerce for six or eight years, without our being able to obtain redress. Negotiation and remonstrance were finally exhausted, and we were compelled to resort to war as the last alternative of civilized nations.

The reader will pardon the assurance that whatever other deficiencies may be found in this volume, there has been no lack of a sincere intention to adhere to the strictest truth in its statements, and rather to incur the charge of scanty than exaggerated description of the exploits of our private armed service.

Message of the President

From the National Intelligencer Extra.

4 o'clock p.m., June 18, 1812.

The injunction of secrecy was about an hour ago removed from the following message, report or manifesto, and act.

To the Senate and House of Representatives of the United States:

I communicate to Congress certain documents, being a continuation of those heretofore laid before them, on the subject of our affairs with Great Britain.

Without going back beyond the renewal in 1803, of the war in which Great Britain is engaged, and omitting unrepaired wrongs of inferior magnitude, the conduct of her government presents a series of acts hostile to the United States as an independent and neutral nation.

British cruisers have been in the continued practice of violating the American flag on the great high way of nations, and of seizing and carrying off persons sailing under it; not in the exercise of a belligerent right, founded on the law of nations against an enemy, but of a municipal prerogative over British subjects. British jurisdiction is thus extended to neutral vessels in a situation where no laws can operate but the law of nations and the laws of the country to which the vessels belong; and a self-redress is assumed which, if British subjects were wrongfully detained and alone concerned, is that substitution force, for a resort to the responsible sovereign, which falls within the definition of war. Could the seizure of British subjects in such cases be regarded as within the exercise of a belligerent right, the acknowledged laws of war, which forbid an article of captured property to be adjudged without a regular investigation before a competent tribunal, would imperiously demand the fairest trial where the sacred rights of persons were at issue? In place of such a trial, these rights are subjected to the will of every petty commander.

The practice, hence, is so far from affecting British subjects alone, that, under the pretext of searching for these, thousands of American citizens, under the safeguard of public law, and of their national flag, have been torn from their country and from everything dear to them; have been dragged on board ships of war of a foreign nation, and exposed, under the severities of their discipline, to be exiled to the most distant and deadly climes, to risk their lives in the battles of their oppressors, and to be the melancholy instruments of taking away those of their own brethren.

Against this crying enormity, which Great Britain would be so prompt to avenge if committed against herself the United States have in vain exhausted remonstrances and expostulations. And that no proof might be wanting of their conciliatory dispositions, and no pretext left for a continuance of the practice, the British government was formally assured of the readiness of the United States to enter into arrangements, such as could not be rejected, if the recovery of British subjects were the real and sole object. The communication passed without effect.

British cruisers have been in the practice also of violating the rights and the peace of our coasts. They hover over and harass our entering and departing commerce. To the most insulting pretensions, they have added the most lawless proceedings in our very harbours; and have wantonly spilt American blood within the sanctuary of our territorial jurisdiction. The principles and rules enforced by that nation, when a neutral nation, against armed vessels of belligerents hovering near her coasts, and disturbing her commerce, are well known. When called on, nevertheless, by the United States to punish the greater offences committed by her own vessels, her government has bestowed on their commanders additional marks of honour and confidence.

Under pretended blockades, without the presence of an adequate force, and sometimes without the practicability of applying one, our commerce has been plundered in every sea; the great staples of our country have been cut off from their legitimate markets; and a destructive blow aimed at our agricultural and maritime interests. In aggravation of these predatory measures, they have been considered as in force from the dates of their notification; a retrospective effect being thus added, as has been done in other important cases, to the unlawfulness of the course pursued. And to render the outrage the more signal, these mock blockades have been reiterated and enforced in the face of official communications from the British government, declaring, as the true definition of a legal blockade "that particular ports must be actually invested, and previous warning given to vessels bound to them, not to enter."

Not content with these occasional expedients for laying waste our neutral trade, the cabinet of Great Britain resorted, at length, to the sweeping system of blockades, under the name of orders in council, which has been moulded and managed as might best suit its political views, its commercial jealousies, or the avidity of British cruisers.

To our remonstrances against the complicated and transcendent injustice of this innovation, the first reply was that the orders were reluctantly adopted by Great Britain as a necessary retaliation on decrees of her enemy proclaiming a general blockade of the British Isles, at a time when the naval force of that enemy dared not to issue from his own ports. She was reminded, without effect, that her own prior blockades, unsupported by an adequate naval force, actually applied and continued, were a bar to this plea; that executed edicts against millions of our property could not be retaliation on edicts, confessedly impossible to be executed; that retaliation, to be just, should fall on the party setting the guilty example, not on an innocent party, which was not even chargeable with an acquiescence in it.

When deprived of this flimsy veil for a prohibition of our trade with her enemy, by the repeal of his prohibition of our trade with Great Britain, her cabinet, instead of a corresponding repeal, or a practical discontinuance of its orders, formally avowed a determination to persist in them against the United States, until the markets of her enemy should be laid open to British products; thus asserting an obligation on a neutral power to require one belligerent to encourage, by its internal regulations, the trade of another belligerent; contradicting her own practice towards all nations, in peace as well as in war; and betraying the insincerity of those professions which inculcated a belief that having resorted to her orders with regret, she was anxious to find an occasion for putting an end to them.

Abandoning still more all respect for the neutral rights of the United States, and for its own consistency, the British government now demands, as pre-requisites to a repeal of its orders as they relate to the United States, that a formality should be observed in the repeal of the French decrees, nowise necessary to their termination, nor exemplified by British usage; and that the French repeal, besides including that portion of the decrees which operates within a territorial jurisdiction, as well as that which operates on the high seas against the commerce of the United States, should not be a single special repeal in relation to the United States, but should be extended to whatever other neutral nations unconnected with them, may be affected by those decrees.

And, as an additional insult, they are called on for a formal disavowal of conditions and pretensions advanced by the French government, for which the United States are so far from having made themselves responsible, that, in official explanations, which have been published to the world, and in a correspondence of the American minister at London with the British minister for foreign affairs, such a responsibility was explicitly and emphatically disclaimed.

It has become, indeed, sufficiently certain that the commerce of the United States is to be sacrificed, not as interfering with the belligerent rights of Great Britain, not as supplying the wants of her enemies, which she herself supplies, but as interfering with the monopoly which she covets for her own commerce and navigation. She carries on a war against the lawful commerce of a friend, that she may the better carry on a commerce polluted by the forgeries and perjuries which are, for the most part, the only passports by which it can succeed

Anxious to make every experiment short of the last resort of injured nations, the United States have withheld from Great Britain, under successive modifications, the benefits of a free intercourse with their market, the loss of which could not but outweigh the profits accruing from her restrictions of our commerce with other nations. And to entitle these experiments to the more favourable consideration, they were so framed as to enable her to place her adversary under the exclusive operation of them.

To these appeals her government has been equally inflexible, as if willing to make sacrifices of every sort, rather than yield to the claims of justice, or renounce the errors of a false pride. Nay, so for were the attempts carried, to overcome the attachment of the British cabinet to its unjust edicts, that it received every encouragement within the competency of the executive branch of our government, to expect that a repeal of them would be followed by a war between the United States and France, unless the French edicts should also be repealed. Even this communication, although silencing forever the plea of a disposition in the United States to acquiesce in those edicts, originally the sole plea for them, received no attention.

If no other proof existed of a predetermination of the British government against a repeal of its orders, it might be found on the correspondence of the Minister Plenipotentiary of the United States at London, and the British Secretary for Foreign Affairs in 1810, on the question whether the blockade of May, 1806, was considered as in force or as not in force. It had been ascertained that the French government, which urged this blockade as the ground of its Berlin decree, was willing, in the event of its removal, to repeal that decree; which, being followed by alternate repeals of the other offensive edicts, might abolish the whole system on both sides. This inviting opportunity for accomplishing an object so important to the United States, and professed so often to be the desire of both the belligerents, was made known to the British government.

As that government admits that an actual application of an adequate force is necessary to the existence of a legal blockade, and it was notorious, that if such a force had ever been applied, its long discontinuance had annulled the blockade in question, there could be no sufficient objection on the part of Great Britain to a formal revocation of it; and no imaginable objection, to a declaration of the fact, that the blockade did not exist. The declaration would have been consistent with her avowed principles of blockade, and would have enabled the United States to demand from France the pledged repeal of her decrees; either with success, in which case the way would have been opened for a general repeal of the belligerent edicts; or, without success, in which case the United States would have been justified in turning their measures exclusively against France.

The British government would, however, neither rescind the blockade nor declare its non-existence; nor permit its non-existence to be inferred and affirmed by the American Plenipotentiary. On the contrary, by representing the blockade to be comprehended in the orders in council, the United States were compelled so to regard it in their subsequent proceedings.

There was a period when a favourable change in the policy of the British cabinet was justly considered as established. The Minister Plenipotentiary of his Britannic Majesty here proposed an adjustment of the differences more immediately endangering the harmony of the two countries. The proposition was accepted with a promptitude and cordiality corresponding with the invariable professions of this government. A foundation appeared to be laid for a sincere and lasting reconciliation. The prospect, however, quickly vanished. The whole proceeding was disavowed by the British government without any explanations which could at that time repress the belief that the disavowal proceeded from a spirit of hostility to the commercial rights and prosperity of the United States. And it has since come into proof, that, at the very moment when the public minister was holding the language of friendship, and inspiring confidence in the sincerity of the negotiation with which he was charged, a secret agent of his government was employed in intrigues, having for their object a subversion of our government, and a dismemberment of our happy union.

In reviewing the conduct of Great Britain towards the United States our attention is necessarily drawn to the warfare just renewed by the savages on one of our extensive frontiers; a warfare which is known to spare neither age nor sex, and to be distinguished by features peculiarly shocking to humanity. It is difficult to account for the activity and combinations which have for some time been developing themselves among tribes in the constant intercourse with British traders and garrisons, without connecting their hostility with that influence; and without recollecting the authenticated examples of such interpositions heretofore furnished by the officers and agents of that government.

Such is the spectacle of injuries and indignities which have been heaped on our country: and such the crisis which its unexampled forbearance and conciliatory efforts have not been able to avert. It might at least have been expected that an enlightened nation, if less urged by moral obligations, or invited by friendly dispositions on the part of the United States would have found, in its true interest alone, a sufficient motive to respect their rights and their tranquillity on the high seas; that an enlarged policy would have favoured that free and general circulation of commerce, in which the British nation is at all times interested, and which in times of war is the best alleviation of its calamities to herself as well as the other belligerents; and more especially that the British cabinet would not, for the sake of the precarious and surreptitious intercourse with hostile markets, have persevered in a course of measures which necessarily put at hazard the invaluable market of a great and growing country, disposed to cultivate the mutual advantages of an active commerce.

Other councils have prevailed. Our moderation and conciliation have had no other effect than to encourage perseverance, and to enlarge pretensions. We behold our seafaring citizens still the daily victims of lawless violence, committed on the great common and highway of nations, even within sight of the country which owes them protection. We behold our vessels freighted with the products of our soil and industry, or returning with the honest proceeds of them, wrested from their lawful destinations, confiscated by prize courts, no longer the organs of public law, but the instruments of arbitrary edicts; and their unfortunate crews dispersed and lost, or forced or inveigled, in British ports, into British fleets: whilst arguments are employed in support of these aggressions, which have no foundation but in a principle equally supporting a claim to regulate our external commerce in all cases whatsoever.

We behold, in fine, on the side of Great Britain a state of war against the United States; and on the side of the United States a state of peace towards Great Britain.

Whether the United States shall continue passive under these progressive usurpations, and these accumulating wrongs; or, opposing force to force in defence of their natural rights, shall commit a just cause into the hands of the Almighty Disposer of events, avoiding all connections which might entangle it in the contests or views of other powers, and preserving a constant readiness to concur in an honourable re-establishment of peace and friendship, is a solemn question, which the constitution wisely confides to the legislative department of the government. In recommending it to their early deliberations, I am happy in the assurance that the decision will be worthy the enlightened and patriotic councils of a virtuous, a free, and a powerful nation.

Having presented this view of the relations of the United States with Great Britain and of the solemn alternative growing out of them, I proceed to remark that the communications last made to Congress on the subject of our relations with France will have shown that since the revocation of her decrees as they violated the neutral rights of the United States, her government has authorized illegal captures, by its privateers and public ships, and that other outrages have been practised on our vessels and our citizens. It will have been seen also, that no indemnity had been provided, or satisfactorily pledged for the extensive spoliations committed under the violent and retrospective orders of the French government against the property of our citizens seized within the jurisdiction of France. I abstain at this time from recommending to the consideration of Congress definitive measures with respect to that nation, in the expectation that the result of unclosed discussions between our minister plenipotentiary at Paris and the French government, will speedily enable Congress to decide, with greater advantage, on the course due to the rights, the interests, and the honour of our country.

    Washington June 1, 1812.   James Madison.

The Committee on Foreign Relations,

To whom was referred the message of the President of the United States, of the 1st of June, 1812.

Report—

That after the experience which the United States have had of the great injustice of the British government towards them, exemplified by so many acts of violence and oppression, it will be more difficult to justify to the impartial world their patient forbearance, than the measures to which it has become necessary to resort, to avenge the wrongs, and vindicate the rights and honour of the nation. Your committee are happy to observe, on a dispassionate view of the conduct of the United States, that they see in it no cause for censure.

If a long forbearance under injuries ought ever to be considered a virtue in any nation, it is one which peculiarly becomes the United States. No people ever had stronger motives to cherish peace: none have ever cherished it with greater sincerity and zeal.

But the period has now arrived, when the United States must support their character and station among the nations of the earth, or submit to the most shameful degradation. Forbearance has ceased to be a virtue. War on the one side, and peace on the other, is a situation as ruinous as it is disgraceful. The mad ambition, the lust of power, and commercial avarice of Great Britain, arrogating to herself the complete dominion of the ocean, and exercising over it an unbounded and lawless tyranny, have left to neutral nations an alternative only, between the bare surrender of their rights, and a manly vindication of them. Happily for the United States, their destiny, under the aid of Heaven, is in their own hands. The crisis is formidable only by their love of peace. As soon as it becomes a duty to relinquish that situation, danger disappears. They have suffered no wrongs, they have received no insults, however great, for which they cannot obtain redress.

More than seven years have elapsed, since the commencement of this system of hostile aggression by the British Government, on the rights and interests of the United States. The manner of its commencement was not less hostile, than the spirit with which it has been prosecuted. The United States have invariably done everything in their power to preserve the relations of friendship with Great Britain. Of this disposition they gave a distinguished proof, at the moment when they were made the victims of an opposite policy.

The wrongs of the last war had not been forgotten at the commencement of the present one. They warned us of dangers, against which it was sought to provide. As early as the year 1804, the Minister of the United States at London was instructed to invite the British government to enter into a negotiation on all the points on which a collision might arise between the two countries, in the course of the war, and to propose to it an arrangement of their claims on fair and reasonable conditions. The invitation was accepted. A negotiation had commenced and was depending, and nothing had occurred to excite a doubt that it would not terminate to the satisfaction of both the parties. It was at this time, and under these circumstances, that an attack was made, by surprise, on an important branch of the American commerce, which affected every part of the United States, and involved many of their citizens in ruin.

The commerce, on which this attack was so unexpectedly made, was between the United States and the colonies of France, Spain, and other enemies of Great Britain. A commerce just in itself; sanctioned by the example of Great Britain in regard to the trade with her own colonies; sanctioned by a solemn act between the two governments in the last war; and sanctioned by the practice of the British government in the present war, more than two years having elapsed, without any interference with it.

The injustice of this attack could only be equalled by the absurdity of the pretext alleged for it. It was pretended by the British government, that in case of war, her enemy had no right to modify its colonial regulations, so as to mitigate the calamities of war to the inhabitants of its colonies. This pretension peculiar to Great Britain, is utterly incompatible with the rights of the sovereignty in every independent State. If we recur to the well-established and universally admitted law of nations, we shall find no sanction to it, in that venerable code. The sovereignty of every State is co-extensive with its dominions, and cannot be abrogated, or curtailed in rights, as to any part, except by conquest.

Neutral nations have a right to trade to every port of either belligerent, which is not legally blockaded; and in all articles which are not contraband of war. Such is the absurdity of this pretension, that your committee are aware, especially after the able manner in which it has been heretofore refuted, and exposed, that they would offer an insult to the understanding of the house, if they enlarged on it, and if anything could add to the high sense of the injustice of the British government in the transaction, it would be the contrast which her conduct exhibits in regard to this trade, and in regard to a similar trade by neutrals with her own colonies.

It is known to the world that Great Britain regulates her own trade in war and in peace, at home and in her colonies, as she finds for her interest—that in war she relaxes the restraints of her colonial system in favour of the colonies, and that it never was suggested that she had not a right to do it; or that a neutral in taking advantage of the relaxation violated a belligerent right of her enemy. But with Great Britain everything is lawful. It is only in a trade with her enemies that the United States can do wrong. With them all trade is unlawful.

In the year 1798, an attack was made by the British government on the same branch of our neutral trade, which had nearly involved the two countries in a war. That difference, however, was amicably accommodated. The pretension was withdrawn and reparation made to the United States for the losses which they had suffered by it. It was fair to infer from that arrangement that the commerce was deemed by the British Government lawful, and that it would not be again disturbed.

Had the British government been resolved to contest this trade with neutrals, it was due to the character of the British nation that the decision should be made known to the government of the United States. The existence of a negotiation which had been invited by our government, for the purpose of preventing differences by an amicable arrangement of their respective pretensions, gave a strong claim to the notification, while it afforded the fairest opportunity for it. But a very different policy animated the then Cabinet of England.

The liberal confidence and friendly overtures of the United States were taken advantage of to ensnare them. Steady to its purpose and inflexibly hostile to this country, the British government calmly looked forward to the moment, when it might give the most deadly wound to our interests. A trade just in itself, which was secured by so many strong and sacred pledges, was considered safe. Our citizens, with their usual industry and enterprise had embarked in it a vast proportion of their shipping, and of their capital, which were at sea, under no other protection than the law of nations, and the confidence which they reposed in the justice and friendship of the British nation.

At this period the unexpected blow was given. Many of the vessels were seized, carried into port, and condemned by a tribunal, which, while it professes to respect the law of nations, obeyed the mandates of its own government. Hundreds of other vessels were driven from the ocean and the trade itself in a great measure suppressed. The effect produced by this attack on the lawful commerce of the United States was such as might have been expected from a virtuous, independent and highly injured people. But one sentiment pervaded the whole American nation. No local interests were regarded; no sordid motives felt. Without looking to the parts which suffered most, the invasion of our rights was considered a common cause, and from one extremity of our Union to the other, was heard the voice of an united people, calling on their government to avenge their wrongs, and vindicate the rights and honour of their country.

From this period, the British government has gone on in a continued encroachment on the rights and interests of the United States, disregarding in its course, in many instances, obligations which have heretofore been held sacred by civilized nations.

In May, 1806, the whole coast of the Continent, from the Elbe to Brest inclusive, was declared to be in a state of blockade. By this act, the well-established principles of the law of nations, principles which have served for ages as guides, and affixed the boundary between the rights to belligerents and neutrals, were violated: By the law of nations, as recognized by Great Britain herself no blockade is lawful, unless it be sustained by the application of an adequate force, and that an adequate force was applied to this blockade, in its full extent, ought not to be pretended.

Whether Great Britain was able to maintain, legally, so extensive a blockade, considering the war in which she is engaged, requiring such extensive naval operations, is a question which it is not necessary at this time to examine. It is sufficient to be known, that such force was not applied, and this is evident from the terms of the blockade itself, by which, comparatively, an inconsiderable portion of the coast only was declared to be in a state of strict and rigorous blockade. The objection to the measure is not diminished by that circumstance. If the force was not applied, the blockade was unlawful, from whatever cause the failure might proceed.

The belligerent who institutes the blockade cannot absolve itself from the obligation to apply the force under any pretext whatever. For a belligerent to relax a blockade, which it could not maintain, it would be a refinement in injustice, not less insulting to the understanding than repugnant to the law of nations. To claim merit for the mitigation of an evil, which the party either had not the power or found it inconvenient to inflict, would be a new mode of encroaching on neutral rights. Your committee think it just to remark that this act of the British Government does not appear to have been adopted in the sense in which it has been since construed. On consideration of all the circumstances attending the measure, and particularly the character of the distinguished statesman who announced it, we are persuaded that it was conceived in a spirit of conciliation and intended to lead to an accommodation of all differences between the United States and Great Britain. His death disappointed that hope, and the act has since become subservient to other purposes. It has been made by his successors a pretext for that vast system of usurpation, which has so long oppressed and harassed our commerce.

The next act of the British government which claims our attention is the order of council of January 7, 1807, by which neutral powers are prohibited trading from one port to another of France or her allies, or any other country with which Great Britain might not freely trade. By this order the pretension of England, heretofore claimed by every other power, to prohibit neutrals disposing of parts of their cargoes at different ports of the same enemy, is revived and with vast accumulation of injury. Every enemy, however great the number or distant from each other, is considered one, and the like trade even with powers at peace with England, who from motives of policy had excluded or restrained her commerce, was also prohibited.

In this act the British government evidently disclaimed all regard for neutral rights. Aware that the measures authorized by it could find no pretext in any belligerent right, none was urged. To prohibit the sale of our produce, consisting of innocent articles at any port of a belligerent, not blockaded, to consider every belligerent as one, and subject neutrals to the same restraints with all, as if there was but one, were bold encroachments. But to restrain or in any manner interfere with our commerce with neutral nations with whom Great Britain was at peace, and against whom she had no justifiable cause of war, for the sole reason, that they restrained or excluded from their ports her commerce, was utterly incompatible with the pacific relations subsisting between the two countries.

We proceed to bring into view the British order in Council of November 11th, 1807, which superseded every other order, and consummated that system of hostility on the commerce of the United States which has been since so steadily pursued. By this order all France and her allies and every other country at war with Great Britain, or with which she was not at war, from which the British flag was excluded and all the colonies of her enemies, were subjected to the same restrictions as if they were actually blockaded in the most strict and rigorous manner, and all trade in articles the produce and manufacture of the said countries and colonies and the vessels engaged in it were subjected to capture and condemnation as lawful prize.

To this order certain exceptions were made which we forbear to notice, because they were not adopted from a regard to neutral rights, but were dictated by policy to promote the commerce of England, and so far as they related to neutral powers, were said to emanate from the clemency of the British Government

It would be superfluous in your committee to state, that by this order the British government declared direct and positive war against the United States. The dominion of the ocean was completely usurped by it, all commerce forbidden, and every flag driven from it, or subjected to capture and condemnation, which did not subserve the policy of the British government by paying it a tribute, and sailing under its sanction. From this period the United States have incurred the heaviest losses and most mortifying humiliations. They have borne the calamities of war without retorting them on its authors.

So fix your committee has presented to the view of the house the aggressions which have been committed under the authority of the British government on the commerce of the United States. We will now proceed to other wrongs which have been still more severely felt. Among these is the impressment of our seamen, a practice which has been unceasingly maintained by Great Britain in the wars to which she has been a party since our revolution. Your committee cannot convey in adequate terms the deep sense which they entertain of the injustice and oppression of this proceeding.

Under the pretext of impressing British seamen, our fellow-citizens are seized in British ports, on the high seas, and in every other quarter to which the British power extends, are taken on board British men-of-war and compelled to serve there as British subjects. In this mode our citizens are wantonly snatched from their country and their families, deprived of their liberty, and doomed to an ignominious and slavish bondage, compelled to fight the battles of a foreign country, and often to perish in them. Our flag has given them no protection; it has been unceasingly violated, and our vessels exposed to danger by the loss of the men taken from them.

If our committee need not remark that while the practice is continued, it is impossible for the United States to consider themselves an independent nation. Every new case is a new proof of their degradation. Its continuance is the more unjustifiable because the United States have repeatedly proposed to the British government an arrangement which would secure to it the control of its own people. An exemption of the citizens of the United States from this degrading oppression, and their flag from violation, is all that they have sought

The lawless waste of our trade, and equally unlawful impressment of our seamen, have been much aggravated by the insults and indignities attending them. Under the pretext of blockading the ports and harbours of France and her allies, British squadrons have been stationed on our own coast, to watch and annoy our own trade. To give effect to the blockade of European ports, the ports and harbours of the United States have been blockaded. In executing these orders of the British government, or in obeying the spirit which was known to animate it the commanders of these squadrons have encroached on our jurisdiction, seized our vessels, and carried into effect impressments within our limits, and done other acts of great injustice, violence and oppression. The United States have seen with mingled indignation and surprise, that these acts, instead of procuring to the perpetrators the punishment due to their crimes, have not failed to recommend them to the favour of their government

Whether the British government has contributed by active measures to excite against us the hostility of the savage tribes on our frontiers, your committee are not disposed to occupy much time in investigating. Certain indications of general notoriety may supply the place of authentic documents; though these have not been wanting to establish the fact in some instances. It is known that symptoms of British hostility towards the United States, have never failed to produce corresponding symptoms among those tribes. It is also well known that on all such occasions, abundant supplies of the ordinary munitions of war have been afforded by the agents of British commercial companies, and even from British garrisons, wherewith they were enabled to commence that system of savage warfare on our frontiers, which has been at all times indiscriminate in its effects on all ages, sexes and conditions, and so revolting to humanity.

Your committee would be much gratified if they could close here the details of British wrongs; but it is their duty to recite another act of still greater malignity, than any of those which have been already brought to your view. The attempt to dismember our union, and overthrow our excellent constitution, by a secret mission, the object of which was to foment discontents, and excite insurrection against- the constituted authorities and laws of the nation, as lately disclosed by the agent employed in it, affords full proof that there is no bound to the hostility of the British government towards the United States; no act, however unjustifiable, which it would not commit to accomplish their ruin.

This attempt excites the greater horror from the consideration that it was made while the United States and Great Britain were at peace, and an amicable negotiation was depending between them for the accommodation of their differences through public ministers regularly authorized for the purpose.

The United States have beheld, with unexampled forbearance, this continued series of hostile encroachments on their rights and interests, in the hope that, yielding to the force of friendly remonstrances, often repeated, the British government might adopt a more just policy towards them; but that hope no longer exists. They have also weighed impartially the reasons which have been urged by the British government in vindication of these encroachments, and found in them neither justification or apology.

The British government has alleged, in vindication of the orders in council that they were resorted to as a retaliation on France, for similar aggressions committed by her on our neutral trade with the British dominions. But how has this plea been supported? The dates of British and French aggressions are well known to the world. Their origin and progress have been marked with too wide and destructive a waste of the property of our fellow-citizens, to have been forgotten. The decree of Berlin of Nov. 21st, 1806, was the first aggression of France in the present war. Eighteen months had then elapsed, after the attack made by Great Britain on our neutral trade with the colonies of France and her allies, and six months from the date of the proclamation of May, 1806.

Even on the 7th of January, 1807, the date of the first British order in council, so short a term had elapsed, after the Berlin decree, that it was hardly possible that the intelligence of it should, have reached the United States. A retaliation, which is to produce its effect by operating on a neutral power, ought not to be resorted to, till the neutral had justified it by a culpable acquiescence in the unlawful act of the other belligerent. It ought to be delayed until after sufficient time had been allowed to the neutral to remonstrate against the measure complained of, to receive an answer, and to act on it, which had not been done in the present instance; and when the order of November 11th was issued, it is well known that a minister of France had declared to the Minister Plenipotentiary of the United States at Paris, that it was not intended that the decree of Berlin should apply to the United States. It is equally well known, that no American vessel had then been condemned under it, or seizure been made, with which the British government was acquainted.

The facts prove incontestably, that the measures of France, however unjustifiable in themselves, were nothing more than a pretext for those of England. And of the insufficiency of that pretext, ample proof has already been afforded by the British government itself, and in the most impressive form. Although it was declared that the orders in council were retaliatory on France for her decrees, it was also declared, and in the orders themselves, that owing to the superiority of the British navy, by which the fleets of France and her allies were confined within their own ports, the French decrees were considered only as empty threats It is no justification of the wrongs of one power, that the like were committed by another; nor ought the fact, if true, to have been urged by either, as it could afford no proof of its love of justice, of its magnanimity, or even of its courage.

It is more worthy the government of a great nation to relieve than to assail the injured. Nor can a repetition of the wrongs by another power repair the violated rights, or wounded honour, of the injured party. An utter inability alone to resist, would justify a quiet surrender of our rights, and degrading submission to the will of others. To that condition the United States are not reduced, nor do they fear it. That they ever consented to discuss with either power the misconduct of the other, is a proof of their love of peace, of their moderation, and of the hope which they still indulged, that friendly appeals to just and generous sentiment, would not be made to them in vain. But the motive was mistaken, if their forbearance was imputed, either to the want of a just sensibility to their wrongs, or of a determination, if suitable redress was not obtained, to resent them.

The time has now arrived when this system of reasoning

must cease. It would be insulting to repeat it. It would be degrading to hear it The United States must act as an independent nation, and assert their rights and avenge their wrongs, according to their own estimate of them, with the party who commits them, holding it responsible for its own misdeeds, unmitigated by those of another.

For the difference made between Great Britain and France, by the application of the non-importation act against England only, the motive has been already too often explained, and is too well known to require further illustration. In the commercial restrictions to which the United States resorted as an evidence of their sensibility, and a mild retaliation of their wrongs, they invariably placed both powers on the same footing, holding to each in respect to itself, the same accommodation, in case it accepted the condition offered, and in respect to the other, the same restraint, if it refused.

Had the British government confirmed the arrangement, which was entered into with the British Minister in 1809, and France maintained her decrees, with France would the United States have had to resist, with the firmness belonging to their character, the continued violation of their rights? The committee do not hesitate to declare, that France has greatly injured the United States, and that satisfactory reparation has not yet been made for many of those injuries. But that is a concern which the United States will look to and settle for themselves. The high character of the American people is a sufficient pledge to the world that they will not fail to settle it, on conditions which they have a right to claim.

More recently, the true policy of the British government towards the United States has been completely unfolded. It has been publicly declared by those in power, that the orders in council should not be repealed, until the French government had revoked all its internal restraints on the British commerce, and that the trade of the United States with France and her allies, should be prohibited until Great Britain was also allowed to trade with them. By this declaration, it appears, that to satisfy the pretensions of the British government, the United States must join Great Britain in the war with France, and prosecute the war, until France should be subdued, for without her subjugation, it were in vain to presume on such a concession.

The hostility of the British government to these states has been still further disclosed. It has been made manifest that the United States are considered by it as the commercial rival of Great Britain, and that their prosperity and growth are incompatible with her welfare. When all these circumstances are taken into consideration, it is impossible for your committee to doubt the motives which have governed the British ministry in all its measures towards the United States since the year 1805. Equally is it impossible to doubt, longer, the course which the United States ought to pursue towards Great Britain.

From this view of the multiplied wrongs of the British government, since the commencement of the present war, it must be evident to the impartial world, that the contest which is now forced on the United States is radically a contest for their sovereignty and independence. Your committee will not enlarge on any of the injuries, however great, which have had a transitory effect. They wish to call the attention of the House to those of a parliamentary nature only, which entrench so deeply on our most important rights, and wound so extensively and vitally our best interests, as could not fail to deprive the United States of the principal advantages of their revolution, if submitted to.

The control of our commerce by Great Britain, in regulating at pleasure, and expelling it almost from the ocean; the oppressive manner in which these regulations have been carried into effect by seizing and confiscating such of our vessels, with their cargoes, as were said to have violated her edicts, often without previous warning of their danger; the impressment of our citizens from on board our own vessels, on the high seas, and elsewhere, and holding them in bondage until it suited the convenience of these oppressors to deliver them up, are encroachments of that high and dangerous tendency which could not fail to produce that pernicious effect, nor would those be the only consequences that would result from it. The British government might for a while be satisfied with the ascendency thus gained over us, but its pretensions would soon increase. The proof, which so complete and disgraceful a submission to its authority would afford of our degeneracy, could not fail to inspire confidence, that there was no limit to which its usurpations and our degradations might not be carried.

Your committee, believing that the freeborn sons of America are worthy to enjoy the liberty which their fathers purchased at the price of much blood and treasure, and seeing in the measures adopted by Great Britain, a course commenced and persisted in which might lead to a loss of national character and independence, feel no hesitation in advising resistance by force, in which the Americans of the present day will prove to the enemy and to the world, that we have not only inherited that liberty which our fathers gave us, but also the will and power to maintain it Relying on the patriotism of the nation, and confidently trusting that the Lord of Hosts will go with us to battle in a righteous cause, and crown our efforts with success—your committee recommend an immediate appeal to arms!

John C. Calhoun, Chairman.

Committee: Porter,	Harper,
Grundy,	Rey,
Smilie,	Desha,
Randolph,	Saver,

An Act declaring war between the United Kingdom of Great Britain and Ireland, and the Dependencies thereof and the United States of America, and their Territories.

Be it enacted by the Senate and House of Representatives of the United States of America, in Congress assembled. That war be, and the same is hereby declared to exist between the United Kingdom of Great Britain and Ireland, and the dependencies thereof, and the United States of America and their territories; and that the President of the United States be, and he is hereby authorized to use the whole land and naval force of the United

States, to carry the same into effect, and to issue to private-armed vessels of the United States commissions, or letters-of-marque, and general reprisals, in such form as he shall think proper, and under the seal of the United States, against the vessels, goods and effects of the government of the same United Kingdom of Great Britain and Ireland, and of the subjects thereof.

    Approved,   James Madison.
    June 18th, 1812.

On the final passage of the act in the Senate, the vote was 19 to 13: in the House, 79 to 49.

By the President of the United States of America

A Proclamation.

Whereas the Congress of the United States, by virtue of the constituted authority vested in them, have declared by their act, bearing date the 18th day of the present month, that war exists between the United kingdom of Great Britain and Ireland, and the dependencies thereof and the United States of America and their territories: Now therefore, I, James Madison, President of the United States of America, do hereby proclaim the same to all whom it may concern: and I do specially enjoin on all persons holding offices, civil or military, under the authority of the United States, that they be vigilant and zealous, in discharging the duties respectively incident thereto.

And I do moreover exhort all the good people of the United States, as they love their country; as they value the precious heritage derived from the virtue and valour of their fathers; as they feel the wrongs which have forced on them the last resort of injured nations; and as they consult the best means, under the blessing of Divine Providence, of abridging its calamities; that they exert themselves in preserving order, in promoting concord, and in maintaining the authority and the efficacy of the laws, and in supporting and invigorating all the measures which may be adopted by the constituted authorities, for obtaining a speedy, a just, and an honourable peace.

{SEAL.}

In testimony whereof I have hereunto set my hand and caused the seal of the United States to be affixed to these presents.

Done at the City of Washington, the nineteenth day of June, one thousand eight hundred and twelve, and of the Independence of the United States the thirty-sixth.

(Signed)
>By the President,
>>James Madison.

(Signed)
>>James Monroe,
>>>Secretary of State.

I insert here the following letter of the venerable patriot John Adams, former President of the United States, to his friend Elkenah Watson, Esq., of Pittsfield, and think his opinion of the war is deserving the respectful consideration of every dispassionate American.

>"Quincy, July 6th, 1812.

"Dear Sir,—I have received the favour of your letter of the 28th of last month, which has revived the recollection of our former acquaintance in France, England and Holland, as well as in several parts of our own country. I think with you. that it is the duty of every considerate man to support the national authorities, in whose hands so-ever they may be; though I will not say whatever their measures may be.

"To your allusion to the war, I have nothing to say but that it was with surprise that I hear it pronounced, not only by newspapers, but by persons in authority, ecclesiastical and civil, and political and military, that it is an unjust and unnecessary war, that the declaration of it was altogether unexpected, etc.

"How it is possible that a rational, a social, or a moral creature can say that the war is unjust, is to me utterly incomprehensible.

"How it can be said to be unnecessary is very mysterious. I have thought it both just and necessary, for five or six years.

"How it can be said to be unexpected is another wonder; I

have expected it for more than five and twenty years, and have had great reason to be thankful that it has been postponed so long. I saw such a spirit in the British Islands, when I resided in France, in Holland, and in England itself that I expected another war much sooner than it has happened. I was so impressed with the idea, that I expressed to Lord Lansdowne (formerly Lord Shelburne), an apprehension that his lordship would live long enough to be obliged to make, and that I should live long enough to see another peace made between Great Britain and the United States of America. His lordship did not live long enough to make the peace, and I shall not probably live to see it; but I have lived to see the war that must be followed by a peace, if the war is not eternal.

"Our Agricultural Societies may not be so much regarded, but the great interest of agriculture will not be diminished by the war. Manufactures will be promoted.

"The Minister of St. Petersburg will be informed of your opinion of the utility of some bushels of Siberian wheat, not kiln dried.

"Yours truly,

"John Adams."

Tardy Justice

Extract from the *Boston Chronicle*.

"The American seamen who were taken from the frigate *Chesapeake*, on the 22nd June, 1807, by the British ship-of-war *Leopard*, were this day, Saturday, June 13, 1812, restored to the same ship in the harbour of Boston.

"They were conducted on board by Lieutenant Simpson, a British officer, and received at the gang-way by Lieutenant Wilkinson, of the *Chesapeake*, who made the following pertinent address:

"Sir,—I am commanded by Commodore Bainbridge to receive these two American seamen, on the very deck from which they were wantonly taken in time of peace, by a vessel of your nation, of superior force.' Midshipman Saunders conducted the men to Commodore Bainbridge, upon the quarter-deck—the Commodore received them with these appropriate and truly American observations.'My lads I am glad to see you—from this deck you were taken by British outrage—for your return to it you owe gratitude to the government of your country. Your country now offers you an opportunity to revenge your wrongs; and I cannot doubt but that you will be desirous of doing so on board of this very ship. I trust the flag that flies on board of her, shall gloriously defend you in future.' Three cheers were given by a numerous company of citizens and seamen, assembled to witness the interesting transaction.

"There were four men taken out of the *Chesapeake*; one, they tell us, has since died two they now restore, and one they hung at Halifax."

Introduction

I commence my plea, soliciting public approbation in favour of privateersmen, and for those who served in private armed vessels in the war of 1812, 1813, and 1814. And in order to show the state of public opinion at that period, I will here insert an article, written by Mr. Jefferson, dated July the 4th, 1812:

"What is war? It is simply a contest between nations, of trying which can do the other the most harm. Who carries on the war? Armies are formed and navies manned by individuals. How is a battle gained? By the death of individuals. What produces peace? The distress of individuals. What difference to the sufferer is it that his property is taken by a national or private armed vessel? Did our merchants, who have lost nine hundred and seventeen vessels by British captures, feel any gratification that the most of them were taken by His Majesty's men-of-war?

"Were the spoils less rigidly exacted by a seventy-four gun ship than by a privateer of four guns; and were not all equally condemned? War, whether on land or sea, is constituted of acts of violence on the persons and property of individuals; and excess of violence is the grand cause that brings about a peace. One man fights for wages paid him by the government, or a patriotic zeal for the defence of his country; another, duly authorized, and giving the proper pledges for his good conduct, undertakes to pay himself at the expense of the foe, and serve his country as effectually as the former, and government drawing all its supplies from the people, is, in reality, as much affected by the losses of the one as the other, the efficacy of its measures depending upon the energies and resources of the whole. In the United States, every possible encouragement should be given to privateering in time of war with a commercial nation.

"We have tens of thousands of seamen that without it would be destitute of the means of support, and useless to their country. Our national ships are too few in number to give employment to a twentieth part of them, or retaliate the acts of the enemy. But by licensing private armed vessels, the whole naval force of the nation is truly brought to bear on the foe, and while the contest lasts, that it may have the speedier termination, let every individual contribute his mite, in the best way he can, to distress and harass the enemy, and compel him to peace."

To arrive at the odium entertained against privateering by the honest and virtuous part of the world, I must carry my readers back to the piratical age of the reckless buccaneers, which continued for a period of twenty or thirty years, say from 1610 to 1640.

Although these piratical vessels occasionally infested almost every sea, their principal resorts were along the coast of the Spanish Main, and among the West India Islands.

These desperate buccaneers committed all sorts of barbarous acts, and were, in fact, a terror to the commercial portion of all civilized nations. They spared neither friend nor foe, and were alike regardless of age or sex.

Their only object was robbery and plunder, and by these means to enrich themselves, at the expense of the honest and industrious portion of mankind. These ruthless bravadoes, by the habitual practice of rapine and murder, became so hardened in sin and crime that they seemed to riot and rejoice over the sufferings of their innocent victims.

No wonder, then, that a strong and deep feeling of enmity should still continue to be felt against privateering for centuries after it was abolished. In Europe, where a large portion of every community is uneducated, it requires many long years to eradicate a deep-rooted prejudice from among the masses, long after the enlightened classes are convinced that such transactions are no longer in existence. Even in our own intelligent country, there exists a strong prejudice against privateering, from the same cause as before stated, namely, by associating it with the bygone days of the reckless buccaneers. It is to be hoped, however, that our late war with England has created a more favourable feeling on this subject, and that a more liberal sentiment will be cherished towards privateersmen, and to those who were employed in private armed vessels. The American people must be convinced that, in our last war with England, it was carried on by privateers and private armed vessels in a spirit of honourable warfare, and generally by gentlemen of high and patriotic sentiments, and in most instances with marked humanity, coupled with acts of generosity and kindness toward their avowed enemy, and, as I believe, with a sincere desire to soften the rugged features of war.

It is true that every honourable device was practised to cripple our enemy, by diminishing his means and power to injure us, and thus compel him to an honourable peace.

It must always be borne in mind that the war on our part was strictly confined to the injury of Great Britain, and that in no instance was a single neutral nation involved in loss or insult by our privateers.

In this age of traffic and moneymaking, when patriotism is measured by dollars and cents, remarks prejudicial to those who sailed in privateers and letters-of-marque are made by some, without much reflection or knowledge on the subject. Others assert that they were a mercenary set of *desperadoes*, only bent on enriching themselves with the spoils of their adversaries, possessing little honour, and less patriotism. Now if there be a single respectable individual possessed of this opinion, I shall be happy to disabuse his mind on the subject, for I can assure him, that there never was a viler slander imputed to such a noble class of men.

I am happy to say I was personally acquainted with scores of the captains and officers, who sailed in privateers and letters-of-marque, during our war with England, and am confident, that a large proportion of those who commanded these vessels, as well as their officers and seamen, would favourably compare with the same class of military men in any army or navy in the world.

The following captains of privateers and letters-of-marque I knew personally, both at home and abroad, and some of them I was proud to acknowledge as intimate friends:

I cannot at this moment, call to mind many other captains of privateers and letters-of-marque, who figured conspicuously in the trying conflict for the liberty of the seas.

All the persons here enumerated were captains in the merchant service, and were consequently thrown out of employment by the war, and obliged to command these vessels, or remain inactive spectators on shore. They, no doubt, like most other men, had a double motive in the contest, *viz.*, to be remunerated for their privations, and to serve their country in distressing the enemy, who strove to drive them off the ocean.

Vessels.	Captains.	Where belonging.
Saratoga,	Wooster, afterward Guy R. Champlin,	New York.
Rossie,	Commodore Barney,	Baltimore.
Midas,	Chayter,	Baltimore.
General Armstrong,	Sam. C. Reid,	New York.
Brig Ida,	Jeremiah Mantor,	Boston.
Rattlesnake,	David Maffet,	Philadelphia.
Globe,	John Murphy,	Baltimore.
Scourge,	Samuel Nicoll,	New York.
Dolphin,	W. S. Stafford,	Baltimore.
American,	Richardson,	Baltimore.
Jack's Favorite,	Miller,	New York.
Benj. Franklin,	Ingersol.	New York.

Can any man of common sense, imagine that these worthy men would risk their lives and reputation, for a mere mercenary hire, without an ardent love of their country, and a desire to revenge themselves upon the tyrants of the seas, who had insulted and abused the most of them for many years? On the contrary, they were, with hardly an exception, a dashing, brave set of disinterested men, and an honour to their country. Many of their well-fought battles and hair-breadth escapes will favourably compare with our most brilliant naval engagements.

Contrast the relative inducements of the officers of the United States Navy and of the captains of private-armed ships and vessels. The former are cherished and supported by the whole nation; have fame and honour meted out for every meritorious act. If wounded, they receive pensions, and are provided for in sickness and old age. Now look at the other side of the picture: What had the captains and officers of privateers and letters-of-marque to expect from their country? Nothing; and from the enemy, nothing but hard knocks, prison-ships, and free lodgings in Dartmoor.

Notwithstanding the disadvantages here enumerated, we have often seen them engaging the enemy's ships-of-war, where they had nothing to hope for but revenge for past injuries, or for the honour of the flag under which they sailed, and their ardent attachment to their beloved country. In many instances we have known their prospects of a cruise broken up and ruined because they would not fly from their haughty foe until they had inflicted a severe punishment on his boasted superiority. It is well known to those Americans who lived through the war of 1812, and to all the reading portion of our extensive country, that the privateers and letters-of-marque were the great thorn in the side of our inveterate enemy, that they harassed and annoyed their adversaries in every quarter of the globe, yes, and even at the entrance of their own ports, in old England itself.

They fought and captured ships and vessels off the North Cape, in the British and Irish Channels, on the coasts of Spain and Portugal, in the East and West Indies, off the Capes of Good

Hope and Horn, and in the Pacific Ocean. In a word, they were harassing and annoying British trade and commerce wherever a ship could float, Yes, they took and destroyed millions of property, and were, beyond all doubt, the happy instruments under God, in bringing about a permanent peace with a proud, haughty, overbearing nation. And now is it not astonishing how soon the services of these brave and gallant men are forgotten, and how lightly their heroic acts are appreciated by our general government?

While Congress has given thousands and tens of thousands of broad acres to all those individuals who fought, or were mustered into service in all our wars since 1790, as a reward for their services to their country, not one foot of land, or any other compensation has been given to privateersmen, and those who served in private armed vessels in the war of 1812, or to their widows and orphan children.

No wonder that the present generation does not appreciate their services, or cherish their memory when the Congress of the United States neglects to notice their claims on the nation.

I complain not at what the government has given to all those who have served in any war for their country's honour or interest, but I do complain of the gross and palpable injustice of the government of the United States towards those brave men, and their widows and orphan children. Many of the privateersmen, and those who served in letters-of-marque, suffered severely in their private fortunes, many were killed and wounded, and not a few were confined in filthy English prisons.

And, what is the reply to all their petitions? Why forsooth, these men were engaged in cruising for prize-money and not for the interest of the country. That assertion is not true; on the contrary, it is a base slander upon the good name and fame of these worthy and gallant defenders of their country's rights and of its honour and glory. "Tell it not in Gath; publish it not in the streets of Askelon." The writer of these pages asks nothing for himself, for, thank God, he has, through his industry, prudence, and economy, sufficient to live on in a modest, unpretending way, and wishes it to be clearly understood, that this appeal is in behalf of the few remaining individuals who have survived the war, the tempest, and the storm, and who are now tottering on the brink of the grave. Yes, it is for them and their widows and orphan children that I make this strong and last appeal to the Government of the United States, to do justice to these much injured men and their families.

When the peace was made with England, the officers of the navy used to say among themselves, that they were looked upon by the people as pillars in war, but as caterpillars in peace. If such was the case with them, with what redoubled force will it apply to the captains of privateers.

I deem it unnecessary at present to add any more on the subject of the unrequited claims of privateers-men and those who served in private-armed vessels, but hope and trust that the Congress of the United States will, ere long, reflect that it is unwise and unjust to exclude those worthy and deserving patriots from an equal participation in the public bounty, which has been so liberally bestowed upon all other classes of citizens, who have served their country in any of its wars during the last sixty-five years.

With these closing remarks, I will now proceed to enumerate a few of the many wrongs and abuses practised upon our commerce and country by British ships-of-war, for a period of at least six or eight years. For it is well known that they took and captured from us more than a thousand ships and vessels bound to France and other European countries, while we were at peace with them. And thus from time to time they continued to heap insult upon insult, with their men of war lying at the mouths of our harbours, and searching and detaining our merchant ships in every part of the world.

On the 26th of April, 1806, off Sandy Hook, the frigate *Leander* fired a cannon-shot into a little harmless, unarmed vessel, by which a seamen was killed, in our own waters. This created an immense sensation, and every citizen throughout the United States felt that it was a gross insult to the nation. Spirited remonstrances were made by our government, and reparation was promised; but the resentment of the people had scarcely time to cool down from this outrage, when, in about a year afterward, a dastardly attack was made by the two-decked ship-of-war, *Leopard*, upon the United States frigate *Chesapeake*, at a period of profound peace, when, from peculiar causes, the latter ship was in a defenceless state.

This cowardly act aroused throughout the Union a spirit of retaliation, which the government found it difficult to repress. This insult, however, like the one preceding it, passed off without any serious consequences, and it was hoped, by a considerable portion of the people. that England would refrain from further aggressions.

This hope, however, was delusive, and so far from making reparation for past injuries, the captains of our merchant ships were often ill-treated and abused by upstart, subaltern officers, for daring to assert their legitimate rights.

The longer we submitted, the more provoking the British government became. A large portion of the American people were opposed to open warfare; not from a fear of its ultimate success, or of the pecuniary losses and sacrifices it would necessarily produce; nor from a timid fear of meeting our adversary in fair and open combat, but from a religious and conscientious feeling of shedding human blood, more especially that of the nation from which we sprung; both professing the same religion, and speaking the same language.

It was, therefore, a most perplexing alternative, and the question was, shall we any longer submit to injury and insult?

We were taunted and reviled on every side; accused of parsimony and cowardice; England boasting that a few broadsides from her "wooden walls" would drive our "paltry, striped bunting" from the ocean.

Our seamen were impressed by the English in every part of the world; dragged on board of their floating hells; made to serve against their will the haughty tyrants placed over them, and were often flogged for refusing to fight against other nations with whom we were at peace.

Many legitimate voyages were broken up and ruined by their piratical cruisers, simply because they had the power to do it.

Their scurrilous newspapers never ceased to accuse us of want of spirit, because we would not unite with them in a crusade against France, and the other nations of Europe.

Our appeals for justice were not listened to; remonstrances and diplomatic negotiations were found useless. Non-intercourse and embargoes were resorted to, in order to prevent war; but the more reluctant we were to engage in open conflict and bloodshed, the more over-bearing our adversary became.

At length, when every resource to obtain justice was exhausted, we had no choice left us but to declare war against our oppressors, or tamely submit to degradation, not only in our own eyes, but in those of the whole civilized world.

In conclusion, I would say, that I think no one, with a sound mind, and possessed of honourable feelings, will doubt that if war is right under any circumstances, ours against England in 1812 was a righteous one.

Chapter 1

Preparation for War

This chapter principally treats of the preparations for the war; the fitting out of small privateers, the embargo, etc., with a full account of the United States frigate *Constitution*, Captain Isaac Hull, his being chased for three days by an English fleet, and finally making his escape, and his safe arrival at Boston; also, his cruise, and capture of his Majesty's frigate *Guerriere*, on the 19th of August, 1812.

The Privateer brig *Anaconda*, named in this chapter, was a beautiful vessel; she was built in Middletown, Connecticut, and owned in New York. She carried sixteen carriage guns, and one hundred and sixty men. She was commanded by —— Shaler, and made a great many valuable prizes, but was finally captured by a large number of British boats, while at anchor at Ocracock, N.C.

Although the clouds of war had, for a long time, been gathering in the political horizon, and everything looked dark and threatening, still there was a secret feeling in the bosom of a large portion of the nation that they would be dispelled, and that something would eventually transpire to divert the wide-spread calamity and distress that war, and its evil attendants, would inevitably produce.

But, alas! this hope was delusive, and the consequence was, when it did actually arrive, it found the country quite unprepared to meet the conflict or to carry it on with energy and success for a considerable time. We had everything to do, and but a short time to perform the work.

The general government called upon the States for men and money, and requested them to organize their militia, and prepare to protect their own States, and, if necessary, to march at a moment's warning to any point where their services might be required, particularly along the Atlantic seaboard. The merchants were, of course, anxious to get home their ships and vessels from every quarter of the globe before they should become a prey to the enemy.

Very soon, a small dispatch pilot boat was sent out in haste to Gottenburg, with news of the war, and with directions to all our commercial marine in the harbours of Sweden, Denmark, Prussia, and Russia, to remain in port until the war should cease.

This enterprise fortunately succeeded, so that the greatest part of our ships and vessels in the north of Europe were saved from capture. When the war was declared, we had but a few sharp, fast sailing clipper vessels suited for privateers and letters of marque.

There were, however, a few in the most of our Atlantic ports, namely, at Boston, New York, Philadelphia, and Baltimore, and these were brigs and schooners which had been employed in a sort of forced running trade to France, and to the islands in the West Indies: for even before the war, such vessels were preferred, on account of their speed, to avoid the British cruisers, for in numberless instances it happened, that when our merchant vessels had made a distant voyage, and were returning home with the fruits of their enterprising industry, they were often detained, and sometimes captured and sent into British ports for adjudication, and if permitted to escape condemnation, their voyages were broken up, and ruined by the exorbitant expenses in what were falsely called their courts of justice.

Fortunately, we still had several of these vessels, which together with the pilot boats belonging to our principal ports, very soon enabled our merchants to be on the alert, and ready to assail our adversary. Several of these small pilot boats were forthwith dispatched to sea in search of British merchantmen.

One large centre gun, commonly called "Long Tom", with a crew of fifty or sixty men, and a suitable number of muskets, sabres, and boarding pikes, etc., was quite enough to capture almost any British merchantman, at this stage of the war. Of this character were the pilot boats *Teazer*. Captain Dobson; *Black Joke*, Captain Brown; *Jack's Favourite,* Captain Johnson, and several other privateers, which were fitted out of the port of New York. These small vessels were only suitable to make short cruises about the Gulf of Florida, and among the islands in the West Indies.

The same course was pursued by Boston, Salem, and other eastern ports. At the first breaking out of the war, these privateers from the eastern ports were dispatched to cruise along the coast of Nova Scotia, Newfoundland, and among the British Windward Islands in the Caribbean Sea. On the 1st of July, I find the following notice in the newspapers of that day:

"The people in the eastern States are labouring almost night and day to fit out privateers. Two have already sailed from Salem, and ten others are getting ready for sea. This looks well, and does credit to our eastern friends."

A Baltimore newspaper, dated July the 4th, 1812, remarks that:

"several small, swift privateers, will sail from the United States in a few days. Some have already been sent to sea, and many others of a larger class, better fitted and better equipped, will soon follow."

About the middle of October, say four months after the declaration of war, I find the following list of privateers belonging to the port of New York alone.

At this period there was quite a number of large brigs and schooners, on the pilot-boat construction, being built at New York, and also at different ports in Connecticut.

On the 3rd of April, 1812, seventy-five days previous to the declaration of war, the American Government wisely laid an

PRIVATEERS.	CAPTAINS.	L. TONS.	GUNS.	MEN.
Teazer	Dobson	1	2	50
Paul Jones	Hazard	1	16	120
Marengo	Ridois	1	6	50
Eagle	Beaufon	—	1	45
Rosamond	Campan	1	12	132
Benjamin Franklin	Ingersol	1	8	120
Black Joke	Brown	1	2	60
Rover	Ferris	1	1	35
Orders in Council	Howard	—	16	120
Saratoga	Riker	—	18	140
United We Stand	Storey	1	2	50
Divided We Fall	Cropsey	1	2	50
Governor Tompkins	Skinner	1	14	143
Retaliation	Newson	1	6	100
Spitfire	Miller	1	2	54
General Armstrong	Barnard	1	18	140
Jack's Favorite	Johnson	1	4	80
Yorktown	Storey	—	18	160
Tartar	King	;	6	80
Halkar	Rowland	—	16	100
Anaconda	Shaler	—	16	160
Patriot	Merrihew	1	2	50
Union	Hicks	—	1	24
Turn Over	Southmead	—	1	50
Right of Search		1	—	60
Bunker Hill	Lewis	1	4	—
Twenty-six.		18	194	2233

embargo on all American ships and vessels in our own ports, which judicious law doubtless prevented a large amount of property from falling into the hands of our enemies.

I will now proceed to quote from a Baltimore paper of the same date, the number of privateers and letters of marque belonging to that place. The list is as follows:—

SCHOONERS.	CAPTAINS.	L. TONS	GUNS, NO.	MEN.	METAL
Rossie	Barney	1	13	120	12's 24's 6's
Comet	Boyle	2	12	128	9's 12's
Dolphin	Stafford	2	10	100	9's 12's 6's
Nonsuch	Lovely	—	12	100	12's
High Flyer	Grant	1	7	100	12's 6's
Globe	Murphy	1	7	90	9's 12's 18's
America	Richardson	2	14	115	9's 24's 6's
Bona	Damerson	1	6	80	12's 6's
Tom	Wilson	2	14	130	12's 18's 9's
Sparrow	Burch	1	5	80	12's 6's
Revenge	Miller	2	14	160	8's 12's 24's
Rolla	Dooley	1	5	60	12's
Joseph and Mary	Wescott	2	4	83	18 & 24 poun.
Wasp	Taylor	1	1	50	9 poun.
Sarah Ann	Moon	1	1	50	9 "
Liberty	Pratt	1	1	50	9 "
Hornet	Frost	1	1	50	9 "

Notwithstanding the numerous British ships of war on our coast and off the entrance of our harbours, a great portion of our merchant ships and vessels were fortunate enough to evade capture by the enemy, and get safe into port, where they were generally dismantled and laid up during the war. This circumstance enabled the commanders of privateers and letters-of-marque to obtain seamen to man them, and together with a sufficient number of landsmen for marines, they were soon ready for a cruise.

In addition to the privateers, there were at sea twenty-five fast sailing letter-of-marque schooners, carrying from six to ten guns, and from thirty to fifty men each, exclusive of officers. Besides what has been already enumerated, there were ten large schooners, on the pilot boat construction, three of which were from three hundred and thirty to three hundred and fifty tons burden. They were probably the largest vessels ever built of this description. Baltimore had sent to sea since the declaration of war forty-two armed vessels, carrying about three hundred and thirty guns, and from 2,800 to 3,000 men.

It is worthy of remark that up to this date not one of our privateers had been captured, though frequently chased by British vessels of war. And here I would observe, that although Baltimore took the lead in fitting out privateers and letters of marque, and was more active and patriotic in annoying the enemy than most other cities in the United States, still I add with pleasure that the same spirit was evinced in most of our Atlantic ports, for even the small commercial cities furnished more or less of these enterprising, mischievous privateers. Witness the famous privateer *Yankee* and several others from Bristol. Rhode Island. and the notorious little schooner *Saucy Jack* from Charleston, S. C, beside the large and famous privateer-schooner *Decatur*. Captain Dominique Diron of the same port; both of which vessels I shall take occasion to notice in their proper place.

The reader will observe by these preliminary observations that a portion of the small privateers and letters-of-marque were sent to sea to cruise for British merchantmen a few weeks after the declaration of war, and that numerous larger ones were preparing to follow in the same pursuit.

They were all, of course, commissioned by the United States Government to take, burn, sink and destroy the enemy wherever he could be found, either on the high seas or in British ports.

I will therefore leave them for the present to annoy the foe, and attempt to give an account of the escape of the frigate *Constitution*, Captain Isaac Hull, from a British fleet off the west end of Long Island, in about twenty-five fathoms water, just out of sight of land.

But before I proceed further on the subject I shall digress a little, and make a few preliminary observations, in order to bring up the witnesses of this interesting chase from both parties, and, like old Mrs. Slipslop in the play, "go on to tell the story in my own way." At this period, the writer of these pages commanded a merchant ship called the *America*, and was then in Lisbon, in which port were quite a number of American merchant ships and vessels bound to the United States. And, though there was no certainty that war would soon be declared, still there was much excitement on the subject, and all were anxious to return home for fear of capture. There were at that time four large ships, belonging to the house of Archibald Gracie & Sons, of New York, lying in this port. *viz.* the *Briganza*, *Eliza Gracie*, *Oronoko*, and the *America*. The last three of these ships, together with many other merchant vessels, sailed out of the Tagus with a fine, fresh, easterly breeze, on the 14th of June, 1812, all bound to their respective ports in the United States.

During the first day out there was no material difference in the sailing of the three ships. We all pushed to the westward taking about the same course. At nightfall, I edged the ship off a couple of points to the southward in order to get clear of the fleet, wishing to pursue my destiny alone, whether for weal or woe, and at daylight the next morning there was nothing in sight. We had favourable winds for several days and proceeded rapidly on our course until we reached lat. 40° 10' North, longitude 32° West, that is to say a little to the west of the Western Islands.

There we met with light airs and calms, which continued for five consecutive days. During that time we did not make fifty miles distance. The calm weather which I at this time considered as a great misfortune, proved in the result the salvation of the ship. The two other ships *viz.*, the *Eliza Gracie*, Captain James Brown, and the *Oronoko*, Captain John Richards, steered their ships on a more northerly parallel, and had a fresh breeze from the north-east, while my ship lay becalmed for nearly a week. And thus, while I fortunately escaped the enemy, they fell in with a British fleet from Halifax, bound to the westward to cruise off the port of New York, with the intention, no doubt, of intercepting and capturing American men-of-war and merchant vessels bound into that port.

This fleet was composed of the following ships, *viz.*, the *Africa*, 64, Captain Bastard; *Shannon*, 38, Captain Broke, senior officer of this squadron; the *Guerriere*, 38, Captain Dacres; *Belvidera*, 36, Captain Byron, and the *Æolus*, 32, Captain Lord James Townsend.

All these ships were united at this time in the hope of falling in with Commodore Rodgers who had sailed with a small squadron from New York on the 21st of June, three days after the declaration of war. When the *Eliza Gracie* and the *Oronoko* fell in with this fleet, they knew nothing of the war, but they soon found to their sorrow that they were all prisoners of war. After removing the captains, officers and crews from the ships, they burned the *Eliza Gracie* (a beautiful new ship) and sent the *Oronoko* into Halifax. This circumstance occurred about a week previous to the memorable chase by the before-named English fleet of the frigate *Constitution*.

The witnesses of the pursuit and escape of that frigate are as follows: Captain James Brown of New York, on board of the *Shannon*; Captains Richards and Rodgers, on board of the other frigates. These gentlemen witnessed the whole proceedings of both parties with the most intense interest and anxiety for the honour and escape of the *Constitution*. They related to me personally all they saw and felt during the whole period of Captain Hull's unparalleled nautical skill, and masterly seamanship, which I will relate in the course of this narrative.

On the 12th of July the *Constitution* left Annapolis, and on the 16th of the same month left the capes of the Delaware, and was soon out of sight of the land, steering along the coast towards Sandy Hook, at no great distance from the shore, with a light breeze from the northward, under easy sail. On the 17th, at one p.m., sounded in twenty-two fathoms of water, and in about an hour after made four large sail to the northward. At four, discovered a fifth sail to the northward and eastward, which looked like a man-of-war. This ship being further to the eastward, and a little detached from the other four, the *Constitution* made sail, and at six p.m., the wind being light from the southward, the *Constitution* now wore round with her head to the eastward, which brought her to the windward of the enemy. She then set her light studding sails and stay sails, and at half-past seven p.m., towards evening, beat to quarters and cleared ship for action, in hopes of cutting off the nearest ship.

The wind continued very light from the southward, and the two ships were slowly nearing each other until eight o'clock. At ten, the *Constitution* shortened sail and showed the private signal of the day. After keeping the lights aloft for about an hour, and receiving no answer from the British frigate, the *Constitution*, at a quarter past eleven, took in the signal lights and made sail again, hauling aboard her starboard tacks, and stood to the eastward under easy sail.

During the whole of the middle watch the wind was light from the southward and westward. Just as the morning watch was called, the frigate, which subsequently proved to be the *Guerriere*, tacked, and then wore entirely round, threw a rocket and fired two guns, no doubt as a signal to the rest of the British fleet that an enemy's frigate was near. As the day dawned, three of the enemy's ships were seen on the starboard quarter of the *Constitution*, and two were astern.

This then, was the squadron of Commodore Broke, all of which had been gradually closing with the American frigate during the night, and was now just out of long gun-shot. As the mist of the morning entirely cleared away, the *Constitution* found she had two frigates on her lee quarter and a ship-of-the-line, two frigates, a brig, and a schooner astern. All these ships and vessels had English colours flying, and immediately gave chase to the American frigate. It soon, however, fell quite calm, and now came the tug of war. All the fleet were in hot pursuit, and the trial commenced of seamanship, skill and nautical activity;

in fine, every feeling of national honour and ardent patriotism was aroused, and brought into requisition on both sides. And this was soon to be the grand crisis, whether we should lose at the commencement of the war one of our finest frigates, or whether she should escape and hereafter shed a halo of glory on the flag under which she sailed, and on the nation to whom she belonged. Every arm was nerved, and every heart beat high for the honour of both the belligerent parties.

The *Constitution* hoisted out her boats, and sent them ahead to tow the ship out of the reach of the enemy's shot. Four of her long twenty-fours were run out as stern chasers, *viz.*, two on the gun-deck, and two on the spar deck. Although it was found necessary to cut away some of the wood-work of the stern frame, in order to make room to work the guns, still this was soon done, and no time lost.

While the boats were towing ahead, Captain Hull discovered that the *Shannon*, one of the enemy's swiftest ships, had not only all her own boats ahead towing, but was assisted by a number from the other ships. As it was quite calm, the *Shannon* appeared to gain a little on the chase. Soon after, the *Shannon*, being the headmost ship, began firing her bow guns, which she kept up for about ten or fifteen minutes, when finding her shot fall short, she ceased firing. And now what should be done to widen the distance between the pursuers and the pursued?

It was evident to Captain Hull and his officers that the superior number of towing boats would soon endanger them to the fire of the enemy's whole fleet. It then occurred to him to sound, which was done at half-past six p.m. When it was found that they were in twenty-six fathoms of water, the *Constitution* mustered her hawsers and all the spare rope that could be found fit for the purpose. They were then payed down into the cutters, when a kedge was run out a long distance ahead and let go. The crew then clapped on and walked away with the ship with such life and animation that the enemy was astonished how the *Constitution* could leave them so fast, having not half the number of boats that were towing the *Shannon*. And thus while one kedge was run up, another was carried ahead. In this manner the enemy's ships were fast losing ground.

My friend Captain Brown, who was a prisoner on board the *Shannon*, told me that with a spy-glass he soon discovered what was going on on board the *Constitution*, but of course he kept the secret to himself. He said, however, that some hours after this, an officer with a glass from aloft discovered that the American frigate was kedging. They also resorted to the same expedient, but, alas! their knowledge came too late. The same gentleman said it was amusing to hear Captain Broke and his officers converse about the *Yankee* frigate. At one period of the chase they were so confident of capturing her that a prize officer and crew were already appointed to conduct her in triumph to Halifax. To all their questions of taking the *Constitution*, Captain Brown had but one answer to make, and that was, "Gentlemen, you will never take that frigate."

At half-past seven in the evening, the *Constitution* was favoured with a light air, when she set her ensign, and fired a shot at the *Shannon*, the nearest ship astern. At eight, it fell calm again, when further recourse was had to the boats, and kedging. At nine, the *Shannon*, on which the English had put most of their boats, was fast nearing the *Constitution* again. There was now a fair prospect, notwithstanding the steadiness and activity of Captain Hull and his gallant officers and crew that the *Shannon* would get near enough to cripple their ship, when her capture by the rest of the squadron would he inevitable.

At this trying moment, the best spirit inspired the whole ship's company. Everything was stopped, and Captain Hull was not without hope that should he even be forced into action by the *Shannon* that he would be able to silence her, and still escape from the fleet. He knew also that the enemy dare not venture too near with his boats, as it would be an easy matter to sink them with his stern guns, so that neither his officers nor men showed the least disposition to despondency. They relieved each other regularly at the trying duty of the ship, and, while the officers caught short naps on deck, the seamen slept at their guns.

But now had arrived the most critical moment of the chase. The *Shannon* was fast closing, the *Guerriere* was almost as near on the larboard quarter, so that one hour more promised to bring the long struggle to an issue; when suddenly, at nine minutes past nine, it pleased God to send a light air from the southward which struck the ship and thus brought her to windward of her adversaries. The manner in which this advantage was improved was truly a beautiful sight, and must have been highly exciting to nautical men, and I have no doubt it was so even in the bosom of the enemy. As the wind increased the sails were trimmed to the breeze, and it was then that Old Ironsides walked away from the enemy like a thing of life.

As soon as she was under command and brought up to the wind on the starboard tack, the boats were temporarily hoisted to their places. As the *Constitution* came by the wind, she brought the *Guerriere* nearly on her lee beam, when that frigate opened a fire from her broadside, but being at so great a distance, her shot fell harmless into the water. In about an hour, however, it fell calm again, when Captain Hull ordered a quantity of water to be started, in order to lighten the ship. More than two thousand gallons were pumped out, and the boats were sent ahead to tow. The enemy now put nearly all the boats of the fleet on the *Shannon*, the nearest ship astern. A few hours of prodigious exertion followed; the crew of the *Constitution* being obliged to supply the place of numbers by their activity and zeal. The ships were close-haul upon the wind, and every sail that would draw was set, but still the *Shannon* was slowly but steadily forging ahead.

About noon this day, there was a little relaxation from labour, owing to the occasional occurrence of light airs or cats-paws. By watching these baffling airs closely, the ship was urged gently through the water, but at a quarter past twelve the toilsome work of towing and kedging was renewed. At one o'clock a strange sail was discovered, nearly to leeward. At the same time the four frigates of the enemy were about one point on the lee quarter of the *Constitution*, at long gun-shot distance, the Africa and the two prizes being on the lee beam. As the wind was constantly baffling, any moment might have brought a change and placed the enemy to windward. At seven minutes before two, the *Belvidera*, then the nearest ship, began to fire with her bow guns, and the *Constitution* opened with her stern-chasers. On board the latter ship, it was however soon found to be dangerous to use the main-deck guns from the cabin windows—the transoms having so much rake, the windows so high and the guns so short, that every explosion lifted the upper deck, and threatened to blow out the stern frame. Perceiving, moreover, that his shot did little or no execution, Captain Hull ordered the firing to cease, at half past two.

For several hours the enemy's frigates were nearly within gunshot; sometimes towing and kedging, and at others endeavouring to close with the light puffs of air that occasionally passed. At seven o'clock in the evening, the boats of the *Constitution* were again ahead; the ship steering S. W. ½ W. with an air so light as to be almost imperceptible. At half past seven, she sounded in twenty-four fathoms.

For four hours the same toilsome duty was going on, until a little before eleven, when a light air from the southward struck the ship, and the sails, for the first time in many weary hours, were asleep. The boats instantly dropped alongside, hooked on. and were all run up, with the exception of the first cutter. The top-gallant studding sails and stay sails were set, as soon as possible, and for about an hour the people caught a little rest. But at midnight it fell calm again, though neither the pursuers nor the pursued had recourse to the boats, probably from their unwillingness to disturb their crews.

At two a.m. it was observed on board the *Constitution* that the *Guerriere* had forged ahead, and was again on their lee-beam. At this time, the top-gallant studding-sails were taken in. In this manner passed the night. and on the morning of the next day it was found that three of the enemy's frigates were within long gunshot, on the lee quarter, and the other at about the same distance on the lee beam. The *Africa* and the prizes were much further to leeward. A little after daylight, the *Guerriere*. having drawn ahead sufficiently to be forward of the beam of the *Constitution*, tacked, when the latter ship did the same, in order to preserve her position to windward. An hour later, the *Æolus* passed on the contrary tack, so near that it was thought by some who observed the movement that she ought to have opened her fire upon the *Constitution*. But as that vessel was only a twelve-pounder frigate, and she was still at a considerable distance, it is very probable her commander acted judiciously.

By this time there was sufficient wind to induce Captain Hull to hoist in his first cutter. The scene on the morning of this day was beautiful in the extreme. The weather was mild and lovely, the sea was as smooth as a mill-pond. There was quite wind enough to remove the necessity of any extraordinary means of getting ahead, that had been so freely used during the previous eight and forty hours. All the English ships were on the same tack with the *Constitution*, and the five frigates had everything set from their trucks to the water's edge, and appeared like beautiful white clouds as they gently ploughed through the unruffled deep.

Including the American frigate, eleven sail were in sight, and shortly after a twelfth appeared to windward, which was soon ascertained to be an American merchantman. But the enemy was too intent on capturing the *Constitution* to regard anything else, and though it would have been easy to take the ships to leeward, no attention appears to have been paid to them. With a view, however, to deceive the ship to windward, they hoisted American colours, when the *Constitution* set an English ensign by way of warning the stranger to keep aloof from the fleet.

Until ten o'clock the *Constitution* was making every preparation to carry sail hard, should it become necessary, and now sounded in twenty fathoms of water. At noon the wind died away again to a moderate breeze, though it was found while the wind lasted that she had gained on all the enemy's ships; more, however, on some than others. The nearest ship was the *Belvidera*, which vessel was exactly in the wake of the *Constitution*, distant about two-and-a-half miles, bearing N.N.W. The two other frigates were on the lee quarter, distant about five miles, and the *Africa* was hull down to leeward on the opposite tack.

This was a vast improvement on the state of things that had existed the previous day, and it allowed the officers and men to catch a little rest, though no one left the decks. The latitude, by observation this day, was 38° 47' North, and the longitude, by dead reckoning, 73° 57' West.

At meridian the wind began to blow a pleasant breeze, and the sound of the water was heard rippling under the bows of the noble old ship. From this moment the *Constitution* slowly, though steadily, drew ahead of all her pursuers, every sail was watched and tended in the best manner that experience and seamanship could dictate. At four p.m., the *Belvidera* was more than four miles astern, and the other ships were left behind in the same proportion, though the wind had again become very light.

In this manner both parties kept pressing ahead and to windward as fast, is possible, profiting by every little change of wind to force their ships through the water. At a little before seven a.m. there was every appearance of a heavy squall attended by rain, when the *Constitution* prepared to meet it with the coolness and discretion which had been displayed throughout the whole affair. The men were stationed, and everything was kept fast to the last moment, when, just before the squall struck the ship. the order was given to "clew up" and "clew down."

In an instant all the light sails were furled, the mizzen-topsail was reefed, and the ship brought under short sail in a few minutes. The English ships saw the threatening force of the squall; without waiting for the wind, began to clew up and haul down, and keep off from the wind, so that when the rain subsided and the weather cleared a little, they were seen steering in different directions. On the other hand, after the *Constitution* had received the force of the squall, she sheeted home, and hoisted her fore and main-top-gallant sails, and in a few moments after, was flying away from the enemy on an easy bowline at the rate of eleven knots.

In a little less than an hour after the squall had struck the ship it had entirely passed off to leeward, and another sight was again obtained of the enemy. The *Belvidera*, the nearest ship, had altered her bearing in that short period nearly two points more to leeward, and was a long way astern. The next nearest vessel was still further to leeward and more distant; while the two remaining frigates were fairly hull down, and the *Africa* was barely visible in the horizon!

All apprehensions of the enemy now were at an end, still it was deemed prudent to carry sail on the ship to increase the distance, and also to preserve the weather gage. At half-past ten the wind backed further to the southward, when the *Constitution*, which had been steering free for some time, took in her lower studding-sails. At eleven the enemy fired two guns, and the nearest ship could just be discovered like a speck on the water. As the wind continued light and baffling, the enemy still persevered in the chase, but at daylight the nearest ship was hull down astern and to leeward.

Under the circumstances, it was thought advisable to use every exertion to lose sight of the English frigates, and as the wind was falling light, the *Constitution's* sails were wet down from the sky-sails to the courses. The good effect of this care was soon visible, as at six a.m. the topsails of the enemy's nearest ships were beginning to dip in the water. At a quarter past eight the English ships all hauled to the northward and eastward, and gave up the chase; fully satisfied, by a trial that had lasted nearly three days and as many nights, under all the circumstances that attend nautical manoeuvres, from reefing topsails, to towing and kedging, that they had no hope of overtaking their enemy.

Thus terminated a chase that has become celebrated for its length, perseverance, coolness, and activity, and stands unparalleled on the pages of nautical history. On board of the *Constitution*, during the whole of this exciting period, there was no confusion or disorder, every order was judiciously given, and promptly obeyed. To effect her escape the *Constitution* lost not a spar, nor a sail, no anchor was cut away, no gun lost, no boat destroyed, and nothing was thrown overboard except some gallons of water. A few days after losing sight of the enemy, the noble old ship arrived safe at Boston. In conclusion I have only to add a just eulogy to her brave commander, the heroic Hull. He was cool, resolute, and discreet throughout the whole affair, and was nobly sustained by his gallant officers and crew. They are therefore entitled to their country's everlasting gratitude.

On Captain Hull's arrival at Boston, after his escape from the English squadron, he was heartily greeted by his friends, and the people of that city, on which occasion he entered the following notice on the coffee-house books:

> "Captain Hull, finding his friends in Boston are correctly informed of his situation when chased by the British squadron off New York, and that they are good enough to give him more credit for having escaped them than he ought to claim, takes this opportunity of requesting them to make a transfer of a great part of their good wishes to Lieutenant Morris, and the other brave officers, and the crew under his command, for their many great exertions and prompt attention to orders while the enemy were in chase.
>
> "Captain Hull has great pleasure in saying, that notwithstanding the length of the chase, the officers and crew being deprived of sleep, and allowed but little refreshment during the time, not a murmur was heard to escape them."

After the memorable chase of the *Constitution* by the British fleet, they were allowed to separate and cruise singly on and off our coast, in order to destroy all manner of American vessels; and it so happened that not long after the separation, when off the coast of Nova Scotia, the little merchant-ship *John Adams*, on her return home to New York from Lisbon (she having a British license,) fell in with the *Guerriere*, when Captain Dacres endorsed the following challenge on her register:—

> "Captain Dacres, commander of his Britannic Majesty's

frigate *Guerriere*, of forty-four guns, presents his compliments to Commodore Rodgers, of the United States frigate *President*, and will be very happy to meet him, or any other American frigate of equal force to the *President*, off Sandy Hook, for the purpose of having a social *tête-à-tête*."

On the arrival of the John Adams at New York, Captain Dacres' challenge was copied into all the newspapers of the day, and had a wide circulation all over the United States.

Captain Hull remained with the *Constitution* in the port of Boston about a week, just long enough to fill up his water, reprovision the ship, and refresh his officers and crew, when we find by his letter to the Hon. Paul Hamilton, Secretary of the Navy, dated August the 2nd, 1812, that he left port on that day and stood to the eastward, along the coast, in hopes of falling in with one of the enemy's frigates which was reported to be cruising in that direction.

He then ran off Halifax and Cape Sable, and after remaining near there for three or four days, without seeing anything which determined him to change his cruising-ground towards Newfoundland, bore up, and ran to the eastward, under full sail, passing near the Isle of Sable, and then hauled in and took a station off the Gulf of St. Lawrence, near Cape Race, to intercept the ships of the enemy bound either to or from Quebec or Halifax, and to be in a situation to recapture such of our vessels as they might be sending into British ports.

On the 10th of August, being off Cape Race, he fell in with a light English brig bound to Halifax, from Newfoundland, and as she was not worth sending in, he took out the crew and burned her. On the 11th he took the British brig *Adiona*, from Nova Scotia, bound to England, loaded with ship timber; took out the crew, set her on fire, and made sail to take a station nearer Cape Race, where he continued to cruise until the morning of the 15th.

At daylight five sail were in sight ahead of them, apparently a small convoy. He gave chase under a press of sail, and soon found he gained on them very fast, and discovered that one of them was a ship-of-war. At sunrise they hove about, and stood on the same tack with him. By this time he discovered that the ship of war had a brig in tow.

At six, coming up very fast with the ship, she cast off her tow and set her on fire, and had ordered a second brig to stand before the wind to separate them, the ship-of-war making sail to the windward. He then gave chase to a ship which appeared to be under her convoy, but when he came up with her she proved to be a British prize to the *Dolphin* privateer of Salem. She had been spoken by the ship-of-war, but he came up with them before they bad time to put men on board and take charge of her.

While the *Constitution's* boats were boarding this vessel, the ship-of-war had got nearly hull down from him, and understanding from one of the prisoners that she was a very fast sailer, he found it would not be possible to come up with her before night, or perhaps not then; he therefore gave chase to the brig that ran before the wind, determined to destroy all her convoy.

He soon found he came up fast with the brig, and that they were making every exertion to get off, by throwing overboard all the lumber, water-casks, etc., etc. At two p. m. he brought-to, the chase, and found her to be the American brig *Adeline*, from Liverpool, loaded with dry goods, etc. Took the prize-master and crew out, and put Midshipman Madison and a crew on board, with orders to proceed to the nearest port in the United States. From the prize-master of this vessel he learned, that the brig burned by the sloop-of-war, belonged to New York, and was loaded with hemp, duck, last from Jutland, having gone in there in distress.

Having chased, so far to the eastward as to make it impossible to come up with the sloop-of-war, he determined to change his cruising-ground, as he found by some of the prisoners that came from this vessel, that the squadron that chased him off New York, was on the western edge of the Grand Bank, not far distant from him. He accordingly stood to the southward, intending to pass near Bermuda, and cruise off our southern coast—saw nothing till the night of the 18th; at half-past nine, p.m., discovered a sail very near, it being dark; made sail and gave chase, and could see that she was a brig. At eleven brought her to, sent a boat on board, and found her to be the American privateer *Decatur*, belonging to Salem, with a crew of one hundred and eight men, and fourteen guns, twelve of which she had thrown overboard while we were in chase of her.

The captain came on board, and informed us that he saw the day before, a ship-of-war standing to the southward, and that she could not be far from us. At twelve a.m. made sail to the southward, intending, if possible, to fall in with her. The privateer stood-in for Cape Race, to make that her cruising-ground, and take ships by boarding, as she had lost all her guns but two.

The above is the substance of a journal kept by Captain Hull; on board the *Constitution*, from the time he left Boston up to this date, namely, August the 18th.

As Captain Hull is once more on his own element, and on the best cruising-ground he could select for English men-of-war, I will leave him there for the present, and return on shore to take a view of public opinion. With respect to naval battles; on the one hand, the Americans had generally been accustomed to think the English navy invincible. They had so long triumphed over the French and Spanish ships-of-war, and gained so many easy victories by their superior seamanship, that the English themselves believed, or affected to believe, that one of their sloops-of-war was a match for a frigate of any other nation.

Their old sea-songs had inspired them with a feeling of vanity which rendered them obnoxious to all other nations, and it seemed to be the will of Providence that young and inexperienced America should be the first nation to humble their pride, and break the spell that had so long caused them to domineer over States less powerful than themselves. In view of all these causes, there was an intense feeling of hope and fear for the result of the first naval battle; the whole nation, as it were, drew a long breath of anxious suspense.

There were, however, some honourable exceptions to the

general feeling of doubt on the subject; there was a little band of nautical men, whose self-reliance never wavered, and whose hearts beat high with ardent desire to wipe off the stain of the attack on the *Chesapeake*, and other numerous wrongs and insults so long endured, that almost every seaman, to a man, throughout the whole length and breadth of the United States, panted for revenge, and they only wished for an opportunity to meet the foe upon equal terms.

Everybody knew of Captain Hull's escape from the British fleet, and every man, woman, and child in the country-knew he had gone to sea again to pick a quarrel with the first English frigate he could meet with, and as this was not long after the commencement of the war, the honour of the whole nation seemed involved in the result of the first naval battle. Hundreds were running to the post-office to catch the first news from the frigate *Constitution*.

The present generation cannot conceive of the intense feeling of anxiety that pervaded the public mind at that period. The writer of these pages was at Charleston, S.C, soon after the affair of the *Constitution* and *Guerriere*, when a patriotic lady of that city, in describing her feelings of anxiety for the safety of the *Constitution* after leaving Boston, she told the ladies and gentlemen present, that her heart beat pit-a-pat so loud that everyone could have heard it quite across the room; and such was the inspiring love of country, that old and young partook of the same patriotic enthusiasm; how then can it astonish any one that victory succeeded victory, whenever our ships met the enemy with anything like equal force?

The reader will observe, that I have brought the cruise of the *Constitution* down to the day before the action between the two frigates. I will here insert the following information supplied me by Captain William B. Orne,[1] (who was on board the *Guerriere* during the action), extracted from his own private journal,

---

1. Captain Orne, at this time, May the 1st, 1856, is still living in the city of Brooklyn, N.Y. He is highly esteemed and beloved by all who know him. He is considered a man of truth and veracity, and his naked word is as good as his sealed bond.

which commences thus:—

"I commanded the American brig *Betsey*, in the year 1812, and was returning home from Naples, Italy, to Boston. When near the western edge of the Grand Bank of Newfoundland, on the 10th of August, 1812, I fell in with the British frigate *Guerriere*, Captain Dacres, and was captured by him. Myself and a boy were taken on board of the frigate; the remainder of my officers and men were left in the *Betsey*, and sent into Halifax, N. S., as a prize to the *Guerriere*.

"On the 19th of the same month, when in latitude 41° 41' North, longitude about 55° 40' West, the wind being fresh from the northward, the *Guerriere* was under double-reefed topsails during all the forenoon of this day. At two p. m., we discovered a large sail to windward, bearing about North from us. We soon made her out to be a frigate. She was steering off from the wind, with her head to the south-west, evidently with the intention of cutting us off as soon as possible. Signals were soon made by the *Guerriere*, but as they were not answered, the conclusion of course was, that she was either a French or an American frigate.

"Captain Dacres appeared anxious to ascertain her character, and after looking at her for that purpose, handed me his spy-glass, requesting me to give him my opinion of the stranger. I soon saw from the peculiarity of her sails, and from her general appearance, that she was, without doubt, an American frigate, and communicated the same to Captain Dacres. He immediately replied, that he thought she came down too boldly for an American, but soon after added: 'The better he behaves, the more honour we shall gain by taking him.'

"The two ships were rapidly approaching each other, when the *Guerriere* backed her main-topsail, and waited for her opponent to come down, and commence the action. He then set an English flag at each mast-head, beat to quarters, and made ready for the fight. When the strange frigate came down to within two or three miles distance, he hauled upon the wind, took in all his light sails, reefed his topsails, and deliberately prepared for action. It was now about five o'clock in the afternoon, when he filled away and ran down for the *Guerriere*. At this moment, Captain Dacres politely said to me: 'Captain Orne, as I suppose you do not wish to fight against your own countrymen, you are at liberty to go below the water-line.'

"It was not long after this before I retired from the quarter-deck to the cock-pit; of course I saw no more of the action until the firing ceased, but I heard and felt much of its effects; for soon after I left the deck, the firing commenced on board the *Guerriere*, and was kept up almost constantly until about six o'clock, when I heard a tremendous explosion from the opposing frigate. The effect of her shot seemed to make the *Guerriere* reel, and tremble as though she had received the shock of an earthquake. Immediately after this, I heard a tremendous crash on deck, and was told the mizzen-mast was shot away. In a few moments afterward, the cock-pit was filled with wounded men.

"At about half-past six o'clock in the evening, after the firing had ceased, I went on deck, and there beheld a scene which it would be difficult to describe: all the *Guerriere's* masts were shot away, and as she had no sails to steady her, she lay rolling like a log in the trough of the sea. Many of the men were employed in throwing the dead overboard. The decks were covered with blood, and had the appearance of a butcher's slaughterhouse; the gun tackles were not made fast, and several of the guns got loose, and were surging to and fro from one side to the other.

"Some of the petty officers and seamen, after the action, got liquor, and were intoxicated; and what with the groans of the wounded, the noise and confusion of the enraged survivors on board of the ill-fated ship, rendered the whole scene a perfect hell."

After having related Captain Orne's statement of the battle, I will now proceed to give Captain Hull's account of the action, with a few additional incidents and remarks, which the gallant Commodore was too modest to insert in his official report. He wrote to the Secretary of the Navy, that on the 19th of August, 1812, being in latitude 41° 41' North, longitude 55° 48' West,

Battle Between the *Constitution* and the *Guirriere* on the 19th August, 1812

at two p.m., a sail was discovered from the mast-head, bearing from him E.S.E., but at so great a distance he could not tell what she was. All sail was however immediately made in chase, and he soon found he gained upon her; at three p. m. could plainly see that she was a ship under easy sail, standing close upon the wind on the starboard tack; at half-past three made her out to be a frigate.

He continued the chase until within about three miles distance to windward of the enemy. Captain Hull then hauled to the wind, and deliberately took in all his light sails, and prepared for action; he also took a second reef in his topsails, as the wind was blowing fresh from the northward; he then sent down royal-yards, hauled up his courses, cleared ship, and beat to quarters. At this time the chase lay with her main-topsail aback, evidently waiting for the American frigate to come down to commence the action.

At five p.m. the *Guerriere* hoisted an English ensign at each mast-head, when the *Constitution* set her colours, bore up and ran to leeward in order to close in with the enemy to the best advantage. As the *Constitution* neared the *Guerriere*, say when within long-gun shot, the latter ship opened her fire, wearing and yawing about to rake and prevent being raked. The first two broadsides fired from the Englishman, however, were at so great a distance that little or no damage was received by the American frigate.

Up to this time, Captain Hull had reserved his fire, all his guns being double-shotted, that is to say with one round shot and a canister of grape. At six in the evening, the English frigate bore up, and ran off the wind under her three topsails and jib, with the wind on the quarter, to invite his adversary to a combat at close quarters. Immediately after this, say at a quarter after six, the *Constitution* set her main-top-gallant-sail and fore-sail, to range alongside and close in with the enemy.

As she approached the *Guerriere*, that ship hulled the *Constitution* several times, and killed or wounded a few men. At this period Mr. Morris, Captain Hull's first lieutenant, came aft on the quarter-deck (where Captain Hull was walking, and attentively observing every movement of his adversary), and inquired of his commander whether he should not return the fire of the enemy. He said the men were very eager to fire, and that it was difficult to restrain their ardent desire to commence the action. His answer to his lieutenant was, not to fire till he gave the order, or in plainer English, "Mr. Morris I'll tell you when to fire, therefore stand ready, and see that not a shot is thrown away."

At this moment the naval hero was watching the exact position of the two ships, and as the Constitution gradually ranged up within half pistol shot, and began to double on the quarter of his opponent, Captain Hull peremptorily ordered Mr. Morris to give him the first division. "The next, sir, pour in the whole broadside," was the reiterated order. He saw the effect of this terrible broadside, and at the same moment exclaimed to those about him, "by Heavens that ship is ours."

As the two frigates now lay nearly abreast of each other, they both kept up a constant cannonading for about ten minutes, when the mizzen-mast of the Englishman was shot away not far above the deck. The *Constitution* still continued to range slowly ahead of his adversary, keeping up a tremendous fire. She then luffed short round the bows of the *Guerriere* to prevent being raked, when unfortunately, in executing this manoeuvre, she shot into the wind, got stern-way upon her, and fell foul of her antagonist, so that the *Guerriere's* bowsprit came in contact with the mizzen shrouds of the American frigate.

In this situation both parties prepared to board, but as each ship kept up a brisk fire of musketry, while they were in collision, Lieutenant Morris, Mr. Alwyn, the sailing-master, Mr. Bush, the marine officer, and others, sprang upon the taffrail to board or repel boarders. Several of them were shot. Mr. Morris received a musket ball in the abdomen, but remained at his post. Mr. Bush fell dead by a musket ball passing through his head, and Mr. Alwyn was wounded in the shoulder. At this moment there was considerable sea on, when the fore and main masts of the English frigate went by the board, leaving the *Guerriere* a helpless wreck, wallowing in the trough of the sea.

The two ships soon separated, when the *Constitution* at once made sail, hauling on board her fore and main tacks, and ran off a short distance to windward, when she rove new braces, and cleared ship to renew the action.

The *Guerriere* having the stump of the mizzen-mast still standing, hoisted upon it an English Jack, and when Captain Dacres saw his adversary preparing to come down athwart his bows to give him the raking *coup-de-grâce,* he very wisely hauled down his flag, and surrendered to the frigate. Thus ended the first naval battle of any consequence in the war of 1812; but which was the prelude to many other glorious victories.

After the flag was struck, Captain Hull sent Mr. Reid, his third Lieutenant, on board the prize to ascertain what ship it was, when the boat was immediately sent back to report that the captured ship was the *Guerriere,* 38, Captain James R. Dacres, one of the frigates that had so lately chased the *Constitution* off New York.

Captain Hull remained near his prize during the night to watch over her safety. The next morning at daylight, the officer in charge of the prize hailed to say, that the *Guerriere* had four feet water in her hold, and that there was much danger of her sinking. Consequently, the first thing to be done was to remove all the wounded prisoners to the *Constitution* as soon as possible, for the first impulse of a brave man, after the battle is over, is to comfort and soothe the wounded and the dying. Captain Hull accordingly sent all his boats, and commenced transporting the officers and men of the *Guerriere* to his own ship, and, as the weather had now become moderate, by noon on the 20th this duty was accomplished. At three o'clock in the afternoon the prize crew was recalled, having previously set the wreck on fire, and in a quarter of an hour after she blew up.

The disparity between the two ships in killed and wounded was almost unparalleled in the history of naval battles, and was by the official accounts as follows:

The loss of the *Guerriere* in killed was fifteen; missing,

twenty-four: wounded, sixty-two. Total killed and wounded, and missing, one hundred and one.

The loss on board the *Constitution* was seven killed and seven wounded.

Remarks on this Important Action

Captain Dacres was the son of a British Admiral, and no doubt a brave, high-minded, honourable man, but unfortunately for him, he made three grand mistakes in this affair. The first was, in holding his enemy too cheap, a very common fault among his countrymen, even down to the present day. Witness the attack of the British light-cavalry at the battle of Balaklava. The second error was, in boasting, before the battle. Had he remembered the injunction of the infallible old book,

Let not him that girdeth on his armour boast himself as he that putteth it off,

it would, doubtless, have saved him much pain and mortification throughout his afterlife. The third mistake was, in firing too soon, for it is agreed on all hands, that he threw away two entire broadsides. This last mistake evinced a great want of cool, deliberate judgement.

On the part of Captain Hull, I should say, as a nautical man, he also made one mistake in allowing the *Constitution* to get into the wind, and, consequently making a stern-board, she should have been kept under good steerage-way, for under some circumstances this getting foul of the enemy might have involved the safety of his ship. I will not, however, judge too severely, perhaps it was unavoidable. The wheel-ropes might have been injured, or some other cause connected with the steering of the ship may have occurred, which has not been related in the official account of the action.

With respect to the relative size of the two ships, there can be no doubt that the *Constitution* was the heavier, and that the weight of metal was also in favour of the American frigate. Still, under these circumstances, it would not have made a shade of difference if the *Guerriere's* main-deck guns had been twenty-fours in lieu of eighteens.

It matters not how large a shot may be, if it is badly directed and thrown into the water, or, the gun so elevated as to have the shot pass through the upper air, or the lofty sails of the enemy. It will be observed, that Captain Hull received the random shot of his adversary as he closed in with him. He, no doubt, expected to suffer some damage before he should, as it were, crush his enemy, for it will be recollected, his guns were all double-shotted, *viz.*, with round grape and canister, and as soon as he poured in the first destructive broadside he saw that the game was his, and, that he had given the *Guerriere* a death blow.

Hair-splitting casuists may weigh straws and solve probable results, and cavil about the great disparity of the two ships, but the common sense conclusion is, that the English had met a new enemy in the American seamen, and were disappointed and confounded; they found the American officers and men fully equal in bravery and seamanship to themselves.

They had for years been accustomed to vanquish the French and Spanish ships-of-war, by their superior skill in sailing and manoeuvring their ships: not that they excelled the French in bravery, for there is no braver people on the face of the earth: neither can the English excel them in gunnery, for they are great cannoneers, and can vie with them in everything pertaining to war, except practical seamanship.

It had long been the custom with the English, in their engagements with the French and Spanish, both in fleets and with single ships, as they approached their adversaries, to fire a gun or two as feelers, to ascertain whether they were near enough for their shot to take effect, and then manoeuvre so as to rake their enemy, and gain the victory with but little loss to themselves. It is therefore more than probable, that Captain Dacres acted on the same old principle with the *Constitution*, not dreaming that she would so soon close in with him, with a determination to conquer or sink.

From the commencement to the end of the war. the same practice and determination were carried out with all our ships-of-war. The old-fashioned way of playing at long balls, for several hours with their enemy, does not suit the nature or taste of the Americans. They make up their minds on a subject, and then, to use a familiar phrase, "go-ahead," regardless of consequences. And so it will ever be with republicans, each individual feels as though the honour of the flag and of the country rested upon his shoulders; that he is a citizen of the United States; is fighting for the land that gave him birth, and not for a tyrannical master, who has no feelings in common with him.

The American seamen in this trial of strength, and in most other naval battles during the war, went into action dancing at their guns, and telling their officers, "Gentlemen, you take care of the flags and the quarter-deck, and we will do the fighting."

Captain Hull, finding his ship filled with prisoners, many of whom were suffering from their wounds, made sail for Boston, where he arrived on the 30th of the month, after a cruise of just twenty-eight days.

On his return to Boston, after his glorious victory, and destruction of the *Guerriere*, he was welcomed with heart-felt joy by all classes of people. An artillery company was posted on the wharf, and greeted him with a federal salute, which was returned by the *Constitution*.

An immense number of citizens received him with loud and unanimous huzzas in every part of the city. The principal streets were beautifully decorated with American flags, and men of all ranks and distinctions appeared to vie with each other to do him honour. A splendid entertainment was given by the inhabitants of Boston to Captain Hull and the brave officers belonging to his ship. The citizens of New York raised a sum of money for the purpose of purchasing swords, which were to be presented to him and his gallant officers.

The people of Philadelphia also subscribed funds to purchase two superb pieces of plate to be given to the naval hero and his first lieutenant, the gallant Morris. In Baltimore the flags of all the vessels in the harbour were displayed in honour of Captain Hull's victory over the *Guerriere*, and a grand salute fired. In fine, the whole country was electrified, and the entire heart of the Nation beat high in his praise.

CHAPTER 2

Captures and Prizes

When I commenced writing the history of the privateers and letters-of-marque, it was not my intention to enter deeply into the exploits and achievements of our gallant little navy, either on the broad ocean or on our extensive lakes, but merely to intersperse my book with a few of the most brilliant combats between single ships. But, as I advance, I find the two subjects so intimately connected, that it is with great difficulty I am able to proceed without giving a sketch, or short outline of the war.

In following up the chain of events from its commencement, it will be necessary to insert here a list of the American frigates, that were well-manned and efficient, when the war was declared, on the 18th of June, 1812.

Constitution,	44 Guns.
President,	44 "
United States,	44 "
Congress,	38 "
Constellation	38 "
Chesapeake,	38 "
Essex,	32 "

Beside the above seven frigates, there were some twelve or fifteen sloops-of-war and smaller vessels, lying in the naval dockyards. Some of these ships were repairing, others unseaworthy, and not fit for present service. Consequently, it followed that the before-named seven frigates were left to contend with the whole British navy, amounting in number, at that period, to one thousand and sixty sail,[1] eight hundred of which were efficient cruising ships, and a large portion of them at sea,

Against such an overwhelming disparity of numbers, while numerous merchant-vessels were spread over almost every sea, what was the best policy for the American government to pursue? The question is easily answered. Send these frigates immediately to sea to protect our own merchant-ships, and order them to take, burn, sink, and destroy the enemy, wherever he should be found, Also, tell them that if they meet a man-of-war of equal or even superior force, should the disparity not be too great, to attack him forthwith, regardless of consequences.

For the result of such a determination, I refer the reader to Cooper's *Naval History,* and to the official government documents on that subject.

After these remarks respecting the United States' Navy, I will go on to record the daring exploits of the privateers and letters-of-marque.

Before I commence with the prizes made by the privateers, I will just stop to notice that the first English merchantman captured, was a British ship from Jamaica, bound to London (she was probably taken off Cape Hatteras), and sent into Norfolk by a revenue cutter. This occurred about the 1st of July, say twelve days after the declaration of war.

On the 10th of July, the British government schooner *Whiting,* Lieutenant Maxey, with despatches from his government to the government of the United States, was taken while lying in Hampton Roads (he not having heard of the war), without resistance, by the privateer *Dash,* of Baltimore, Captain Carroway. The *Dash,* at this time, was ready for sea, and bound on a cruise for British merchantmen.

On the 18th of July, the letter-of-marque schooner *Falcon,*

---

1. The British Government publishes annually a list of its whole navy with a particular description of the ships composing It, commencing with a first-rate, carrying 120 guns, down to the cutter of 4, with all the intermediate rates. I refer the reader to Steel's *List of the Royal Navy,* for the years 1811 and 12, as my authority, and also to Fenimore Cooper's *History of the United States Navy* of the same date.

belonging to Baltimore, on her passage from Boston to Bordeaux, with four guns and sixteen men, when on the coast of France, was engaged with the British cutter *Hero*, with five guns and fifty men for two hours and a-half, and finally beat her off, with considerable loss on both sides, after repulsing the enemy three times in his attempts to board.

On the next day, the *Falcon* was attacked by a British privateer of six guns and forty men, and although considerably injured by her engagement with the cutter the day previous, the privateer commenced a heavy fire on the *Falcon*, which she bravely returned for an hour and a-half, when the captain and several of the crew of the *Falcon* being wounded, she was carried by boarding, while her colours were still flying. They were carried into Guernsey, where the wounded were taken on shore.

I find the following in a New York paper, dated July 14th:

"We believe that in sixty days from the day on which war against England was declared, there will be afloat from the United States not less than one hundred privateers, carrying upon an average six guns and seventy-five men. If these are successful, their number will probably be doubled in a short time. At any rate, sixty-five were at sea on the 16th, and many others are probably out from different ports which have not been reported.

"*Philadelphia, July the 20th.*—This day four privateers of considerable force left the capes of the Delaware on a cruise, and others are preparing to follow. In the latter part of this month, prizes were almost daily pouring into most of the Atlantic ports."

PRIZES TAKEN BY PRIVATEERS DURING THE MONTH OF JULY.

The privateer *Paul Jones*, of New York, captured the British brig *Ulysses* from the West Indies for Halifax, and sent her into Norfolk.

The letter-of-marque *Gypsey* of New York for Bordeaux, was captured by a British cruiser, and retaken by her crew and carried safely into France.

Successful Cruise.—"Salem, July 10th.—Last evening the privateer schooner *Fame*, Captain Webb, returned to port, having taken a ship of near 300 tons, loaded with square timber, and a brig of 200 tons, loaded with tar. The ship had two four-pounders, but was prevented from firing or making any defence by our boarding her so suddenly."

July 14th, the British government transport, No. 60, having two guns, musketry, etc., with twelve men, prize to the *Madison* privateer, was sent into Gloucester; she was from Halifax, bound to St. Johns. The transport was under convoy of the *Indian*, British sloop-of-war, but observing a privateer (supposed to be the sloop *Polly*), she gave chase to her, and while she was absent, the *Madison* pounced upon the transport and took her. On board of the transport were found one hundred casks of gunpowder, eight hundred and eighty suite of uniform for the 104th British Regiment Light Infantry, some bales of superfine cloths for officer's uniforms, ten casks of wine, drums, trumpets, and other camp equipage. She was a fine brig, 290 tons burthen, and with her cargo, was supposed to be worth $50,000.

Arrived at Salem, July 15th British sloop *Endeavour*, Newman, of Bermuda from Newfoundland, bound to St. Andrews, with sugar, prize to the privateer-sloop *Polly*, of that port. The prize-master of the *Endeavour* reported that off Cape Sable, the *Polly* and *Dolphin* privateers discovered a ship and brig in company, both of which they took to be merchantmen, and their determination was in the first place to board the ship, but having proceeded nearly within gun-shot of her, discovered she was an English sloop-of-war of twenty-two guns (probably the *Indian*), when she immediately crowded all sail and stood for the *Polly*, firing several shots, which, however, did not reach her.

It afterwards became calm, when the sloop-of-war manned out her launch, and several boats, with about forty men; coming within musket-shot, she gave three cheers, and commenced a brisk fire of musketry and one four-pound cannon, which the *Polly* immediately returned with such a tremendous fire of musketry and langrage, that in a few minutes the launch was silenced and struck her colours, and the other boats were glad to return to their ship. The sloop-of-war being nearly within gun-shot, the privateer took to her sweeps and succeeded in making her escape.

The loss of the Englishman could not be ascertained, but it must have been severe. The launch came up to the *Polly* with sixteen sweeps—only five could be seen when she returned to the ship.

The sloop sustained no injury! The brig in company was the transport which was sent into Gloucester, having been captured by the *Madison*, while the sloop-of-war was in chase of the *Polly*.

A British schooner which had arrived at Amelia Island, about the middle of July, from New Providence, with $20,000 specie on board was detained by the revenue-cutter. The prizes lately made in that neighbourhood at that time, were of great value.

The privateer *Madison* of Gloucester, Mass., captured a British ship of twelve guns. Ten or twelve prizes had already reached Salem. Seven privateers sailed from Baltimore, on or about the 10th of July, on a cruise. One of them, the schooner *Rossie*, was commanded by the celebrated Commodore Barney. Several others were fitting out, and were expected to sail in a few days.

The American ship *Margaret*, on her passage from Liverpool to the United States, loaded with a valuable cargo of salt, earthenware, and ironmongery. A fine new coppered vessel was captured by a British cruiser, and afterwards recaptured by the privateer *Teazer*, of New York. She was sent to Portland, where she safely arrived. The ship and cargo were said to be worth $50,000.

A British brig, four schooners and a *shallop*, laden with dry goods, were sent into Salem, prizes to the privateers *Jefferson* and *Dolphin*.

Three Nova Scotia *shallops,* prizes to the *Lion* privateer, laden with West India produce, and also a few thousand dollars, arrived at Marblehead.

The *Madison* also captured the British brig *Eliza*, of six guns, after a sharp engagement. The privateer had but one gun; she had two men wounded. The captain of the *Eliza* was badly wounded.

An English brig, laden with sugar, together with six or seven small vessels from Eastport, had recently been captured, and sent into various eastern ports.

By order of Governor Mitchell, of Georgia, seventeen English vessels, laden with timber for the use of the British navy, were captured at St. Mary's and at Amelia Island, as soon as he knew the declaration of war.

A fine English brig from Liverpool, bound to St. John's, arrived at Marblehead, a prize to the privateers *Lion* and *Snowbird*. The brig had six guns, but made no resistance.

The first English vessel that arrived at Baltimore was on the 26th of July, *viz.*, a British schooner, loaded with sugar, a prize to the *Dolphin*. Her cargo was valued at $18,000.

EXTRACT FROM A BALTIMORE PAPER, DATED JULY 18.

"We are pleased to observe the spirit that prevails in the eastern States. Though England has many friends in that region, a large majority of the people are full of patriotism, and are determined to carry on the war with enterprise and vigour, knowing that the more they distress the enemy, the sooner we shall have a permanent peace. There is not, perhaps, one port in the whole of the eastern States where they have not one or more privateers, and the most of them have sailed in pursuit of the enemy. We believe the whole number afloat up to this day is about one hundred."

OPINION OF THE ENGLISH PRESS ON THE WAR.

I herewith insert the following article extracted from the *London Statesman* newspaper, dated June the 10th 1812, eight days previous to our declaration of war against England. This article will serve to show that the opposition or liberal party in Britain knew something of the American character, while the

Tory aristocracy were not only blind to justice, but also to their own interest:

"It has been stated, that in a war with this country, America has nothing to gain. In opposition to this assertion it may be said, with equal truth, that in a war with America, England has nothing to gain, but much to lose. Let us examine the relative situation of the two countries. America cannot certainly pretend to wage a maritime war with us. She has no navy to do it with. But America has nearly 100,000 as good seamen as any in the world, all of whom would be actively employed against our trade on every part of the ocean in their fast-sailing ships-of-war, many of which will be able to cope with our small cruisers; and they will be found to be sweeping the West India seas, and even carrying desolation into the chops of the channel.

"Everyone must recollect what they did in the latter part of the American war. The books at Lloyd's will recount it; and the rate of assurances at that time will clearly prove what their diminutive strength was able to effect in the face of our navy, and that, when nearly one hundred pendants, were flying on their coast. Were we then able to prevent their going in and out, or stop them from taking our trade and our store-ships, even in sight of our garrisons? Besides, were they not in the English and Irish channels, picking up our homeward bound trade, sending their prizes into French and Spanish ports, to the great terror and annoyance of our merchants and ship owners?

"These are facts which can be traced to a period when America was in her infancy, without ships, without seamen, without money, and at a time when our navy was not much less in strength than at present. The Americans will be found to be a different sort of enemy by sea than the French. They possess nautical knowledge, with equal enterprise to ourselves. They will be found attempting deeds which a Frenchman would never think of; and they will have all the ports of our enemy open, in which they can make good their retreat with their booty. In a predatory war on commerce, Great Britain would have more to lose than to gain, because the Americans would retire within themselves, having everything they want for supplies, and what foreign commerce they might have, would be carried on in fast-sailing armed ships, which, as heretofore, would be able to fight or run away, as best suited their force or inclination.

"Much is also to be apprehended from the desertion of our seamen, who will meet with every encouragement in the United States, by protecting laws made in their favour, perhaps large *douceurs* offered for their disaffection, and it is well known the predilection which our sailors have for the American shores. These are considerations which by far outweigh any advantages that ought partially to arise to individuals from a few scattering prizes that might be taken by our cruisers. Their harvest seems much more abundant under those wretched and impolitic regulations, called the Orders in Council, the existence of which gives rise to the present differences between the two countries, has drained our treasury, and is starving thousands of our manufacturing brethren.

" America could sustain no possible injury, but internal taxation, from a war with this country, which would not bear any proportion to what we might feel from the circumstances already mentioned, and from which we would most seriously have to apprehend; for our ships, without a large military force, durst not enter the ports of the United States, and that military force, in our present situation, is nowhere to be found. The probable consequence would be the starvation of our West India colonies, and the loss of Upper, if not of Lower Canada; while the total want of specie (which latterly has been wholly drawn from the United States) to pay our troops at Halifax and Quebec, could not fail to accelerate the mischief."

Prizes taken during the month of August.

The British vessel *Wabisch*, laden with timber, and sent into Salem by the privateer-schooner *Dolphin*.

Schooner *Ann* sent into Charleston, by the privateer *Nonpareil* of that place.

Ship *Jarrett*, with two guns and eighteen men, in ballast. from

Bristol, England, for St. Andrews, sent into Salem by the *Fair Trader*, of that port. The *Fair Trader* had one gun and fifteen men. The Englishmen refused to fight, and four of them entered on board the privateer.

Three schooners laden with pork, wine, furs, cordage, etc., sent into Salem.

Schooner ——, captured by the *Dolphin* of Salem, and released, after taking from on board of her $1,000 in specie, and a quantity of beaver skins.

Schooner *Ann Kelly*, of Halifax, with an assorted cargo, sent into Salem by the same.

Brig from St. Andrews for England, sent into Salem by the *Dolphin*.

Schooner ——, sent into Marblehead by the *Lion*, of that port, laden with lumber and naval stores.

Schooner ——, laden with sugar and indigo, sent into Portland by the *Argus* of Boston.

Schooner *Fanny*, from St. Croix for St. Andrews, in ballast, sent into Baltimore by the *Dolphin*, valued at $18,000.

Ship *Mary*, from Bristol, England, for St. John's carrying fourteen heavy guns, a valuable vessel, having on board a considerable quantity of arms and ammunition, sent into Salem by the *Dolphin*.

Schooner ——, laden with provisions, sent into Wiscasset, by the *Fair Trader*.

Schooner *Diligent*, with fifty-five pipes of brandy, sent into Salem by the *Polly*.

Two schooners with cargoes of provisions, pork, corn, etc., sent into Salem by the *Snowbird*, of that place.

Schooner *Jane*, from the West Indies for Halifax, sent into Marblehead by the *Dolphin*.

Ship *Ann Green,* of four hundred and thirty tons, carrying eight twelve-pounders, and two long-sixes, an excellent vessel, from Jamaica for Greenock, with a cargo of rum, etc., valued at $50,000, sent into Boston by the *Gossamer*, of that port.

Barque *St. Andrews*, carrying eight guns, sent into Portland, by the *Rapid* of Boston.

Schooner *Nelson*, laden with oil, furs, fish, etc., sent into Salem by the Buckskin

Schooner ——, sent into Machias by the *Fame*.

Schooner *Three Brothers*, sent into Boston by the *Wiley Reynard*, of that port.

Barque ——, sent into Portland, by the *Catherine* of Boston.

Brig ——, in ballast, captured by the *Polly*, ransomed after taking out a few bales of dry-goods.

Schooner *Eliza*, of Halifax, from Jamaica, sent into Salem by the *Polly*.

Brig *Lady Sherbrook*, two hundred and fifty tons burthen, armed with four six-pounders, laden with lumber and fish, sent into New York by the *Marengo* of that port.

Brig *Elizabeth and Esther*, from St. Johns, for Bermuda, with a cargo of fish, pork, and some dry goods, sent into Philadelphia, by the *Governor McKean* of Philadelphia.

Brig *Ranger*, from St. Domingo for London, carrying six guns, laden with coffee and log-wood, captured by the *Matilda* of Philadelphia, and sent into that port, after a short engagement, in which the British Captain was mortally wounded.

Schooner *Polly*, sent into Boston by the *Wiley Reynard*.

A ship and two brigs sent into Wiscasset, by the *Wiley Reynard*.

Sloop *Mary Ann*, laden with three thousand bushels of salt, sent into Philadelphia by the *Paul Jones,* of New York.

Ship *Hassan*, of London, from Gibraltar for Havana, carrying 14 guns, and twenty men, laden with wines, dry goods, etc., worth $200,000, captured after half an hour's combat, with the loss of her captain, and a boy wounded, by the *Paul Jones*, then of three guns. The guns of the *Hassan* were transferred to the privateer, and the vessel ordered for Savannah.

Brig *Harmony*, from Greenock for Quebec, a fine vessel, two hundred and fifty tons burthen, carrying four heavy guns, laden with a cargo, of dry-goods, etc., sent into New York by the *Yankee*, of Bristol, R. I.

Brig ——, captured by the *Yankee*, and given up for the purpose of disposing of her prisoners.

Ship *Braganza*, from Port-au-Prince, for London, mounting twelve guns, burthen four hundred tons, deeply laden with coffee and log-wood, captured and sent into Baltimore by the *Tom* of that port, after a running fight of fifty-five minutes.

Brig *Peter Waldo*, from Newcastle, England, for Halifax, with a full cargo of British manufactures, clearing for the captors $100,000, sent into Portland by the *Teazer*, of New York.

Ship *Prince Adolphus*. from Martinique for Falmouth, England, mounting eight guns, with thirty-six men, among whom were the Governor, collector, and postmaster of Demarara, sent into Philadelphia by the *Governor McKean,* of that port.

Brig *Ceres*, a valuable vessel, sent into Salem by the *John*, of that port.

Brig ——, laden with timber, taken by a Salem privateer, recaptured by the English, and retaken and sent into Gloucester by a Lynn privateer.

Brig *William*, from Bristol, England, for St. Johns, with a cargo of coal, butter and sundries, sent into Boston by the *Rossie*, Commodore Barney, of Baltimore.

One ship, five brigs and a schooner, all laden with fish and timber, captured by the *Rossie* and burned.

Brig *Mary*, from Scotland for Newfoundland, captured by the *Yankee* and released, to dispose of her prisoners, forty-seven in number.

Schooner *Venus*, with one hundred and nineteen puncheons of rum, a quantity of sugar, fruits, etc., sent into Portland by the *Teazer*.

Ship *Osborne*, ten guns, eighteen pounders, twenty-six men, from Gibraltar for St. Andrews, in ballast, burthen five hundred tons, sent into Portland by the *Teazer*, after a long fight, in which no person on either side was injured. It is said the government of Nova Scotia offered $30,000 for the *Teazer*. This privateer carried only two guns, and at the time she captured the *Osborne*, had not thirty men.

Brig *Eliza*, from Jamaica for Halifax, laden with rum and sugar, sent into New York by the *Marengo* of that port.

Brig *Richard*, three hundred tons, laden with timber, sent into Marblehead by the *Industry* of Lynn.

Brig *Nancy*, with a full cargo of provisions, sent into Salem by the *Fair Trader*, of that port.

Brig ———, from Quebec for the West Indies, laden with flour, sent into New York by the *Bunker Hill*.

Schooner ———, sent into Providence by the *Leander*, of Providence, R. I.

Brig *Leonidas*, of fourteen guns; a first-rate vessel, from Jamaica for Belfast, laden with about two hundred and thirty hogsheads of sugar, seventy-five puncheons of rum, coffee, pimento, etc., sent into Savannah by the *Mars*, of Norfolk. The brig was carried by boarding after a short resistance, in which she had one man wounded.

Schooner *Skylark*, from Quebec for Martinique, laden with provisions, sent into the port of New York by the *Bunker Hill*.

Brig *Lady-Provost*, from Halifax for Jamaica, sent into New York by the *Marengo*.

Brig *Friends*, sent into Boston by the *Benjamin Franklin*.

Brig *Mary*, from Pictou, for England, sent into Boston by the *Benjamin Franklin*.

Ship *Jenny*, twelve guns, and eighteen men, from Liverpool for St. Johns, with salt, sent into Salem by the *Rossie*.

Schooner ———, of one hundred and seventy tons, from Pointe-à-Pitre for Halifax, a very valuable vessel, laden with sugar and rum, sent into Portland by the *Teazer*.

Desperate encounter between the Privateer-Brig Yankee and the British Letter-of-Marque ship Royal Bounty.[2]

The privateer *Yankee* was cruising off the coast of Nova Scotia, on the 1st of August, 1812. At noon, she saw a large ship on her lee bow, about four miles distant, and made all sail in chase. At one p.m. she prepared for action. The privateer being

---

2. See Appendix.

to windward, she ran down on the ship's weather-quarter, and gave her the first division, and soon after, as she doubled on the enemy, gave her the entire broadside.

The ship soon returned the compliment, and the action was continued with spirit on both sides. The two vessels being near each other, the *Yankee's* marines poured a continued volume from her small arms, which was very destructive to her adversary.

The privateer's shot soon cut the ship's sails and rigging to pieces, and killed the helmsman. In a few moments after, the ship became unmanageable. The *Yankee* then ran off a short distance and luffed-to athwart the bows of the foe, and gave him a raking broadside, keeping up at the same time a constant shower of musketry, which soon compelled the enemy to strike his colours.

The ship proved to be the *Royal Bounty*, Captain Henry Gambles. She was a fine ship of 658 tons, mounting ten guns, with twenty-five men. She was from Hull, in ballast, seven weeks out, and bound to Prince Edward's Island. The privateer took out the prisoners, and manned the prize for the United States.

The *Yankee* had three men wounded, with her sails and rigging somewhat damaged.

The *Royal Bounty* had two men killed; the captain and six officers and seamen wounded.

The action lasted one hour.

The ship was terribly cut up in her sails and rigging. All her boats were stove, and more than one hundred and fifty shot of different sizes passed through her sails, or lodged in her hull and spars.

The wounded prisoners were carefully attended by the *Yankee's* surgeon.

Prizes Captured by Privateers.

One brig and a schooner captured by the *Rossie*, and sent to Newfoundland, with the crews of the above vessels, one hundred and eight in number, on parole and receipt for exchange.

Commodore Barney sent his compliments to Admiral Sawyer, desiring the poor fellows might be fairly treated, and promising a larger supply very soon.

Schooner *Perseverance*, from St. Augustine for Nassau, in ballast, sent into Charleston by the *Nonsuch*, of Baltimore.

Ship *Sir Simon Clark*, sixteen guns, thirty-nine men, from Jamaica for Leith, with a cargo of sugar, rum, coffee, etc., worth from $100,000 to $150,000, sent into Norfolk by the *Globe*; she was gallantly carried by boarding, after a brisk cannonade of a few minutes.

The British ship had four men killed, with the captain and three others severely wounded. The second lieutenant and drummer were killed on board the *Globe*, and one wounded.

Brig *Honduras Packet,* two guns and twelve men, with a valuable cargo of rum and dry-goods, from Jamaica for the city of St. Domingo, sent into Charleston by the *Mary Ann* of that port.

Brig *Amelia*, ten guns and seventeen men, from Malta for Havana, with a valuable cargo of wine, castile soap, oil, etc., etc., sent into Charleston by the *Mary-Ann* carried but one gun and fifty men.

Schooner *Mary*, from Gonaives for Jamaica, laden with cotton, captured by the *Mary Ann*, and burnt.

Schooner ———, (armed) after a smart brush taken by the *Mary Ann*, and discharged to release her prisoners.

Schooner *Union*, from Jamaica for Quebec, with 146 puncheons of rum; vessel and cargo worth $30,000, sent into Salem by the *John*, of that port.

Brig *Elizabeth*, from Gibraltar for Quebec, in ballast, burthen 300 tons, four guns and twelve men, sent into Salem by the *John*.

Three brigs, laden with lumber, taken by the *John* and released.

A schooner and a sloop, from St. Johns for Halifax, laden with lumber, sent into Gloucester by the *Orlando*, of that port.

Brig ———, from Jamaica for Halifax, with a full cargo of rum, sent into Charleston, by the *Bunker Hill*, of New York.

Brig *James*, sent into Falmouth, by the *Bunker Hill*.

Ship *Apollo*, eight guns, burthen 400 tons, sent into Salem by the *John*.

In Long Island Sound, a deeply laden brig, from Jamaica, prize to the *Teazer* privateer.

A schooner, from Jamaica, with 160 puncheons of rum, prize to the *John*.

The *John* had taken three new brigs, bound from Halifax to England, laden with lumber. Also one ship of 400 tons, coppered, in ballast; having eight eighteens. The *John* was left in chase of a ship from England of 400 tons, laden with dry goods.

Schooner *Sally*, of Cape Ann, from Cayenne, with a full cargo of molasses, was sent into Newport on the 10th of July, by a privateer belonging to that place.

The privateer ship *Alfred*, of sixteen guns and one hundred and thirty men, sailed from Salem on a cruise the 16th of August.

Philadelphia, August 20th.—"The privateer-schooner *Shadow* is below. She put into port in distress, having been damaged in an action with a letter-of-marque. Captain Taylor had two men killed and twelve."

Privateer *Globe*, of Baltimore, arrived at Hampton Roads, accompanied by a very large British ship, showing twenty-two guns. She was from Jamaica, bound for Glasgow, and richly laden. The ship came up the bay, and the *Globe* proceeded again to sea as quickly as possible.

Schooner *Ann*, another prize to the *Globe*, carrying four guns, laden with log-wood and mahogany, arrived at Baltimore. It is stated that several of the crews of these prizes entered as seamen on board of the *Globe*.

The *Eliza Ann*, from Liverpool, for Baltimore, with a full cargo of British goods, has been sent into Boston by the privateer *Yankee*. Several other vessels in like circumstances have been sent into port by our privateers.

The privateer *Benjamin Franklin* arrived at New York, with twenty-eight prisoners, after a month's cruise, during which she captured seven British vessels, most of them armed, and bound to England with lumber.

The privateer *John*, Captain Crowninshield, of Salem, of sixteen guns and one hundred and sixty men, returned to port after a short cruise of about three weeks. During this time, she made eleven captures; two had arrived, three were destroyed, one retaken, and the rest not then heard of.

EXTRACT FROM A SALEM PAPER.

"The privateer *Buckskin*, of Salem, has taken four loaded schooners, one of them with fish and English goods. She has also retaken a Kennebeck brig. The *Buckskin* spoke yesterday in the bay a prize to the sloop *Polly*, loaded with fifty-five pipes of brandy and two cases of pocket-books. Among the prizes taken by the *Buckskin* was a schooner from Halifax for Quebec, laden with military stores, on board of which was Colonel Pearson of the British army, his lady and family. The *Buckskin* also recaptured the brig *Hesper*, taken by the *Maidstone* frigate.

"The privateer *Dolphin*, after a successful cruise of twenty days, returned to Salem on the 23rd of July. The *Dolphin* has taken six prizes without receiving the smallest injury. She was repeatedly chased by the English, and at one time for twenty-four hours, but finally escaped. She has treated her prisoners with the greatest kindness. In rowing away from men-of-war, she found great aid from their voluntary assistance. The prisoners said they had much rather go to America than return on board a British man-of-war."

EXTRACT FROM THE LOG-BOOK OF THE SCHOONER *HIGHFLYER*, OF BALTIMORE.

"On the 26th of July, off the Double-headed Shot Keys, at half-past four p.m., discovered a sail standing North and West; gave chase. At seven p.m. came up with and boarded the British schooner *Harriet*, in ballast from New Providence, bound to Havana. She carried three black men and one boy, two gentlemen and one lady passengers. Put on board Captain Taylor as prize-master, and ordered her for the first port in the United States. The next day the captain of the *Harriet* informed Captain Gavet that there was money concealed on board we boarded her, and found $8,000 in specie.

"Next day, stood through the Gulf. On the 19th August, latitude 9° 22', at six a.m., discovered a fleet bearing S.S.W., distant two leagues; wore ship and made sail, endeavouring to get to the windward, for the purpose of reconnoitring them. Next day, at half-past one p.m., the frigate from the fleet gave chase to us, steering various courses. At five p.m. dropped him, still pursuing the squadron. At six saw them bearing North. The next day, 21st, at five p.m., the wind moderate, brought-to and boarded the British ship *Diana*, Captain Harvey, one of the Jamaica fleet, bound to Bristol, burthen 353 tons, laden with rum, sugar, coffee, etc. Took out her crew, sent a prize-master and ten men on board, and ordered her for the first port in the United States.

"At the same time two other sail in sight; at six a.m., bore down on them, fired three or four shots at them, which were returned by both ships. 22nd, at two p.m., engaged the two ships at half gun shot, and after firing on them upwards of sixty shots, the breeze blowing fresh, not thinking it safe to board them, at four p.m. hauled off. Next day, at four p.m., wind moderating, bore down, and engaged the stern-most ship, called the *Jamaica*, of Liverpool, Captain Neil, of seven guns, twenty-one men, 365 tons, in company with the ship *Mary and Ann*, of London, Captain Miller, mounting twelve guns, eighteen men, and 329 tons burden. When within musket shot, we commenced a brisk fire from our great guns and musketry, which was returned with great courage and resolution from both ships. The engagement lasted twenty minutes, when we boarded and carried the *Jamaica*, the *Mary and Ann* striking her colours at the same time.

"It is with pleasure we state that every man and officer acted with great courage and determined resolution, but we are sorry to announce that Captain Gavet was unfortunately wounded about the middle of the action, by a musket ball, which passed through his right arm; also one ordinary seaman, slightly wounded in the cheek. The *Highflyer* received several shot in her sails; her gib and flying jib-stay were shot away, and her foremast wounded. Manned both ships; put Mr. Brown (prize-master) and eight men on board the *Mary and Ann,* and Mr. Grant and fourteen men on board the *Jamaica*, and ordered them for the first port in the United States. Both ships were richly laden with sugar, rum, coffee, log-wood, etc. Several of their seamen were wounded, but none killed. The prizes arrived safely."

EXTRACT FROM THE JOURNAL OF THE
PRIVATEER *GLOBE*, OF BALTIMORE.

"On the 24th July, the *Globe* left the Capes of the Chesapeake Bay, in company with the letter-of-marque *Cora*, and proceeded to sea. The *Globe* was well manned, having a crew of eighty seamen, all in good spirits.

"On the 25th, spoke the ship *Marmion*, from New Orleans for Baltimore.

"*26th*—Spoke the ship *South Carolina*, from the same port, bound for the same place. Boarded a large ship from Havana for New York, all well.

"*27th*—Boarded a schooner from the West Indies, for New England, which had fallen in with four sail of merchantmen, without convoy, three days before. Brought-to schooner *Polly* of Boston, from Havana for New York, examined her papers, etc.

"*30th*—Brought-to ship *Camilla*, of Philadelphia, from Cadiz for the same port. Boarded a Swedish schooner from St. Bart's, for Norfolk, and while overhauling her, being at the mast-head, discovered a sail ahead, which we gave chase to, but lost her in the night.

"*31st*—Saw a sail to which we gave chase, and in about three hours were within gun-shot, when we commenced firing. She hoisted British colours, and returned fire with her stern-chasers, two long-nines, which was continued for about forty minutes, against our long nine (midships), that being the only gun we could get to bear, as it was blowing fresh and she crowded all sail; when we got close enough we began to fire broadsides (charged with round shot, double shotted, and then with langrage and round), which she returned, broadside for broadside; when we got within musket-shot and fired several volleys into her she struck, after a brisk engagement of an hour and a half.

"She proved to be the English letter-of-marque ship *Boyd*, from New Providence, for Liverpool, laden with coffee, dyewoods, and cotton, mounting ten guns, *viz.*, two long-nines, two short-twelves, and six long-sixes. None hurt on either side. Our sails and rigging very much cut up. Their boats were destroyed, rigging and sails cut to pieces, and several shot in the hull; took out all the crew except the mate and two men, put a prizemaster and eight men on board, and ordered her for Baltimore; arrived at Philadelphia. The prisoners treated as well as our own crew.

"*August 1st*—Parted with the *Boyd*, and went in quest of two other English vessels which we expected this way. Repaired damages; seven prisoners entered as seamen. Saw a schooner and gave chase, but lost her in the night; saw another sail the same night, which also escaped.

"At eleven a.m. saw *Bermuda*, we passed within gunshot; cruised off under British colours.

"*3rd.*—At sunset, saw a sail ahead, standing toward us, when we got near enough, manoeuvred for two hours; she appeared to be an English sloop-of-war; she gave chase, but soon gave it up, as she did not make any way with us.

"*4th*—Saw a schooner to windward, and chased all day, sweeps out from four to eight p.m.; she altered her course, and escaped under cover of the night.

"*8th*—Officers and men put on an allowance of three quarts of water per day, for cooking, etc.

"*9th*—The seamen exchanged their liquor, quart for quart, for water.

"14th—Saw a sail ahead to which we gave chase, and captured without resistance. She proved to be the British schooner *Ann*, from the City of St. Domingo for Guernsey, laden with mahogany and log-wood; mounts four guns, and carries nine men, (arrived.)"

Prizes Captured by Privateers.

Ship *Elizabeth*, ten guns, twelve-pounders, from Jamaica for England, laden with three hundred and twenty-three hogsheads of sugar, some tierces and barrels of do., with a quantity of coffee and ginger, etc.; sent into Charleston by the *Sarah Ann*, of Baltimore, after a smart action, in which four men were wounded on board the ship, and two on board the privateer.

Schooner *James*, from Porto Rico for Martinique, in ballast, sent into Baltimore by the *Dolphin*, of that port. The *Dolphin* destroyed several droggers.

Brig *Pursuit*, from Poole for St. Andrews, sent into Portland by the *Rapid*, privateer.

Brig *Tay*, from Dundee for Pictou, N. B., sent into Portland by the *Rapid*.

Ship *Britannia*, six guns, 350 tons, a new vessel in ballast, from Portsmouth, England, for Halifax, sent into —— by the *Thrasher*, privateer.

Brig *Howe*, six guns, in ballast, from Penzance for Pictou, sent into Portland by the *Dart*, of that port.

Brig *Elizabeth*, of Liverpool, 165 tons, laden with coal, sent into Newport, R. I., by the *Decatur*, privateer.

Ship ——, from Jamaica, for London, sent into Cape Ann.

Ship ——, fourteen guns and twenty-five men, burthen 450 tons, laden with 449 hhds. of sugar, 140 puncheons of rum, etc., sent into Portland by the *Revenge*, privateer.

Brig *Ocean*, seven guns, twenty-six men, from Jamaica, for White Haven, laden with sugar and rum, sent into New York by the *Saratoga*, of that port.

Ship *Esther*, twelve guns, twenty-five men, a valuable vessel, sent into Gloucester by the *Montgomery*, of Salem.

Ship *Quebec*, from Jamaica, sixteen guns, fifty-two men, burthen 400 tons, laden with sugar, etc., valued at $300,000, sent into New York by the *Saratoga*. Her cargo consists of 334 hhds. of sugar, 59 puncheons of rum, 636 bales of cotton, 52 tierces of coffee, 52½ tons of log-wood, 70 tons fustic, one ton ebony, a quantity of old copper, a quantity of hides and spars. The *Saratoga* returned to port with between seventy and eighty prisoners on board, nearly as many as her crew at present consists of.

Ship *Richmond*, fourteen guns, twenty-five men, beside officers, 800 tons burthen, deeply laden with West India produce, worth $200,000, captured on her voyage from Jamaica for London, and sent into Portsmouth by the privateer *Thomas*.

Ship *Adonis*, of Greenock, twelve guns and twenty-five men, a valuable vessel, in ballast from Newfoundland, for Nova Scotia, sent into Salem by the *Montgomery*, privateer.

Ship *Falmouth*, fourteen guns, thirty men, from Jamaica, for Bristol (E.), with a cargo valued at $200,000, sent into Portsmouth by the *Thomas*, of that port.

Brig *Two Friends*, sent into Boston by the *Benjamin Franklin*, privateer,

Ship *Friends*, six guns, burthen 290 tons, laden with timber, sent into Boston by the *Dart*.

Schooner *Trial*, sent into Salem by the *Leader*, of Providence.

Schooner *John and George*, sent into Boston by the *Regulator*, privateer.

Ship ——, chiefly laden with rum, sent into Wilmington, North Carolina, by the *Poor Sailor*, of Charleston.

Brig ——, with 260 hhds. of rum, sent into Portland by the *Dart*.

Schooner *Mary Ann*, with a cargo of rum and coffee, sent into Norfolk by the privateer *Black Joke*, of New York.

Brig *Hannah*, from Oporto for Quebec, with rum and fruit, sent into Salem by the *Montgomery*.

Schooner *Mary*, from Lisbon for Halifax, with some specie, sent into Salem by the same.

Brig ——, sent into Castine by the *Dart*.

Brig *Pomona*, two guns, captured by the *Decatur* and sent to Halifax as a cartel with prisoners.

Brig *Devonshire*, laden with fish, captured by the same, and sent to France to sell her cargo.

Brig *Concord*, captured by the *Dart* and burnt.

Brig *Hope*, captured by the same, and sent to Halifax with prisoners, as above.

The *Decatur* returned to port after a cruise of forty-seven days, during which she captured eleven vessels, several of them very large and valuable.

Schooner *Minorca*, from Jamaica, for Cuba, sent into Savannah by the *Wasp*, of Baltimore.

Barque *William and Charlotte*, sent into Boston by the *Decatur*, privateer.

EXTRACT FROM A NEW YORK NEWSPAPER, DATED AUGUST 20.

"We observe with much pride and pleasure, that the conduct of our privateersmen is in general so correct and liberal as to command the respect of their enemies, and to afford no room for the clamour of those opposed to the system of privateering."

"Magnanimity—Arrived at New York on the 24th instant, the schooner *Industry*, Captain Renncaux, prize to the *Benjamin Franklin*, privateer.

"The *Industry* is laden with pickled salmon, is worth about $2,000, and was captured near the Anglo-American coast, in order to prevent her giving information to some British cruisers of the *Benjamin Franklin's* being in those seas.

"The owners of the privateer, on being apprised that the *Industry* belonged to a poor widow who had a family, promptly directed her to be restored. We are informed that they have also taken such measures as will prevent the consequences of the war from operating in this instance to the injury of the indigent and unfortunate."

Portsmouth, August 18th—The privateer-schooner *Thomas*, Captain Shaw, eleven guns and one hundred men, and privateer-sloop *Science*, Fernald, sailed from this port on a cruise. Two other privateers were fitting out at the same time.

Norfolk, Sept. 3rd—The schooner *Hornet*, a privateer fitted out in Baltimore, was run ashore nineteen miles to the South of Cape Henry, by a British man-of-war, and bilged.

Commodore Barney arrived at Newport on the 30th of August, in his schooner *Rossie*, from a short but successful cruise of forty-five days, along the eastern coast of the United States. During his absence he captured fifteen vessels, nine of the number he burned or sunk. The vessels captured amounted to about 2,914 tons, and were manned by 166 men. The estimated value of these vessels was $1,289,000. Commodore Barney remained in this port about eight or ten days to water, provision, and refresh the crew of his privateer, for another cruise.

During his stay in this port, the writer of these pages had the pleasure of lodging in the same hotel with him, and dining daily at the same table in his society. He was very agreeable and gentlemanly in conversation, full of life and animation, very enthusiastic in character, and was in every sense of the word a patriotic hero. If fighting was the order of the day, he was always sure to be found in the midst of it. On his return to Baltimore I shall give an extract from his journal in its proper place.

The *Lewis*, of New London (she had but four guns and forty-five men), was sent into Halifax, but previous to her capture she fell in with, and seized a most valuable English ship of eight guns, richly laden, for Quebec, which paid the privateersmen very abundantly for their losses.

Extract from the log-book of the Privateer-Schooner *Shadow*, of Philadelphia.

"On the 3rd of August, at half-past twelve (meridian), discovered a sail; called all hands to quarters, and made all necessary sail in chase. At half-past five p.m., came up with the chase, and perceived she was a British man-of-war; took in the square-sail and stay-sail, and hauled by the wind; at the same time she tacked for us, commencing a brisk fire. At eight p.m. lost sight of her.

"On the 4th of August, at half-past twelve (meridian), saw a sail to the eastward standing westward; made all necessary sail in chase. At half-past five p.m. carried away the square-sail boom; cut the wreck adrift; rigged out the lower studding-sail boom, and set her square-sail again, coming up with the chase. At six p.m., being within gun-shot, she commenced firing from her stern guns. At seven p.m. came up with her, and commenced an action; at half-past seven the ship hoisted a light in her mizzen rigging, which was answered by a light from us; at the same time hailed her. She hailed from Liverpool, when Captain Taylor ordered her to send her boat on board with her papers, which she in part complied with, by sending her boat with an officer and two men, whom we detained, and gave directions to man the boat with our crew, board the ship and demand her papers.

"These orders were delivered by Mr. Thomas Yorke, who received for answer, that such a demand would not be complied with, at the same time handing him a note addressed to Captain Taylor, purporting that his ship was a British letter-of-marque, called the *May*, from Liverpool, bound to St. Lucia, commanded by Captain Affleck, mounting fourteen guns and fifty men. He also stated that the Orders in Council had been rescinded, and a change of ministry taken place in England. The note was handed to Captain Taylor. The boat was again sent on board, with a note from our captain, demanding his papers, which were refused. At half-past eight o'clock, a brisk fire commenced on both sides, during which time, William Craft, sailmaker, was wounded. At ten p.m., dropped astern, with the intention of lying by all night within gun-shot; at intervals kept up a brisk fire; weather squally and dark.

"At daylight, ranged up under her stern and commenced a severe action, when we received a shot in our starboard bow which shattered the wooden ends, started the plank shear, and broke several timbers. At half-past seven a.m. received another in our larboard bow; struck the larboard after-gun-carriage; killed six men and wounded three. At half-past eight a.m., our commander received a ball in his left temple, which instantly terminated his existence, to the inexpressible regret of all hands. About the same time a shot struck under the larboard fore-chains, between wind and water, which caused the vessel to leak badly; found three feet water in the hold on sounding the pumps."

The *Shadow* arrived at Philadelphia, was refitted, and soon sailed on another cruise.

PRIZES CAPTURED BY PRIVATEERS

Ship *Grenada*, eleven guns, thirty men, 700 tons burthen, laden with 700 hhds. of sugar, with large quantities of cotton and coffee, from Pointe-à-Pitre, Guadaloupe, for London, sent into Charleston by the *Young Eagle*, of New York.

Schooner *Shadock*, also armed, from Antigua, for Liverpool, laden with molasses, in company with the *Grenada*, sent into New York by the *Young Eagle*. The *Eagle* carried but one gun and forty-two men. She engaged the *Grenada* and *Shadock* at the same time, and in an hour and a-half captured them both. The captain of the *Shadock* was killed, and two of his men wounded; three men were wounded on board the ship; no person hurt belonging to the privateer.

Brig *Roebuck*, with a full cargo of rum, from Grenada, for Jersey, sent into Norfolk by the *Rosamond*, of New York. The *Roebuck* is a very valuable vessel, formerly belonging to the United States, but peaceably captured under the Orders in Council.

Brig *Henry*, from Gibraltar, sent into Newport, R. I., by the *Yankee*, of Bristol.

Ship *Hopewell*, fourteen guns, twenty-five men, from Surinam, for London, burthen upwards of 400 tons, laden with 710 hhds. of sugar, 54 hhds. of molasses, 111 bales of cotton, 260 bags and casks of coffee and cocoa, captured by the *Comet*, of Baltimore, and sent into that port after an obstinate engagement, in which one man was killed and six wounded on board the ship; two of the privateer's men were wounded. The *Hopewell* sailed from Surinam, in company with five other ships, from which she parted but two days before; the *Comet* went in search of them, every sail set. The *Hopewell* was worth $150,000. Her late captain bears the most honourable testimony to the bravery of the crew of the *Comet.*

Brig *Hazard,* from Newcastle, for Newfoundland, in ballast, burthen 233 tons, carrying six twelve pounders. An excellent vessel, first captured by the *Dolphin,* of Salem, recaptured by the *Æolus* frigate, and sent into Boston by the United States ship *Wasp.*

Schooner *Forebe and Phoebe,* sent into Portsmouth, N. H., by the *Squando* of that port.

Brig *Thetis,* by the *Yankee* of Bristol, burnt.

Brig *Alfred,* by the *Yankee,* destroyed also.

Brig *Antelope,* by the *Dolphin* of Salem, sent into that port.

Ship *Kitty,* by the *Rossie,* of Baltimore, sent into an eastern port.

Schooner *Spunk,* by the *Fair Trader,* of Salem, sent into that port.

Schooner *Providence,* captured by the *Wiley Reynard,* of Boston, and sent into an eastern port.

Ship *Guayana,* carrying eight guns, burthen 300 tons, from Liverpool, for New York, with salt, crates, etc., sent into Salem by the *Dromo,* of Boston. This was an American Ship and British property.

Barque *Duke of Savoy,* eight guns, twenty men, sent into Salem by the *Decatur,* of Newburyport. The *Decatur* having thrown over her guns when chased by the *Constitution,* rearmed herself from the prize.

Ship *Pursuit,* with 600 hhds. of sugar, sent into Philadelphia by the *Atlas* of that port.

Ship Evergreen, sent into Salem by the Dolphin.

Brig *New Liverpool,* four guns, from Minorca, for Quebec, with a full cargo of wine, sent into New York by the *Yankee.*

Ship *Mary Ann,* from Jamaica, for London, a very valuable vessel, carrying twelve guns and eighteen men, deeply laden with sugar, etc., sent into Charleston by the *Highflyer,* of Baltimore.

Sent into Baltimore the first-class British ship *Henry,* 400 tons burthen, coppered to the bends, mounting four twelve-pounders and six six-pounders, bound from St. Croix for London. She was captured by the privateer *Comet*, Captain Boyle, of Baltimore. The *Henry's* cargo consisted of 700 hogsheads of sugar, and thirteen pipes of old Madeira wine; this vessel and cargo produced a clear profit to the captors of more than $100,000.

Also arrived, the English schooner *Alfred*, sent in by the privateer *Spencer*, of Philadelphia, from Bermuda for New Providence, with an assorted cargo of brandies, rum, and claret wine.

The *Teazer* privateer, of New York, captured an English Brig from Gibraltar, in ballast, and sent her into an Eastern port.

The English brig *Resolution* arrived at Portland, a prize to the privateer *Nancy*, of Portsmouth, N. H.

New York, August 4th.—The brig *Nerina*, Stewart, from Newry, for New York, arrived at New London.

The *Nerina* was captured by a British cruiser, and all the crew, except the captain, taken out, and a British prize-master and crew put on board the brig. Previous to her capture, the captain secreted all his passengers, numbering about fifty, in the hold. After getting out of sight of the English man-of-war, Captain Stewart suggested the propriety of opening the hatches to air the vessel, when all the passengers rushed on deck, and retook the brig without resistance.

The British, about this time, captured five of our small privateers, belonging to Salem, and other Eastern ports.

The famous Commodore Barney, after his first successful cruise in the privateer-schooner *Rossie*, of Baltimore, arrived at Newport, on the 30th of August, 1812.

A Card.

Mrs. Elizabeth Bell, of Nova Scotia, passenger on board the schooner *Ann*, Kelly, master, from Halifax, taken and sent into Salem by the Privateer *Dolphin*, begs leave to acknowledge, with much gratitude, the gentlemanly and humane treatment of the captain and prize-master of the *Dolphin*, in returning her $900, together with all her personal effects, etc.

On the 1st December, the privateer-schooner *Jack's Favourite*,

Captain Miller, of New York, was lying at the island of St. Bart's, where he had put in for water and refreshments. A few days after his arrival, his Majesty's schooner *Subtle* came into the same port, and while there threatened, in the presence of the merchants and others, "that he would follow, and take the damned *Yankee* privateer, if he went to hell for her."

When Captain Miller was ready, he sailed out of the harbour, on a cruise among the islands; the Englishman soon followed to put his threat into execution. Immediately after leaving port, the privateer not wishing to engage a man-of-war, made sail to avoid his enemy; soon after the chase commenced a terrible squall arose, and raged with fury for a considerable time, both vessels, of course, carrying all the sail they could possibly bear during the continuance of the terrific gust. It soon, however, expended itself, and when it cleared away, behold there was nothing to be seen of the *Subtle*.

She having so suddenly disappeared, Captain Miller, moved, by motives of humanity, tacked ship and sailed over the same ground from which his adversary had so recently disappeared, and all that was left of the gallant *Subtle* were a few hats, caps, and hammock-cloths floating on the surface of the water. The writer of this article was personally acquainted with Captain Miller, and two of his crew. These two individuals were young men of respectability, belonging to Milford, Connecticut, and have related to me all the circumstances here narrated, and I have no doubt that their statement is true, to the spirit and the letter.

Prizes Captured by Privateers.

Brig ——, ten guns, with a very valuable cargo of dry-goods, sent into Savannah by the privateers *United we Stand*, and *Divided we Fall*.

Transport ship *Lord Keith*, four guns, from Lisbon for England, sent into Newport by the *Mars*.

Transport ship *Canada*, twelve guns, one hundred soldiers, and forty-two horses, captured by the *Paul Jones*, and ransomed for £3,000 sterling, after disarming the men.

Brig *John and Isabella*, of Berwick-on-Tweed, captured by the same, and given up to discharge her prisoners.

The large ship *Neptune*, of 690 tons, sent into New Orleans by the *Saratoga*. This is probably one of the most valuable ships taken during the war.

Brig ———, of twelve guns, with an assorted cargo from St. Michaels, sent into New London by the *Dolphin*, of Salem.

Schooner ———, worth $10,000, sent into New Orleans by the *Lovely Lass*, of Wilmington, N. C.

Brig ———, sent into Chatham by the *Paul Jones*.

Ship *Mentor*, of London, twelve guns, with a cargo invoiced at £60,000 sterling, sent into New Orleans by the *Saucy Jack*, of Charleston.

Schooner *Huzzar*, sent into Savannah by the *Liberty* of Baltimore, laden with turtle, etc., supposed as presents for Admiral Warren and his officers.

Brig *Antrim*, from Ireland, with dry-goods, etc., valued at $60,000, sent into New Orleans by the *Saucy Jack*.

Schooner ———, 100 tons, laden with beeswax and redwood, arrived at Tarpaulin Cove, a prize to the *Yankee*.

Gallant Exploits.

Extract of a letter from Captain Le Chantier, of the privateer *Hazard* to a gentleman in Charleston, from St. Mary's, Georgia.—

"I have just arrived here with my prize, the ship *Albion*, which I captured on the 1st of February, longitude 64° West, latitude 16° North. On the 23rd of February, being on *Savannah* bar, having lost sight of her in a fog, she was retaken by a privateer from *New Providence*, mounting eight pieces of cannon, after which we fell in with her again, the privateer in company, which we engaged, and after an action of seven hours and a half, the privateer struck, and we retook the ship. If we had had half an hour more of daylight, I should have brought in the privateer; but fearing to lose my prize, I was forced to abandon her. My lieutenant and carpenter were wounded dangerously, and five seamen slightly. It is surprising we had so few wounded, considering how severely our vessel was crippled by the grape shot of the enemy. Our force was twenty-eight fighting men, while that of the enemy, including both vessels, the prize and the privateer, was twenty guns and sixty men. I hope the privateer *Caledonia* will long remember the little *Hazard*.

"Among the naval exploits of the present war, there is none which reflects more credit on American gallantry than the battle of the privateer-brig *Montgomery*, Captain Upton, of Boston, with a large British brig off Surinam, on the 6th of December. This vessel, along side of which the *Montgomery* lay for half an hour, was no less than His Majesty's brig *Surinam*, carrying eighteen thirty-two pound carronades and two long-nines, while the *Montgomery* had only twelve guns, ten sixes and two eighteen-pound carronades. Notwithstanding this disparity of force, the *Surinam* had received such shocks that she was evidently glad to get off, and instead of going direct to the common rendezvous at Barbadoes, she first put into an out-port to refit, having had her foremast badly wounded. What further damage she sustained we have not heard."

"Britannia needs no bulwark,
No towers along the steep;
Her march is o'er the mountain waves,
Her home is on the deep."

GALLANT ACTION FOUGHT BETWEEN THE PRIVATEER-SCHOONER *SARATOGA*, CHARLES W. WOOSTER, COMMANDER, AND THE BRITISH LETTER-OF-MARQUE BRIG *RACHEL*, OFF LAGUIRA, ON THE 13TH OF DECEMBER, 1812.

On the 9th December, the private armed schooner *Saratoga*, commanded by Charles W. Wooster, made her appearance off this place, (Laguira.) The same day the first lieutenant came on shore. He said they were twenty-four days from New York, and had seen nothing. On the 10th, Captain Wooster ran down and anchored in the roads, but in a few minutes was advised in a note, from the

American consul, to weigh and keep out of the reach of the batteries, as the commandant had said he would sink her if she came to. He immediately complied with this advice, and stood off. He soon discovered a schooner standing down the coast, some miles to, windward of Laguira. He boarded and captured her. She was a schooner, with dry-goods on board to the amount of $20,000.

The next day, at nine a.m., after the fog cleared off, we saw the *Saratoga* some miles to leeward, in-shore of a brig, but neither near enough to fetch in. At eleven a.m., the brig tacked off shore, and soon after, the schooner did the same. It was known on shore the brig was well armed and manned, and it was generally believed she would take the *Saratoga*, or at all events beat her off. All the inhabitants, from the commandant to the beggar, left their business to see the engagement.

The brig being so far from the schooner, it was some time before she came up with her. Both vessels were so far off, we could but just discern them from the housetops, and just as we had given up all hopes of seeing the battle, we discovered, they both tacked in-shore again. They continued standing in until within two leagues of the town, when the *Saratoga* commenced the action from her starboard bow-guns, which was returned from the brig's larboard quarter. The action now became furious, so that both vessels were hid from us in columns of fire and smoke. In a few minutes, however, the firing ceased.

When the smoke cleared off, we could see no colours flying except the American on board the *Saratoga*, which was victorious. (May it always remain so.)

On the 13th the second mate and twenty-five seamen arrived at Laguira in the brig's long-boat, which Captain Wooster had given them, together with every article belonging to them. The second mate was the only officer that was alive after the action, there being great slaughter on board the brig. On board the *Saratoga* they had but one man slightly wounded. The brig was the *Rachel*, from Greenock, mounting twelve long-nine-pounders, and carrying sixty men. She had on board a cargo of dry-goods, etc., invoiced at £15,000, sterling.

Battle Between the Schooner *Saratoga* and the Brig *Rachel* on the 15th December, 1812

CHAPTER 3

Conflict with the English

BATTLE BETWEEN THE UNITED STATES FRIGATE *UNITED STATES* AND THE BRITISH FRIGATE *MACEDONIAN*

On the 26th October, in latitude 29° North, longitude 29° 30' West, in the neighbourhood of the Western Islands, Commodore Decatur was cruising alone to intercept the enemy, and no doubt wishing to meet a single ship of equal or somewhat superior force, it was his good fortune to make a large sail to windward. It was then blowing a strong breeze, with a high sea on, and as the sail was. dead to windward, the Frigate *United States* was brought to the wind, in order to near, and ascertain the character of the ship in sight.

It was soon discovered that the stranger was a frigate, and no doubt an enemy, who being to windward, bad of course, his choice of distance and time for commencing the conflict. As the stranger did not choose to approach within good fighting distance, Commodore Decatur was obliged to hug the wind, in order to bring the enemy within the range of his guns.

At length, drawing up under his lee, he ordered a broadside to be given to the foe, but observing that most of the shot fell short of the enemy, he reserved his fire, keeping his luff so that he was soon enabled to get near enough to have his main-deck guns take effect. Although at too great a distance to reach his opponent with his carronades and musketry, a heavy cannonade with their long-guns was kept up for the space of half an hour, by both parties. It was then apparent that the American frigate was hulling and cutting her antagonist to pieces, while she herself received but little injury, as the greatest portion of the shot from the English ship passed over her, and through her upper sails.

As a matter of course, the English frigate gradually drifted to leeward, while the American kept her luff. They naturally neared each other, and as the American frigate had ranged far enough ahead to gain a favourable position, she tacked and passed under the lee of the enemy.

The mizzen-mast of the English ship having been previously shot, at this moment fell overboard, taking with it the fore and main top-masts, while the main-yard was hanging in the slings in two pieces. There were no colours flying, for there was nothing left to set them upon.

In this situation, the disabled ship could do no more, and any further resistance would have been a useless sacrifice of human life. As a matter of course, the firing ceased on both sides.

When the *United States* came up under the lee of the disabled ship, demanding her name, and whether she had surrendered, her answer was that it was the *Macedonian* frigate, of thirty-eight guns, Captain Carden, and that she had struck.

On taking possession of the *Macedonian*, she was found frightfully cut to pieces, having received about one hundred round shot in her hull. Her rigging and sails were rent in tatters. Of a crew of three hundred men, thirty-six were killed and sixty-eight wounded, numbering together one hundred and four put *hors de combat;* a fearful destruction of human life in the short space of an hour and a half.

The *Macedonian* was a fine ship of her class; rated thirty-eight, but carrying forty-nine guns: eighteens on her gun-deck, and thirty-two pound carronades on her spar-deck. She was only four years old, and had not been long at sea.

It is but fair to acknowledge that the *United States* was a larger ship than her opponent. She also carried five more guns, and heavier metal, with a larger number of men; still it is surprising how little she suffered in comparison with her adversary; she having had but five men killed, and seven wounded.

Among the killed was the third lieutenant, Mr. John M. Funk, a promising young officer. No other officer was hurt in the combat.

The rigging and sails of the American frigate were somewhat injured, but not so much as to prevent her from continuing her cruise, had it not been deemed advisable for her to convoy her prize into port.

Mr. Allen, the first lieutenant of the *United States*, was appointed to the command of the prize. They rigged a jury mizzenmast, repaired the sails and rigging, and soon the English frigate was transformed into an American barque, and proceeded on her passage to "the land of the free and the home of the brave."

REMARKS ON THE BATTLE.

I am aware that it is much easier to criticize than to fight, still, as a seaman, I think Captain Carden made a mistake in keeping at so great a distance, and, as it were, lying like a target to be cut to pieces.

Had he bore down close to his enemy, he could at least have done him a great deal of damage, and no one knows but some lucky shot might have disabled his opponent in her rudder or some other vital part.

As he was to windward during the whole fight, he had the advantage of choosing his own distance, and could but have been beaten at last.

I am happy to add, however, that it is agreed on all hands, both by friends and foes, that Captain Carden was a brave, humane, honourable man, with the polished manners of gentleman.

The writer of these pages was in New York at the time of the arrival of the *Macedonian* at the navy yard in Brooklyn, and immediately repaired on board the captured ship.

She was, of course, somewhat battered in her hull and spars, but still a fine fast-sailing frigate, and was soon repaired and fitted to cruise under the stars and stripes, against those who had until this war been in the habit of treating our flag with contempt and derision. I will here observe that every American was rejoiced at the capture of another British frigate; still there was no disposition to triumph over an unfortunate foe. Captain Carden had never been bullying and blustering on our coast, and carrying fire and destruction in his path against defenceless plantations and fishing towns, like the notorious Cockburn, and several other ruffians of the same stamp of character.

On the contrary, Captain Carden was looked upon as a gentleman, and every honourable man felt a sympathy for his misfortunes. It may appear somewhat surprising to the present generation to learn how soon the public and private character of nearly all the British officers that commanded on our coast at that period was known to the public at large. Some of them were respected and esteemed even by their enemies, for their kind and humane acts of generosity, while others were despised and hated for their coarse brutality. As the most of those who figured in the war against us have gone to their rest, I deem it unwise to name any more of them, as it can do no good, and may perhaps injure the feelings of their children and grandchildren.

Notwithstanding the reiterated proclamations by Admiral Warren (commander-in-chief of His Majesty's naval forces on the coast of North America), declaring the greatest part of our sea coast under a strict and rigid blockade; and though numerous line-of-battle ships and frigates were stationed at the entrance of our principal ports, striving to intercept and annihilate our trade and commerce; still, with all their force and vigilance, they could not prevent our privateers and letters-of-marque from entering and leaving our ports almost daily.

If the enemy's ships were to leeward, and a strong breeze blowing, our privateers and private armed vessels would slip out in spite of them, even at midday.

If such an opportunity did not offer, they had only to wait for darkness, or thick, stormy weather, and thus, while the enemy was waiting to catch our mischievous privateers near our own ports, they were annoying and capturing British ships and vessels in almost every part of the world; in defiance of their eight hundred ships of war.

Before hostilities commenced, their oft-repeated boast was, that in six months after war should exist between the two nations, not a single American flag would be seen on the ocean. And such was their inflated vanity that they counted on very little resistance, either from our navy or private armed vessels. What then must have been their disappointment when single ships met? and when, with their numerous ships of war, and cruising vessels, they were unable to keep a handful of frigates, in combination with our privateers and private armed vessels, from perpetually harassing their shipping, even at the mouths of their own ports in the British and Irish channels.

No one acquainted with the English character can justly accuse them of timidity, or want of courage. On the contrary, they are a daring, brave people, but sadly deficient in good manners, and civility in their intercourse with other nations. This is certainly a grave charge, but it is nevertheless true.

Prizes Captured by Privateers.

Ship *Marianna*, from St. Croix for London, six hundred tons, laden with sugars, etc., found deserted at sea, by the *Governor McKean*, of Philadelphia, and towed into Norfolk.

Brig ——, laden with salt, sent into Portland by the *Teazer* privateer.

Brig ——, captured by a whale-boat privateer, and brought into Portland. After the capture, the boat was hoisted on the deck of the prize, and carried into port.

Brig *Isabella*, two hundred and five tons, one year old, laden with crockery ware, iron, etc., sent into Portland by the *Teazer*.

Ship ——, laden with timber, bound for England, sent into Marblehead by the *Decatur* privateer.

Brig *Diana* from London sent into Portland by the *Dart*.

Three vessels captured by the *Dolphin* of Baltimore, and burned.

Ship *John*, fourteen guns, thirty-five men, four hundred tons burthen, from Demarara for Liverpool, laden with 742 bales of cotton, 230 hogsheads of sugar, 100 puncheons of rum, 50 casks and 300 bags of coffee, with a large quantity of old copper and dye-wood, worth at least $150,000, sent into Baltimore by the *Comet*, of that port.

Ship *Commerce*, fourteen guns, long-nines, —— men, from four hundred to five hundred tons burthen, from Demarara for London, very richly laden with sugar, rum, cotton, coffee—a very valuable prize—sent into Portland by the *Decatur*, of Newburyport. The captain and several of the crew were killed by the first broadside from the privateer.

Privateer-schooner *Frances*, of Nassau, N. P., four guns and thirty men, a fine, fast-sailing vessel, sent into Baltimore by the *Dolphin*.

A small English privateer, taken by the *Rapid*, of Charleston, and burnt.

Brig *Tor Abbey*, laden with dry fish, sent into Cape Ann by the *Thrasher*, privateer. A valuable vessel.

Schooner ——, laden with sugar, flour, etc., an assorted cargo, sent into Portland by the *Teazer*, privateer.

Brig ——, from Madeira for London, laden with choice wine, sent into Newburyport by the *Marengo*, of New York.

Brig *Orient*, from Quebec for England, laden with timber, sent into Portland by the *Teazer*, privateer.

Extract from the Log-Book of the Schooner *Atlas*, Captain David Maffet.

August 3rd, in latitude 37° 30', North, longitude 46° West, at half-past eight a.m., made two sail to the westward, standing to the north-east; tacked to the southward; at half-past nine tacked to the northward; at ten a-m. beat to quarters and cleared for action.

At half-past ten, bore away for both ships, and hoisted the American ensign and pendant; at three-quarters past ten the smallest ship fired a shot at us, both ships at this time having English colours flying.

At eleven a.m., the action commenced by a broadside and

Battle Between the Schooner *Atlas* and the British Ships on the 5th August, 1812

musketry from the *Atlas*, which continued (engaging both ships at the same time) until noon, when the small ship struck her colours. We then directed the whole of our fire against the large ship, but to our utmost surprise, the small ship again opened her fire on us, although her colours were still down.

We again commenced firing on her, and in a few minutes drove every man off her decks. At twenty minutes past meridian the large ship struck, and we immediately took possession of them both; one proved to be the ship *Pursuit*, Captain Chivers, of London, of 450 tons, sixteen guns, eight and nine pounders, with a complement of thirty-five men; the other, the ship *Planter*, Captain Frith, of Bristol, of 280 tons, twelve guns, twelve pounders, and fifteen men; both with valuable cargoes of sugar, coffee, cotton and cocoa, thirty days out from Surinam, bound to London. We took out the prisoners, put a prize-master, mate and crew on board of each of them, and steered to the southward in company.

During the action we had two men killed and five wounded. Every one of the shrouds on the larboard side were shot away, some of them in two of three places; the running rigging and sails very much cut. In consequence of the disabled condition of our rigging, and the fore-yard being gone, Captain Maffet determined on convoying the prizes to the first port in the United States to refit; kept in company with the prizes until Wednesday, the 2nd of September, when at half-past four a.m., we made a large ship to the eastward, standing to the southward; at half-past five she tacked, and gave chase for us.

We bore down, and spoke the *Pursuit*, and ordered the prize-master to tack to the southward, and make the first port he could. At six spoke the *Planter*, and informed him that the ship in chase was probably an enemy, and ordered him to make sail to the northward. At ten the *Pursuit* was out of sight to the southward. At eleven backed the main topsail, the strange sail coming up fast with the *Planter*. At meridian tacked to the southward. At half-past one p.m., the frigate fired five guns at the *Planter*, which obliged her to bring-to. Supposing her to be a British frigate, as she kept English colours flying, we made sail to the westward. At half-past three p.m., the frigate and the prize, *Planter* still in sight, lying-to, the *Planter* with American colours flying at the mizzen peak.

The frigate alluded to in this report must have been an American, as I find it subsequently stated that both these prizes had arrived at a port in the United States.

Although the English about this period, September, 1812, captured several of our small privateers, I observe, by a New York paper, that their places were soon filled by a larger and better class, which were then fitting for sea, namely, *Captain Bulkely*, an old revolutionary cruiser, equipped a privateer, to carry twenty guns, at New London, Connecticut. There were also at New York, getting ready for a cruise, ship *Volunteer*, of twenty-two guns; *Chinese*, eighteen guns; the schooner *Isaac Hull*, seventeen guns; and the schooner *Swallow*, of six guns.

The *James Madison*, privateer, had been recently captured by the English frigate *Jason*.

Prizes Captured by Privateers

The privateer *Paul Jones* was said to have captured lately, some twelve or fifteen British vessels near the Island of Porto Rico, some of them of considerable value.

It is also stated in a New York newspaper of this date, that from the 6th of April to the 22nd of August, 266 merchant vessels had arrived safe into that port, *viz*., 142 ships, 84 brigs, and 40 schooners. Fortunately, these vessels have escaped from the fangs of the enemy, while their own merchantmen are bleeding at every pore.

The Common Council of the city of New York, on the 18th of June, presented to Captain Isaac Hull, the freedom of their city in a gold box.

Boston, October 13th.—"Privateer-schooner *Fame*, Captain Green, from a cruise of fifteen days, returned on Saturday evening last, has taken two schooners, one loaded with salmon, oil, etc., (considered valuable), the other a new vessel, ballasted with sugar; parted with them to the westward of Halifax. It is worthy of remark, that the *Fame* was privateering in the Revolutionary war."

Schooner *Jenny*, laden with gum, sugar, etc., sent into Portland by the *Teazer*.

Schooner *Adela*, from Martinique, under Spanish colours, laden with sugars, sent into New York by the *Rosamond*, of that port.

Brig *Point-Shares*, from St. Johns, New Brunswick, for Barbadoes, captured by the letter-of-marque schooner *Baltimore*, of Baltimore, on her voyage to France, and sent into port. The brig was laden with fish.

Brig *San Antonio*, (under Spanish colours) from Guernsey, for Jacquemel, captured on the coast of Africa by the *Marengo* of New York. This vessel was richly laden, and supposed to be British property. She arrived at Philadelphia.

Schooner *Single-Cap*, sent into the Mississippi by the *Matilda*, of Philadelphia.

Schooner *Fame*, from Trinidad for Cayenne, laden with dry-goods, oil, etc., sent into Savannah by the *Nonsuch*, of Baltimore.

Ship *Phoenix*, twelve guns, seventeen men, from Bermuda for Jamaica, cargo, one hundred pipes Fayal wine; sent into Charleston by the *Mary Ann*, of that port.

Brig *Favourite*, 222 tons, two guns, from Cork for Pictou, in ballast, sent into Lynn by the *Industry*, of that port.

Brig *Sir John Moore*, from Dublin for Prince Edward's Island, 177 tons burthen, sent into Lynn by the *Industry*.

Brig *Lord Sheffield*, from Tenerife for Quebec, burnt by the *Marengo*, after taking out a few small articles.

Schooner *Betsey Ann*, from the West Indies, laden with sugar, captured in sight of Halifax harbour, by the *Fame*, privateer, and sent into Salem.

Brig *Henry*, from Liverpool for Halifax, laden with crates, salt and coal; a valuable vessel, sent into Salem by the *John*, of that port.

Schooner *Four Brothers,* from the West Indies for Newfoundland, sent into Salem by the *Fame,* privateer.

Schooner *Four Sons,* from the Bay of Chaleur, laden with fish and furs, sent into Salem by the *Fame,* of that port.

Two schooners sent into Portland by the *Dart,* privateer, one in ballast, the other with live stock.

Schooner *Antelope,* of Curracoa, sent into Charleston by the *Rosamond.*

Schooner *Dawson,* captured off the Island of Jamaica, laden with sugar, rum, and coffee; sent into Savannah by the *Wasp* of Baltimore.

Many American vessels, with goods from England, have been sent into port by our privateers, on suspicion of having British property on board. These have not been noticed in our list, but it appears the facts were, in many instances, as they were supposed, and when proper proofs were furnished, condemnations to a great amount took place. It is positively stated, that one of the *Yankee's* prizes of this description, afforded the captors the enormous sum of $200,000.

Fair Haven, Mass., *October 23rd.*—"The beautiful new privateer *Governor Gerry,* of 250 tons, pierced for 18 guns, was launched from the ship yard in this village, on Wednesday last. She is a most beautiful vessel, built of the best materials, and good judges are of opinion that she will be a remarkably swift sailer. The keel of this vessel was laid only forty-eight days previous to the launch."

A specimen of English vanity—

"The winds and seas are Britain's wide domain,
And not a sail but by permission spreads."
British Naval Register.

The gallant Commodore Barney has recently returned home to Baltimore, in his privateer-schooner *Rossie,* on the 10th of November, from a second successful cruise, and had the audacity to traverse over a pretty large space of ocean water, without asking permission of his Britannic Majesty.

I herewith extract from the journal of the brave commodore, the substance of his late cruise. It proceeds as follows:—

July 12th.—Sailed from Baltimore.

July 15th.—Left Cape Henry.

July 17th.—Spoke ship *Electra*, of Philadelphia; informed her of the war.

July 21st.—Spoke brig *Triton*, of Portsmouth; informed her of the war. Spoke ship *Rising Sun,* of Baltimore; informed her of the war.)

July 22nd.—Seized the brig *Nymph*, of Newburyport, for breach of the non-importation law; spoke ship *Reserve*, of Bath; spoke a brig from Lisbon for New London; informed her of the war.

July 23rd.—Was chased by a frigate, fired twenty-five shots at us, out-sailed her.

July 30th.—Chased by a frigate, out-sailed her.

July 31st.—Took, and burned the ship *Princess Royal.*

August 1st.—Took and manned the ship *Kitty.*

August 2nd.—Took and burnt the following: brig *Fame*, brig *Devonshire*, schooner *Squid*; and took the brig *Brothers*, put on board of her sixty prisoners, and sent her to St. Johns, to be exchanged for as many Americans.

August 3rd.—Took and sunk the brig *Henry* and schooner *Race Horse*: burned the schooner *Halifax*, manned the brig *William* (arrived), and gave the schooner *Two Brothers* forty prisoners, and sent them to St. John's on parole.

August 9th.—Took the ship *Jenny*, after a short action, she mounting twelve guns; sent her to the United States (arrived).

August 10th.—Seized the brig *Rebecca*, of Saco, from London, for a breach of the non-importation law (arrived).

August 14th.—Spoke brig *Hazard*, from Cadiz; informed her of the war.

August 17th.—Spoke brig *Favourite*, from Cadiz to Boston.

August 20th.—Spoke brig *John Adams*, who had been captured and plundered by the *Guerriere*, and let go.

August 28th.—Seized the ship *Euphrates*, of New Bedford, for breach of the non-importation law (arrived).

August 29th.—Spoke a brig, prize to the *Benjamin Franklin*; spoke ship *Jewell*, of Portland; informed her of the war.

August 30th.—Spoke schooner *Ann and Mary*, of New London; informed her of the war.

September 7th.—Spoke a brig from Providence, R. L, in distress; left her under the care of the *Revenue Cutter*, of Newport.

September 9th.—Chased by three ships of war, which did not continue long, for we out-sailed them without difficulty.

September 10th.—Spoke ship *Joseph*, from Bonavista; informed her of the war.

September 11th.—Spoke a brig, prize to the schooner *Saratoga*, of New York.

September 12th.—Chased by a frigate six hours; out-sailed her.

On the 16th September, Commodore Barney, in the privateer-schooner *Rossie*, fell in with his Britannic Majesty's packet-ship *Princess Amelia*, when a severe action commenced between the two vessels at close quarters. It lasted nearly an hour, and during the greatest part of the time within pistol shot distance. Captain Barney's first lieutenant, Mr. Long, was severely wounded, six of his crew were also wounded in the conflict, but not severely, as the most of them soon after recovered. The *Rossie* suffered considerably in her rigging and sails, but nothing in her hull.

The loss of the *Princess Amelia* was, her captain, sailing-master, and one man killed; the master's mate and six seamen wounded. The packet was terribly cut to pieces in her hull, sails and rigging.

September 16th.—Fell in with three ships and an armed brig; exchanged shot with the *Commodore*, received an eighteen pound shot through our quarter, wounded a man, and lodged in our pump; continued to dog and watch the above vessels four days in hopes of separating them, but in vain.

September 23rd.—Spoke the private-armed schooner *Globe*, Captain Murphy, of Baltimore; went in pursuit of the above English vessels, but could not fall in with them.

September 25th.—Spoke a Spanish brig bound to Porto-Rico.

October 8th.—Took (in company with the *Globe*) the schooner *Jubilee*, and sent her into port.

October 9th.—Spoke a Spanish schooner from Palma for Porto-Rico.

October 10th.—Chased and spoke the privateer-schooner *Rapid*, of Charleston, S. C, fifty-two days out; had taken nothing.

October 22nd.—Seized the ship *Merrimack* for a breach of the non-importation act. The result is, 3,698 tons of shipping, valued at upwards of $1,500,000, and 217 prisoners.

Brig *Diamond*, 220 tons, twelve guns, with a full cargo of cotton and log-wood, and $2,500 in gold; sent into Salem by the *Alfred*, privateer.

Brig *George*, 270 tons, laden with sugar and cotton, sent into the same port by the *Alfred*, both of these vessels were from Brazil, and were valued at $120,000.

Brig *Neptune*, a prize to the *John*, of Salem, arrived at that port.

Ship *Jane*, of Port Glasgow, a prize to the *John*, also arrived at Salem.

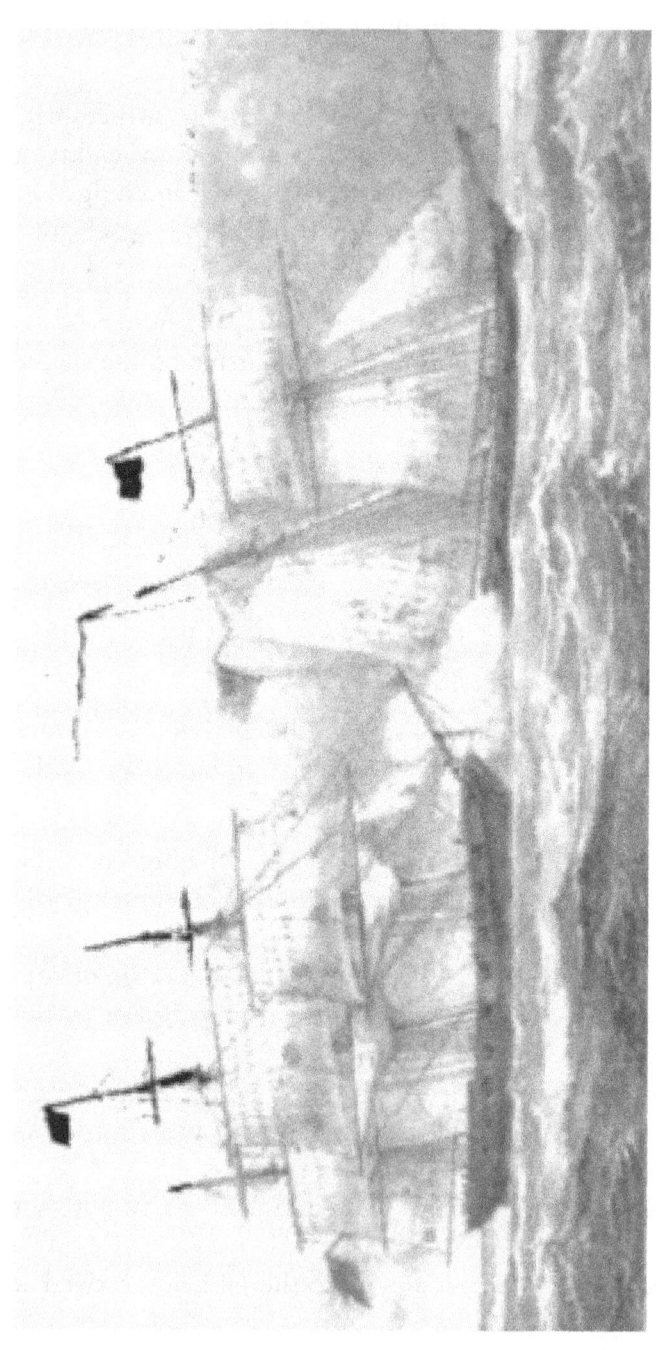

Battle Between the Schooner *Rossie* and the Ship *Princess Amelia* on the 10th September, 1812

A schooner laden with timber, taken by the *Saucy Jack,* of Charleston, and given up to release the prisoners she had taken.

Sloop *Louisa Ann*, laden with molasses, seized and captured by a boat from the *Benjamin Franklin* privateer, with seven men, in Trinity Harbor, Martinique, under the guns of a battery of twelve eighteen pounders.

A Gallant but Unprofitable Conflict.

Captain Levely, of the privateer *Nonsuch*, of Baltimore, had a severe engagement with an English ship and schooner, off Martinique, on the 28th of September. The following is an extract of the action from the logbook of the *Nonsuch*:

"The *Nonsuch* privateer, of Baltimore, Captain Levely, carrying twelve twelve-pound carronades, and (at that time) between eighty and ninety men, on the 28th of September, fell in with a ship and schooner under British colours, the ship carrying sixteen eighteen-pound carronades and two hundred men, including soldiers; and the schooner six four-pounders and sixty men. When within reach of the ship, she gave us a broadside. We bore down upon her and hoisted American colours, and returned ten broadsides, accompanied each time with a heavy volley of musketry, the ship and schooner keeping up a heavy fire upon us with their great guns and musketry. The engagement lasted three hours and twenty minutes, when the bolts and breachings of our guns, fore and aft, were carried away both sides.

"We could then only use our musketry, or we should certainly have captured them both. We dismounted several of the ship's guns, and damaged her very much in her hull and rigging. From the confusion which appeared on board, we judge that we must have killed and wounded a considerable number of men; she bore away for Martinico; we being much crippled in our sails and rigging, could not pursue her. After getting our decks cleared a little, we hauled to the northward, not only to repair our sails and rigging, but to refit gun carriages, and attend to the sick and wounded.

"During the action, we received several shot in our hull, and some two or three between wind and water, which caused the schooner to leak considerably, until we had time to plug them up and make suitable repairs.

"Our crew all fought like true Americans, Officers wounded: Mr. Wilkinson, dangerously in the body, since dead; Mr. Williams, prize-master, severely in the feet. Seamen killed: Samuel Christian, Lewis Riley, David McCarthy; we had also six seamen wounded.

"We subsequently learned that after the action the ship arrived at Barbadoes, and that she had seven of her crew killed and sixteen wounded. Among the former were some persons of distinction."

Prizes Captured by Privateers

Sloop *Venus*, of Jamaica, burnt by the *Two Brothers*, of New Orleans.

Brigs *Jane* and *Charlotte*, laden with salt, coals, crates, and a few bales of dry-goods, sent into Salem by the *America*, privateer.

Brig *Francis*, from St. John's, Porto-Rico, for Martinique, laden with bullocks, sent into Charleston by the *Nonsuch*, of Baltimore.

Brig *Porgie*, from Antigua, laden with rum and molasses, sent into Norfolk by the *Highflyer*, on her second cruise.

Ship *Ned*, of Glasgow, ten guns, nine-pounders, sixteen men, laden with timber, sent into Salem by the *John and George* privateer of that place, after a smart action. The *John and George* carries one twelve and two three-pounders. She had on board thirty-eight men, including officers.

Schooner ———, captured in the Bay of Fundy, laden with oil, seal skins, etc., sent into Salem by the *Fame*, of that port.

The following memorial to Congress will evince the state of public sentiment in favour of privateering, at this period of the war.

To the Honourable, the Senate and House of Representatives of the United States of America, in Congress assembled.

The memorial of the subscribers, owners of and agents for twenty-four private armed vessels, fitted out of the port of New York, and other citizens of the city of New York, respectfully sheweth: That your memorialists, convinced that the successful issue of the present war against Great Britain materially depends upon the effectual annoyance of the enemy, have, many of them, engaged in the equipment of private armed vessels. The extent to which such enterprises may be carried, to the injury of the foe, is incalculable; for no bounds can be prescribed to the hardihood and daring of American seamen. The great advantages of this cheap and effectual mode of warfare, peculiarly entitle it, in the opinion of your memorialists, to the serious regard and fostering care of Congress; the effect of promoting or discouraging it, will be felt, not only by those immediately concerned, but throughout every department and member of the war.

To the bold and successful efforts of our private armed vessels, we may attribute, in a great degree, a growing confidence in every class of citizens, in our ability to contend, at least on equal terms, with the self-styled mistress of the ocean. The examples of heroism in our seamen of the east, cannot fail to inspire with a corresponding ardour our soldiers of the north and west, producing a rivalship of patriotism and courage, ensuring a war of glory, terminating in an honourable and lasting peace.

The spirit with which our maritime citizens have engaged in such adventures, and which if properly excited and encouraged, would prove so destructive to the enemy, is in danger of being extinguished, unless Congress interpose immediately and effectually for its preservation.

For this object, a diminution of the high duties imposed on prize goods is indispensable. The captured property, loaded with these duties, in addition to the charges attending its condemnation and sale, produces, even at this early period, and under the most favourable circumstances, net profits utterly inadequate to the risk and danger of such enterprises, and in some instances is attended with an absolute loss to the captors. The cases in which profit is obtained must daily lessen as adventures increase, until all hope of advantage being precluded, a stop will effectually be put to further attempts.

Your memorialists believe, that as a means of revenue, it will eventually prove its own destruction, for though large sums may at present be obtained from it, by diminishing the expectation of profit, it will soon, not only prevent the increase of private armed vessels, but drive them from the ocean as a hopeless speculation or certain loss. A reduction of the duties by encouraging additional adventurers, would soon more than indemnify the treasury for any temporary loss it might sustain, in the increased number of subjects of duty which it would produce.

In addition to the burden of the high duties above complained of, these enterprises are subject to other grievances, which we respectfully hope will meet a speedy and complete redress.

By the 4th section of the act concerning letters-of-marque, prizes, and prize-goods, it is provided:

> "That all captures and prizes of vessels and property shall be forfeited, and shall accrue to the owners, officers and crews of the vessels by whom such captures and prizes shall be made, and on due condemnation had, shall be distributed according to any agreement which shall be written between them, and if there be no such agreement, then one moiety to the owners, the other to the officers and crew, as nearly as may be, according to the rules prescribed for the distribution of prize-money, by the act entitled 'An act for the better government of the Navy of the United States.' To this section no other construction can, in the opinion of your memorialists, reasonably be given, than that the capture, when ascertained to be a lawful prize, is to be at the disposal of the captors, to be by them distributed according to the provisions of the law."

The object of the interference of the Court of Admiralty, is simply to inquire into the character of the prize, which, if enemy's property when captured, "accrues" and "is forfeited" by the taking to the captors, whose property therein is affirmed, not acquired, by the act of condemnation. This property is, in the opinion of your memorialists, the undoubted right of the owner, derived from all moral and political rules of law and justice, to dispose of as he deems proper; a right not to be divested but by delinquency or crime. In the district of New York, of which your memorialists are inhabitants, the Court of Admiralty has decided, that prizes when condemned shall, in every instance, be sold by the marshal, and the proceeds deposited in the hands of the clerk of the court, to be by him distributed.

Whilst your memorialists submit with respect to the authority whence this decision emanates, they must complain of the hardness of its consequences, from which they respectfully hope Congress will see the necessity of affording immediate relief. It is manifest that sales by the marshal must, in almost every instance, be conducted hastily, and without regard to the value of the property, which will often be sold at times and places unfavourable to the sale of the commodity. The owners will thus be enforced and passive spectators of the total sacrifice of valuable property, which, in their own hands, would yield a certain profit, were they permitted to dispose of it at such times and places, on such terms of credit, and in such quantities as are accommodated to the demand.

By this proceeding, not only are the captors deprived of the common right of managing their own concerns in their own way, but when their property is sacrificed at any price, the proceeds are loaded with commissions of officers for making that very sacrifice. Of these commissions the marshal receives one and a-quarter *per cent* on the gross amount of sales, which includes the duty and the humane fund, established for the support of disabled seamen and their families, and constitutes tax upon tax. This gross amount, so stripped of one and a-quarter per cent., then passes into the hands of the clerk, where it again suffers a diminution of one and a-quarter per cent. for receiving and paying over.

After these deductions, the payment of the duties, the costs of condemnation, together with the extra ministerial and indispensable charges of the two per cent, invalid fund, agency, wharfage, etc., the owners, officers, and crew are presented with a lean account of profit, if not of absolute loss, chilling to the hopes and unnerving the arm of private enterprise. Your memorialists trust that it is unnecessary to enlarge on the utter impossibility of aiding the country by a continuance of services burdened with such grievous impositions. To Congress they confidently look for legal provisions, that may secure to owners of private armed vessels an adequate return for their expense and risk, to the brave officers and crew the reward of their gallant services, and to their widows and orphans the humane fund, established by law, unimpaired by official exactions. Your memorialists would suggest the expediency of shortening the time for effecting the condemnation of prizes, and of limiting the ordinary fees of officers of the prize court to a certain sum, as was formerly done in this country, when a colony of Great Britain.

Your memorialists, while they direct the attention of Congress to the foregoing evils, would respectfully further suggest the propriety and importance of granting to the owners, officers and crews of private armed vessels, a bounty for the destruction of enemy's property. It will often be expedient to destroy vessels and goods captured to prevent almost certain recapture. Thus, whilst it promotes the object of the war in distressing the enemy, produces no benefit to the captors. A bounty, proportioned to the tonnage of the vessels destroyed would prompt to much activity and vigilance, and insure the loss of much valuable property to the enemy, in situations whence it could not safely be carried into port, or not without the deduction of a force disabling the captors for other operations of equal or greater importance.

To redress the evils above complained of, and to encourage and promote a system of maritime warfare so beneficial to the country, and so mischievous to the enemy, your memorialists would earnestly recommend that provision be made by law—For reducing the duties on prizes; for delivering the prize property or condemnation to the captors, to be by them disposed of and distributed; for shortening the time necessary to procure condemnation; for limiting the fees of the officers of the prize courts to a certain sum; and for authorizing prize owners or their agents to order prizes arrived in one port to any other port at their discretion, at any time before the actual libelling of such prizes.

Your memorialists are convinced that such legal provisions, aiding and encouraging the patriotic spirit of our citizens, will soon cover the ocean with an active, hostile armament, which no vigilance can elude, and from which no force, however great, can effectually protect.

  (Signed)   Thomas Farmer,
              Thomas Jenkins.

New York, Nov. 20th, 1812.

The above memorial was signed by a large number of the most respectable merchants belonging to New York.

Prizes Captured by Privateers

Schooner *Robin*, sent into Portland by the *Revenge*, of Salem.

Schooner *Sally*, of Curacoa, sent into Charleston by the *Black Joke*, of New York, and *George Washington*, of Norfolk.

Sloop ———, belonging to Tortola, sent into Charleston by the *Saucy Jack*.

Brig *John*, ten guns, twelve-pounders, from Laguira for Gibraltar; a new and valuable vessel, laden with coffee and cocoa, sent into Charleston by the *Benjamin Franklin*, of New York.

Schooner *Three Sisters*, 120 tons burthen, laden with plaster, sent into Salem by the *Fame*, privateer. The *Fame* is only thirty tons burthen.

Schooner *Comet*, two guns and small arms, captured on the south side of St. Domingo, sent into Savannah by the *Rapid*, of Charleston. She was laden with sugar, beeswax, tobacco, and dry-goods.

Schooner *Searcher*, a New Providence privateer, of one gun and twenty men, captured by the *Rapid*, and burnt.

Schooner *Mary*, of St. Thomas, captured by the *Rapid* and ransomed, not having men to spare to send her home.

Brig *Union*, from Guernsey for Granada, in ballast, sent into Old Town by the *General Armstrong*, privateer, of New York. The *Union* carried six guns;

Schooner *Neptune*, with a cargo of fish, salt, and oil, taken by the *Revenge*, of Salem, and sent into Cape Ann.

Barque *Fisher*, from Rio Janeiro, with a very valuable cargo, and considerable specie, sent into Portland by the *Fox*, of Portsmouth.

Brig *James Bray*, with rum and pimento, arrived at Boston, a prize to the *Bunker Hill*.

Brig *Lady Harriot*, with a cargo of wine from Cadiz, sent into New York by the *Orders in Council*, a privateer of that place. Good!

Three vessels captured by the same and ransomed.

Brig *Freedom*, 700 hhds. of salt, from Cadiz for St. Johns, sent into Marblehead by the *Thorn*, privateer.

The schooner *America*, of Newburyport, sent into Salem by the privateers *Fame*, *Industry*, and *Dromo*, laden with salt.

These privateers passing Indian Island, a British post, were fired upon by the enemy. They, returned the compliment, and determined to seize all the vessels then lying there. They succeeded only in getting their own neighbour's vessel out, the rest being run on shore. She is a good prize, having been trading with the enemy,

Brig *Fancy*, for Jamaica, a valuable vessel, sent into New London by the *Joel Barlow*, privateer.

Schooner *John Bull*, a king's packet out of New Providence, chased on shore on Crooked Island by the *Rover*, of New York.

Ship *John Hamilton*. 550 tons, mounting ten guns, twelve pounders, and thirty men, from Honduras for London, laden with 700 tons of mahogany, sent into Baltimore by the *Dolphin* privateer of that port, after a smart action, but without loss of a single life on either side, though several were wounded. A fine prize.

Schooner *Loreen*, from Martinique for St. Martin's, laden with sugar and coffee, sent into Philadelphia by the *Revenge*, of that port.

Brig *Bacchus*, of Port Glasgow, in ballast, sent into Salem by the *Revenge*, privateer.

Brig *Venus*, from Brazil for London, ten guns, richly laden with 562 bales of cotton, fustic, etc., sent into Savannah by the privateer *Polly*, of Salem.

Nine British vessels sunk, burnt and destroyed, by the *Patriot*, of New York, during a cruise of fifty-six days.

Packet *Townsend*, from Falmouth (England), for Barbadoes, heavily armed, captured by the *Tom*, of Baltimore, after a severe engagement, in which the captain of the *Townsend* and four of her men were killed and several wounded. The *Tom* was but little injured, and had only two men wounded. The mail was thrown overboard, but recovered by the *Bona*, and brought to Baltimore a few days after.

Brig *Burchall*, a packet from Barbadoes for Demarara, with an English commissary and his lady on board, was captured by the *Highflyer*, of Baltimore, and sent into that port. The *Highflyer* has captured a number of *droggers*, (coasting vessels), plying between the islands of the West Indies; she released one of them with the commissary and seventy-two prisoners, and sent her as a flag of truce into Demarara. The Governor (Carmichael) returned a complimentary letter to her captain for his kind treatment of them.

Brig *Criterion*, sent into New York.

Schooner ——, driven ashore on the coast of Nova Scotia, and burnt by the *Revenge*, of Salem.

Sloop *Nelly and Parmelia*, captured by the *Revenge*, of Philadelphia, was wrecked on Chincoteague Shoals; crew and cargo saved.

Schooner ——, from Quebec, sent into New York by the *Retaliation*, of that port.

Ship ——, of twenty-two guns, and full of men, driven on shore after an engagement of thirty-five minutes, at the mouth of the Demarara River, by the *General Armstrong*, of New York. This privateer has returned to port after a brilliant cruise, having captured among others, three heavily armed and very valuable vessels, neither of which had been heard of when she arrived. She also seized and gave up several small vessels.

Brig *Two Brothers*, sent into New York by the *Benjamin Franklin*, privateer.

Brig *Active*, of ten guns, valuable, sent into Charleston, S. C, by the *Highflyer*, of Baltimore.

Brig ———, sent into Portland by a letter-of-marque brig from that port for France.

Brig *Pomona*, from Lisbon for Newfoundland, a valuable vessel, carrying eight twelve-pounders, sent into Belfast, Maine, by the letter-of-marque *Leo*, on her voyage to France.

Ship *Betsey*, ——— guns, for Glasgow, supposed to have a quantity of specie on board, sent into Wilmington, N. C., by the *Revenge*, of Baltimore.

Brig *Dart*, eight guns, of and from Port Glasgow, richly laden with rum, cotton, and cocoa, captured near the Western Islands by the *America*, of Salem, and sent into that port. The *America* had captured two other very valuable vessels, and at the time the prize left her, had upwards of seventy prisoners on board.

Ship *Queen*, sixteen guns and forty men, from Liverpool, with a cargo invoiced at from £70,000 to £100,000, sterling, captured by the *General Armstrong,* of New York, but unfortunately wrecked off Nantucket. She was, perhaps, the most valuable prize yet made. This ship was bound to Surinam, and was bravely defended, the captain, his first officer, and nine of his crew being killed before she was surrendered. The *General Armstrong* was not much injured in the contest.

Schooner ———, laden with dry goods, etc., from Jamaica for the Spanish Main, valuable, sent into Savannah by the *Liberty*, of Baltimore. The prize carried two guns and had thirty men; the privateer had only one gun and forty men.

Brig *Lucy and Alida*, a very valuable prize to the *Revenge*, of Norfolk, and sent into that port. The brig was first taken by the *General Armstrong*, of New York, retaken by the British letter-of-marque ship *Brenton*, of Liverpool, and then fallen in with by the

Revenge, by whom she was sent into port. She has a full cargo of dry-goods.

The schooner sent into Savannah by the *Liberty* is said to be worth $60,000.

Three vessels captured and destroyed by the privateer *Jack's Favourite*.

Schooner *Swift*, of Plymouth (England), from St. Michael's, taken by the *Rolla*, of Baltimore, and burnt. In a severe gale of wind, Captain Dewley was compelled to throw overboard all his guns but one, but the crew, sixty in number, determined to continue the cruise. Near Madeira, from the 12th to the 16th of December, without the loss of one man, the *Rolla* captured, manned, and ordered for the first port, the following immensely valuable vessels, being a part of the Cork fleet:

Ship *Mary*, fourteen guns, of Bristol, laden with hardwares, crates, etc.;

Ship *Eliza*, of ten guns, of *do.*, laden with 20,000 bushels of wheat;

Ship *Rio Nouva,* eighteen guns, of London, laden with dry goods;

Ship *Apollo*, ten guns, deeply laden with king's stores;

Brig *Boroso*, six guns, of Cork, laden with dry goods, beef and candles;

Schooner ———, of Aberdeen, given up to discharge the prisoners ;

Grand total: seven vessels, fifty-eight cannon, 150 prisoners, and property worth between two and three millions of dollars.

Shall the men that dare such deeds as these be stolen from their country? No. "Impressment must cease."

Sloop *Reasonable*, from Porto Rico for Martinique, chased on shore on the north-east end of the former, by the *Liberty*, and destroyed.

Schooner *Maria*, from Jamaica for the Bay of Honduras, in ballast, taken by the *Liberty*, and ransomed.

Schooner *Catharine*, three guns and twenty-four men, cargo, provisions and dry goods, sent into Charleston, a prize to the

Eagle and *Lady Madison*, privateers of that port.

Schooner *Maria*, with a valuable cargo of dry-goods, captured by the above, and released to discharge their prisoners, after removing the cargo.

Schooner *Rebecca*, laden with sugar and molasses, from Trinidad for Halifax, sent into New London by the privateer *Jack's Favourite*.

Ship *Hope*, twelve guns, from St. Thomas for Glasgow, 400 tons burthen, with a full cargo of rum, sugar, cotton, etc., valuable, sent into Marblehead by the *America*, of Salem.

Ship *Ralph*, from Quebec for London, a very large vessel, mounting eight guns, laden with timber, etc., sent into Portland by the same.

Brig *Euphemia*, ten guns, from Laguira for Gibraltar, laden with 400,000 pounds of coffee, sent into Portland by the *America*.

A brig and a schooner, captured by the *Decatur*, off Madeira, and sent to France.

Schooner *Meadow*, captured by the *Sparrow*, and released, after divesting her of a quantity of dry-goods.

Schooner *Erin*, from Curacoa for Jacquemel, laden with dry goods, sent into Charleston by the *Eagle*, of that port.

Schooner *Mary*, with an assorted cargo, from Porto Rico for St. Jago de Cuba, sent into Charleston by the *Eagle*, of that port.

Brig *Peggy*, of Barbadoes, from St. John's (Newfoundland), for St. Lucia, taken from under the convoy of two British sloops of war, by the *Hunter*, privateer, and sent into Boston.

Ship *Arabella*, of 500 tons, eight guns, coppered, laden with coal, plantation utensils, etc., from Bristol, (England), for the West Indies, sent into New London by the *Growler* privateer.

A schooner and sloop, taken on the coast of Africa, and released, after dispossessing them of 452 ounces of gold dust.

Brig ——, captured by the *Growler*, privateer, and released after dispossessing her of many valuables.

Schooner ——, captured by the *Gallinipper*, privateer, and

ransomed.

Ship *Neptune*, ten guns, from London for Rio Janeiro, with a very rich cargo of brandy, wine and dry-goods, sent into New London by the *Decatur*, privateer. The *Neptune* was a large ship, coppered, and of the first class. Her cargo was 500 pipes of brandy and wine, twenty bales of dry-goods, and ten cases of watches. The *Decatur* had taken two other vessels and sent them to France.

Ship ———, from Quebec for London, laden with timber, comprising the whole frame of a ship of seventy-four guns, sent into Kennebeck by the *America*. The timber was doubtless duly seasoned, and was just in time.

Ship ———, twenty guns, laden with mahogany and log-wood, sent into New Orleans by the privateer *Spy*, of that port.

Schooner *Prince of Wales*, captured by the *Growler*, and released after taking out a few pipes of Madeira wine, etc.

Ship *Aurora*, twelve guns, with a valuable cargo of dry-goods, worth $300,000, sent into Newport by the privateer *Holkar*, of New York.

Two vessels captured by the *Mars*, privateer, and sent into England as cartels. The *Mars* arrived at New London after a cruise of one hundred days, during which time she took eleven prizes, some of them-valuable. She only fired seven shots during her cruise. She had on board one hundred thousand dollars in cash, taken out of the different vessels, whose arrival was daily looked for at that time.

Brig *Pelican*, from London for Gibraltar, with a cargo of iron and fish, sent into Charleston by the *Mars*, of New London.

Sloop ———, laden with hides, sent into Newbern, N.C, by a privateer of that port.

Brig *Emu*, ten guns, twenty-five men, from Portsmouth for Botany Bay, with forty-nine women-convicts, the brig was sent into New York by the *Holkar*, of that port. The convicts and prisoners were landed on the Island of St. Vincents (one of the Cape de Verds), with a stock of provisions sufficient to last them four months. On this island there is no want of water.

The brig *Ann*, 10 guns, from Liverpool for New Providence, richly laden with dry-goods and crates, worth $100,000, sent into Marblehead by the *Growler*.

The privateer *Hunter*, of Salem, captured an English transport carrying ten guns, laden with military stores, but unfortunately this vessel was recaptured, and sent into Halifax.

The *Paul Jones* privateer captured on the 15th of April, the British ship *Lord Sidmouth*, having on board a valuable cargo, besides $80,000 in specie, which was removed to the privateer.

About the 1st of June the privateer *Decatur*, Captain Nichols, of Newburyport, was captured by the British frigate *Surprise*.

A Severe Combat

While Captain John Murphy, in the privateer *Globe*, of Baltimore, was cruising off the coast of Portugal, he fell in with an Algerine sloop-of-war, when a severe engagement ensued between them. Although the action was continued for a period of three hours, at half-gunshot distance, it is strange to relate that the *Globe* lost not a man, and had but two wounded. The shot of the Algerine almost invariably passed over her adversary, the *Globe* having received no less than eighty-two shot through her sails. How much the sloop-of-war suffered was not ascertained, but from all appearances, she must have been terribly hulled and cut to pieces.

The *Globe* hauled off to repair damages, and the Algerine seemed unwilling to renew the conflict, so that both parties probably esteemed it a drawn battle, and accordingly separated.

CHAPTER 4

A Coup de Main

The privateer-schooner *General Armstrong,* belonged to New York, and was a formidable vessel. She made a great many prizes, was commanded by Captain Guy R. Champlin, who had a severe battle with a British frigate off Surinam river, on the 11th of March, 1813, and after receiving much damage, made her escape. This vessel was subsequently commanded by Captain Samuel C. Reid, who made an unparalleled defence against the English, in the harbour of Fayal, where she was finally destroyed by British men-of-war, in a neutral port, on the 27th of October, 1814.

FROM A CHARLESTON PAPER OF APRIL 5TH.

"Unequalled Bravery.—Arrived at this port, yesterday, the privateer-schooner *General Armstrong,* Guy R. Champlin, Esq., commander, of New York, from a cruise. The following is an extract from her log-book:

"*March 11th,* 1813.—These twenty-four hours commence with moderate breezes and cloudy weather. At half-past 5 a.m., tacked to the southward and eastward. At 7 discovered a sail bearing S.S.E. At half-past 7 discovered her to be at anchor under the land. At 8, she got under way, half-past 8, she got sail on her, and stood to the northward; she fired three guns at us and hoisted English colours. We were then in five fathoms water, and about five leagues to the eastward of the mouth of Surinam river. At ten minutes past 9, we fired the centre gun and hoisted

American colours.

"At forty-five minutes after, she tacked and stood as near us as the wind would permit, keeping up a brisk fire on us from her main-deck guns. At a quarter-past 10. we standing to the northward, and having the advantage of reconnoitring her with our spy-glasses, were of opinion she was a British letter-of-marque, and unanimously agreed to bear down and board. At half-past 10, put our helm up, and bore down on her with intention to give her our starboard broadside, and to wear ship, and give her our larboard broadside, which was all ready for the purpose, and board her.

"This was all done with the exception of boarding; we found she was a frigate, pierced for fourteen guns on the main-deck, six on the quarter-deck, and four on the forecastle; she had her starboard tacks on board. The wind being light, and keeping up a constant fire, our vessel lay ten minutes like a log; we shot away her fore-topsail tie, and her mizzen-gaff halyards, which brought her colours down, and her mizzen and main-stay. We thought she had struck, and ceased firing, but we soon saw her colours flying again. We recommenced the action. She lay for a few minutes apparently unmanageable, but soon got way on her, and opened a heavy fire on us from her starboard broadside and maintop, no doubt with the intention of sinking us.

"We lay for the space of forty-five minutes within pistol-shot of her; our captain standing by the centre gun, fired one of his pistols and snapped the other, when he was wounded by a musket ball from the ship's maintop. The ball passed through his left shoulder. He walked aft to the doctor, and had his wound dressed. We luffed to windward, and fore-reached on her. In this action we had six men killed and sixteen wounded, and all the halyards of the head-sails shot away, the foremast and bowsprit one-quarter cut through, and all the fore and main shrouds but one shot away; both mainstays and running rigging cut to pieces; a great number of shot through our sails, and several between wind and water, which caused our vessel to leak. There were also a number of shot in our hull. In this situation we began to make sail from her; got the fore-sheet aft, and the jib and top-gallant-sail on her, and by the assistance of our sweeps, we soon got out of gunshot. During the time we were getting away from her, she kept up a well-directed fire for our foremast and fore-gaff, but without effect."

Compliment to Valour

At a meeting of the stockholders of the private armed schooner *General Armstrong*, Guy R. Champlin, Esq., commander, convened at Tammany Hall, pursuant to public notice, on Wednesday evening, 14th of April, 1813, the following resolutions were unanimously adopted:

"Resolved, That the agents be requested to transmit the thanks of this meeting to Captain G. R. Champlin, his officers, and crew, for their gallant defence in an action sustained between the *General Armstrong* and a British frigate, off Surinam.

"Resolved, That the agents present Captain G. R. Champlin with a sword, at the expense of the stockholders, for his gallant conduct in the *rencontre* above mentioned.

"Resolved, That the above resolutions be published.

      "Thomas Farmer, *Chairman*.

"Thomas Jenkins, Secretary."

Remarks on the Action

The writer was intimately acquainted with Captain Guy R. Champlin for many years. He was a native of New London, Connecticut. A more worthy and brave patriot, it would be difficult to find in any country. In the year 1806, we sailed from Leghorn to New Orleans, myself as chief mate, and Mr. Champlin as second mate of the ship *Marshall*, of New York.

Soon after this period we both became ship-masters in the merchant service, and continued our intimacy for more than ten years.

In a conversation with him about his action with the British frigate off Surinam, he said that when the Englishman's gaff-haul-yards were shot away, and his colours down, he thought, for a moment, she had struck. This circumstance occurred while the privateer lay within half pistol-shot of the enemy's cabin windows, and had his colours been flying, he should have poured a double charge of round and grape from his long-torn into his cabin windows, which would have raked the frigate's decks fore and aft.

A person on board of the *General Armstrong* told me, that after Captain Champlin was faint with the loss of blood from his wounded arm, he was persuaded to retire into the cabin, and while lying there on the floor, with a loaded pistol in his hand, directly above the magazine, he overheard something said on the quarter-deck about striking the colours. The heroic Champlin immediately requested the doctor to go on deck, and "tell the officers and men, that if any one of them dare to strike the colours, he would immediately fire into the magazine, and blow them all to hell together."

Every person on board knew the character of their commander, they consequently had the choice of two evils; therefore, with what sails they had left, and by the help of their sweeps, they made short tacks to windward, and soon got out of the reach of the enemy's shot.

None but a man of a resolute and daring character would have escaped capture under like circumstances. And although my friend has been dead many years, I am happy, even at this late day, to bear witness to the heroic bravery of this distinguished American, who was an honour to his State and country, and richly merits a national monument to perpetuate his devoted patriotism.

Fleet Sailing

For the information of those unacquainted with fleet sailing, I will endeavour to sketch its practice with the English, in the years 1812, '13, and '14. It had long been their general custom when at war with other nations, to send their merchant vessels to sea in fleets, especially so when engaged in war with France, or the United States, so that when hostilities commenced between us, in this instance, their old practice was rigidly pursued.

For this purpose, large numbers of ships and vessels of every description were collected from Scotland, Ireland, and from their own ports, to some convenient *rendezvous* in the English or Irish Channels, generally at Portsmouth, Plymouth, or Cork.

To collect a large fleet in this way often occupied several months. When a considerable number were thus got together, a suitable force was appointed to convoy them to the East or West Indies, or to whatever part of the world might be their destination.

If the fleet was large and valuable, they generally sent a line-of-battle ship, commanded by an *Admiral*, with one or two frigates, and as many sloops-of-war or gun-brigs. If only a small fleet of merchantmen, then a smaller force was sent for its protection, say a frigate and one or two sloops-of-war.

When nearly ready for sea, a signal was made from the *Admiral* or Flag-ship, for all the captains of merchant-vessels sailing in the fleet to repair on board, to receive written instructions how to sail under his convoy, and also to understand the necessary signals. These instructions are familiarly called "sailing orders."

After leaving port the order of sailing is as follows: The *Admiral* or flag-ship takes the lead, and proceeds a short distance ahead. She is called the van-ship. To bring up the rear, they appoint a fast-sailing frigate, so that if necessary she may be able to tow up any dull-sailing ship, to prevent her being left astern of the fleet On each side, or what a soldier would call "the flanks," is placed a sloop-of-war or a gun-brig.

In this manner they sail from England, and return there from their foreign ports. The first order is for no ship to go ahead of the admiral, and to watch and obey all the signals made by the flag-ship. The second and never-failing signal is constantly repeated, *viz.*, for the headmost ships to shorten sail and for the stern-most to make all sail and keep up with the fleet. Every now and then, one of the frigates or sloops-of-war is ordered to tow up some dull sailer ahead of the squadron. To do this, a large hawser is made fast to the fore-mast of the merchantman, when she is towed quite ahead of the fleet, that is to say just under the stern of the *Admiral.*

Towards evening, or at nightfall, a signal is given to close convoy, and sail in close order, or in other words to huddle together near the stern of the leading bully. This manoeuvre reminds one of a hen gathering her chickens together to protect them from a ravenous hawk.

When a fleet of merchant vessels was collecting in the windward or leeward West India islands, either at Tortola or Jamaica, the fact was generally known to the American privateers, in time to place themselves on the *qui-vive* to catch as many of them on their passage home as they possibly could.

These homeward-bound ships were generally laden with sugar, coffee, and other valuable goods, and were, of course, objects of great temptation to their adversaries; consequently they were frequently dogged and watched from the time of their leaving the harbours in the West Indies, until their arrival at their own ports at home.

Two privateers in company stood a much better chance of success than one alone; for while a man-of-war was sent in pursuit of one of them, the other was ready to pounce upon some of the merchantmen.

The prize crews should be ready at a moment's warning to be thrown on board of the prizes, and after taking possession of them they are ordered to run to leeward of the fleet, separate and steer in different directions, so as to divide the attention of the enemy; for while one of the frigates is in chase of the privateer, the enemy must retain one or more ships to protect the fleet; so that the prizes have time to make their escape.

At other times it happens that, when the captured vessel is too closely pursued by the enemy, the prize-crew are obliged to leave in their boats, and return in hot haste to the privateer.

It not unfrequently occurs that a privateer may run into the midst of a fleet, and have only time to capture one vessel, place the crew into their own boats, apply the torch, and leave it to burn in defiance of their adversaries.

Then again it may happen that, after chasing a fleet for several days, and even for weeks, if the weather is fine, no opportunity will offer to take a single ship; but should thick weather or a strong gale of wind intervene and separate them, then the privateers have capital picking, and have only to select the most valuable of the ships, for they are in truth like sheep without a shepherd.

In such cases, the privateersmen generally seize upon the specie and the most valuable goods they can find, and remove them to the privateer for fear of recapture, and then are governed by circumstances in disposing of the captured vessels. If valuable, and they can spare men, they send them into port; if not, destroy them; and if encumbered with too many prisoners, they frequently give up some of the prizes to them, and allow them to return home, or proceed to the nearest land.

At the commencement of a cruise, before one gets hardened to the business, it seems harsh and cruel thus to distress our fellow-men; but such is war. Whether by sea or land, its features are certainly rough and unchristian-like, and to smother rising feelings of philanthropy, one is obliged to call to remembrance the fact that England had been preying upon most other nations during the last two centuries; and towards the last of this war, their burning Washington was a sort of watchword to inspire retaliation and revenge for past injuries.

In the year 1810, two years previous to this war, the writer of this sketch commanded an American vessel, and sailed in a fleet of about 600 sail of merchantmen, professing to be neutral vessels, bound from Gottenburg into the Baltic Sea, to different ports in Russia, Prussia, and Sweden.

We left Gottenburg on the 24th of October, passing through the Great Belt, and did not get into the Baltic until the 1st of November. We were convoyed by the *St. George*, a line-of-battle-ship. and two frigates. The *St. George* led the van, while the two frigates were placed on each side. There were also several sloops-of-war in the rear, all to protect the fleet from the Danish gun-boats that constantly threatened us on all sides.

For the particulars of this passage, see *Coggeshall's Voyages*, published in 1852.

Besides the merchant vessels that sailed to and from England in fleets at that period, under convoy of British men-of-war, there was a class of private armed ships that relied on their own strength to defend themselves. These were called running ships, and were insured to prosecute their voyages out and home without waiting for convoy. The owners of this class of vessels, of course, paid a higher rate of premium of insurance against capture than those who sailed under the protection of ships-of-war. It therefore followed that many of our largest privateers were fitted out almost expressly to capture this class of ships; and it was with them that many a hard-fought battle occurred.

After the first year of the war, it was found, with few exceptions, that small pilot-boat-privateers were too weak to make many captures, the enemy's vessels being too well manned and equipped to be captured by these small craft. Still there were a few of them that continued to I make short cruises. These small pilot-boat-privateers I were so well adapted to low latitudes, where the winds are light, and the weather fine—as is almost invariably the case along the coast of Florida, and among the West India Islands—that several of them, like the *Saucy Jack,* of Charleston, and a few others of like character from Baltimore, continued to annoy the British coasting trade among the islands, and occasionally to capture a straggling ship in the Gulf Stream which had separated from her convoy; and thus did these mischievous little vessels continue to harass and vex the enemy, until the peace was ratified by both nations.

Prizes Captured by Privateers

The privateer *Yankee* arrived at Newport, R. I., after a cruise of about 150 days, during which time she had scoured the whole western coast of Africa, taken eight prizes, sixty-two guns, 196 men, 496 muskets, and property worth $296,000. The *Yankee* had on board thirty-two bales of fine goods, six tons of ivory, and $40,000 worth of gold dust. She looked in at every port, river, town, factory, harbour, etc., on the coast; touched at several Portuguese Islands for water and supplies. The following is a list of her prizes:—

Sloop *Mary Ann*, Sutherland, of London, coppered, four guns, eleven men; having on board gold dust, ivory, and camwood, worth $28,000; took out the cargo and burnt the vessel.

Schooner *Alder*, Crowley, of Liverpool, coppered, six guns, nine-pounders, twenty-one men; 400 casks, muskets, flints, bar lead, iron, dry-goods, etc. Vessel and cargo worth $24,000. Ordered to the first port in the United States. In the contest an explosion occurred, which blew up her quarter-deck and killed her captain and five of her men.

Brig *Fly*, Tydeman, of London, six guns, fourteen men; with gold dust, ivory, gunpowder, iron, dry-goods, and sundries; ordered to the first port in the United States. Vessel and cargo worth $36,000; taken under Fort Appolonia, of 50 guns.

Brig *Thames*, Toole, of Liverpool, eight guns, fourteen men; with ivory, dry-goods, and camwood; worth $40,000; ordered to the first port in the United States.

Brig *Harriet and Matilda*, Inman, of Maryport, from Cork for Pernambuco, eight guns,. fourteen men; with fine cloths, linens, iron, salt, porter, etc.; worth $41,000.

Brig *Shannon*, Kendall, from Maranham for Liverpool, ten guns, fifteen men; worth $50,000.

Andalusia, Kenall, ten guns, 100 men, (eighty-one free blacks); vessel and cargo worth $34,000; arrived at Savannah.

Schooner *George*, cut out of Tradestown; cargo, rice, part taken out, and vessel given up to the prisoners; worth $2,500.

Three vessels captured on the Spanish Main by the *Snap-Dragon*, of Newbern, N. C.; divested of their valuables, and burnt.

Three vessels taken by the same; valuable articles removed, and all given up to release the prisoners.

Sloop ———; a fine copper-bottomed vessel; taken by the *Snap-Dragon*, and fitted out as a tender and store-ship.

Two vessels captured by the privateer *Divided We Fall*, and ransomed.

One vessel taken by the same privateer, and sunk.

Three vessels taken by the *Divided We Fall*, and given up.

The above prizes, we presume, were West India trading vessels, commonly called "*droggers.*" What may be called the coasting trade of the West Indies, was a very valuable branch of the British commerce, and appears to have been severely handled.

Port of New York, *April 24th.*—Arrived, letter-of-marque schooner *Ned*, Captain Dawson, of Baltimore, forty-two days from La Teste (through Long Island Sound). In lat. 44° 54' N. long. 15° W., fell in with the English letter-of-marque brig *Malvina*, of Aberdeen, mounting 10 guns—six and nine pounders—and after a close action of fifty-two minutes, succeeded in capturing her. The captain of the *Malvina* was killed. The *Ned* had seven men badly wounded. The *Malvina* was from the Mediterranean for London, laden with wine. Put Captain Penderson, as prize-master, and a crew on board of her, and ordered her into an American port.

On the 18th inst., the *Ned* was chased off the *Chesapeake* by a seventy-four and a frigate; on the 19th was chased off the Delaware; on the 20th was chased off Sandy Hook; and on the 21st got in at the east end of Long Island, through four or five ships-of-war. She touched at New London for a Sound pilot.

Brig *Tartar*, with 160 hhds. of rum, sent into Georgetown, S. C, by the *General Armstrong*, privateer. The *Tartar* being chased by a British government brig, was wrecked on the bar; people and cargo saved.

Schooner *Fox*, a British tender of three guns, commanded by the first lieutenant of a seventy-four, captured by the *Hero*, of Stonington, Conn., fitted out for the occasion, and manned by volunteers.

Brig *London Packet,* from London for St. Michael's, taken by the *Paul Jones*, and wrecked on Nantucket.

Brig *Return*, of London, from Cumana; sent into Chatham by the *Paul Jones.*

Schooner *Farmer*, of Nassau, N. P., laden with cotton, captured by the *Sparrow*, of Baltimore, but given up.

The captain of the *Farmer* speaks in the handsomest terms of the liberal conduct of Captain Burch, of the *Sparrow*. The most trifling article was not permitted to be touched. He would not even receive some poultry without paying for it.

Schooner ———, sent into Machias by the *Wasp*, of Salem.

Schooner *Crown*, a British privateer, captured off Waldoboro by a sloop fitted out at that place, and manned by volunteers.

Ship ———, sent into Brest (France), by the privateer *True-blooded Yankee*, said to be worth from $400,000 to $500,000. This privateer had taken five other valuable prizes. One loaded with dry-goods and Irish linens had been ordered for the United States.

Brig *Charlotte*, ———, with a cargo of dye wood, etc., captured off the English Channel by the *Montgomery*, of Salem, and sent into that port.

Privateer schooner *Richard*, ——— guns, captured by the *Holkar*, of New York, and sent into Savannah.

Privateer sloop *Dorcas*, taken by the same; armament, etc. destroyed, and given up to exchange the prisoners.

Brig *Edward*, eight guns, from Brazil for London, laden with 180 bales of cotton, etc.; a valuable prize, sent into Salem by the *Alexander*, of that port. The *Alexander* had also captured a brig of sixteen guns, laden with dry-goods, gunpowder, etc.

Schooner ———, taken by the *Alexander*; her valuable articles taken on board the privateer, and then given up to the prisoners.

Brig *Mars*, from Jamaica for Halifax, laden with rum; sent into Portsmouth, N. H., by the *Fox*, privateer.

Ship *Nancy*, ——— guns, sent into Bristol, R. I., by the *Yorktown*, of New York.

Schooner *Delight*, from Bermuda for Halifax, laden with wine and silks; sent into Machias by the privateer-boat *Fame*, of Salem.

King's packet *Mary Ann*, twelve guns, from Malta, having touched at Gibraltar, for England, captured after an obstinate battle by the *Governor Tompkins*, of New York, and sent into Boston. $60,000 in gold and bullion, and the mail, were among the spoils of the conquerors. The privateer had no person hurt. One man was killed and several wounded on board the packet.

Ship *Dromo*. 12 guns, from Liverpool for Halifax, with a cargo invoiced at $70,000, sterling, sent into Wiscasset by the *Thomas*, of Portsmouth.

Brig ———, sent into Boothbay by the same, with a very valuable cargo. It is said these two vessels produced the captors more than $500,000.

The corvette ship *Invincible Napoleon*, 16 guns, sent into Portland by the *Young Teazer*, of New York.

Packet *Ann*, of 10 guns, a valuable prize, sent into Portland by the *Young Teazer*.

Schooner *Greyhound*, laden with fish and oil, sent into Portland by the same.

Brig ———, sent into Portsmouth by the *Governor Plumer*, privateer of that port.

British packet *Express*, captured off the coast of Brazil by the *Anaconda*, of New York, divested of her specie, $80,000, and given up to discharge the prisoners.

Brig *Mary*, 8 guns, laden with wine, valuable, sent into New Haven by the *Anaconda*.

Ship *William*, 10 guns, with a valuable cargo of dry-goods, crates, wine, etc., from Cork for Buenos Ayres, captured by the *Grand Turk*, of Salem, and sent into that port.

Brig *Harriet*, with a cargo of hides, tallow, etc., from Buenos Ayres, sent into New Bedford by the *Anaconda*, of New York.

Schooner *Pearl*, from Curacoa, for St. Croix, with a cargo of corn meal, etc., sent into Savannah by the *Liberty*, of Baltimore.

Sloop ———, a British privateer of ——— guns, captured by the *Liberty*, and divested of her armament and valuable articles, and then given up for want of room for the prisoners.

Brig ———, captured and burnt by the *Governor Plumer*, privateer. She was bound from Hull to Halifax.

Brig ———, from Lisbon to London, with a cargo of cotton,

taken by the letter-of-marque schooner *Sabine*, of Baltimore, on her way to France, and burnt.

Brig *Kingston Packet*, with a valuable cargo of rum, etc., brought into Ocracock, North Carolina, by the *Globe*, of Baltimore.

Schooner *Britannia*, from St. Johns for the West Indies, sent into Portland by the *Grand Turk*.

Ship *Loyal Sam*, 10 guns, from Nassau, N. P., for England, captured by the letter-of-marque schooner *Siro*, of Baltimore, on her passage from France, and ordered to a southern port. The *Loyal Sam* had $23,500 in specie on board, and a quantity of indigo which came safe to Portland, where the *Siro* arrived soon after.

Ship *Venus*, 14 guns, from Cadiz for Newfoundland, with a full cargo of salt, sent into Beaufort, S. C, by the *Globe*.

Brig *David*, from Waterford for Halifax, laden with provisions, sent into Portsmouth by the *Governor Plumer*, privateer.

Brig *Ajax*, 2 guns, captured by the *Governor Tompkins*. The prize did not arrive, but a handsome quantity of dry goods that were on board of her having been transferred to the privateer, came safe to New York.

Brig *Hartley*, 2 guns, from Gibraltar for St. Salvador, taken by the *Governor Tompkins* and burnt.

Transport ship from Lisbon for England, captured by the letter-of-marque *Bellona*, of Philadelphia, on her passage from France. The prisoners were paroled for exchange, and the vessel ransomed.

Brig *General Prevost*, from Halifax for Demarara, captured by the *Rolla*, of Baltimore, and sent into New Orleans.

Schooner *Brown*, of London, captured by the letter-of-marque *Bellona*, of Philadelphia, and ransomed.

The noted schooner, *Liverpool Packet*, of —— guns, carried into Portsmouth by the *Thomas* of that port.

Brig ——, from South America for London, with a valuable cargo of hides, tallow, etc., sent into Providence by the *Yorktown*, of N.Y.

Ship *Susan*, of Liverpool, from Gibraltar for that port, captured by an American letter-of-marque, and carried into Marennes, France.

Ship *Seaton*, captured by the *Paul Jones*, and afterward burnt by the *Globe*, at the request of the prize-master, she not being seaworthy.

Schooner *Elizabeth*, from Lisbon for London, captured by the *Globe*, and burnt.

Ship *Pelham*, from Lisbon for Figaro, laden with rum, captured by the *Globe*, and burnt. The *Globe* captured and ordered into port several valuable vessels.

Brig *Margaret*, 220 tons, 10 guns, laden with 1000 hhds. of salt, from Cadiz for Newfoundland, captured by the *America*, of Salem, and sent into that port.

Brig *Morton*, 12 guns, from London for Madeira, captured by the *Yorktown*, divested of her dry-goods, worth £7,000, sterling, and sent into Wilmington, N. C.

Three schooners captured by the *Young Teazer*, and sent into Portland, one laden with salt, the other two with 146 puncheons of Jamaica rum, and some mahogany.

Brig *Sally*, Budford, of London, from Plymouth to Pictou, in ballast, with some cordage and crockery— mounting 4 four-pounders—by the *Benjamin Franklin*.

Brig ——, from Jamaica, sent into New York; prize to the *Teazer*.

Brig *Hero*, from St. Andrews, sent into Castine by the *Teazer*.

Brig *Resolution*, with flour, arrived at Portland, prize to the *Nancy*, Captain Smart.

Brig ——, from Jamaica for Madeira, laden with wine, arrived at New London, a prize to the *Marengo*.

Brig ——, from the Leeward Islands to Guernsey, mounting six guns, with a full cargo of West India produce, arrived at Martha's Vineyard, a prize to the *General Armstrong*.

Brig ——, with salt, cut out of Turk's Island, by the *Orders in Council*, arrived at New York.

Brig ——, a new, light vessel, from Gibraltar to Halifax, a

prize to the *John*, arrived at Boston.

Brig *Ann*, prize to the *Teazer*, arrived at an Eastern port.

Brig *Thomas*, from Aberdeen for the River St. Lawrence, mounting two guns, in ballast, captured by the *Decatur*, and sent as a cartel to Halifax.

Brig *Tulip*, British property under American colours, sent into Philadelphia by the *Atlas*, Captain Maffet.

Brig ———, 14 guns, arrived at New York, sent in by the *Holkar*.

Bark ———, captured and burnt by the *Dolphin*, Captain Endicott, on her second cruise.

Ship *Eliza Ann*, from Liverpool, arrived at Boston, prize to the *Yankee*.

Schooner *Success*, from Newfoundland for New Brunswick, 250 barrels of salmon, prize to the *Benjamin Franklin*.

Schooner *Lady Clark*, arrived at New York, August 31st, prize to the *Bunker Hill*.

Schooner *Sally*, from Sidney, N. S., arrived at Boston, a prize to the *Wiley Reynard*.

Schooner *Blonde*, from Dominico for St. Johns, N. F., prize to the *John*.

Schooner ———, from Jamaica, with 160 puncheons of rum, arrived at Salem, prize to the *John*.

Armed schooner *Dorcas*, taken by the *Liberty*, of Baltimore, divested of her dry-goods, etc., and released.

Extract from a New York Paper July 6th, 1818.
"A Coup De Main."

"Yesterday forenoon a fishing-smack was sent out from Mosquito Cove by Commodore Lewis, who has the command of a flotilla of gun-boats, stationed off the Hook, for the purpose of taking by stratagem the sloop *Eagle*, tender to the British 74 *Poictiers*, cruising on and off Sandy Hook light-house, which succeeded to a charm.

"The smack, named the *Yankee*, was borrowed of some fishermen at Fly market, and a calf, a sheep, and a goose, purchased, and secured on deck. Between thirty and forty men well armed with muskets, were secreted in the cabin and fore-peak of the smack. Thus prepared, she stood out to sea, as if going on a fishing-trip to the Banks—three men only being on deck, dressed in fisherman's apparel, with buff caps on.

"The *Eagle*, on perceiving the smack, immediately gave chase, and after coming up with her, and finding she had live stock on deck, ordered her to go down to the *Commodore*, then about five miles distant. The watch-word 'Lawrence,' was then given, when the armed men rushed on deck from their hiding places, and poured into her a volley of musketry, which struck her crew with dismay, and drove them all down so precipitately into the hold of their vessel, that they had not time to strike their colours.

"Seeing the deck was cleared of the enemy, Sailing-Master Percival, who commanded the expedition, ordered his men to cease firing—upon which one of the enemy came out of the hold, and struck the colours of the *Eagle*. She had on board a thirty-two-pound brass howitzer, loaded with canister shot; but so sudden was the surprise, they had not time to discharge it. The crew of the *Eagle* consisted of H. Morris, master's-mate of the *Poictiers*, W. Price midshipman, and eleven marines. Mr. Morris and one marine were killed; Mr. Price mortally, and one marine severely wounded.

"The *Eagle*, with the prisoners, was brought up to town yesterday afternoon, and landed at Whitehall, amidst the shouts and plaudits of thousands of spectators assembled on the battery, celebrating the Fourth of July."

PRIZES CAPTURED BY PRIVATEERS

Brig *Union*, from Ireland, laden with provisions, sent into Abrevrehe, (France), by the *True Blooded Yankee*.

Ship *Aurora*, from Belfast for London, sent into Roscoff, (France), by the same.

Ship ———, of 20 guns, chased on shore, on the coast of Africa, by the *Rambler*, of Bristol.

Ship *Integrity*, from Waterford to Lisbon, captured between Waterford and Cork, by the *True Blooded Yankee*, and carried into Norway.

Brig *Avery*, from Magadore, 12 guns, laden with gums, almonds, beeswax, etc., sent into New- Bedford by the *Yorktown*, valued at $200,000.

Schooner *Leonard*, taken and sunk in Dublin Bay, by the *True Blooded Yankee*.

Brig *Betsey*, with a full cargo of wine, raisins, etc., from Malaga for St. Petersburg, sent into Plymouth by the *Jack's Favourite*, valued at $75,000.

Schooner *Three Sisters*, of Bermuda, with a cargo of flour, etc., sent into St. Mary's by the *Saucy Jack*, of Charleston.

Schooner *General Horseford*, of 210 tons, with a valuable assorted cargo, sent into Savannah by the *Decatur*.

Brig *Nelly*, from Cork for Newfoundland, captured by the *Fox* of Portsmouth, and burnt after dispossessing her of her valuable articles.

Sloop *Peggy*, from Greenock for Limerick, captured by the same and ransomed.

Schooner *Brother and Sister*, from Liverpool for Westport, captured by the same and burnt.

Brig *Louisa*, captured by the *Fox*, and ransomed.

Sloop *Fox*, from Liverpool for Limerick, valuable, captured by the privateer *Fox*, and sent to Norway.

Sloop *William and Ann*, from Newcastle for Galloway, captured by the same, and sent to France.

Sloop *James and Elizabeth*, captured by the same and ransomed.

Brig *Chance*, from Liverpool for Newfoundland, captured by the *Fox* and sent to Norway.

Brig *Mary*, from Cork for Pictou, captured by the same privateer and burn.

Ship *Venus*, an American vessel, sent into Salem by the *Dolphin* privateer, enemy's property, condemned to the amount of $60,000.

Terrific Explosion

In June, 1813, the privateer *Young Teazer,* belonging to New York, was destroyed by a *desperado* by the name of Johnson.

This man had formerly commanded the *Old Teazer.* When that vessel was captured by Admiral Warren's fleet, Johnson was released on his parole. Not long after he had obtained his liberty, without waiting to be regularly exchanged, he entered as first lieutenant on board of the *Young Teazer.*

By letters from several of the crew (prisoners in Halifax) to the agents of the privateer, we learn the following particulars of the sad catastrophe:

> While the *Teazer* was closely pursued by an English man-of-war, and in great danger of being taken, Captain Dawson (who commanded the privateer), called his officers aft to consult on what had better be done. While they were deliberating on the subject, one of the sailors called aloud to the captain, that Lieutenant Johnson had just gone into the cabin, with a live brand of fire in his hand. In another instant, the *Young Teazer* was blown up. All the crew perished with her, except seven seamen who were standing on the forecastle, one of whom died soon after.
>
> Had Johnson blown his own brains out, or tied a gun about his neck, and thrown himself overboard, some would have mourned for him, and none found fault. By all accounts he was not one of the most amiable men living; on the contrary, the desperate wretch must have been possessed of the devil, to have plunged so many human beings into eternity without a moment's warning. Many of them, it is said, had wives and children to mourn their untimely fate.
>
> *July 31st.*—The privateer sloop *Wasp,* Captain Ervin, of Salem, carrying 2 guns, with small arms, etc., fought the British Government schooner *Bream,* of 10 guns, upwards of nine hours, *viz.,* a running fight for 8 hours, and at close quarters for about 45 minutes, and was afterwards taken. The lieutenant

commanding the British schooner being a gentleman, treated Captain Ervin and his crew with great kindness, for their bravery in defending their little vessel so resolutely.

Remark

The conduct of the British officer towards his prisoners in this little action, is an infallible sign of a brave, kind-hearted man.

Prizes Captured by Privateers

Three vessels captured by the *America*, of Salem, and given up to dispose of her prisoners, she being incommoded by too great a number.

Schooner ———, from the Falkland Islands for Lisbon, captured by the *Fox*, of Portsmouth, and her cargo of skins taken on board the privateer.

Brig ———, heavily laden, sent into Bristol, R. I., by the *Yankee*, of that port.

Ship *London Trader*, 2 guns, from Surinam for London, sent into Charleston by the *Decatur*, laden with 209 hhds. of sugar, 140 tierces of molasses, 55 hhds. of rum, 700 bags of coffee, 50 or 60 bales of cotton, and some other articles.

Brigs *Good Intent, Venus, Happy*, barque *Reprisal*, and schooner *Elizabeth*, captured by the *Snap-Dragon*, of North Carolina, and destroyed or given up.

The privateer, when last seen, had in company the brig *Ann*, from England for Nova Scotia, with a full cargo of cloths, cassimeres, etc., valued at $500,000.

The Yankee's Cruise

May 20th.—Left Newport. *23rd.*—Recaptured brig *William*.

June 22nd.—Close in with Ireland, took the cutter-sloop *Earl Camden*, valued at $10,000; ordered for France.

June 30th.—Took brig *Elizabeth*, 2 guns, laden with cotton, valued at $40,000; ordered for France. Same day, took brig

Watson, laden with cotton, valued at $70,000; ordered her for France.

July 2nd.—Ireland in sight, took brig *Mariner*, laden with rum, sugar, etc., valued at $70,000; ordered her for France.—Arrived at Providence, R. I., Aug. 19th.

The *Yankee* had not a man killed or wounded during her cruise.

Prizes Captured by Privateers

Barque *Henrietta*, sent into Beaufort, N. C, by the *Snap-Dragon*, of Newbern.

Brig *Ann* ——, with a cargo of dry-goods, worth $500,000, captured by the *Snap-Dragon,* and the most valuable part of the cargo taken on board the privateer, which vessel safely arrived at Newport.

The *Saucy Jack* arrived at St. Mary's from her third cruise. She captured the schooner *Two Sisters,* laden with flour and fish; ship *Eliza*, of 10 guns, with flour, beef, etc. On the 17th July, fell in with the ship *Louisa*, and brig *Three Brothers,* of 10 guns each, and captured them both without loss. The *Saucy Jack* also took and gave up some small vessels. She was the cause of the loss of the enemy's sloop-of-war *Persian*, which was wrecked on the Silver Keys, June 29th, while in chase of this famous little privateer.

Brave Defence of the Letter-of-Marque Schooner *Lottery*, in the Chesapeake Bay.

The letter-of-marque schooner *Lottery*, of Baltimore, with 6 guns and thirty-five men, on the 15th of February, 1813, while at anchor in Chesapeake Bay (being outward bound), was captured by nine British barges, containing 240 men ; after fighting them off for an hour and a half, it was supposed that more Englishmen were killed and wounded than the whole crew of the letter-of-marque. Captain Southcomb of the *Lottery*, being badly wounded, the enemy boarded the schooner, and pulled down the colours themselves.

Interesting Battle Between the Privateer *Dolphin*, Captain W. S. Stafford, and the English Ship *Hebe*, and with her Consort the —— Brig, from Malta, off Cape St. Vincent.

Captain Stafford had been for some days cruising off the coasts of Spain and Portugal, and when off Cape St. Vincent, on the 25th of January, 1813, he fell in with a large ship and a brig, and gallantly engaged them both. The combat was sustained with considerable spirit until the captain of the *Hebe* and eight men being wounded, they both struck their colours, and were manned for the United States.

The privateer lost but four men in this gallant affair. The force of the *Dolphin* was ten guns and sixty men.

The *Hebe* carried 16 guns and forty men, the brig 10 guns and twenty-six men; making together twenty-six guns and sixty-five men. They were both richly laden, and were very valuable prizes.

The *Dolphin* then proceeded homeward. She passed through the British squadron in the Chesapeake Bay, and arrived safe at Baltimore, on the 15th of February, after a very fortunate cruise. The captain of the British ship, smarting from his wounds, said "he did not expect to find a d——d Yankee privateer in that part of the world," but was given to understand that, by-and-by, captures might be made in the Thames; at which he wondered greatly!

The following is honourable to all parties concerned in it— we should be glad to see such things from the other side of the water.

A Card

"W. A. Brigham, lately captured in the British merchant ship *Hebe*, late under his command, by the United States privateer *Dolphin*, Captain W. S. Stafford, after a severe contest, begs to make public, and gratefully acknowledge the sense he has of the very kind and humane treatment he and his crew experienced

Battle Between the Schooner *Dolphin* and the British Ship *Hebe* and a Brig off Cape St Vincent on the 25th January, 1815

on board the *Dolphin*, during a passage of five weeks, from the time of capture till our arrival at this port. All wearing apparel and private property were given up to the prisoners, and the wounded (eight in number), most diligently and tenderly attended. W. A. Brigham being badly wounded by a musket-shot, and much burnt, experienced a very great share of this attention from Dr. Chidester, the surgeon, which, together with the tender sympathy and goodness of Captain Stafford, added much to his recovery and happiness. Should the fortune of war ever throw Captain Stafford, or any of his crew into the hands of the British, it is sincerely hoped he will meet a similar treatment."

Baltimore. Feb. 16th, 1813.

The writer of these pages was personally acquainted with Captain W. S. Stafford, when at Bordeaux, in the year 1814. And it is with pleasure, he adds, that he always found him a modest, unassuming, gentlemanly man; no one can, for a moment, doubt his unflinching bravery and gallant bearing, when he reflects on the many battles he has gained over the enemies of his country. To be convinced that Captain Stafford was generous, kind, and humane, the reader has only to refer to the fact of Captain W. A. Brigham's voluntary certificate, after his capture, and during the time he was a prisoner on board the *Dolphin*.

When the writer of the following article calls to mind the spirit and acts of the Baltimoreans during our last war with England, he is inspired with a feeling of esteem and veneration for them, as a brave and patriotic people, that will endure with him to the end of his existence.

During the whole struggle against an inveterate foe, they did all they could to aid and strengthen the hands of the general government, and generally took the lead in fitting out efficient privateers and letters-of-marque to annoy and distress the enemy, and even to "beard the old lion in his den," for it is well known that their privateers captured many English vessels at the very mouths of their own ports in the British channel.

When their own beautiful city was attacked by a powerful fleet and army, how nobly did they defend themselves against the hand of the spoiler! The whole venom of the modern Goths seemed concentrated against the Baltimoreans, for no other reason but that they had too much spirit to submit to insult and tyrannical oppression. Many of the eastern people made a grand mistake in counting on the magnanimity of the British nation to do them justice by mild and persuasive arguments.

In making these remarks in praise of Baltimore, I do not mean to disparage the noble patriotism of many other cities of our glorious Union, but I do mean to say, that if the same spirit that fired the hearts and souls of the Baltimoreans, had evinced itself throughout our entire country, it would have saved every American heart much pain and mortification, and would, in my opinion, have shortened the war. For while the English believed we were a divided people, they were slow to relinquish their unreasonable demands.

With these obvious reasons, can anyone possessed of the least knowledge of human nature, believe there can ever be any real friendship between an English Aristocrat, a High-Church Tory, and an American Republican; the very idea of such a friendship is preposterous to the last degree. It therefore follows, that we have only to rely upon our own strength and union, to repel aggression from whatever quarter it may come. Would the English, if they had succeeded in taking Baltimore, have shown more mercy in sparing it than they did Washington? I have no patience with such fallacious reasoning. Are they not the same people, and playing the same game now, on the shores of the Baltic, and in the White and Black Seas?

Should we have another war with them, would they not perform the same unnatural acts as were perpetrated at Hampton, in 1813, if they had the power to do it? Talk not of British magnanimity to any one acquainted with their history; were it not for the religion and virtue of the middle classes in England, "the hands of the aristocracy would be against every man, and every man's hand against them." The writer was in Baltimore shortly after the English retreated from that place, and when he saw the American flag, with its beautiful stars and stripes, wave gracefully in the breeze on Fort McHenry, the impression made upon his mind was indelible. He will not attempt to describe the feeling, it being much better expressed in Key's immortal *Star Spangled Banner.*

Interesting Cruise of the Famous Captain Boyle, in the Privateer-Schooner *Comet,* on the Coast of Brazil, and Among the West India Islands.

Captain Boyle left Baltimore in Dec. 1812, and on a dark, stormy night passed through the midst of the British blockading squadron, at the mouth of the Chesapeake. After getting to sea, Captain Boyle proceeded to the coast of Brazil, without meeting with any remarkable incident until he arrived off Pernambuco, on the 9th of January, 1813. At this point his *Journal* proceeds as follows:

"On this day I spoke a coaster from Pernambuco, who informed me of some English vessels who were to sail in a few days from that place. On the 11th, spoke the Portuguese brig *Wasa,* from St. Michael's for Pernambuco. 14th, at 1 p. m., discovered four sail standing out of the harbour—laid-by to give them an opportunity to get offshore, and then to cut them off; at 3 p. m., they were upon the wind, standing S.E., and about six leagues from the land; bore up and made all sail in chase; at 5, we were coming up with them very fast; at 6, discovered one of them to be a very large man-of-war brig; called all hands to quarters; loaded all the guns with round and grape; cleared the decks, and got all ready for action.

At. 7 p. m., close to the chase, hoisted our colours, and sheered close up to the man-of-war brig, who had also hoisted her colours. The captain hailed us, and said he would send his boat on board; accordingly I hove to and received it. The officer informed me that the brig was a Portuguese national vessel, mounting twenty 32's, and 165 men; that the three others were English, for Europe, under his protection, and that I must not molest them. I informed him that I was an American cruiser, and insisted on his seeing my authority to capture English vessels, which he did.

I then informed him I would capture those vessels if I could; that we were upon the high seas, the common highway of all nations; that he had no right to protect them. That the high seas, of right, belonged to America as much as any other power in the world; and, that at all events (under those considerations), I was determined to exercise the authority I possessed. He said he should be sorry if anything disagreeable took place; that he was ordered to protect them, and should do so. I answered him, that I should feel equal regret that anything disagreeable should occur; that if it did, he would be the aggressor, as I did not intend to fire on him first. That if he did attempt to oppose me, or fire on me when trying to take these English vessels, we must try our respective strength, as I was well prepared for such an event, and should not shrink from it.

He then informed me those vessels were well armed, and very strong. I told him I valued their strength but little, and should very soon put it to the test. He then left me to go on board the man-of-war brig, to communicate our conversation to his captain, with a promise of again returning, which, however, he did not do. Finding he did not mean to return, I spoke the man-of-war immediately, and asked him if he intended sending his boat back; he said he would speak to his convoy, and requested me to send my boat on board. Entertaining some suspicion of his motives for thus asking for my boat, I told him that I did not make a practice of sending my boat from my vessel in the night, and should not now do it. I then again told him of my determination very distinctly, so that he should not misunderstand me.

The English vessels were ahead of us, consisting of a ship of 14 guns, and two brigs of 10 guns each, making in all a force of 54 guns! I made sail immediately for them, came up with the ship (the three, in fact, were close together), hailed her, and ordered them to back the main top-sail; he gave little or no answer. Having quick way at the time, I shot ahead, but told him I should be alongside again in a few minutes; and if he did not obey my orders, I would pour a broadside into him. After a few minutes I tacked, the man-of-war close after me; this was about half past 8, p. m. I then ran alongside the ship, one of the brigs being close to her, and opened my broadside upon them both; we were all carrying a crowd of canvas, and I was, from superior sailing, frequently obliged to tack, and should have profited much by it, had not the man-of-war been so close, who now opened a heavy fire upon us, with round and grape, which we returned.

Having now the whole force to contend with, I stuck as close as possible to the English vessels, they frequently separating to give the man-of-war a chance, and I, as frequently, poured whole broadsides into them, and at times, into the man-of-war. About 1, p. m., the ship surrendered, being all cut to pieces, and rendered unmanageable. Directly after, the brig *Bowes* surrendered, she being very much disabled. I then proceeded to take possession of her, and, as the boat was passing, the man-of-war gave us a broadside, and was near sinking the boat, which was obliged to return.

I then renewed the action with the man-of-war, who sheered off at some distance; I followed a little, and then made the third vessel surrender, she being also cut to pieces. I was now proceeding to take possession of the *Bowes* again, when I spoke the ship, the captain of which I ordered to follow me, who informed me his ship was in a sinking condition, having many shot-holes between wind and water, and not a rope but what was cut away; but for his own safety, he would, if possible, follow my orders.

At half past 1, p. m., took possession of the *Bowes*, and manned her. The man-of-war brig, however, continued to interfere with my taking possession of the three English prizes, so that I was occasionally obliged to exchange broadsides with him. After this, the man-of-war fired a broadside into the prize, and passed her. The moon was now down, and it became quite dark and squally, which caused us to separate from our prizes. At 2 a. m., he stood to the south; it being quite dark, we were out of sight of the brig and ship, which were in a southern direction. I now thought it prudent to take care of the prize till daylight, the captain of which informed me that the ship and the other brig were loaded with wheat.

At daylight, we were close to the prize, the man-of-war standing for us. I immediately hove about, and stood for him, or rather for the ship and brig; he tacked likewise, and made signals for the convoy to make the first port. Considering the situation of the ship and brig, I determined not to take possession of them, but to watch their manoeuvres. They both bore up before the wind, for the land, in company with the man-of-war, which appeared also much damaged. I followed for some time, taking particular notice of them. It appeared to me that great exertions were made to keep the ship from sinking, which, with the brig, settled in the water.

The man-of-war appeared occasionally to render them assistance; the ship was called the *George*, of Liverpool, Captain Wilson, and the brig the *Gambia*, of Hull, Captain Smith. At 10 a.m., went in pursuit of the *Bowes*, and at meridian spoke her. I have since learned from several vessels which I boarded from Pernambuco, that the man-of-war brig [1] was damaged very much, besides having her first lieutenant and five men killed, and a number wounded. Among the latter was the captain, who had his thigh shot off, and has since died of his wounds. The ship's masts scarcely lasted to carry her to Pernambuco; her cargo was nearly all damaged; she was dismantled, and obliged to get new top-sides. The brig was nearly in the same situation, the greater part of her cargo being damaged, and it was with difficulty they kept her from sinking, before they reached Pernambuco harbour.

Soon after the fight and capture of the three British vessels, the gallant Boyle fell in with, and took the Scotch ship *Adelphi*, belonging to Aberdeen. She was from Liverpool bound for Bahia, of 361 tons, mounting 8 long twelve-pounders, laden with

---

1. Some three or four months after Captain Boyle's engagement with this fleet, the Portuguese man-of-war brig here alluded to, arrived at Lisbon. The author of this book being there at the time, had the curiosity to examine her, in company with his friend Richard M. Lawrence, Esq., of New York, and several other American gentlemen We found her a very large vessel, with high bulwarks, a very formidable battery, and to all appearance big enough to hoist the *Comet* on her decks.

salt and dry-goods; manned her, with orders to proceed to the United States. He was subsequently chased by the famous British frigate *Surprise*, which he easily out-sailed, and continued on his cruise down among the West India Islands.

On the 6th of Feb., at daylight, being off the Island of St. Johns, distant two leagues, he discovered two brigs to leeward, when he made all sail in chase of them; called all hands to quarters; soon made out the nearest brig to be armed. At 6 a. m. she hoisted English colours, fired a gun and then struck her flag; took possession of her. She proved to be the *Alexis*, of Greenock, from Demarara, loaded with sugar, rum, cotton, and coffee, mounting 10 guns; sent Mr. Ball and six men on board, to take her to the United States, and then made sail after the other.

At eight a. m., discovered a man-of-war brig upon the wind, standing to the S.E., apparently from St. Thomas; ascertained from the prisoners that they were a part of a convoy of nine sail from Demarara, bound for St. Thomas; that the most of them had got in during the night, and that the man-of-war brig then in sight had convoyed them, and that she was called the *Swaggerer*. At 9 a.m. hoisted his colours, and prepared to give the brig he was then in chase of, a broadside, when she set English colours, and gave the *Comet* her whole broadside of great guns, which was instantly returned, when down came her colours.

After she had struck they cut away her topsail and jib-haulyards, etc., etc., in addition to the damage the *Comet* had done by her shot, which was very considerable; sent Mr. Cashell, first Lieutenant, and several men, on board, to repair the rigging as quick as possible; took out most of the prisoners, and sent Mr. Gilpin, prize-master, with seven men, to relieve Mr. Cashell; the brig by this time had made sail and filled away in company with the *Comet*.

The man-of-war by this time had gained very much upon them, he therefore thought it prudent to make no delay, but to order Mr. Cashell to make the best of his way through the passage between St. Johns and St. Thomas, as the only possible way of saving the prize brig from recapture. In the mean time Captain Boyle, with the *Comet*, played about the man-of-war brig, to divert his attention until the prizes had time to make their escape. The last brig captured was the *Dominica* packet, of Liverpool, from Demarara bound for St. Thomas, laden with rum, sugar, cotton, and coffee. mounting ten guns.

Captain Boyle then hove to and gave the man-of-war brig time to approach the *Comet*, which he did to within long gunshot; Captain Boyle soon found he could out-sail his opponent with ease, and was able to tantalise and perplex him, and in this way he detained him until his prizes had made their escape through the passage. He kept him in play in this manner until noon, when he found Mr. C. had got through the passage. He had ordered him to steer to the northward, and decided he would follow him as soon as possible.

He then made all sail upon the wind to go around to the windward of St. Johns, the *Swaggerer* in full chase. At two p. m. he had so out-sailed his adversary, that he was at least four miles to leeward. At this time he discovered a sail on the weather bow, and Boon after made her out to be a schooner running before the wind. At 3 p. m., being near her, fired several muskets at her when she hove to. Put Mr. Wild, prize-master, and six men on board, took out the prisoners, and ordered him through the passage between Tortola and St. Johns, and from thence to the United States. She proved to be the schooner *Jane*, from Demarara for St. Thomas, loaded with rum, sugar, and coffee. The *Swaggerer* still in chase, though very far to leeward.

It appears that soon after the capture of these prizes, Captain Boyle made the best of his way home, and returned safe to Baltimore after this successful cruise, on the 17th March, passing through the British blockading squadron, bidding defiance to their vigilance and numbers.

Soon after the termination of this successful cruise, we find the ever-active and gallant Boyle again on the broad ocean in command of the elegant and formidable privateer-brig *Chasseur*, always annoying the enemy, wherever he chanced to steer; sometimes on the coasts of Spain and Portugal, and anon in the

British and Irish Channels, carrying dismay and terror to British trade and commerce, in defiance of their fleetest frigates and sloops-of-war, who strove again and again to capture him, but were never able. He appeared frequently to tantalise and vex them, as if for mere sport, and at the same time convince them, that he could out-manoeuvre and out-sail them, in any trial of seamanship or skill.

It must have been a fine sight to see him handle his beautiful vessel, and to a nautical man, highly exciting, to have witnessed his famous escape in the British Channel, when nearly surrounded by two frigates and two brigs of war, as recorded in the tenth chapter of this work.

He received the fire of one of the frigates and skilfully hauled out from among them, and made good his retreat.

CHAPTER 5

Captain Shaler's Escape

EXTRACT OF A LETTER FROM NATHANIEL SHALER, COMMANDER OF THE PRIVATE ARMED SCHOONER *GOVERNOR TOMPKINS*, TO HIS AGENT IN NEW YORK.—DATED AT SEA, JAN. 1ST, 1813.

Two days after dispatching the *Nereid*, I took a whaleman from London, bound for the South Seas, but as she was of no value, I took out such stores, etc., as 1 could stow, and being much lumbered with prisoners and baggage, I put them on board, and ordered her for Falmouth. The chasing of this ship had taken me some distance from my ground, and owing to calms, I could not regain it until the 25th *ultimo.*, when at sunrise three ships were discovered ahead. We made all sail in chase. The wind being light, we came up with them slowly. On a nearer approach, they proved to be two ships and a brig. One of the ships had all the appearance of a large transport, and from their manoeuvres, seemed to have concerted measures for mutual defence. The large ship appeared to take the bulk of an action. Boats were seen passing to and from her. She had boarding nettings almost up to her tops, with her topmast studding-sail booms out, and sails at their ends, ready for running, as if prepared for a runaway fight.

Her ports appeared to be painted, and she had something on deck, resembling a merchant's boat. After all this what the devil do you think she was? why, have a little patience, and I will tell you. At 3 p.m. a sudden squall struck us from the northward, and the ship not having yet received it, before I could get our light sails in, and almost before I could turn round, I was under the guns, (not of a transport) but of a large frigate! and not more than a quarter of a mile from her.

I immediately hauled down English colours, which I previously had up, set three American ensigns, trimmed our sails by the wind, and commenced a brisk fire from our little battery, but this was returned with woeful interest. Her first broadside killed two men and wounded six others—(two of them severely, one has since died)—it also blew up one of my salt-boxes, with two nine-pound cartridges; this communicated fire to a number of pistols and three tube boxes which were lying on the companion way, all of which exploded, and some of the tubes penetrated through a crevice under the companion leaf, and found their way to the cabin floor, but that being wet, and the fire-screen being up, no further accident took place. This, together with the fire from the frigate, I assure you, made warm work on the Tompkin's quarter-deck, but thanks to her heels, and the exertions of my brave officers and crew, I still have the command of her.

When the frigate opened her fire on me, it was about half-past three. I was then a little abaft her beam. To have attempted to tack in a hard squall, would at least have exposed me to a raking fire, and to have attempted it, and failed to do so, would have been attended with the inevitable loss of the schooner. I therefore thought it most prudent to take her fire on the tack on which I was, and this I was exposed to from the position I have mentioned, until I had passed her bow; she all the while standing on with me, and almost as fast as ourselves, and such a tune as was played round my ears, I assure you, I never wish to hear again on the same key. At four his shot began to fall short of us.

At half-past four the wind dying away, and the enemy still holding it, his ship began to reach us. We got out sweeps, and turned all hands to. I also threw all the lumber from the deck, and about 2,000 lbs. weight of shot from the after hold. From about five p. m., all his shot fell short of us. At twenty-five minutes past five the enemy hove about, and I was glad to get so clear of one of the most quarrelsome companions that I ever met with. After the first broadside from the frigate, not a shot struck the hull of the Tompkins, but the water was literally in a foam all around her.

The moment before the squall struck us, I told Mr. Farnum that she was too heavy for us, and he went forward with his glass to take another look, when the squall struck the schooner as if by magic, and we were up with her, before we could get in our light sails. My officers conducted themselves in a way that would have done honour to a more permanent service. Mr. Farnum, first Lieutenant, conducted himself with his usual vigour. Mr. Atchison, sailing-master, performed his part in the style of a brave and accomplished seaman. Messrs Miller and Dodd, second and third Lieutenants, were not immediately under my eye, but the precision and promptitude with which all my orders were executed, is sufficient proof that they were to be relied upon. Mr. Thomas, boatswain, and Mr. Casewell, master's-mate, were particularly active, and deserve encouragement.

The name of one of my poor fellows who was killed ought to be registered on the book of fame, and remembered with reverence as long as bravery is considered a virtue. He was a black man, by the name of John Johnson; a 24 lb. shot struck him in the hip, and took away all the lower part of his body. In this state the poor, brave fellow lay on the deck, and several times exclaimed to his shipmates, "fire away boys, neber haul de colour down."

The other was also a black man, by the name of John Davis, and was struck in much the same way: he fell near me, and several times requested to be thrown overboard, saying he was only in the way of the others. While America has such sailors, she has little to fear from the tyrants of the ocean. From the circumstance of her shot being 24's, which I assure you was the case, as we have felt and weighed them, I am of opinion that it was the *Laurel*, a new frigate, which I had information of. A gentleman whom I took, told me she was in the fleet; that she was built and manned for the purpose to cope with our frigates; that if she got sight of me, she would certainly take me, as she was the fastest sailer he ever saw.

I send you a list of the killed and wounded; in everything else we are in good order and high spirits.

Killed—John Johnson, John Davis; wounded—six.

Prizes Captured by Privateers.

The British brig *Harriet*, captured by the privateer *General Armstrong*, and sent into Porto Rico, she being short of water; was seized by the Spanish government and given up to the British.

On the 20th of May, 1813, the privateer *Alexander*, of Salem, of 18 guns, was chased on shore in Well's Bay, by two British men-of-war. She was so closely pursued that only twenty of her crew had time to make their escape. It fortunately happened, however, that a large portion of her crew were on board of seven prizes, which she had made previous to her capture.

On the 1st of June the *Yankee* privateer, of 19 guns, with a crew of 200 men, sailed in company with the privateer *Blockade*, of 15 guns, from Newport, R. I., on a fresh cruise.

The privateer *Grand Turk*, of 16 guns, arrived at Portland, after having captured three large, armed, and very valuable ships, on the coast of Brazil, all of which she ordered to proceed to France. On her passage home she also captured a schooner, which she sent to the United States.

Extract from the London Courier.

I herewith insert the following extract from the *London Courier*, dated June the 17th, 1813, in order to show the erroneous opinions entertained in England at that period, with respect to the power and strength of the United States to defend their own territory:

"Policy of taking New Orleans.—There are arguments in our colonial journals, tending to prove that there exists a necessity for our government's taking possession of the province of New Orleans. We extract the following observations on that subject: If Great Britain will only take New Orleans, she will divide the States. By shutting that outlet to the fruits of Western industry, she will make herself known and respected by those States, in spite of the power of the rest of the Union. If in the war of 1755, France had been as superior at sea, as Britain then was, we should never have heard of the United States of America. The back country would have been as well settled before this with Frenchmen, as it now is with the descendants of Britons. We ought at present to take the benefit of former lessons, and make those people our friends, when so much is in our power. Take New Orleans, which is at the threshold of our West India Islands, and which could furnish them with provisions, at half the price they have been accustomed to pay. By such conduct, firm allies would be created on the Continent. Our West India planters would be gratified, and the integrity of the Spanish dominions in America, guaranteed from traitorous insults."

In reply to the policy of taking New Orleans, an American statesman says:

"This is very good, but the editor of the *Courier* seems not to know that two millions of people as hardy, brave and patriotic as the world can produce, are immediately interested in maintaining an outlet to New Orleans, who, like the flood of their own Mississippi, would precipitate themselves on the foe with irresistible force. Should the English attempt to carry out their plan, it would prove to them more disastrous than the Walcheren expedition."

What prophetic words were here announced! In about eighteen months after the above article was written, the English attempted to reduce their beautiful theory to practice. The result is too well known to need one word of comment.

Prizes Captured by Privateers

Schooner *Flying Fish,* taken by the *Saucy Jack,* and released after dispossessing her of goods to the value of $1,000.

Sloop *Catherine,* laden with salt, taken by the *Saucy Jack,* and sent into Cape Henry, Hayti.

Schooner *Kate*, with salt fish, sent into Cape Henry by the same.

Ship *Louisa*, 10 guns, laden with coffee, taken by the *Saucy Jack*, and burned to prevent her falling into the hands of a British man-of-war, in chase.

Brig *Three Brothers*, 10 guns, laden with 2,646 bags and forty tierces of coffee, sent into St. Mary's by the *Saucy Jack*. The bounty on the prisoners when brought in amounted to a very handsome sum.

Among the curious incidents that belong to privateering, we notice the fitting out of a three-masted vessel, at Salem, called the *Timothy Pickering*, apparently for the chief purpose of seizing licensed vessels, and those evading the non-importation law.

Brig *Earl of Moira*, from Liverpool for St. Andrews, in ballast, sent into Machias by the *Industry*, of Marblehead.

Schooner ——, laden with a few hhds. of rum, sent into Eastport by the privateer boat *Terrible*.

Two of the enemy's vessels, trading between the United States and the ports of Nova Scotia, sent into Machias by the privateer boats *Holkar* and *Swiftsure*, worth $5,000.

Schooner *Louisa*, of 202 tons, one gun, and 26 men, from St. Vincents for St. Johns, a first rate vessel, Baltimore built, sent into Newport by the letter-of-marque schooner *Expedition*, of Baltimore, having on board 100 hhds. rum, and thirty barrels sugar,. The bounty on this vessel, cargo and prisoners, allowed by the United States government, was about $4,000.

There were three vessels lately sent into France by the *True Blooded Yankee*.

Two vessels were recently sent into France by the *Leo*, letter-of-marque, Captain T. Lewis, and there sold.

The letter-of-marque schooner *Leo*, Captain T. Lewis, captured a homeward-bound English East India ship, said to be worth £500,000, sterling. Captain Lewis removed from his prize to the *Leo*, bullion and other valuable articles to the amount of $60,000, which sum was fortunately saved, as the *Indiaman* was subsequently recaptured by an English sloop-of-war.

Brig ——, captured by the *Brutus*, letter-of-marque, on her passage to France, and ransomed for $5,000. The *Brutus* also captured another vessel, which was not heard of.

Schooner ——, captured by the *General Armstrong*, on her passage to France, and burnt.

An English schooner from the West Indies, laden with sugar and coffee, bound for Halifax. The mate (being an American), persuaded some of the crew to join him to capture her, which they accomplished without bloodshed, and took the vessel safely into Castine.

The privateer *Snap-Dragon*, of Newburn, N. C, captured the British brig *Ann*, and convoyed her into that port, her cargo consisted of the following articles, namely: 215 bales of cloths, 22 boxes, 18 trunks, 43 casks, 74 packages, and 22 crates of earthenware, all English goods, invoiced at £83,000, sterling. She was truly a rich prize for the captors.

I find it stated, that in September, 1813, the privateer *Matilda*, of Philadelphia, was captured on the coast of Brazil, by the British ship-of-war *Lion*.

A schooner belonging to Penobscot River, sailed from Salem. When off Mount Desert, was captured by the English privateer *Dart*, and an English prize crew put on board. All the American were taken out of the prize, except one young man eighteen years of age; she was ordered for Halifax, and the young American officiated as pilot. In a fog, he adroitly managed to run the schooner into Machias, where she was taken possession of by the revenue cutter.

Ship *Reprisal*, from Scotland for the Bay of Chaleur, captured by the *Frolic*, of Salem, and burnt.

Brig *Friends*, of Bristol for Pictou, captured by the same and burnt.

Brig *Betsey*, taken by the *Frolic*, and burnt.

Brig ——, from Newfoundland, laden with fish, sent into Bordeaux by the letter-of-marque schooner *Pilot*, of Baltimore.

Four vessels captured by the *Lovely Cordelia,* of Charleston, and burnt.

Schooner ——, cut out of Setang Harbour, N. B., by a privateer-boat.

Galliot *Guttle Hoffnung*, of Portsmouth (England.), captured by the *Frolic*, and burnt.

Brig *Jane Gordon*, of London, 8 guns, and twenty men, captured by the same, dispossessed of her valuable articles, and burnt.

Schooner *Hunter*, captured by the same, and converted into a cartel.

Ship *Grotius*, of London, captured by the same, and sent into Portland.

Schooners *Vigilant*, and *Susan*, captured by the same, and given up to the prisoners.

Sloop ——, laden with dry-goods, sent into Ellsworth, by a privateer-boat belonging to Beer Island.

Brig ——, from Lisbon for London, laden with wool, rice, and cotton, captured by the letter-of-marque schooner *Grampus*, of Baltimore, on her passage from France, and burnt.

Two small vessels captured by the privateer-boat *Terrible*, of Salem, and sent into that port.

Schooner *Lilly*, from Port-au-Prince for London, captured by the letter-of-marque schooner *Pilot*, of Baltimore, and given up, after taking out some sugars, etc.

Brig *Mary Ann*, from St. Lucie for St. Johns, N. B., laden with 180 puncheons of rum, and 147 hhds. of molasses, captured by the same, and ransomed for $4,000.

Brig ——, captured by the letter-of-marque *General Armstrong*, on her passage to France, and burnt.

A brig and a sloop sent into Machias, by the *Industry*, of Salem.

The privateer *Rattlesnake*, Captain Maffet, captured the British packet *Lapwing*, and after divesting the prize of her armament, &c. &c, Captain Maffet transformed her into a cartel for prisoners, and sent her to Falmouth, England.

Two English ships taken by the *True Blooded Yankee*, and sent into France.

Sloop *Traveller*, with a cargo of 52 packages of dry-goods, thirteen casks of red wine, 70 crates of crockery ware, 68 casks of copperas, sixteen hhds. of alum, four do. of sugar, sent into Machias by the privateer-boat *Lark*.

Ship *Industry*, sent into Bergen (Norway), by the *True Blooded Yankee*, and there sold.

Ship *London Packet,* 14 guns, from Buenos Ayres for London, laden with 16,000 hides, etc., captured by the letter-of-marque brig *Argus*, of Boston, and sent into that port, where the brig also arrived. The prize was estimated at $160,000.

Brig *Atlantic*, from Trinidad for Cork, laden with 320 hhds. of sugar, 90 *seroons* of indigo, and other valuable commodities, captured by the *Argus*, and ordered for the first port in the United States. The indigo, worth $18,000 or $20,000, was taken out of the prize, and safely brought into port by the *Argus*.

Brig *Jane*, captured by the same, and ransomed to dispose of the prisoners taken in sundry prizes.

Brig *Jane*, in ballast, captured by the *Snap-Dragon*, and given up to dispose of her prisoners.

"His majesty's" packet, *Morgiana*, 18 guns, 9 pounders, two of them long brass pieces, fifty men, burden 400 tons, captured by the privateer *Saratoga*, of 4 guns, and 116 men, by boarding. The *Saratoga*, chased by a frigate, had been compelled to throw overboard 12 of her guns, previous to the action, but took the brass pieces from the packet, and continued her cruise. The *Morgiana* was obstinately defended; had two men killed and five wounded, among the latter, the captain, severely. The *Saratoga* had three men killed and seven wounded. Before the *Morgiana* struck, she threw over the mail. The prize has arrived at Newport, R. I., where her late captain has publicly offered his thanks to the prize-master, for his humanity and kindness during his captivity.

During this same cruise, the *Saratoga* took a brig and a ship, and burnt them both, being of little value.

Schooner ——, of 130 tons, from St. Johns for the West Indies, sent into Machias by the privateer *General Stark.*

Several American privateers were on the British coast about this time. The *Lion* and two others were cruising on the coast of Spain. The *Scourge* and *Rattlesnake* released 180 prisoners, which they took in a fleet from Archangel.

Fifteen vessels, captured off Jamaica by the *Lovely Cordelia,* of Charleston, the valuable articles were taken out, and the vessels destroyed. The *Lovely Cordelia* arrived safely in port, after a fortunate cruise.

A brig, captured by the *Lovely Cordelia,* and manned for the United States, was subsequently wrecked on the coast of Florida.

Schooner *Fame,* from Barbadoes for Berbice, laden with Madeira wine, and government stores, captured by the *Saratoga,* was wrecked on Long Island, her crew and cargo all saved.

Ship *St. Lawrence,* from England, with a British license, full of most valuable British goods, worth from $300,000 to $400,000, captured by an Eastern privateer, and sent into Portsmouth, N. H., where she was condemned. The vessel and property were professedly American, but were ultimately proved to be English, consequently a good prize to the captors.

The Privateer *Yankee,* during her last cruise captured nine vessels, two of which she gave up to dispose of her prisoners and sent them to England as cartels, and after making a successful cruise returned again to Rhode Island.

The letter-of-marque *Water-Witch,* of New York, fell in with a British fleet of merchantmen, and captured three of them, which she manned for the United States.

Brig *President,* with a valuable cargo of sugar, molasses, and rum, sent into Savannah by the *Polly,* of Salem.

The *Yankee,* on her last cruise of forty-nine days, captured the brig *Ann,* with rum, salt, and dry-goods, for Newfoundland, valued at $40,000; brig *Mary,* with salt, etc., worth $20,000; brig *Despatch,* cargo of general English manufactures, invoiced at £80,000, sterling; brig *Telemachus,* with rigging, coals, provisions, etc., $40,000; brig *Favourite,* of little value, given up to release the prisoners; schooner *Katy*, laden with wine; barque *Paris*, 10 guns, captured after 35 minutes fight, a very valuable vessel; brig *Howe*, 6 guns, threw the guns overboard, and gave up the vessel to the prisoners; *John and Mary*, loaded with provisions and other goods, worth $49,000. These loaded vessels were part of a fleet from Cork; two of them were ordered for France, and the rest for different ports in the United States. It is possible the greater part of the *Yankee's* prizes may be recaptured. If she had belonged to the United States, sailing under orders to destroy the commerce of the enemy, the loss of property would have been equal to half a million of dollars on his part, and the gain of 180 prisoners on ours, in the space of forty-nine days.

Thirteen merchant vessels captured on the coast of Spain, by the *Leo* of Baltimore, and burnt.

Copy of a Letter from Commodore Lewis, to the Secretary of the Navy

"Sir, I have the honour to inform you of the recapture of the American schooner *Sparrow*, of Baltimore, from New Orleans bound to this port, laden with sugar and lead. On the 3rd, the enemy's ship *Plantagenet* chased the said vessel on shore, near Long Branch, six miles distant from where the flotilla is stationed, and took possession of her with about one hundred men. A detachment from the flotilla marched against them, attacked them, drove them from on board the vessel, and took possession under a fire from the enemy's ship and barges. In the affair we lost one man; the enemy's loss must have been considerable, as many were seen to fall. The whole cargo, together with sails, rigging, etc., have been saved, vessel bilged.

"The saving of the cargo of the *Sparrow*, was a very gallant affair. The 74 came near enough to fire grape shot at our people, having no sort of shelter, they laid down on the sand, and presented their heads to the enemy; and when his barges neared the shore, they rose and beat them off."

New York, November 7, 1813.

The London papers give a doleful account of the proceedings

of an American privateer off the mouth of the Tagus (Portugal.) They report that she had captured thirty-two British vessels, many of them richly laden, and that their merchant vessels were unable to leave the ports of Great Britain without convoy.

They further add, that the American privateers seemed to increase daily, that they infest every part of Europe, that they were also on the coast of Brazil, and among the West India Islands, and that there was no security for trade and commerce except under the guns of their men-of-war.

I herewith extract from a Salem newspaper, the number and names of all the privateers, lost and taken by the British, belonging to that place and the neighbouring ports, which are as follows:—

Schooner	*Fair Trader*,	Brig *Montgomery*,
"	*Regulator*,	Ship *Alexander*,
"	*Active*,	Schooner *Cossack*,
"	*Dolphin*,	Boat *Owl*,
"	*Buckskin*,	Sloop *Wasp*,
"	*Revenge*,	Schooner *Growler*,
Ship *John*, Schooner,		*Dart*—lost,
Schooner *Enterprise*,		*Gallinipper*—cast-away and lost.

The whole value of the above sixteen privateers, was estimated at $164,100. The sale of prizes brought into Salem, up to this date, amounts to $675,695 93.

Prizes Captured by Privateers.

An American schooner, from one of the Eastern ports, laden with 700 barrels of flour, bound for Halifax, sent into New Bedford by the *Water-Witch* of Bristol, R. I.

Sloop *Eliza Ann*, valuable, sent into Eastport. The commander of the British sloop-of-war *Martin*, had demanded her restoration, under the penalty of destroying the town. The demand was not complied with, and some shot were exchanged between that vessel and the fort, without apparent injury to either party. The *Eliza Ann* was captured by the *Timothy Pickering*.

The schooner *Experiment*, of New York, was captured off Cape Henry; a prize-master and three men were sent on board, and two of the crew taken out, the captain and one man left. The same night the captain recaptured his vessel.

The schooner *Federalist*, taken by the British, was sent into Cape May for ransom. The citizens took possession of the vessel and set the men at liberty.

Captain W. S. Stafford, famous for his defence of the *Dolphin* privateer, in the Chesapeake, during the last summer, was attacked close in with Charleston bar, on the 27th of November, by five boats, from a British brig-of-war, when close upon him, he tore one of the boats to pieces with grape shot, and gave the rest employment in saving their comrades. The brig, after discharging a broadside at him, hauled off. Captain Stafford had one man wounded. The loss of the enemy was not known.

Captain Kennedy, of the sloop *Betsey*, from Maurice River for Newbern, N, C, was captured by the *Lacedemonian*, who put five men and a prize-master on board, leaving Captain Kennedy and another person on board, which two made out to surround the six Englishmen, and take them safely to Newbern. The prize-master promised that no further resistance should be made, and he did not attempt it, he of course was well watched.

The *Timothy Pickering*, privateer, sent into Salem the brig *Dart*. The *Pickering* also about the same period, sent a schooner into the same port.

Sloop *General Hodgkinson*, from Curracoa for Martinique, with salt and some specie, captured by the *Saratoga*, but cast away near Charleston, S. C, where the prize-master and crew arrived safe.

Brig *Edward*, from N. B., laden with oil and fish, was captured and sent into Folly landing by the *Fox* privateer, of Baltimore.

Brig *Lloyd*, from Goree, captured by the *Saratoga*, her cargo of camwood, muskets and pistols taken out, and the vessel burnt.

Ship *Venus*, of 10 guns, from London for Bonavista, captured by the *Saratoga*, divested of her guns and all her valuables, and suffered to proceed with a little "friendly advice," not being worth sending in. The *Saratoga* had thrown ten of her guns overboard, when chased by a British ship-of-war, and now supplied herself very opportunely from the *Venus.*

Schooner *Joseph,* of Surinam, laden with government stores, captured by the *Saratoga,* who took out her cargo, and ransomed the vessel, putting on board twenty-nine prisoners on parole.

Schooner *Lady Cockburn,* with a cargo of indigo and coffee, taken by the same—took out the cargo, and allowed her to proceed to her destined port.

The *Saratoga* has arrived at Wilmington, N. C.; besides the cargoes of the above vessels, she is said to have on board a considerable sum in specie. She watered at the Canary Islands, where she was very civilly treated.

The brig *Sir John Sherbroke,* of 10 guns and forty men, taken by the *Saucy Jack,* after a fight of twenty minutes, in which she had two men killed, and five wounded. The *Saucy Jack* sustained but little injury, except three men slightly wounded.

The valuable ship *Manly,* 4 guns, laden with wine, oil, etc., from Halifax, for the West Indies, sent into Charleston, S. C, by the *Revenge,* of Baltimore.

A brig laden with sugar and molasses, captured by the *Caroline* of Baltimore; was recaptured by the British off Charleston.

We have had the pleasure of noticing the exploits of the *Lion* privateer, of Baltimore, off the coasts of Spain and Portugal. She safely arrived at L'Orient in France, with about $400,000 on board, after having destroyed fifteen or twenty English vessels.

Schooner *Messenger,* from the West Indies, laden with rum and molasses, sent into Wilmington, N. C, by the *Comet,* of Baltimore.

Brig ——, laden with rum, sent into Wilmington, N.C, by the letter-of-marque schooner *Eliza.*

Brig *Agnes,* in ballast, captured by the *Saucy Jack,* on her late cruise, and burnt.

Sloop *John,* divested of her cargo of provisions, etc., etc., taken by the same, and given up.

The *Saucy Jack* took several small British vessels, which the commander gave up "without ransom." The privateer arrived at Charleston ten or twelve days after.

Brig *Abel*, from the West Indies, laden with rum and sugar, sent into North Carolina by the *Caroline*, of Baltimore.

Unfortunate Rencontre Between a British Sloop-of-war, and the Privateer Grampus, of Baltimore

The schooner *Grampus* safely arrived at New York, from an unfortunate cruise among the Canary Islands.

Previous to her leaving her cruising ground, she captured the British brig *Speculation*, from Lanzarote bound to London, but as she was an old vessel of little value, Captain Murphy gave her up to the prisoners.

Soon after he gave up his prize, a British sloop-of-war hove in sight, and was so well disguised as a merchantman, that Captain Murphy was decoyed quite under her guns, before he discovered his mistake. Believing her to be a letter-of-marque, he was, as it were, taken by surprise when the man-of-war opened her ports, and gave the *Grampus* a terrible broadside from her main-deck battery when within half pistol-shot distance. By this destructive discharge Captain Murphy, and one seaman were killed, and several of the crew wounded.

The privateer suffered greatly in her sails and rigging, and it was only by the utmost exertion she was able to make her escape from the enemy.

The writer of this article was personally acquainted with Captain John Murphy; some months previous to this sad event we met at Bordeaux. Captain Murphy was then in command of the *Grampus*.

At that period I commanded the letter-of-marque *David Porter*, which vessel was lying at La Teste, a small port about thirty miles from Bordeaux.

It gives me pleasure to add that Captain Murphy was a brave, worthy man, and an excellent seaman, highly esteemed and beloved by all who knew him. I have no doubt his hard fate drew many a sympathetic tear from the gentle and good of his numerous friends in Baltimore.

"So Sleep the Brave."

Prizes Captured by Privateers.

Sloop *Resolution*, from Jersey for Lisbon, with linen, paper, etc., captured by the letter-of-marque schooner *General Armstrong*, on her passage from France to the United States, dispossessed her of her cargo, and gave her up to the prisoners.

Brig *Phoebe*, from Ireland for Madeira, laden with butter and potatoes, captured by the same, and scuttled. The *General Armstrong* soon after arrived at New York.

Brig *Commerce*, from Martinique for Halifax, laden with rum and molasses, a prize to the letter-of-marque brig *Flirt*, of New York. The prize was partially dismasted, and otherwise so severely damaged as induced the crew to abandon her. She was consequently destroyed.

Schooner *Fanny*, from Trinidad, laden with sugar, carried into Charleston, S. C, by the *Revenge*.

Brig *Victoria*, laden with 250 hhds. of Jamaica rum, 40 hhds. of sugar, and a quantity of coffee, sent into Savannah by the *Rapid*, of Charleston.

British ship *Tryal*, 200 tons, burnt by the *Grand Turk*.

Brig ——, from Lisbon, captured by the same, and ransomed for $8,000.

Schooner ——, from Martinique, laden with 120 hhds. of molasses, sent into Charleston by the *Caroline*. The prize had British and Swedish papers.

Brig *Silena*, captured by the *Revenge* of Baltimore, and burnt.

The elegant privateer-ship *Jacob Jones*, of 600 tons, carrying 20 twelve-pounders, and a picked crew of 127 men, lately sailed from Boston, on a cruise in the East Indies.

Brig ——, from St. Lucia, sent into Elizabeth City, (N. C), laden with 140 hhds. and 200 barrels of sugar, by the *Caroline*.

The Privateer *Rapid*, of Charleston, being chased off the Mississippi, by the British sloop-of-war *Herald*, was unfortunately upset. Her crew, however, were soon picked up, and saved by the boats of the enemy. They were kindly treated as prisoners of war.

I hope no civilized nation would have acted otherwise under similar circumstances.

Brig ——, from Halifax for England, laden with lumber, captured by the *Grand Turk*, and burnt.

The *Grand Turk,* about this time, arrived at Salem. Besides the above vessels, she captured and manned two valuable ships, one brig and one schooner. One of the ships was estimated to be worth $150,000. The *Grand Turk* cruised about twenty days in the mouth of the English Channel. She had no fighting, nor was she chased by a man-of-war during her absence.

Schooner ——, laden with sugar, coffee, etc., sent into Sunbury by the *Patapsco*, letter-of-marque, of Baltimore.

Pink stern-boat, belonging to Herrings Gut, with $20,000 worth of English goods on board, was captured off George's River, by a row-boat privateer, and sent into a neighbouring port.

Ten enemy's vessels, captured by the *Caroline*, (in addition to those whose safe arrival have been noticed,) divested them of their valuable articles, burnt, sunk, etc. The *Caroline* arrived at Charleston, S. C., with a large amount of dry-goods, etc., on board. She caught also two traitor vessels. The following is an extract from her log-book:—

> "*Nov. 20th*—Fell in with the American sloop *Osiris*, Driggs, from Martinique bound to St. Bartholomew, with a cargo of molasses. Captain Driggs, taking the *Caroline* for a British cruiser, showed his British license to Captain Almeda, at the same time informing him, that he had supplied Commodore Oliver, of his Majesty's ship *Valiant*, of New London, with a quantity of potatoes and apples, for which he was paid, and that he had no doubt if he fell in with an American privateer he should be hung. Put Mr. Canoning and a prize-crew on board the *Osiris*, and ordered her for the first American port."

The letter-of-marque *Herald*, arrived at New York on the 26th of December, from Charleston. On the passage she engaged an English schooner, and after having exchanged several broadsides they separated, it being near night when the *rencontre* occurred.

An American privateer of 18 guns, sailed from Bordeaux, in October, bound on a cruise.

DESPERATE ACTION OFF MADEIRA, BETWEEN THE PRIVATEER SCHOONER *GLOBE* OF BALTIMORE, RICHARD MOON, COMMANDER, AND TWO ENGLISH PACKETS.

The *Globe* arrived at Wilmington, N. C., on the 27th of January, 1814, when the captain reported an account of his action. I have rewritten the substance of it in nautical style, as follows:—

On the 1st of November, while cruising off Madeira, we saw a sail to leeward; bore away to ascertain her character. She proved to be a large man-of-war brig, and after exchanging a few shots, I thought it most prudent to haul off. Before we separated, however, we received a nine-pound-shot under our quarter, very near the water-line. After getting clear of the man-of-war, we proceeded off the port of Funchal. We there saw two brigs, backing and filling about the roads, apparently ready to leave port. They probably saw the *Globe* in the offing, and were perhaps waiting for us to leave the Island, to enable them to proceed to sea without molestation.

On the 2nd of November, at nine in the morning, they sailed out of the roads, and steered to the. southward. We gave chase, but as it soon became dark and squally, we lost sight of them.

We however, still continued the pursuit under easy sail, until daylight the next morning.

November the 3rd, at 6 o'clock, we saw the two brigs again bearing S. W. from us, some six or eight miles distant, we continued the chase until half-past 11 a. m., when the largest brig commenced firing upon us with her stern guns, which was soon returned, when the action commenced in good earnest. At half-past twelve noon, we sheered up alongside of our adversary to board him.

The schooner unfortunately fell off, so that only the first and second lieutenants, and three seamen, had time to get on board.

These poor fellows were probably overpowered and killed by the enemy. At this time the *Globe* was very much injured in her sails and rigging. While we were thus engaged with the first brig, the other one bore up, and passing athwart our bows, gave us a terrible raking fire, which completely cut up our sails and rigging.

This broadside added to the injury we had already received from her consort, rendered our schooner for a considerable time quite unmanageable.

We however, continued the fight at close quarters, until we compelled the largest brig to strike her colours, at half-past three o'clock.

The other brig continued the action with great obstinacy, pouring in upon us broadside after broadside within half pistol-shot distance.

The largest brig having surrendered, we managed to get the *Globe* under steerage-way, and return the fire of the second brig, which had so severely injured us. We were now able to return his fire with compound interest, at close quarters, until half-past four o'clock, when we found our vessel almost in a sinking condition; having received seven shot in our hull nearly between wind and water.

Notwithstanding our disabled condition, we managed to haul to windward to take possession of the brig that first struck; when to our surprise, she again hoisted her colours, and gave us a broadside, being aided by her consort. We were obliged to haul off to repair damages, having the greater part of our standing and running rigging shot away, and not a sail but what was completely riddled with shot, and almost useless.

The two brigs were packets. We saw one of them throw her mails overboard during the action.

The largest brig mounted eighteen guns, and the other sixteen twelve-pounders. They were mostly brass pieces.

We found one double-headed shot sticking in our side which weighed 12 lbs.

We have every reason to believe, that the enemy suffered severely, and that great numbers of men were killed on board both these vessels, by our great guns and musketry.

After the action, we proceeded to the Grand Canary Island to repair damages, and refit.

While in that port, we heard from Santa Cruz, Tenerife, that a British packet brig, carrying 18 guns, and another brig of 14, had recently arrived at that port. They reported that a few days before they had a severe engagement with an American privateer, and that they succeeded in beating her off, with great loss to themselves, having had twenty-seven men killed and wounded, besides being terribly cut up in their hulls, sails, and rigging.

The loss of the *Globe* was eight killed, and fifteen wounded. Here follow the names of the killed and wounded:—

Killed.— John Harrison, first lieutenant; John Smith, second lieutenant; Joshua Brown, seaman; Richard Blair, do.; James Thelis, do.; Samuel D. Smith, do.; Sandy Forbes, do.; —— Oliver, do.

Wounded.—Richard Moon, captain; Noah Allen, prize-master; John Frinks, do.; Asa Hart, seaman; Ab. Kinhart, do.; —— Fortune, do.; Job E. Wheeler, do.; P. Short, do.; F. Statt, do.; T. Jifford, do.; J. Arnold, J. Beatly, do.; John Wilson, do.; John Mitchell, do.; Daniel Milton, do.

The force of the *Globe* was one long-torn amidships, and eight twelve-pound carronades, with a complement of ninety men, including officers and marines.

Prizes Captured by Privateers

Hermaphrodite brig *Cossack*, from Martinique for Bermuda, laden with 133 hhds., two tierces, and 68 barrels of sugar, sent into Georgetown, S. C, by the letter-of-marque schooner *General Stark*, of 2 guns and twelve men, on her passage to St. Domingo. The *General Stark* had previously recaptured an American vessel, and ordered her into port, and at the time of capturing the *Cos-*

sack, had only eight men on board, three of whom, with a boy, brought in the prize and her crew (twelve in number), all safe. This is truly "Yankee enterprise." The *General Stark* belongs to Salem. The bounty allowed to our letters-of-marque and privateers, (on the reduction of duties,) on the cargo of this vessel, is equal to nearly $4,000.

Schooner *Jasper*, from Surinam, laden with coffee, sugar and rum, a prize to the *Caroline*, of Baltimore, sent into Georgetown, S. C. It is stated this vessel would have been wrecked and lost on the bar, but for the meritorious exertions of Lieutenant Monk, of the United States Navy.

Schooner *Rebecca*, from Halifax for Bermuda, cargo live stock and provisions, sent into Portsmouth by the *Grand Turk*.

Schooner *Agnes*, from St. Johns, Newfoundland, for Bermuda, laden with fish, sent into France by the same.

Brig *Criterion*, a traitor vessel, laden with 80 hhds. of rum, captured by the *Caroline* of Baltimore, and sent into Stonington, Conn. This vessel was tried and condemned for account of the captors.

Schooner *Henry*, laden with fish, sent into Charleston by the *Roger*, of Norfolk.

Schooner *Maria*, captured by the same, and burnt.

Ship *Nereid*, 280 tons, 10 guns, from London for Buenos Ayres, laden with 250 bales of dry-goods, 263 packages and trunks of the same, 150 casks, hhds. and tierces of hardware and jewellery, 869 bundles of iron hoops, 80 bars of iron, and a quantity of coal, etc., the whole valued at £75,000 sterling, captured off Madeira, by the *Governor Tompkins*, of New York, and sent into that port. The *Governor Tompkins* had also captured two other very valuable vessels, and manned them for the United States, and was left in chase of a ship; all these had belonged to a fleet that sailed under convoy, but separated in a gale. Allowing this vessel's cargo to be worth £75,000, the bounty in the reduction of duties, of itself, is equal to sixty or seventy thousand dollars.

Eight vessels, taken by the *True Blooded Yankee*, and burnt off the coast of Ireland.

The *Castor*, captured by the same, divested of her valuable articles, and given up to the prisoners.

The *True Blooded Yankee* also captured the following British vessels, namely, the *Active*, *Watson*, *Cora*, and *Eliza*, and sent them into France.

Schooner *Traveller*, laden with 119 hhds. and 60 barrels of sugar, besides coffee, etc., and sent into Squam by the *Frolic*, of Salem.

Schooner *George*, laden with dry-goods, and sundries, sent into Ellsworth by the *Fly*, privateer.

Sloop *Experiment*, with dry-goods, hardware, and lumbar, sent into Machias, by the same privateer as above.

The *Fox* privateer has arrived at Salem, having made several valuable captures. The *Fox* was loaded with dry-goods and hardware, and had on board twenty-one English prisoners.

The *Vigilant*, a tender to the *Admiral* of the Windward Island station, captured by the *Comet*, of Baltimore, and sent into Wilmington, N. C.

Schooner ———, laden with sugar and coffee, sent into Savannah by the *Patapsco*, of Baltimore.

The very valuable brig, *Young Husband*, laden with dry-goods, hardware, etc., from Bristol, England, for Madeira, sent into Newport by the *Governor Tompkins*.

Nine vessels captured by the *Comet*, of Baltimore, divested of their valuable articles and sunk. The Comet is stated to have had a handsome amount in cash and rich goods on board. Besides the above, she captured and manned four prizes, one of which had at this time arrived. She had a terrible battle with the ship *Hibernia*, of 800 tons, 22 guns, and a large complement of men, but was beaten off. The fight lasted about eight hours. The great height and strength of the ship probably saved her. The privateer had three men killed, and sixteen wounded. The ship had eight killed, and thirteen wounded. The *Comet* put into Porto Rico to refit, and the *Hibernia* arrived at St. Thomas, both much injured.

Brig *Tullock*, of 200 tons, 10 guns, from Shields for Martinique, with a valuable assorted cargo, sent into Gloucester by the *Fox*, of Salem.

The rich ship *Minerva*, with an assorted cargo, from Bristol (England), for the West Indies, was captured by the *Fox*, and sent into Portsmouth, N. H.

Sloop ——, captured by the *General Stark*. She was subsequently cast away on Cape Cod, and lost.

Schooner *Harmony*, of Yarmouth, N. S., with a few puncheons of rum, captured by the privateer-boat *Terrible*, of Salem, and sent into an Eastern port.

Boat *Humbird*, laden with crockery, etc., taken by the privateer-boat *Surprise*, and sent into Machias.

A valuable brig was captured by the *Fox*, of Salem, on her late cruise, manned and ordered for the United States. Two days after the privateer had left her, she was fallen in with by two French frigates. Captain Damerell, the prize-master, supposing them to be English, hoisted a Swedish flag. But the French commodore sent a boat on board, ordering the officer to set fire to her immediately, as there were three other vessels in sight, which was done, under the belief that she was a Swedish vessel. When the prize-master and his crew were carried on board, and the matter was duly represented, the commodore expressed his regret for what had happened, and told the prize-master that the next vessel he took should be given him in compensation for the brig destroyed. On the same day, the frigates captured the Portuguese brig *Prince Regent*, from New Haven, bound to Cayenne, with a cargo of flour, lumber, etc., and according to promise, she was given up to Captain Damerell and crew, for reasons before stated. The *Prince Regent* being short of water, Captain Damerell put into St. Barts, where he found the owner of the vessel, who immediately claimed her as his property, and after an investigation, the Governor ordered her to be restored to her former owner.

A British vessel laden with sugar, a prize to the *Comet*, of Baltimore, being short of provisions, lately put into Porto Rico for a supply. But the government seized and gave her up to the English claimant.

The privateer *Diomede*, Crowninshield, arrived at Salem, after a short cruise, in which she captured and manned six vessels belonging to the enemy. She also brought in thirty-five prisoners.

The privateer schooner *Viper*, Captain D. Dithurbide, of this port, sailed from Charleston on the 24th of February, on a cruise, and arrived at New; Bedford on Friday, March 4th, having made three prizes, *viz.*, the British ship *Victory*, burthen 300 tons, mounting 10 guns, and thirteen men, from Jamaica for Liverpool, laden with 484 bales of cotton, 140 tons of log-wood, 170 tierces, 280 bags of coffee, sixteen *ceroons* of indigo, (twelve of which she brought in), eight casks of white lead, and three casks of castor-oil. She was a new vessel, coppered to the bends, and cost £13,000, sterling;

British schooner *Nelson*, of Halifax, from St. Thomas, with fifty puncheons of rum;

Spanish schooner, *Rosa*, from Bermuda, with 84 hhds., seventeen *tierces*, and 74 bbls. of sugar, with British license. These vessels were all ordered into port. Captain Dithurbide also brought in fourteen prisoners.

Notwithstanding Admiral Warren had declared the Chesapeake Bay under a strict blockade, still, in March, 1814, from fifty to sixty Baltimore privateers were cruising in almost every sea, laughing at John Bull's paper blockades, and sending rich prizes into the ports along the Atlantic board.

During the week ending March 26th, many valuable American vessels arrived in the ports of the United States.

The privateers *Comet* and *Chasseur*, of Baltimore with other vessels belonging to that port, were doing a great business in the West Indies. It was stated that the former had taken nineteen prizes on her last cruise. The latter had made six prizes, five of which she burnt, after divesting them of their valuable articles. The *Comet* had been into an out-port of Tortola, and cut out several vessels.

The *True Blooded Yankee* was owned by a Mr. Preble, an American gentleman, at that period residing in Paris. She had been thirty-seven days at sea, during which she captured twenty-seven vessels, and made two hundred and seventy prisoners. While on this cruise she took an island on the coast of Ireland, and held it six days; she also took a town in Scotland, and burned seven vessels in the harbour. She was soon after fitted out to make another cruise in company with the *Bunker Hill*, of fourteen eighteen-pounders and 140 men. When the *True Blooded Yankee* arrived in France she was laden with the following spoils:—eighteen bales of Turkey carpets, forty-three bales of raw silk, weighing twelve thousand pounds; twenty boxes of gums, forty-six packs of the best skins, twenty-four packs of beaver skins, 160 dozen of swan skins, 190 hides, copper, etc.

Schooner *Mary*, of Jamaica, captured by the *Macedonian*, letter-of-marque of Baltimore, and ransomed.

Sloop, ——, from Jamaica for the Spanish Main, captured by the *Hope*, arrived at Philadelphia, divested of a quantity of dry-goods, and given up.

Schooner *Curfew*, laden with fish and oil, from Nova Scotia for St. Lucia, sent into Marblehead by the *Alfred* of Salem.

Brig *Tercilla*, laden with fish, from St. John's, Newfoundland for Bermuda, captured by ditto and burnt.

Ship ——, full built vessel of 500 tons, sent into Beaufort, N. C, by the *Chasseur* of Baltimore, from Liverpool for Pensacola, with a large cargo of crockery, hardware, white lead, dry-goods, etc. She was under Swedish colours, but the property was unquestionably British, from the papers found on board of her.

Ship ——, of 400 tons, armed with twelve long twelve-pounders, from Smyrna, with an immensely valuable cargo of Turkey goods, sent into the Isle of Batz, (France,) by the *True Blooded Yankee*.

Ship ——, of 400 tons, 16 guns, nine-pounders, with a full cargo of hides, tallow, etc., from Buenos Ayres, sent into Abrevach, (Prance,) by the *True Blooded Yankee*.

These are in addition to the prizes already stated to have been made by this astonishing vessel. She arrived at Brest full of the richest spoils of the enemy.

Armed schooner from Halifax, formerly the American privateer *Eldridge Gerry*, of Portland, laden with fish and oil, sent into Cape Francois, by a Baltimore letter-of-marque.

Ship ——, laden with dry-goods, etc., captured by the letter-of-marque schooner *Delille*, of Baltimore, on her passage from Bordeaux to New Orleans, and sunk. The *Delille* had previously captured and manned a very valuable vessel, and could not spare hands to navigate the second prize.

Schooner *Mary & Joseph*, from Grenada for St. Thomas, with sixty-six hogsheads of rum and seven of sugar, sent into New York by the *Diomede*.

Brig *Bykar*, laden with earthenware, hollow-ware, etc., sent into Gloucester by the *Fox*.

Schooner *Hope*, sent into Bristol by the *Diomede*, with a cargo of rum, sugar and lime-juice.

Schooner *Susan & Eliza,* of Bermuda, laden with 120,000 lbs. of coffee, sent into Wilmington, N. C, by the *Mars*, of New York.

Schooner ——, called a Spaniard, but with a British license; a good prize, sent into Newport by the *Viper*.

Schooner ——, valuable, laden with dry-goods and provisions, sent into North Carolina by the *Fairy* of Baltimore.

Schooner ——, laden with rum and sugar, sent into Newport by the *Viper*.

Ship ——, under Russian colours, from Pensacola for London, laden with 1,100 bales of cotton, sent into Savannah by the *Saucy Jack*, of Charleston; cargo supposed to be British.

The total number of prizes, for the last four weeks, safely arrived or satisfactorily accounted for, amounts to thirty-nine vessels: estimated value, two millions and seventy thousand dollars, [$2,070,000.]

Brig *Superb*, with a cargo of salt, sent into Charleston, by the *Mars* of New York.

Brig *Friends*, of Halifax, from Grenada, with 112 puncheons of rum; taken by the *Diomede*, of Salem, and chased on shore on Long Island, by three men-of-war. The cargo was saved.

Schooner *Sea-Flower*, captured by the letter-of-marque

schooner *Tuckahoe*, of Baltimore, on her passage to Aux Cayes, and burnt.

Schooner *Hazard*, from Nassau, for St. Domingo, captured by the same, and given up.

The *Tuckahoe* also captured another English vessel, (whose name is not given), which prize she manned and sent into port. The *Tuckahoe* narrowly escaped capture off the east end of Long Island, having been chased for several days by sundry English frigates and brigs-of-war. She, however, by superior sailing, and good management, eluded their grasp, and got safe into Boston, in March, 1814.

Brig *Sovereign*, of and for Liverpool, of 300 tons, with an assorted cargo. Sent into Portsmouth by the *America*, of Salem.

Schooner *William*, laden with sugar, coffee and molasses, from Martinique for St. Thomas. She was captured by the *Diomede*, and sent into Savannah.

The beautiful privateer-schooner *Governor Tompkins*, belonged to New York, and was a very formidable vessel. On her first cruise, she was commanded by Joseph Skinner, of New London, and made many prizes. She subsequently sailed under the command of —— Shaler.

She suffered severely from the shot of a British frigate, but finally made her escape.

The famous brig privateer *True-Blooded-Yankee*, carrying 18 guns, and 160 men, was owned by an American gentleman residing in Paris, by the name of Preble. She was first commanded by —— Hailey, and subsequently by —— Oxnard. She had an American commission, and sailed under the American flag, but always fitted, and sailed out of French ports, *viz.*, Brest, L'Orient, and Morlaix.

This vessel was very successful. She cruised the greatest part of the war in the British and Irish Channels, and made a large number of rich prizes. These she generally sent into French ports; sometimes, however, she sent a few to the United States.

The privateer-schooner *Saratoga*, spoken of in this chapter, belonged to New York. She was a powerful vessel. On her first cruise she was commanded by —— Ricker, who made some prizes. On her second cruise she was commanded by Charles W. Wooster, who captured the British letter-of-marque brig *Rachel*, after a well-fought battle.

Her third commander was the celebrated Guy R. Champlin, who made a great many very valuable prizes. Though this vessel had several battles with the enemy, she ran all the war without being captured.

CHAPTER 6

Voyage to France

DESPERATE BATTLE, FOUGHT BETWEEN THE AMERICAN SCHOONER-PRIVATEER *DECATUR*, OF CHARLESTON, CAPTAIN DOMINIQUE DIRON, AND HIS BRITANNIC MAJESTY'S SCHOONER *DOMINICA* COMMANDED BY LIEUTENANT GEORGE WILMOT BARRETTE.

The well known privateer *Decatur*, of Charleston, figures conspicuously in this chapter.

The schooner *David Porter*, also here spoken of, under the command of George Coggeshall, was a letter-of-marque, and belonged to New York. She made a successful cruise in the Bay of Biscay, and was subsequently sold in Boston, from which port she sailed as a privateer, and made several cruises under the command of —— Fish.

The *Decatur* was armed with six twelve-pound carronades, and one long eighteen-pounder on a pivot amidships, with a crew of 103 men, including the officers.

Captain Barrette's vessel had twelve twelve-pound carronades, two long-sixes, one brass four-pounder, and a thirty-two-pound carronade on a pivot, with a crew of 88 men and officers.

The *Decatur* was cruising in the track of the West India traders, on their return passage to England. On the 5th of August, 1813, when in latitude 23°4' N., longitude about 67°0' W., during the early part of the morning, the *Decatur* was steering to the Northward, under easy sail. At half-past 10 o'clock in the forenoon, the man at the masthead discovered two sail, bearing about South, when the *Decatur* tacked to the southward, to get the weather-gage, and by so doing, ascertain the character of the two strangers.

At eleven o'clock, they were made out to be a ship and a schooner, standing to the northward. At half-past twelve (noon), being a little to the windward, and not far distant, the *Decatur* wore round and ran a little to the leeward, when the strange schooner set English colours.

At one p.m. the privateer wore again, still keeping to windward of his adversary. In the course of about half an hour, the strange schooner fired a shot at the *Decatur*, but without effect. Captain Diron then beat to quarters, and prepared for boarding the enemy.

After having loaded all his great guns and small arms, he hoisted American colours, having previously got on deck all the necessary ammunition, water, etc.

He then ordered all the hatches secured, so that no person could leave the deck, and with his grappling irons ready, bore down upon the enemy. His plan was to discharge all his guns, both great and small, and then board his adversary in the smoke.

For this purpose, at about two o'clock, Captain Diron wore ship, in order to pass under the stern of his opponent, and give him a raking fire. As they neared each other, the Englishman luffed to, and gave the privateer a broadside, but the most of his shot passed over her. At a quarter past two, Captain Diron fired his long Tom which fire the enemy returned from his main-deck battery. Captain Diron continued to discharge his long gun, a second and third time, and being now within half-gunshot distance, it must have done the enemy much damage.

As the English schooner evinced a disposition to run to leeward, Captain Diron was fearful that he wished to make his escape. To prevent this, the *Decatur* filled away to bring his bowsprit over the stern of his antagonist, but to counteract this manoeuvre, the English schooner gave him a whole broadside, which fortunately for him, only injured a portion of his rigging and sails.

The *Decatur* answered the broadside by again giving him a shot from his long-tom, at the same time ordering the boarders to be ready at a moment's warning, to rush on board of the enemy, should an opportunity offer. It was now about a quarter to three o'clock in the afternoon, and as the privateer approached to board, three cheers were given by the crew; when the English schooner gave the *Decatur* a whole broadside, which killed two of her crew, and materially injured the sails and rigging.

In the mean time, the privateer kept up a brisk fire of musketry. The Englishman then kept away, to prevent being boarded, while the *Decatur* followed close under his stern, to avoid another broadside from him, and lose not a moment in boarding him.

In this manner the conflict was kept up, and another attempt made to board, but it was again repulsed. Captain Diron then ordered the drum to beat for the boarders, and the crew cried out to let them board.

The *Decatur's* bowsprit was forced over the stern of the enemy, and her jib-boom pierced through the mainsail of the English schooner. It was now half-past three o'clock. While the fire of the musketry was being kept up by a portion of the privateer's crew, the rest rushed from the bow-sprit on board the *Dominica*. A terrible scene of slaughter and bloodshed then ensued: the men fought with swords, pistols, and small arms, in short, it was a hand to hand combat, and was well sustained on both sides, until Captain Barrette and his principal officers were either killed or wounded.

Mr. Vincent Safifth, first-prize master, and Mr. Thomas Wasborn, quarter-master, were the first two of the *Decatur's* crew who got on board of the English schooner.

This action was one of the hardest contested battles on record. Both parties fought with unparalleled vigour and desperate courage. The decks were covered with the dead and wounded. The conquerors themselves hauled down the English colours. On board the *Decatur* there were five killed and fifteen wounded. On board the *Dominica*, thirteen killed and forty-sev-

Battle Between Schooner Decatur and Schooner Dominica on the 5th August, 1813

en wounded, five of whom died soon after the action; making altogether sixty killed and wounded.

Among the killed was the commander, G. W. Barrette, Mr. J. Sacker, sailing-master, and Mr. D. Brown, purser. Mr. Archer and Mr. Parry, midshipmen, were wounded.

The only officers not killed or wounded were the surgeon and one midshipman. The first lieutenant was on shore sick.

When the two schooners separated, the rigging and sails of both vessels were in a very bad condition. To restore and repair damages, and look after the wounded, was the first care of Captain Diron, his officers, and crew.

On returning to Charleston with his prize, Captain Diron made the land near Georgetown, ran down along the shore, and crossed Charleston bar without meeting an enemy. For several days previous to his arrival, there had been two English men-of-war brigs cruising off the harbour, but fortunately for him, they had steered away to the southward, so that he had time to enter the port without being molested.

Captain Diron was a fortunate man in more respects than one, for the day after capturing the Dominica, he fell in with, and took without resistance the British ship *London Trader,* from Surinam bound to London. She had on board a valuable cargo, consisting of 209 hhds. of sugar, 140 *tierces* of molasses, 55 hhds. of rum, 700 bags of coffee, and 60 bales of cotton. The prize arrived safe in Savannah, on the same day that Captain Diron reached Charleston.

During the combat between the *Decatur* and the *Dominica*, which lasted over an hour, the British government packet *Princess Charlotte* remained a passive spectator of the scene. As soon as the two schooners were disengaged from each other, she tacked about, and stood to the southward. She left St. Thomas bound to England, under convoy of the *Dominica*, to a certain latitude, and from thence to proceed on her course alone.

Remarks on the Battle

The surviving officers of the *Dominica* attributed the loss of their vessel, to the superior skill of the *Decatur's* crew in the use of musketry, and to Captain Diron's adroit manner in manoeuvring his schooner during the action, which rendered their carriage guns in a manner, almost useless.

Captain Barrette was a brave young man, not more than twenty-five years of age. He was wounded early in the action, by two musket-balls in the left arm, but he fought till the last moment, refusing to surrender his vessel, although urged to do so by the few survivors of his crew. He declared several times his determination not to survive the loss of his schooner.

One of the lieutenants of the *Decatur* received a severe sabre wound in the hand, from Captain Barrette, a few moments before he fell.

It was acknowledged by the English prisoners, that during their captivity, they were treated with great kindness and humanity by Captain Diron, his officers and crew; and that the utmost care and attention were paid to the sick and wounded.

The crew of the captured vessel were all fine looking young men. There were among them eight or ten boys. To see this youthful crew on their arrival at Charleston, in their mangled condition, was enough to freeze the blood with horror, of any person not accustomed to such sanguinary scenes.

Among the crew was a small boy, not eleven years old, who was twice wounded while contending for victory on the deck of the *Dominica*.

The writer of this action was in Charleston soon after the *Dominica* was brought into that port, and heard the most of what he has narrated, from those who were acquainted with all the particulars of this bloody conflict. He also saw daily, one of the wounded English midshipmen, with his arm in a sling, who had the privilege of walking about the city, on his parole of honour.

The famous privateer *Decatur*, Captain Diron, sailed from Charleston on a new enterprise, the same day that the writer of this article arrived there.

It was with unfeigned pleasure I witnessed the departure of the brave Diron in pursuit of fresh laurels, and in sincerity wished him a successful cruise.

Voyage to France in the Letter-of-Marque Schooner *David Porter*.

On the 20th of October, 1813, the letter-of-marque schooner *David Porter*, of New York, was lying at Providence, R. I., taking in an assorted cargo for Charleston. She was a fine, fast-sailing vessel of about 200 tons burthen, armed with a long 18 pound centre gun, four six pounders, muskets, boarding pikes, etc., etc., etc., and was commanded by George Coggeshall. At this time the U. S. frigate *President*, Commodore Rodgers, was lying in this port. He had recently arrived from a cruise, and had discharged the most of his men.

From among them I obtained the greatest part of my petty officers and seamen, amounting in all to thirty souls. Having finished loading the schooner, I sailed down the river to Newport, to get ready to leave port, and wait for a favourable opportunity to proceed to sea. At this period there were several English line-of-battle ships and frigates cruising directly off Newport, to blockade Commodore Rodgers and prevent him from going to sea. Wherever there was one American frigate in any of our ports, the English generally kept several seventy-fours and frigates to watch and blockade it.

The merchantmen and letters-of-marque, at this period, when ready for sea, were generally obliged to wait for bad weather or dark nights to leave port. This was my case. After lying a few days at Newport, I sailed towards evening, on the 14th of November, in a thick N.E. snow-storm, and passed through the British fleet in darkness and obscurity, and fortunately, without molestation. I made the best of my way towards Charleston, During the passage I was chased several times by British ships of war, for our coast at that time was lined with these unwelcome visitors. I however was fortunate enough to escape them all,

At daylight, on the morning of the 26th of November in ten fathoms water, off Cape Roman, saw an English man-of-war brig just out of gun-shot, of our weather quarter. He immedi-

Schooner *David Porter* Lying in the Bay of Biscay January 30th, 1814

ately made sail in chase of us.

The wind being off the land, to the N.N.E., the enemy kept to windward, close along shore, in hopes of driving me off to leeward. Just out of sight of Charleston bar, there were stationed two brigs-of-war, but being aware of the trap laid for me, I resolved to hug the wind, and push boldly for the channel at the bar, at the entrance of the port, and defend myself the best way I could.

The chase from off Cape Roman to Charleston bar, lasted about four hours, during which time I had gained but very little on the enemy. When I hauled up for the bar upon the wind, I brought the Englishman upon my weather beam, at long gunshot distance. To ascertain whether I could reach him, I gave him a shot from long Tom, and though it did not quite hull him, I saw the shot strike so near him that it dashed the water all over his larboard quarter.

As the brig's guns were carronades, his shot could not reach us, while I should have annoyed him with our long Tom, had he thought it advisable to continue the action. Just at that moment, however, the famous privateer *Decatur*, Captain Diron, and the letter-of-marque *Adeline*, Captain Craycroft, of Philadelphia, were crossing the bar, and bearing down upon the brig, all three of us, with our ensigns flying. The Englishman probably thought it was most prudent to decline the combat, and speedily squared his yards, and ran out of sight to leeward.

The *Decatur* and *Adeline* steered on their course to the eastward, while I crossed the bar and proceeded up to Charleston. Soon after my arrival, I obtained a full freight for a port in France, consisting of 331 bales of cotton, at twenty-six cents per pound, with five *per cent*, primage. The gross freight and primage on this small cargo of cotton amounted to twenty-three thousand dollars, which, for a pilot-boat schooner of 200 tons, certainly appears like an enormous freight on sea island cotton, when the article could at that time be purchased for twelve or thirteen cents per pound. But when the expense of sailing one of these letters-of-marque is taken into consideration, the freight is not too high. The insurance at that time was from fifteen to twenty *per cent.* and seamen's wages at thirty dollars per month, and other expenses in like proportion.

On the 18th of December, I finished loading, and got all the crew on board. The next day we were ready for sea, but unfortunately the wind blew fresh from the southward, with dark, disagreeable rainy weather.

The Congress of the United States had lately assembled at Washington, and great fears were entertained by many that an embargo would soon be laid. I was, of course, extremely anxious to get out of port, as such a measure would have been ruinous to myself and the other owners of my vessel; and as it was impossible to get over the bar while the wind was blowing strong, directly into the harbour, to avoid being stopped, and to keep my men on board, I judged it best to drop as low down the harbour as possible, and watch the first favourable moment to proceed to sea.

Fortunately the weather cleared up the next day, and with a favourable breeze and fine weather, I left the port of Charleston on the 20th of December, 1813, bound to Bordeaux. I had a good run off the coast, and met with nothing worth remarking until the 27th, about a week after leaving port, when I fell in with a small English brig, from Jamaica, bound to Nova Scotia. As it was about four o'clock in the afternoon, and at the time blowing a strong gale from the N.W., with a high sea running. I did not think it safe to board him until the gale should moderate, and the sea become smoother, and therefore ordered him to carry as much sail as possible, and follow me on our course to the eastward until better weather.

He reluctantly followed, and once before dark, I was obliged to hail, and give him to understand, that if he showed too great a disposition to lag behind, or did not carry all the sail his brig could bear, he would feel the effect of one of my stern-guns. This threat had the desired effect, and he followed kindly at a convenient distance, until midnight, when it became very dark and squally, and we soon after lost sight of our first prize, which

I did not much regret, as I could not conveniently spare men enough to send him into port.

From this time until we got near the European coast we scarcely saw a sail, and did not meet with a single man-of-war. Thus, while the whole coast of the United States was literally lined with English cruisers, on the broad ocean there were very few to be seen: a clear proof that the risk of capture between Newport and Charleston, was infinitely greater than in going to France.

At this period we were not obliged to deliver the goods on freight at any particular place, but at any port in France, from St. Juan de Luce to Ostend. My bills of lading were filled up on this principle, to "Bordeaux, or a port in France," so that on the arrival of the goods, the owners or agents were bound to receive them at any place where the vessel was fortunate enough to enter. My object was to get as near Bordeaux as possible; still I did not like to attempt entering the Garonne, as the English generally kept several frigates and smaller vessels stationed directly off the Cordovan Light, which rendered it extremely difficult and hazardous. I therefore decided to run for the harbour of La Teste.

About a week before we got into port, while in the Bay of Biscay, namely, on the 19th and 20th of January, we encountered one of the most severe gales from the westward that I ever experienced. It commenced early on the morning of the 19th, and blew a perfect hurricane, which soon raised a high cross-sea; at 8 o'clock, a. m., I hove the schooner to under a double-reefed foresail, lowered the fore-yard near the deck, and got everything as snug as possible. At 12 o'clock noon, a tremendous sea struck her in the wake of the starboard fore-shrouds. The force of the sea broke one of the top timbers or stanchions, and split open the plank-sheer, so that I could see directly into the hold. The violence of the blow, and the weight of water that came on board, threw the vessel nearly on her beam-ends. Fortunately the foresail was split, and the bulwarks torn away by the water, and being thus relieved, she gradually righted.

We then threw overboard two of the lee-guns, water-casks, etc., and after nailing tarred canvas and leather over the broken plank-sheer, got ready to veer ship, fearing the injury received in the wake of the starboard fore-shrouds would endanger the foremast. We accordingly got ready to hoist a small piece of the mainsail, and then kept her off before the wind for a few minutes, and watched a favourable, smooth time to bring her to the wind on the other tack.

During the time that the schooner ran before the wind, she appeared literally to leap from one sea to another. We soon, however, brought her up to the wind on the other tack without accident; and thus, under a small piece of the mainsail, she lay to pretty well. As the gale confined to rage violently, I feared we might ship another sea, and therefore prepared, as it were, to anchor the vessel head to wind. For this purpose we took a square-sail boom, spanned it at each end with a new four-inch rope, and made our small bower cable fast to the bight of the span, and with the other end fastened to the foremast, threw it overboard, and payed out about sixty fathoms of cable; she then rode like a gull on the water, and I was absolutely astonished to see the good effect of this experiment. The spar broke the sea, and kept the schooner nearly head to the wind until the gale subsided.

The next day, in the afternoon, January 20th, we again made sail, and on the 26th, six days after this tempest, got safe into La Teste, thirty-seven days from Charleston. While we providentially escaped destruction, other ships were less fortunate; many vessels were stranded and wrecked along the coast; five sail of English transports were thrown on shore near La Teste, and most of their crews perished in the same gale. On my arrival, all my papers were sent up to Paris; and although we were all well, still we were compelled by the government to ride quarantine for six days.

After this was accomplished, I landed all my cotton, and having put it into a large and convenient warehouse, I proceeded directly to Bordeaux. The distance from La Teste to Bordeaux is about thirty miles, and as the roads were in a bad state at this season of the year, it was deemed most advisable to let my cargo remain at La Teste until some favourable change. At Bordeaux everything was in confusion, as the enemies of France were at that time entering the empire in almost every direction. It was reported, while I was there, that a part of the Russian and Austrian armies were within thirty leagues of Paris, and that Lord Wellington, with his army, was in the Landes in pursuit of Marshal Soult, who was on his way to Toulouse; and great fears were entertained that a part of the English army would soon be in Bordeaux. I was therefore extremely anxious to get away at all hazards, not knowing whether the English would respect private persons and private property.

All the American vessels had left Bordeaux for fear of the English, and. had gone down near the mouth of the Garonne; some were bound home to America, and others strove to get to La Rochelle, as that was a strongly fortified town, and would. probably hold out longer than this place. Every day brought us worse news from Paris and other quarters, and from present appearances the country could not hold out much longer.

In this state of things, when all was hubbub and confusion, the merchants were unwilling to advance any portion of the freight on the cotton, I therefore found it difficult to obtain sufficient means to pay my necessary disbursements. I, however, at length prevailed on my consignees, Messrs. Brun *frères*, to purchase for me one hundred casks of wine, and fifty pipes of brandy, to charter a small coasting vessel to carry these articles to La Rochelle, and wait my arrival there. They also agreed to furnish me with sufficient funds to pay my outfit at La Teste. Having made these arrangements, I forthwith proceeded to La Teste on horseback.

Although at this period the Austrian and Russian armies were in the neighbourhood of Paris, and Lord Wellington at the head of a victorious army overrunning the south of France, it was astonishing to see how little was known to the country people of this region about the military state of the empire. Perhaps not a man in a thousand knew that there was a Russian or an English soldier within a hundred leagues of France.

One day, in passing through a small village, I stopped at a house to get some water, and found a poor woman wringing her hands and weeping as though her heart would break. On inquiring the cause of her grief, she said: "Sir, they have just taken away my son to join the army, and I have already lost two of my children in the same way. Oh! I shall never see him again!"

I offered the poor woman all the consolation I could. I told her I was a stranger, and had no right to interfere with the affairs of another nation, but at the same time, if she would keep quiet, I could assure her that there was no danger of losing her son—that the wars were nearly at an end, and that peace, in all human probability, would be concluded in a few weeks, when her son would be restored to her again.

At these words the poor creature was completely overjoyed, and blessed me a thousand times. When I mounted my horse and rode off, I could not but reflect with indignation on what men call military glory; but at the next moment I felt self-reproved, as I too commanded an armed vessel, and expected to go out in a few days to distress the enemies of my country. How strange and inconsistent is poor, short-sighted man, condemning others when committing the same offence for which he would denounce his neighbour.

The state of affairs in France daily grew worse and worse. Lord Wellington was following Marshal Soult day after day, towards Toulouse. We also received bad news from the north, that the Austrians and Prussians were daily advancing on Paris, and were then within twenty leagues of that city.

Under this state of things, I deemed it most prudent to proceed forthwith to La Teste, and get ready for sea as soon as possible. La Teste was a poor, little village, and badly supplied with articles necessary for ship stores. On my arrival there, I found no other ship or vessel lying in the port, and no stone ballast; I was therefore compelled to take in sand in my own boat, and fill up our water casks and take them on board also in the same way. We had no biscuit on board, and there was but one baker of any consequence in the town. I hastened to this important character, and agreed to take all the bread he could make in two days, and thus, by hurrying and driving, I got ready for sea on the 11th of March. At the end of two days I called on the baker for my supply of bread, when, to my great mortification and disappointment, I could get only loaves enough to fill two bags, and this, for a vessel bound to La Rochelle, with a crew of thirty-five in number, was certainly a very small allowance. It is true I had salt beef and pork enough on board, but no vegetables or rice.

On the 11th, in the evening, by letters from Bordeaux, I learned that the day before, the town had surrendered by capitulation to a portion of Lord Wellington's army, that no person had been molested, and that perfect good order was observed through the city. All this appeared very well with respect to Bordeaux, but still I was fearful that the English would come down and take La Teste before I could get to sea. The next day, March 12th. the wind was from the westward, and the pilot would not take my vessel to sea. He said that it was impossible to get out; that there was too great a swell on the bar, etc. The next day (the 13th), the weather was clear and the wind fresh at N.N.E. In the morning I prevailed on the pilot to come on board. He told me that the tide would suit at five .o'clock in the afternoon, and if there should not be too much sea on the bar at that hour he would take the vessel out.

Accordingly, at four o'clock, I requested him to get under way, and be ready to pass the bar at five. I now found he was unwilling to go out at all. He said: "Captain, if we should succeed in getting out, it would be impossible to land me." I then offered him double pilotage, told him I was fearful the English would come down in the morning and make a prize of my vessel, and that I would treble his pilotage, and pledge him my honour, that if I waited a week outside, I would land him in safety. At last my patience was exhausted, and I found the more I coaxed and strove to persuade him to go, the more obstinate he became.

At length I said: "If you will not go to sea, pilot, just get the schooner under way, and go down below the fort, and anchor there within the bar." To this proposition he consented. While getting under way, I went below and put into my pocket a loaded pistol, and again returned on deck. We soon got below the fort, and it was five o'clock, precisely the hour he had named as the most suitable to pass out over the bar. I then placed the pistol to his ear, and told him to proceed to sea, or he was a dead man; and that if the schooner took the ground, his life should pay the forfeit.

The poor fellow was terribly frightened, and said he would do his best; and in less than fifteen minutes from the time we filled away, we were fairly over and outside of this formidable bar. I then discharged the pistol, and assured the pilot I would do him no harm, and that I would wait a week, if it was necessary, for good weather to land him in safety. He now appeared more tranquil and composed, but could not refrain from talking occasionally of his poor wife and children, and seemed to have a lurking fear that I would carry him to America.

I stood off and on during the night, and in the morning, March 14th, the wind was light off-shore, from the eastward; as the sea was smooth, I stood close in to the beach, and got our boat ready to land the pilot. I sent by him several letters to my friends, and an order on my consignees, for a considerable sum over and above his regular pilotage, notwithstanding I had compelled him to take my vessel to sea.

At eight o'clock in the morning, my second officer, with four men, took Mr. Pilot on shore. I gave the officer of the boat positive orders to back the boat stern on to the shore, and let the pilot jump out whenever he could do so with safety. I took a spy-glass, and had the pleasure to see the man land, and scamper up the beach. The boat soon returned, and was hoisted on board, when we made sail and stood off in a N.W. direction.[1] The wind was light from the eastward, and the weather fine and clear. During the night we had not much wind, and of course made but little progress.

---

1. For a more detailed account of this cruise, and the political state of France at that period, the reader will please see *Coggeshall's Voyages.*

At daylight, March 15th, 1814, saw a large ship on our weather quarter. I soon made her out to be a frigate, distant about two miles. We were now in a very unpleasant position, early in the morning with a frigate dead to windward. I manoeuvred for some ten or fifteen minutes in hopes of drawing him down to leeward, so that I should be able to weather him on one tack or the other. This was often done at the commencement of the war, with American schooners, for if the pilot-boats could succeed in getting the enemy under their lee, they would laugh at their adversary. This manoeuvre however did not succeed, he only kept off four or six points, and I have no doubt he thought it impossible for me to elude his grasp. All this time I was losing ground, and the ship not more than two gunshots to windward.

I held a short consultation with my officers on the subject of attempting to get to windward (which would involve our receiving a broadside), or of running off to leeward. They all thought it best to ply to windward, and receive his fire. I stated that we should have to pass him within pistol-shot, and the probability was that he would shoot away some of our spars, in which case we should inevitably be captured. I knew the schooner sailed very fast off the wind, and I thought the chance of escape better to run to leeward. I accordingly gave orders to get the square-sail and studding-sails all ready to run up at the same moment; and thus when everything was prepared, the helm was put up, and every square-sail set in a moment.

The frigate, not dreaming of my running to leeward, was unprepared to chase off the wind, and I should think it was at least five minutes before she had a studding-sail set, so that I gained about a mile at the commencement of the chase. The wind was light from the E.N.E., and the weather very fine. I ordered holes to be bored in all the water-casks except four, and the water pumped into buckets to wet the sails; also, to throw overboard sand ballast, to lighten the schooner.

After this was done, we began to draw away from the frigate, so that at noon, I had gained about eight or ten miles on the chase. At four in the afternoon he was nearly out of sight, and appeared like a speck on the water. We had now time to look into our own situation, when to my great regret, in lieu of having four casks of water, the carpenter, in the confusion, had only left two; and as the wind freshened, I found the schooner so light that it was unsafe to haul upon the wind.

Seafaring men will appreciate what was my unfortunate situation. Thus wide off to sea in the Bay of Biscay, in a light vessel, with scarcely ballast enough to stand upon her bottom, with a crew of twenty-five men, and only two casks of fresh water and a few loaves of soft bread.

The wind was light during the night, and towards morning it became almost calm. At daylight, to our unspeakable joy, we were in the midst of a small fleet of merchant ships. They had left England under convoy of a frigate and a sloop-of-war, and had separated in a gale of wind a few days before I fell in with them. This little fleet was bound to St. Sebastian, and many of them were loaded with provisions for the British army. The first one I captured was a brig, principally laden with provisions. After taking possession, I agreed with the captain, that, if he would assist me with his boats and men to transport his cargo from his vessel to my schooner, I would let him go; otherwise I would take what I wanted and destroy his brig.

Of course he was glad to make the best of a bad bargain ; and thus with the boats of both vessels, in two hours we had provisions enough for a three month's cruise. His cabin was filled with bags of hard biscuit, the staff of life, which we took first, and then got a fine supply of butter, hams, cheese, potatoes, porter, etc., and last, though not least, six casks of fresh water. After this was done, the captain asked me if I would make him a present of the brig and the residue of the cargo, for his own private account, to which I willingly agreed, in consideration of the assistance I had received from him and his men.

I showed him my commission from the government of the United States, authorizing me to take, burn, sink. or destroy our common enemy, and satisfied him that he was a lawful prize to my vessel. I then gave him a certificate, stating that though his brig was a lawful prize, I voluntarily gave her to him as a present. (This, of course, was only a piece of tom-foolery, but it pleased the captain, and we parted good friends).

This was on the 16th of March, the day after my escape from the British frigate.

I had now got as much water and provisions as I wanted, and made sail for a ship and two brigs, a mile or two off on our lee beam. Although the wind was very light, I soon took all three of them, and made the same agreement with them as with the other captain, that if they would assist me with all their boats and men to load my schooner, with such part of their cargo as best suited me, I would let them go, otherwise I would send them into port as prizes, or destroy their vessels. This was a bitter pill, but they had the choice of two evils, and of course, complied with my request.

We soon commenced taking out of these prizes all sorts of stores designed for the British army, *viz.*, officer's and soldier's clothing, cocked hats, epaulettes, small arms, instruments of music, etc. Independent of these warlike stores, we also took a considerable quantity of English cloths, and various other articles of. merchandise. A fresh breeze sprung up from the S.W., and the weather became dark and rainy, which rendered it difficult to continue transporting any more goods from the prizes to our schooner. At five o'clock in the afternoon, a large ship hove in sight to windward. From aloft, with a spyglass, I clearly made her out to be the same frigate that had chased me the day before. I recognized her from the circumstance of her having a white jib; all the sails were dark coloured except this jib, which was bleached.

We of course cleared the decks, and got ready for another trial of speed, but as my schooner was now in good trim, and night coming on, I had no doubt of dodging him in the dark. He came rapidly down, within five or six miles of us, when I ran near my prizes, and ordered them all to hoist lanterns. None of them up to this time had seen the frigate, and thus, while the lanterns showed their positions, I hauled off silently in the dark.

Very soon after this, I heard the frigate firing at his unfortunate countrymen, while we were partaking of an excellent supper at their expense.

The next day, March 17th, it was dark and rainy, with strong gales from the S.W.; saw nothing. Stood to the northward, under easy sail, waiting for better weather, to complete loading my little schooner with something valuable from another prize.

I would here remark, that small guns, six or nine-pounders, are of little or no use on board of small vessels; for if the sea is rough, they cannot be used at all. I have found them of no service, but rather in the way. My only dependence was on my eighteen-pounder, mounted amidships, on a pivot. This gun I could use in almost any weather. With it, and forty small arms, I found no difficulty in capturing merchant ships.

I selected ten of the largest and strongest men on board to work the centre gun. One of them was a huge black man, about six feet six inches in height, and large in proportion. To him I gave the command of the gun. Although so powerful a man, he was the best natured fellow in the world, and a general favourite, both with officers and men.

March 18th.—Still a continuation of bad weather, with a strong gale to the westward. At four p.m., saw a frigate and a brig of war off my lee beam, distant about five miles. They made sail in chase. but under my three lower sails, mainsail, foresail, and jib, I had no fear of them. I showed my ensign for a few moments, and then plied to windward, making short tacks, and in a few hours they gave up the chase, when I again pursued my course to the northward, under easy sail. Next day, March 19th, the wind moderated, but still there was a very high sea, and unpleasant weather.

March 20th.—Moderate breezes from the westward, and unpleasant weather. This day I came to the conclusion to land myself somewhere on the coast of France, and to send my vessel home, under the command of my first officer, Mr. Samuel Nichols; and on examination of a chart of the coast, I concluded to run for L'Isle Dieu. and land there. Accordingly I shaped my course for the Island, and without meeting with any incident worth relating, made the land on the 23rd of March, at four o'clock in the afternoon; at six *ditto*, landed on the island in my own boat. It soon became dark, and I was obliged to remain on shore, with my boat's crew, all night.

I took with me my clearance and other papers from Bordeaux, with sundry newspapers, and was well received by the Governor and Commissary of Marine.

March 21st.—At six o'clock in the morning, although the weather was thick and rainy, and a strong breeze from the S.W., I sent my boat on board the schooner with a pilot, with orders to get the vessel into the roads, near the town, which is situated on the N.E. end of the island. At two o'clock in the afternoon, the schooner came directly off the town, close in within the fort, where with our own boat, we took on board six casks of fresh water, some fresh provisions, and sundry small stores. I then obtained liberty from the public authorities to dispatch my vessel to the United States.

At five o'clock in the afternoon of March 24th, 1814, I repaired on board in a shore boat, and wrote a few hasty letters to my friends in the United States.

After making a short address to my officers and men, I resigned the command to Mr. Samuel Nichols, my first-lieutenant, and promoted my brother, Mr. Charles Coggeshall, who was second-lieutenant, to be first-lieutenant, directing them to proceed directly to the United States. At the same time, I requested the captain to fill the schooner with whatever valuable goods he should be enabled to take from the enemy on his return passage home. I then returned on shore with a heavy heart at parting with my little band of brave and faithful followers.

The schooner was soon out of sight, as she stood round to the south end of the island. And here I should be doing injustice to the memory of these brave men, did I not give my feeble testimony to their good conduct, from the time we left Charleston until parting with them at L'Isle Dieu. I never saw one of them intoxicated in the slightest degree, nor did I ever see one of them ill-treat a prisoner, or attempt to plunder the smallest article. In a word, from the first-lieutenant to the smallest boy on board, they were faithful, good, and true men, and, to the best of my knowledge and belief, were all born and bred in the United States.

After my schooner sailed, I had leisure to look at the island, which lies in latitude 46° 42' north, longitude 2° 27' west. It is five leagues from the continent, directly opposite St. Gilles, and is of a moderate height, about three miles long, and one and a half broad. It numbers about two thousand three hundred souls, and is principally supported by the fishing business. It is defended by a pretty strong fort at the mouth of the harbour, with a garrison of about three hundred men. Its produce is not sufficient for its own support; on the contrary, I was told by several of the inhabitants that it only yields about one quarter part of the breadstuffs that are consumed by its inhabitants. It has a snug little harbour, but only accessible to small vessels of a light draft of water. The principal town is rather pleasant, and many of the houses are commodious and well built.

This little island has become interesting from its historical association.

On the 1st of October, 1795, an English squadron brought here a Bourbon prince and several thousand French emigrants from England, to join the royal party of La Vendée; and after the fleet of men-of-war and transports had remained here until about the 15th of November, the army debarked at St. Gilles, when the fleet returned to England. [2]

When I landed at L'Isle Dieu, I took with me, as one of the boat's crew, the large black man, Philip. I was astonished to see the curiosity expressed here at the sight of a negro. He was followed at every step by a crowd of men, women, and children, all desirous to see a black man; and I soon received a pressing message from the Governor's lady to see him. I accordingly took Philip with me, and repaired to the residence of the Governor,

---

2. See Thiers's *History of the French Revolution*.

where were assembled all the first ladies of the island. They had a great many questions to ask about him, respecting the place of his birth, whether he was kind and good-natured, etc. When their curiosity was gratified, the fellow begged of me as a favour to be allowed to go on board, as he did not like to be exhibited as a show. This request I readily granted, telling the ladies and gentlemen that I had an Indian on board, and that I would send for him. The Indian came directly on shore, but, to my surprise, there appeared but little curiosity on the part of the inhabitants to see the savage. This island had been, as it were, shut out from the rest of the world for twenty-five or thirty years, with little or no commerce or communication with other nations, and it is therefore highly probable that very few of its inhabitants had ever seen a negro, and were, of course, eager to behold one.

L'Isle Dieu, March 25th, 1814.—Throughout this day we had light winds from the westward, and clear, pleasant weather. I got a passport from the Commissary of Marine, and was now only waiting for a passage to St. Gilles.

March 26th.—Light winds from the southward, with rain during the whole day; still waiting an opportunity to leave the island for the continent.

March 27th.—Throughout this day pleasant breezes from the N.N.E., and fine weather. At seven o'clock in the morning I embarked on board the *chasse-marée Mariana*, Captain Brumel, and after a pleasant passage of three hours, arrived safe at St. Gilles—a small seaport town on the west coast of France, lying in latitude 46° 40' North, longitude 1° 51' West. It is an inconsiderable place, and only navigable for small vessels.

At two o'clock in the afternoon I left this place, on horseback, for Sables d'Olonne, at which place I arrived at six o'clock in the evening, and put up for the night. This is a pleasant little seaport town, about five leagues from St. Gilles.

March 28th.—Fresh breezes from the S.E., and cloudy weather throughout this day. At ten o'clock this morning, left this place with the courier, for Napoleon, where I arrived at three o'clock in the afternoon, having travelled seven leagues in a miserable vehicle.

Napoleon is a newly-built town, with several fine houses, and broad streets. I had now got upon the great public road, and after agreeing to pay sixty *francs* for my passage to La Rochelle, left Napoleon in the same vehicle, at five o'clock in the afternoon. At eight o'clock in the evening, we arrived at the small village of Maria, and, after having travelled about five leagues, put up here for the night.

March 29th.—We left Maria at five o'clock in the morning, and travelled on the great public road. We passed through Lucan, and several other towns and villages, and arrived at La Rochelle (eighteen leagues from Napoleon), at five o'clock in the afternoon of the same day.

Here I put up at the Hôtel des Ambassadeurs, where I was delighted to meet with many of my countrymen, and once more to hear the sweet sound of my native language. It was at this place that I became acquainted with Captain Maffet of the brig *Rattlesnake*. He had recently arrived from his northern cruise, and had made many captures. He informed me that not long before he came into this port, he captured the British transport-ship *Mary*, from Sicily bound to England, with some French prisoners on board. There were also several English Army officers and soldiers, sent to guard them.

The *Mary* had several carriage guns, with musketry, etc. The captain of the transport sustained an action with the *Rattlesnake* for about twenty minutes, when himself and two seamen being killed, and three others wounded, the ship struck her colours, and was ordered into a port in France.

The *Rattlesnake* had not a man killed, and but one wounded. That was his marine officer, a handsome young man belonging to New York, who was shot in one of his legs. He was here taken to the hospital. He had the best medical aid, and was tenderly nursed by the Sisters of Charity.

He was advised by surgical men to have the limb amputated,

and was warned of the danger of delay. He would not consent, however, to the operation, giving as a reason that it would spoil his dancing. The good Sisters, seeing the young man daily become weaker and weaker, were extremely anxious that he should become a Christian, (meaning a Catholic).

To gratify them, he consented, at least in appearance. They were rejoiced, thinking no doubt, they had been the means of saving the soul of a heretic.

The poor fellow lingered a few weeks and died. He was followed to the grave by all the Americans in the place.

I subsequently learned; that Captain Maffet's prize-ship *Mary*, was recaptured, and sent to England. I saw it stated afterwards in the English papers, that the officers on board the *Mary* on their arrival in England, greatly extolled the generous conduct of Captain Maffet, in giving them all their personal property. Also, for his kind and humane treatment of them, and of all his other prisoners.

At this period there were lying in this port three American vessels beside the *Rattlesnake*, *viz.*, the letter-of-marque brig *Ida*, of Boston, the schooner *Decatur*, of Philadelphia, and a merchant brig belonging to New York, laid up here during the war.

There was lying in La Rochelle roads an English fleet commanded by Admiral Lord Keith, in the *Queen Charlotte*. Beside the admiral's ship, there were four other line-of-battle ships, several frigates, and sundry brigs and schooners-of-war. The brigs and schooners were anchored close in at the mouth of the harbour, to blockade the Americans, and also to prevent any vessel from going in or coming out of the port.

For several days after my arrival at La Rochelle we were without news from Paris, as all communication had been cut off, and not a diligence was allowed to run on the road between the two cities. The town was placed in a very anxious state of suspense. Everybody knew that the allied armies were in the neighbourhood of Paris, and no one dared to speak a syllable on the subject. At this time the military officers were seen conversing with each other in small groups, and appeared to be the only men that the government could rely upon. At length, on the 2nd of April, 1814, news arrived in town that Paris had been taken by the allied armies on the 30th *ultimo*. The next day official orders arrived from that city proclaiming the change of government. In the capitulation, Bonaparte was sent to Elba, and Louis XVIII. acknowledged King of France.

In a few minutes someone mounted a white cockade, and very soon after it became general; and now it was "*Vive le roi!*" "*Vive Louis XVIII.!*"

Although at that time I was no friend of the emperor, I was absolutely disgusted with several poor devils who, a few days before this great event, had extolled "*Le Grand Empereur*" up to the skies, and now turned against him, and called him "*Le Prince des Tyrants.*" This implication does not apply at all to the military, nor to the respectable part of the inhabitants, but to some hotel keepers and other mean-spirited turncoats, such as infest every part of the globe.

The *chasse-marée*, that I chartered in Bordeaux to bring to this place 100 casks of wine and 50 pipes of brandy, I found lying here waiting orders with respect to its disposition.

The *Ida* was a fine coppered brig of 272 tons burden, mounting eight long nine and twelve-pounders, with a complement of thirty-five men. She was in ballast, and required freight. I soon struck a bargain with Captain Mantor to take the wine and brandy at a low freight, for Boston—say at $45 per ton.

On the morning of the 8th of April, Captain Maffet, in the *Rattlesnake*, Captain Mantor, in the *Ida*, and Captain Brown in the *Commodore Decatur*, all sailed from this place. They ran down on the north side of L'Isle de Ré, namely between the island and the mainland. In this passage they met an English man-of-war brig and a schooner in company, and were all driven back.

The *Rattlesnake* and the *Commodore Decatur* returned into port again. The *Ida* lay-to off the east end of the island long enough to discharge his pilot, and then made a bold dash down the south side of the island, in plain sight of the British fleet that was lying at anchor in the roads, off La Rochelle.

I will here digress from the thread of my narrative, to insert the two following letters. As they have an intimate connection with this subject, I think it is better to place them here than to leave them to a later date:

"Captain Jeremiah Mantor, formerly of the brig Ida, of Boston:

"Dear Sir: Upon the score of old acquaintance, I herewith take the liberty of writing to you on the subject of the scenes through which we passed in our late war with England, in the years 1812, 1813, and 1814. I have been for several months writing a narrative of all the voyages I ever made, namely, from the year 1798, until I retired from the sea, in 1841.

"Now, my dear sir, you doubtless recollect that I commanded the letter-of-marque schooner *David Porter*, of New York, and that after I sent my vessel home from off L'Isle Dieu, coast of France, I went on to La Rochelle, where we met on the 29th of March, 1814; and you will also recollect that I shipped by you in the brig *Ida*, 100 casks of wine and 50 pipes of brandy for Boston. I had no insurance on this property, and was, of course, extremely anxious for your safety.

"I recollect that you sailed from La Rochelle on the morning of the 8th of April, in company with the privateer brig *Rattlesnake*, Captain Maffet, of Philadelphia, and the letter-of-marque schooner *Commodore Decatur*, Captain Brown, also of Philadelphia, and that you all three ran down between L'Isle de Ré and the mainland, and in that passage you met an English man-of-war brig with a schooner in company, sent there to guard and block up the passage, and that you were all driven back. The *Rattlesnake* and *Commodore Decatur* returned into port again, and off the east end of L'Isle de Ré you squared away and dashed down the south side of the island, and had to pass through the British fleet.

"At that time there lay at anchor in the roads off La Rochelle the *Queen Charlotte*, and four ships of the line. I understood that one of these line-of-battle ships slipped her cables and made sail in pursuit of your brig. Although I was at the time of your sailing standing on the quay at La Rochelle, I still have but an imperfect idea of all that passed. And now, my dear sir, you would do me a great favour by giving me a detailed account of all you can recollect of your marvellous escape—namely, the length of your passage home, the number of shot fired at you during the chase, and whether they threw more than one shot on board of your brig, and any other incident you can call to mind, will be gratefully received.

"Your bravery and good conduct in evading the close pursuit of so many ships-of-war, ought to be published to the world. You certainly out-manoeuvred and out-sailed them all, and I am satisfied that your prompt decision and gallant conduct saved the whole of the property entrusted to you.

For this and many other kind favours, I remain your obliged and very grateful friend,

George Coggeshall."

New York, January 5th, 1846.

West Tisbury, Mass.
Martha's Vineyard, Jan. 17th, 1846.

Captain George Coggeshall:

"Dear Sir:—I received your letter of the 5th inst., and am happy to hear from one of my old acquaintances. I often think of them and the scenes I have passed through during the years I have spent on the ocean. The voyage you speak of is well remembered. It would not be possible, after the lapse of so many years, for me to give you a correct account of all my voyages during the late war, but I will write you the particulars of that passage home, and you can make what use of it you think proper.

"I left La Rochelle in company with the *Rattlesnake* and *Commodore Decatur,* and run out north of L'Isle de Ré, with a fair wind. Saw two men-of-war ahead, hauled our wind and stood back to the east end of L'Isle de Ré. I saw there was a risk in returning again into port, and might be taken there; so I determined at once to make a bold push, discharged my pilot, and made all sail to pass the south end of the Island. I saw in a moment several of the men-of-war under way upon my lee quarter. I was looking out for ships ahead, and as I opened the island, a schooner came down on my starboard side within musket-shot; she gave me a broadside and three cheers, shot away my studding-sail boom and main-stay, and some small rigging. I soon passed her, but the men-of-war were coming up under my lee, and the shot flew thick.

"I soon saw another ship bearing down upon my starboard side. There was but one way to escape, which was, up helm, and bring all astern, or sink; this was quickly done, and we crossed the bows of the head ship so near that I could hear them halloo on board plainly.

"The shot went most of it over me: one thirty-two pounder raked my deck and lodged in the bows, one cut my anchor off the bows and cut the chains at the same moment. I cut the cable and let the anchor go. My crew were on the other side of the deck, and in the hold heaving out ballast, which saved many lives.

"The vessels continued the chase until eleven at night, after that I saw no more of them. I think there was as many as eight or ten in pursuit of me. I stood out to sea, and at daylight saw two frigates right ahead, and had just time to haul upon the wind, not knowing but that I should upset, as I had lightened the brig so much that night—I had thrown overboard six nine-pounders during the night, and soon found her ready for another chase.

"At dark I had gained four or five miles upon them; one was on my lee quarter, and the other astern. I was headed into the bay, and dare not risk to get before the wind.

"About nine p.m. the shutter of the binnacle fell, and they saw my light. They made signals one to the other, and that showed me where they were. I immediately bore up before the wind, and at daylight saw them hull down. I now had once more the wide ocean, but my brig was light, which made my passage rather long. I think it was twenty-six days.

Nothing more worth relating took place during our passage. I made two voyages to France, and one to New Orleans in the war, and passed through many scenes which often come to my mind, now I have sat down in my old age to think of the many dangers and escapes that I have passed through.

I shall be happy to hear from you at any time.
Yours with respect,
Jeremiah Mantor,

I will now continue my narrative, and return to the 9th of April, 1814. After the *Ida* had made her escape, and the *Rattlesnake* and *Commodore Decatur* returned into port, these two vessels were watched and blockaded with more vigilance than ever. The English men-of-war anchored nearer the port, while a brig and a schooner were almost constantly within gun-shot of the harbour. Tranquillity having been restored in Paris, all the wheels of government began to move in a more regular train; the mails and diligences commenced running throughout the kingdom as formerly.

In a few days I settled all my business, and left this place in the diligence for Bordeaux, on the 12th of April, 1814, passing through Rochefort and several other towns lying on the great public road, and on the 14th, two days after leaving La Rochelle, I once more had the pleasure to return in safety to Bordeaux. Here I found everything tranquil, and although the city was in the hands of the English, there was no noise or confusion.

The theatres were all open as usual, and well supported, In lieu of seeing French troops and sentinels about the town, there were English and Portuguese soldiers stationed at every military post.

I found my business had been well managed by my good friends Messrs. Brun *frères*; a portion of my freight had been collected, and everything was in a successful train. The English had thus far, respected private persons and private property.

There were no American vessels here; nearly all of them had left this country. There were a few however in the northern ports, namely, three blockaded at La Rochelle as before stated. The letter-of-marque schooner *Kemp*, Captain Jacobs of Baltimore, was lying at Nantes, and the schooners *Lion* and *Spencer* at L'Orient. These were about all the American vessels left in the

Western ports of France, There were several American gentlemen, supercargoes, at Bordeaux and La Rochelle, waiting an opportunity to return home to the United States. Nearly all the American captains and supercargoes at this time in France were well known to each other, and were upon very friendly terms. I found here, as in all parts of the world, that mutual interest and mutual sympathy draw men closely together .[3] We were all devising means to get home, some going to Amelia Island in neutral vessels, others taking passage in letters-of-marque, and some few in ships-of-war.

A few days before I arrived at Bordeaux, on the 10th of April, there was a terrible battle fought between the French and English armies at Toulouse. The French army was commanded by Marshal Soult, and the English by Lord Wellington. This was a most sanguinary conflict. Although the English were victorious, they lost, in killed and wounded, about five thousand men, and the French about three thousand. I saw great numbers of English officers who were brought down to Bordeaux sadly maimed, some with the loss of their limbs, others cut and mutilated in a frightful manner. These sights and scenes were absolutely enough to sicken one with war.

I had now so far arranged all my commercial affairs in Bordeaux with my friends Messrs. Brun *frères*, that I thought seriously of returning to the United States, by the first good opportunity. Thus, after staying in this city six days, I left it again on the 21st of April, to return to La Rochelle in search of a passage home. I took the diligence and travelled on the great public road along the sea-coast, and arrived in two days at La Rochelle. Here I found the *Rattlesnake* and *Commodore Decatur* still blockaded, and, as it appeared altogether uncertain when they would be able to get to sea, after remaining here a fortnight, I concluded to proceed to Nantes.

---

3. For example, a gentleman who witnessed the great earthquake at Carraccas, in March, 1812, told me, that at that time he saw men embrace each other who had not spoken together for years, and that the whole community buried their private animosities in face of the general danger.

I accordingly left La Rochelle on the 10th of May; travelled on the grand route, and passing through Morcilles, Napoleon, and several towns and villages, arrived at Nantes on the 11th of May. The distance from La Rochelle to this place is 100 miles. I stopped at the Hôtel de France for a few days, and then took private lodgings with Captain Jacobs, of the letter-of-marque schooner *Kemp*, of Baltimore. His schooner was anchored at Paimbœuf, near the mouth of the river Loire, about thirty miles below Nantes. I made frequent excursions with Captain Jacobs down to Paimbœuf, and found the river very shallow and full of flats and sand bars, and very difficult to ascend except for small vessels. There is, however, water enough at the port of Paimbœuf, and the anchorage is good and safe.

The shores and meadows along the river in the summer season are beautiful. The grounds are highly cultivated, and the houses and cottages are neat and pretty. Nantes is a fine old city, lying in lat. 47° 13' N., long. 1° 33' W., about 210 miles in a direct line S.W. of Paris. By Orleans, Blois, Tours and other towns on the Loire, the distance is about 300 miles. It is generally well built, and has a great many public squares. The quays along the river are very fine, and shaded by rows of large elm trees, which render them delightful promenades.

Nantes was formerly one of the largest, if not the largest, commercial town in France, and is still a place of considerable importance in a commercial point of view. It numbers from one hundred and eighty to two hundred thousand inhabitants, and is, in my opinion, the most moral town of its size in the kingdom. Provisions are cheap, and taking everything into consideration, it is a very desirable residence, and strangers in pursuit of health and reasonable living, will find themselves quiet and comfortable in this highly favoured place. At the time I visited this town, there appeared to be about three women to one man; the male population had been taken away in great numbers for the last twenty years, to fill up the armies of France, which of course left a very large proportion of females.

I came on here for the purpose of obtaining a passage to

the United States; but in this I was disappointed: there were no other American vessels here but the Kemp and she was preparing to return home as a cruising vessel—that is to say, to pick up a cargo from the enemy on the ocean, if possible, and perhaps man and send into port a fast-sailing rich prize or two, if fortunate enough to meet with such. This mode of cruising, although pleasant enough as a captain did not meet my views as a passenger or a volunteer. I therefore concluded to return to Bordeaux, and wait a more favourable opportunity to get home.

I found Captain Jacobs a pleasant, gentlemanly man, and parted with him with sincere regret. After spending about a month of perfect leisure at Nantes, I left this agreeable place in the diligence for Bordeaux, on the 13th of June, 1814. The distance between the two cities is 216 miles. We were two days on the road, and arrived in Bordeaux on the 15th, without accident. I now had abundance of leisure, not only to look after my commercial affairs in Bordeaux, but to partake of its various amusements, and enjoy its hospitable society.

On the 9th of August I received the account sales of my cottons, with a statement of what was due me, and also the balance due for freight, all of which was now settled to my entire satisfaction. I forthwith remitted to my owners in New York, in sundry bills of exchange, $8,692, besides leaving a large balance in the hands of my worthy friends, Messrs. Brun *frères*. I am happy to say, I surmounted one difficulty after another, until things began to wear a brighter aspect; and as I was unable to obtain a passage from any of the ports on the western coast, I decided to go up to Paris and spend a few weeks, and try to get a passage home from some of the northern ports of France.

Before leaving this place, it would be ungrateful in me not to speak of the kind hospitality I received in this town; even amidst war and confusion, the rites of hospitality are here never forgotten. The kind treatment to strangers by the inhabitants of Bordeaux is proverbial, and needs no repetition from me. Still, I am happy to bear my feeble testimony, and time will never efface from my memory the happy days I have spent in this delightful city.

On the 15th of August, I left Bordeaux in the diligence for the capital. We passed through Angoulême, Poictiers, Tours, and along the pleasant banks of the Loire to Blois, Orleans, and from thence to Paris. The time occupied in performing this journey was five days, and the distance 130 post leagues, and the whole expense, including the fee to the conductor, postillion, servants, etc., etc., was 196 *francs*. I put up at the Hotel Strasbourg, in the Rue Notre Dame des Victoires. We got into the vicinity of this magnificent city just before the dawn of day. A young American friend was my travelling companion, and we were at daylight on the *qui vive* to catch the first glimpse of this vast metropolis, when just as the sun was rising we ascended a hill, and behold! the famed city of Paris was in full view.

Among the many objects of admiration that caught the eye, the dome of the Hôtel des Invalides was the most conspicuous; it was newly gilded, and when the sun shone upon this splendid object, the effect was truly enchanting. I was young and enthusiastic at that time, and shall never forget the impression made on my mind by this, my first view of this astonishing city.

It was absolutely like transporting one to another world. I had read its history from my boyish days, and now, for the first time, beheld it in all its magnificence. Since that time I have visited many parts of the globe, and, even down to this date, 1856, I have never met its equal. London, certainly, covers a greater space, and has almost double the number of inhabitants; still, there never was, nor ever will be, but one Paris.

Immediately on my arrival in Paris, I wrote the following letter to the several owners of the *David Porter*.

"Paris, 20th August, 1814.

"Messrs. Lawrence & Whitney, James Lovett, Esq., and the other owners of the *David Porter:*

"Gentlemen:—I have this moment arrived here from Bordeaux. I came here in hopes of obtaining a passage home in the ship *John Adams,* from Amsterdam, which ship, I am informed, is to sail in about a week from this day for America. I need not tell you my disappointment to learn from several American gentlemen who are here, that they, with several others in London, have applied to our minister for a passage in said ship, and have been refused, and that it is absolutely impossible to obtain a passage in the *John Adams* on any terms.

"How, or in what way, I shall get home, I am not able to say, but assure you I shall embrace the first opportunity. It was not until the 9th instant that I got my business settled with Brun *frères*. Enclosed I send you one set of bills of exchange, amounting, together, to $8,691, all of which, I trust, will be paid, without any difficulty; if they are not, the persons from whom I bought them are fully able to pay them, should they be returned. I enclose you, also, account sales of our cotton. Independent of what I now remit you, I have left in the hands of Messrs. Brun *frères* about 40,000 *francs*. What I now remit you, with what I have left in the hands of Brun *frères*, all belongs to the joint concern of the owners of the *David Porter*, when the voyage is settled, except a small sum due to my officers.

"As you may suppose, I am very much fatigued after so long a journey; but for fear my letter will not be in time to go by the *John Adams*, I am obliged to write this in haste, which I hope you will receive as an apology for my not writing more particularly.

"I hope before long to find a passage home some way or other, when I trust I shall have the pleasure to explain everything to your satisfaction.

"As I am too late to write any of my friends by this opportunity, please advise them of the substance of this letter, and oblige

"Your obedient servant,
"George Coggeshall."

After having delivered several letters of introduction from my friend in Bordeaux, I occupied myself for some days attending to commercial business, and among other things, purchased five thousand *francs* worth of French silks, shawls, silk stockings, etc. These articles were all carefully packed and dispatched to Bordeaux, to be shipped, by the first fast-sailing American schooner that should leave that place for the United States. When this was accomplished, I commenced visiting the various museums, libraries, public gardens, palaces, etc. It being a fine season of the year, I also made excursions to St. Cloud, Versailles, St. Germain, St. Denis, and other places in the neighbourhood of the metropolis.

There are in this great city so many objects of curiosity, that a stranger may spend several months with pleasure and profit in visiting them.

The day before I left Paris, I wrote the following letter:

"Paris, September 8th, 1814.
"Messrs. Archibald Gracie & Sons:

"Gentlemen:—I send you enclosed a bill of exchange for $991, on James Williams, Esq., of Baltimore. This is the net proceeds of your fifty-one bales of cotton. By the ship *John Adams*, I forwarded you one set of these bills and account sales. I also sent one copy to L'Orient, to be forwarded. This I shall send to England, to go by the *Cartel*, which, I am told, is now fitting for the United States.

"I am extremely sorry, gentlemen, your shipment of cotton has turned out so much to your disadvantage. I however hope you will do me the justice to believe I have done the best I could in the business. I came on here for the purpose of getting a passage in the *John Adams* from Amsterdam, but was disappointed, as they are not allowed to take passengers. I am also informed that the *Cartel*, which is now fitting away from England, takes none but prisoners. I shall, therefore, leave here tomorrow morning for Bordeaux, and endeavour to get a passage to Amelia Island, or the West Indies, and from thence home, when I hope I shall have the pleasure to explain everything relating to your shipment to your satisfaction.

"I am, gentlemen, with respect and regard,
"Your obedient servant,
"George Coggeshall."

"P. S. I wrote by the schooner *Commodore Decatur*, brig *Rat-*

tlesnake, and Commodore Perry, which letters I fear you have never received, as it is here reported that all those vessels have been captured.

"Yours truly,
"G. C."

At this period there was but a small number of American gentlemen in Paris, consequently they were generally known to each other.

The Ambassador from the United States, residing here, was the Hon. Wm. H. Crawford, He was highly respected and esteemed by the Americans, and seemed to take pleasure in acts of kindness and benevolence to his countrymen. From a turbulent state of war and confusion, Paris had lately become quiet and tranquil. Louis XVIII., and other members of the royal family, used almost daily to show themselves from the balcony of the Tuileries, and I frequently saw the Duke and-Duchess of Angoulême riding on horseback in various parts of the city.

The theatres and all public places of amusement were open, and appeared to be well patronized and supported. There were vast numbers of strangers here from different parts of Europe, and everybody seemed to be in pursuit of pleasure.

After having spent twenty days amidst these gay scenes, I left Paris on the 9th of September, 1814, in the diligence, and returned by the same route by which I came up, passing through Orleans and down along the banks of the Loire, and so on to Bordeaux, where I arrived on the 13th of September, without accident.

I had many kind friends in this city, and returned to it with pleasure, but found those from America were daily diminishing; some returning home in neutral ships, by way of the West Indies and Amelia Island; others going to Holland to take passage from that country. My friend R. Stewart, Esq., of Philadelphia, after waiting several months for a passage to the United States, had left this place for L'Orient, in hopes of getting a passage from that city to the United States with Captain Blakely, in the *Wasp*. This ship after having captured the British sloop-of-war *Rein-*

deer, put into L'Orient for supplies, and here Mr. Stewart joined her. They sailed from that place on the 27th of August, 1814, bound on a cruise for several months, and at the expiration of the appointed time intended to return to the United States.

A few days after leaving port she made several prizes and on the evening of the 1st of Sept, she engaged and captured the British sloop-of-war *Avon*, of 18 guns. A few minutes after this ship had surrendered, the English brig-of-war *Castilian*, of 18 guns, fired one broadside into the *Wasp*, and then hauled off and escaped in the darkness of the night. There is scarcely a doubt that the *Wasp* would have taken the *Castilian* also, if they had been favoured with daylight. While on board the *Wasp*, Mr. Stewart joined the marine corps, as a volunteer, and thus assisted under the brave Blakely to vanquish the enemies of his country.

About the middle of September, the *Wasp* took and destroyed two British brigs; and on the 21st of the same month, in latitude 33° 12' North, longitude 14° 56' West, she captured the British armed brig *Atalanta*. This being a valuable prize, Captain Blakely determined to send her into port. He put on board of her as prize-master, Midshipman Geisinger, and a prize-crew. In this brig, Mr. Stewart went as passenger. She arrived safely at Savannah on the 14th of November, 1814. These two gentlemen and the prize-crew are all that escaped from the ever-to-be-lamented *Wasp* and her gallant crew.

I take pleasure in stating these facts, that the patriotic conduct of my friend may be known to the world, as I have never seen his name mentioned in connection with the ill-fated *Wasp* (in any official account), and I deem it but a matter of common justice to record my knowledge of these facts. There were very many patriotic individuals during our late war with England who rendered essential service to their country and are entitled to its gratitude, whose acts, I am sorry to say, are almost entirely unknown; for instance, my worthy friends Mantor, of the *Ida*, and Stewart, who was a volunteer on board the victorious *Wasp*.

While in Bordeaux, I heard the gratifying news of the safe arrival of the schooner *David Porter*, at Gloucester, Cape Ann, and also of the arrival of the brig *Ida*, at Boston. After I left the *David Porter,* at L'Isle Dieu, under the command of Mr. Nichols, he captured on his passage home several British prizes, from which vessels he loaded the schooner, and carried with him into port ten prisoners. Soon after his arrival at Cape Ann, he proceeded with the *David Porter* to Boston, at which place the vessel and cargo were consigned to the respectable house of Messrs. Munson & Barnard, at that place. These gentlemen sold both vessel and cargo at high prices. They also sold the brandy and wine, by the brig *Ida*, at a very good profit, and closed the whole concern to the entire satisfaction of all parties. I think the schooner sold for $10,000, and was soon fitted out as a regular privateer, and I believe was afterwards very successful

Messrs. Munson and Barnard also received from the government of the United States, $1,000 as a bounty on the ten prisoners.

The trunk of goods which I purchased in Paris for 5,000 *francs*, or say $1,000, was shipped by my friends in Bordeaux, on board the Baltimore schooner *Transit*, Captain Richardson. This vessel arrived in New York on or about the 8th of March, 1815, and this trunk of goods sold at auction for $2,075.

Bordeaux, Oct. 1st., 1814

I had now closed the voyage of the *David Porter,* so far as it devolved upon me, and will here close the subject with a few remarks.

When it is considered how many obstacles we met with, from the commencement of the voyage on the 14th day of Nov., 1813, until its conclusion, I think it will be conceded that we triumphed over many difficulties, and ultimately made a good voyage; and I am happy to add, to the entire satisfaction of all the owners of the fortunate little schooner.

I will here insert the following letter to my brother Charles Coggeshall, second lieutenant of the letter-of-marque *David Porter*, at Milford, Connecticut.

"Bordeaux, Oct. 21st., 1814

"Dear Charles:—I am now on the eve of leaving this place for L'Orient, to take command of the elegant American schooner *Leo*. I have been waiting several months to obtain a passage home to the United States, and have consented to take charge of this schooner, to proceed from France to Charleston or some other southern port.

"Your cotton netted 903 *francs*. The account sales I have sent to Messrs. Lawrence and Whitney, and desired them to pay you the amount, together with the gain on the exchange, which is about ten *per cent*.

"You may, perhaps, ask why I did not invest the amount in French goods, that you might have gained a larger profit. I answer that I did not feel myself authorized to hazard your property without your consent, the risk of capture being in my opinion very great.

"I was very happy to hear of your safe arrival in the *David Porter*. Both Captain Nichols and yourself, and in fact, all the officers and men deserve a great deal of praise, and I do assure you I shall never forget your faithful and very friendly conduct during the whole voyage. Yes, Charles, although I sometimes scold a little when we are together, I need not tell you how dear you are to me, and that your faithful and brave conduct has entirely won my heart. I hope you will study navigation, and improve your mind by reading while you remain at home, and thus qualify yourself to command a ship when the war is ended. Should the enemy dare to molest the part of the country where you may be, I hope and trust you will be among the first to drive them into the sea. Our father fought them in 1775, before he was as old as you are, and I hope he has not left a son who would not defend his country, if necessary, with his heart's blood.

"We hear nothing from America but degrading defeats and losses of every kind. Washington City burnt, our armies on the frontiers beaten in one place or another, and everything appears to be going to the devil. If things go on no better, I shall be ashamed to acknowledge myself an American,

"I shall write to mother and sister by the same vessel that conveys this to you.

"Remember me affectionately to our brothers James and Francis, and believe me, my dear Charles,

"Your sincere friend and brother,

"George Coggeshall."

CHAPTER 7

A Narrow Escape

SUCCESSFUL CRUISES MADE BY THE PRIVATEERS *SCOURGE* AND *RATTLESNAKE*, OFF THE NORTH CAPE, AND COAST OF NORWAY

The privateers *Scourge* and *Rattlesnake* appear to merit something more than a passing remark. As they were often in company in a distant sea, on the same cruising ground, and as they were very fortunate in capturing and annoying the enemy's trade and commerce, I shall devote a separate notice to them as their just due.

Though the worthy captains of both these vessels have passed away from earthly scenes, I hope their acts and deeds in their country's service will ever be appreciated, while bravery and patriotism are held in high regard by civilized nations.

The *Rattlesnake* belonged to Philadelphia, and was commanded by Captain David Maffet, an excellent seaman, and a brave, honourable man.

Captain Maffet commanded a privateer from the commencement of the war to its termination, and was always active and vigilant. In the early part of the war, he commanded the *Atlas*, and I think one other (of this, however, I am not sure), until he took command of the *Rattlesnake*, in 1818.

She was a fine fast-sailing brig, carrying 14 guns, suitably equipped, and well supplied with able officers and men.

After leaving the United States Captain Maffet proceeded to cruise off the North coast of England, and from thence to the coast of Norway, where having made many valuable prizes, and inflicted much injury upon British commerce, he put into La Rochelle about the middle of March, 1814, to refresh his officers and crew, and refit for another cruise.

The *Scourge* was owned in New York, and commanded by Captain Samuel Nicoll, a native of Stratford, Connecticut. He was a worthy, intelligent, enterprising man, and a good patriot.

The Scourge was a large schooner privateer, mounting fifteen carriage guns, with musketry, etc., and suitably officered and manned for a long cruise. She sailed from New York in April 1813, for the north coast of England and Norway.

Captain Nicoll was a man of sound judgement, and a good financier. After he had made one or two successful cruises, he found it more to his advantage to remain on shore in the different ports of Norway, where he sent in most of his prizes, and attend to the sale of them than to go to sea, and leave the management of his rich prizes in the hands of dishonest or incompetent persons. Consequently, he occasionally appointed one of his lieutenants to command the *Scourge*, to cruise under his direction. This accounts for Captain Nicoll's name not appearing more frequently in the public journals at that period.

On the 19th of July, while Captain Nicoll was off the North Cape, in the *Scourge*, he fell in with and cruised for several days in company with Commodore Rodgers, in the United States frigate *President*, who was then cruising in those high northern latitudes.

After Commodore Rodgers left that region for a more southerly one, the *Scourge* proceeded off the coast of Norway, and alternately off the North Cape, to intercept British ships sailing to and from Archangel.

The following list comprises a portion, but by no means all the prizes captured by the *Scourge* and *Rattlesnake*. A great number were sent into the different ports in the United States and Norway, particularly into the harbour of Drontheim, and many others were disposed of in various ways.

"The winds and seas are Britain's wide domain,
And not a sail, but by permission spreads."

British Naval Register.

British barque *Concord*, West, 187 tons, and two guns, from London for Archangel, in ballast.

Ship *Liberty*, Sugden, 253 tons, and 8 guns, from Liverpool for the same place, in ballast.

Brig *Jolly Bachelor*, Struthon, of 119 tons, from Archangel, laden with tar, bound for Aberdeen.

Brig *Ruby*, of 4 guns, 138 tons, taken by the *Rattlesnake*.

Hartford, 260 tons, from London, and Sutherland, for Archangel, in ballast, by the *Rattlesnake*.

Brig *Brunswick*, Lewis, 249 tons, 4 guns, from Dublin for the same port, taken by the Rattlesnake.

Latona, of Shields, by the *Scourge*.

Experiment, of Aberdeen, by the *Scourge*.

Brigs *Nottingham*, 266 tons and 4 guns, and *Britannia*, 4 guns, both from Onega, Russia, for Hull, cargoes lumber; after an action of fifteen minutes—no lives lost—taken by the *Scourge*.

Prosperous, 260 tons and 4 guns, in ballast, from Newcastle; given up to dispose of the prisoners, by the *Scourge*.

Ship *Brutus*, taken by the *Scourge* and *Rattlesnake*; given up to dispose of the prisoners.

Westmoreland, from London, partly laden with sugars; taken by the *Scourge*.

The *Brothers*, of 126 tons, from Lancaster; by the *Scourge*.

Brig *Betsey*, 186 tons and 4 guns; by the *Rattlesnake*.

Brig *Pax*, of 200 tons; by the *Rattlesnake*.

Galliot *Perseverance*, 167 tons and 4 guns; by the *Rattlesnake*.

Sloop *Fame*, 94 tons; by the *Rattlesnake*.

Brig *Burton*, Ludlin, of 266 tons, and 4 guns, from Onega for Hull; by the *Scourge*.

Brig *Thetis*, 114 tons; by the *Rattlesnake*.

Diligent, 250 tons and 4 guns; by the *Rattlesnake*.

Friend's Adventure, 245 tons and 4 guns; by the *Rattlesnake*.

Brig *Hope*, 260 tons, 4 guns, cargo of linseed; also the *Economy*, of 181 tons, and 2 guns, with tar; both from Archangel for England; by the *Scourge*.

All the before-named prizes were ordered for Drontheim, and arrived safe at that port, except two which were given up to the prisoners, one laden with sugar, which was unfortunately cast away on her passage to Drontheim; 140 hhds. of sugar, however, were saved, in a damaged state.

The *Scourge* arrived in Drontheim in company with the *Rattlesnake*, after having captured the above vessels.

The aggregate tonnage of these vessels, sent into Norway, amounted to 4,505 tons, numbering 60 guns.

At Drontheim, the *Scourge* was refitted, and rigged into a brig, for a new cruise, under the command of Captain J. R. Perry. Captain Nicoll remained in Drontheim to look after the prizes.

Here follows a continuation of prizes made by the *Scourge*, and other incidents relating to the privateer schooner *Fox*, Brown commander.

The *Scourge* sailed from Drontheim on the 10th March, and on the 1st of April, off Cape Wrath, captured the British ship *Symetry*, a fine vessel, from Liverpool, 350 tons, coppered, laden with salt, crates, hardware, etc.; in company with ship *Winchester*, of 400 tons, from the same place, laden with salt, crates, porter, etc.; and brig *Union*, 200 tons, from the same port, cargo, tobacco; all bound to Long Hope, for convoy: burnt all of them. Same day, boarded a Swedish ship from Liverpool, and put part of the prisoners on board of her.

British barque *Brothers*, 260 tons, from Liverpool for Long Hope, cargo salt, etc.; and manned her for the United States. Next day, captured a sloop from London; put on board a number of prisoners, and gave her up.

7th.—Chased a Greenland whale ship, and fired ten broadsides at her, which appeared to cut her up considerably. A sloop-of-war in chase, close in shore on the coast of Scotland, was obliged to give up the pursuit, and haul off to get clear of a shoal. The sloop continued the chase six hours. In the chase, the *Scourge* sprung her fore-topmast badly.

About the 17th of April, carried away both topmasts (blowing no more than a good breeze), by which accident one man was killed and three wounded.

About the 22nd, lat. 50° N., lon. 30° W., captured the British ship Caledonia, 300 tons, from Greenock for Nova Scotia, in ballast; put on board twenty-six prisoners, and gave her up. A few days after, captured a brig from Dublin for Quebec, with salt, etc.; sunk her. Same day, captured a brig from St. Johns, N. B., for Liverpool, cargo lumber, etc., having on board a number of women and children, passengers; took out some rigging, sails, etc.; put ten prisoners on board, and gave her up.

May 1st,— lat. 47°, lon. 32°, captured a brig from Dublin for N. P., cargo cordage, duck, fishing gear, etc.; ordered her for the United State.

9th,—lat. 46° N. lon. 44° W., boarded the privateer schooner *Fox*, Brown, forty days from Portsmouth, who had made four prizes; destroyed two, and ordered two into port She had thrown ten guns overboard while being chased by a frigate. She had chased a disguised sloop-of-war, and did not discover the mistake until close aboard her, when she opened her ports, and fired two broadsides into the *Fox*; she, however, effected her escape. Several shot struck her, and one went through her arm chest, and broke several muskets. No one was injured.

The *Scourge*, on her homeward passage from Norway, after leaving the coast of Scotland, made the following prizes.

Brig *Nancy*, from Leghorn, with an exceedingly rich cargo of silks, oil, sulphur, marble, etc.; sent her into New York.

Ship *Lord Hood,* from Quebec for London; burnt.

Brig *Trident*, from the same place for the same port; burnt.

Brig *Haddock*, from Quebec for London; also burnt.

Brig *Belfield*, from Quebec for London; also destroyed.

During this cruise, the *Scourge* made 420 prisoners, and arrived at Chatham, Cape Cod, in May, after having been absent from the United States about a year. This vessel was very appropriately named, for she was, in truth, a severe scourge to the enemy. She inflicted a chastisement upon the commerce of Great Britain that will cause her name to be remembered for several generations.

Prizes Captured by Privateers

British brig *Brothers*, captured by the ship *America*, of Salem, and sent into Fontarabia, a port in Spain, and there sold, by the consent of the government.

The privateer *Caroline*, of Baltimore, captured the English brig *Elizabeth*, for Kingston, (Jamaica,) and sent her into Charleston. Though the *Elizabeth* was nominally in ballast, she had on board a quantity of British goods, which were removed to the privateer, and taken by her into Charleston. She has recently sailed on a second cruise.

The ship *Annette Catharine*, said to be a Swedish vessel, cleared out at Boston, in ballast for the West Indies, but found to have had on board a cargo of provisions. She was captured by the *Saucy Jack*, and sent into Charleston.

The *Saucy Jack* also captured the British schooner *Nimble*, laden with log-wood, and sent her into Beaufort.

The *Caroline* captured the schooner *Jason*, of Nassau, N. P., divested her of her cargo, and set her on fire,

Schooner ———, with dry-goods and other valuable articles, captured by the *Kemp*, of Baltimore, and carried into Cape Francois, where the prize and her cargo were disposed of.

Schooner *Trinitaria*, sent into Savannah by the *Saucy Jack*, of Charleston.

Nine valuable British vessels, captured by the privateer *Prince of Neufchâtel* (belonging to New York), on the enemy's coast; they were sent into France, or destroyed.

Nine vessels captured by the *Comet*, of Baltimore, in the West Indies, divested of their valuable articles and destroyed.

Four vessels captured by the same, and ransomed in money.

Two vessels captured by the same, and sent into North Carolina. The privateer arrived at Newbern, N. C.

Brig *Apollo*, 250 tons, 6 guns, of Poole, England, laden with 1,000 hhds, of salt, sent into Salem by the *America*, of that port.

Brig *Ann*, captured by *ditto*, and given up to release the prisoners.

Cutter *Patty*, from Scotland, taken by *ditto*, and sunk.

Brig ——, captured by *ditto* and sunk.

Ship ——, in ballast, from Liverpool for Antigua, sent into Wilmington, N. C, by the *Invincible*, of Salem.

Schooner *Encouragement*, from Antigua for Nova Scotia, laden with 20 hhds. of sugar, 20 hhds. of molasses and five of rum, captured by the *Frolic* of Salem and destroyed.

British brig *Two Sisters*, from Malaga for Holland. richly laden with wine and fruits, etc., captured off Cape Finnisterre by the *Wasp*, of Philadelphia, and sent into that port.

Schooner *Hope*, from St. Andrews for Barbadoes, laden with lumber, beef, oil, etc., captured by the *America*, of Salem, and burnt.

Schooner *Sylph*, of Liverpool, N. S., laden with fish, oil, etc., captured by *ditto*, and burnt.

The *America* took twelve prizes in all, several of which were very valuable. She had arrived at Salem, with fifty prisoners on board. She had also forty packages of dry-goods, and some other articles taken from her prizes, several of which are yet to be heard of. This was the third cruise of this truly fortunate vessel. She has captured in the whole twenty-six prizes; and the property taken and safely got into port amounts to about $1,100,000.

Schooner *Eclipse*, laden with salt, captured by the *Wasp*, of Philadelphia, but lost on Rockaway beach, Long Island.

Schooner *Cobham*, of Bermuda, sent into Wilmington, N. C., by the *Jonquilla*, of New York.

Brig *Louisa*, laden with oil and fish, sent into Elizabeth City, Va., by the *Kemp*, of Baltimore, ship *Hebe*, from Halifax for Bermuda, with coal, lumber, etc., captured by the *Surprise*, of Baltimore, the third day after she left the Chesapeake, and sent into a southern port.

Brig *Nimble*, with a cargo of West India produce, captured by the *Invincible*, letter-of-marque, and sent into Tenerife, where, as the vessel was not sea-worthy, the cargo was sold.

Brig *Ceres*, in ballast, captured in the Bay of Biscay by the *Grampus*, of Baltimore, from Bordeaux, on her way home, and burnt.

Schooner ——, laden with 70 hhds. of sugar, captured off Martinique, and sent into New Bedford by the *Saratoga*, of New York.

Schooner *Friends' Adventure*, laden with 60 hhds. of rum, 58 hhds. of molasses, 13 hhds. of sugar, captured by the *Fox*, of Portsmouth, and sent into Wiscasset.

Brig *Fanny*, of London, laden with fish, captured by the letter-of-marque ship *Galloway*, of New York, on her passage from France, and sent into Nantes.

Brig ——, laden with lumber, captured by the *Fox* of Portsmouth, and burnt.

Schooner *Kentish*, with a full cargo of sugar, sent into Fair Haven by the *Saratoga*.

Schooner *Prince Regent*, 10 guns, captured by the *Invincible*, of N.Y.; divested of her armament, etc. and given up. Cutter *Lyon*, with dry-goods, hardware, etc., captured by the same; divested of the most valuable part of her goods, and given up. Brig *Portsea*, 8 guns, captured by the same; divested of her valuable goods, and given up. Brig *Conway*, 10 guns. with a cargo, of dry-goods, captured by the same; took out 44 trunks, 35 cases, and 23 bales; she was manned, and ordered for the United States.

Schooner *Francis & Lucy*, laden with fish, oil, and lumber, captured by *ditto*, and given up to the prisoners.

The *Invincible* also captured, close in with Tenerife, the brig *Margaretta*, laden with wine; she was given up. as having been taken within the Spanish jurisdiction, for which, when the *Invincible* put into Santa Cruz, the captain and crew were well received by the governor. The privateer arrived in Charleston full of valuable goods.

The letter-of-marque schooner *Siro*, of Baltimore, bound to France, has been captured by the English, and sent into Plymouth, England.

The very valuable brig *Henry*, 6 guns, 200 tons, coppered, from Liverpool for Buenos Ayres, laden with 300 packages of dry-goods and other valuable articles, invoiced at £40,000 sterling; sent into New York by the *Governor Tompkins*, of that port.

The bounty (or the reduction of duties) allowed by the United States on this prize amounted to about $35,000.

The cargo of the prize ship *Nereid* has been disposed of at New York. The gross amount of the sales, exclusive of the jewellery, was $270,000.

Schooner ——, sent into Beaufort, N. C, by the *Snap Dragon*; laden with mahogany.

The privateer *York*, of Baltimore, when off the coast of Nova Scotia, on the 18th of April, had a severe engagement with the British transport ship *Lord Somers*. During the action, Captain Staples, of the *York*, and five of his men were killed, and twelve wounded. In this disabled situation, the privateer was obliged to haul off, and give up the contest.

About the 15th of May, the *Mammoth*, *Revenue*, and *Fairy*, all of Baltimore, were cruising off St. Bartholomews.

Brig *James*, from the Isle of France for England, captured by the *Young Wasp*, of Philadelphia; divested of part of her cargo, manned, and ordered into port.

Two vessels captured by the same; one was destroyed, the other given up to release the prisoners. The *Young Wasp* arrived at Philadelphia, (May 28th), with a quantity of valuable goods on board.

Ship *Union*, from Jamaica, laden with sugar and coffee, captured by the *Rambler*; recaptured by the *Curlew*, but lost near Sambo lighthouse.

Brig *Fair Stranger*, with a cargo of fish, oil, etc., sent into Portsmouth by the *Fox* of that port.

Brig ——, from Lisbon for Passage, with provisions for the English troops, captured and destroyed by the *Expedition*, of Baltimore.

Schooner *Miranda*, captured by the *Chasseur*, of Baltimore; divested of some dry-goods, and burnt. Sloop *Martha*, laden with government stores, captured by the same; divested of the most valuable part of her cargo; the other part of it was destroyed: she was then made a cartel of, to release the prisoners. Two other vessels were captured by the *Chasseur*, and destroyed;

one of them had on board a quantity of money in gold.

The very valuable schooner *Adeline* arrived at New York, from Bordeaux. She was captured four days out. by a British frigate, but recaptured by the *Expedition*, six days after. The *Adeline* had dispatches for government and 4,000 letters, all of which were thrown overboard previous to her capture by the enemy.

Brig *Experience*, from Jamaica for Gonaives captured by the *Caroline*, of Baltimore, but lost on the island of Cuba, being chased ashore. Crew saved.

The very valuable ship *Experience*, from England for Amelia Island, with a full cargo of dry-goods, glassware, etc., etc., 300 tons burthen; sent into Savannah by the privateer *Rapid*. This vessel and cargo was valued at $250,000.

Schooner ———, laden with rum, cocoa, etc., sent into the Delaware by the *Perry*, of Baltimore.

Schooner *Francis*, with bullocks for the British army, captured off the French coast by the letter-of-marque schooner *Midas*, of Baltimore, on her passage home, and burnt.

Schooner *Appallodore*, laden with 450 boxes of fruit, captured by ditto, and sunk.

Schooner *William* and sloop *Irwin*, captured by the same, and sent in as cartels, with 59 prisoners.

Brig *Bellona*, laden with Madeira wine and fruit, captured by the *Globe*, of Baltimore, and by stress of weather, compelled to enter Barracoa, (Cuba), where, being condemned as unseaworthy, the vessel and cargo were disposed of.

Sloop ———, cut out of Carracoa by the boats of the *Saratoga*, and sunk.

Sloop *Cygnet*, from Jamaica, with a cargo of rum, sent into Wilmington, N. C, by the *Saratoga* of New York.

Schooner *Diligence*, from Halifax for St. Johns, captured by the York, of Baltimore, and destroyed.

Sloop *Bonita*, captured by the *Delisle*, of Baltimore, and destroyed.

Brig *Robert*, with fish and lumber, from St Johns for Jamaica, captured by the *Zebec Ultor*, of Baltimore, and sent into Charleston.

Ship *Equity*, from London for Limerick, captured by the *Rattlesnake*, and burnt.

Ship *Adston*, captured by the same, and sunk.

The letter-of-marque schooner *David Porter*, of New York, was obliged to hurry off from La Teste, near Bordeaux. During a short cruise of fifteen days in the Bay of Biscay she made several captures, when the captain landed on L'Isle Dieu, and sent his first lieutenant home with the vessel. On her return passage, she made two or three more prizes, and, after obtaining a full cargo from them, she arrived safe at Boston, with ten or fifteen prisoners on board. Her crew of officers and men only numbered twenty-five or thirty souls.

Brig ——, laden with rum and sugar, sent into Portsmouth, N. H., by the *Rattlesnake*, of Philadelphia.

Ship *James*, captured by the *Young Wasp*, divested of $24,000 in specie. The *James* was subsequently recaptured.

Brig *Swift*, 4 guns and fifteen men, bound for Halifax, with a cargo of sundries, sent in by the *Zebec Ultor*, of Baltimore.

Brig *Camelion*, coppered, from the West Indies for New Brunswick, laden with rum and molasses, sent into an eastern port by the *Mammoth*, of Baltimore.

Two vessels captured by the *Caroline*, of Baltimore, divested of their valuable articles and destroyed. The *Caroline* arrived at Charleston; she captured three other vessels, which were manned and ordered into port.

Ship *Fortuna* (under Russian colours), from Havana for Riga, with 1,520 boxes of sugar, sent into Beaufort by the *Roger*, of Norfolk. The cargo was the property of the enemy, consequently condemned.

Schooner *Phoebe*, with rum and molasses, sent into Wilmington, N. C, by the *Hawk*, of Washington.

Brig *Kutozoff*, of 6 guns, from Laguira for Gibraltar, laden with coffee, cocoa, and hides, captured after a very severe action, and carried by boarding, sent into Frankfort, Maine by the *Surprise*, of Baltimore. She was worth $50,000.

Schooner *Young Farmer*, from Laguira, laden with indigo, worth $40,000, captured by the letter-of-marque *Henry Guilder*, of New York, and brought into that port

Two vessels captured by the letter-of-marque *James Monroe*, on her passage from L'Orient to Savannah, and burnt.

British Polacca ship, *Joanna*, of Malta, from Constantinople for Lisbon, with a cargo of wheat and barley, worth $30,000, captured by the *Chasseur*, and sunk.

The *Chasseur* captured several other valuable vessels on the same cruise.

The elegant ship *Pelham*, of 540 tons, carrying 12 guns; a vessel of the first class from London for Port-au-Prince, laden with an assorted cargo, 494 packages of India and British goods, captured after a smart action by boarding, by the *Saucy Jack,* of Charleston, and convoyed into that port.

The passengers of the ship *Pelham*, captured by the *Saucy Jack*, and sent into Charleston, have publicly offered their grateful thanks to Captain Chazel and his officers, for the very kind treatment they experienced whilst in their possession, and for the means afforded for their liberation.

The Baltimore privateers *Patapsco, Grampus,* and *Syren*, had recently sailed from New York.

Schooner *Hope*, from St. Johns, Newfoundland, laden with fish, was sent into Saco by the *Pike*, of Baltimore.

Schooner *Pickrel*, from Dartmouth, England, bound to Quebec, laden with dry-goods, teas, etc., captured by the same, divested of her cargo and destroyed.

Ship *Askew*, from Palermo for Belfast, captured by the *True Blooded Yankee*, and sent into France.

Schooner *Brilliant*, with 6 guns, an elegant vessel of 157 tons, late a New Providence privateer, laden with 116 casks of *spermaceti* oil, 41 bales of cotton, log-wood, etc., sent into Boston by the privateer *Scourge*, of New York, on her return to the United States.

The *Scourge* took two other valuable vessels on the same cruise, *viz*., on her return from Norway.

Brig *Dove*, laden with lumber, from Liverpool for Nova Scotia, captured by the *Fox*, of Portsmouth, and burnt.

The *Fox* also captured the ship *Jane*, in ballast, from Scotland, for Marsmashea, divested and given up to release the prisoners.

Ship *Mermaid*, sent into Damariscotta, Maine, laden with salt and coal, by the *General Pike*, of Baltimore.

Ship *Commerce*, from Limerick for Bilboa, laden with 180 tons of barley, and 100 tons of oats, for the British army, captured by the *Lawrence*, of Baltimore. The *Commerce* arrived at Portland, Maine.

The British ship *Upton*, from Cork, bound for Newfoundland, was captured by the privateer *Diomede*, of Salem, and sent into Wiscasset. The *Upton* was 270 tons burthen, armed with 16 guns, and 104 men (many of them were, however, passengers). She made considerable resistance, and had one man killed and another wounded before she surrendered.

The brig *Providence*, from Maryport, England, bound for Nova Scotia, captured by the *Diomede*, and sunk.

Brig *Harmony*, from Maryport, England, was also captured by the same vessel, and destroyed. The *Harmony* was bound to some port in Nova Scotia.

Brig *Recovery*, from Halifax for St. Andrews, driven ashore by the *Diomede*, and destroyed,

Brig *Melpomene* of 6 guns laden with 260 pipes of wine, sent into Newport, R. I. by the *Chasseur* of Baltimore.

Brig *Britannia*, from Tenerife, laden with wine, sent into Beaufort by the same.

Brig ——, laden with rum and sugar, from Jamaica for England, sent into a southern port by the *Roger*, of Norfolk.

Schooner ——, sent into Newport by a Baltimore privateer.

Ship *Henry Dundas*, for Lisbon, captured by the *Rattlesnake*, and released after divesting her of the most valuable part of her cargo.

Brig *Indian Lass*, from Liverpool for St. Michaels, with dry-goods, etc., captured by the *Grand Turk*, of Salem, divested of her dry-goods, and ordered into port. She arrived safely at Salem with the balance of her merchandise, which was worth. $65,000. She also brought in thirty prisoners.

Brig *Catharine*, from Lisbon for London, captured by the *Grand Turk*, recaptured by the British brig *Bacchus*, she was again captured by the *Grand Turk* and subsequently burnt.

Sloop *Caroline*, from London for St. Michaels, laden with dry-goods, etc., captured by the same, divested of her cargo and then given up.

The *Grand Turk* took several other vessels, which she ordered into port.

Schooner *Traveller*, with 174 puncheons of rum. etc., sent into Thomastown by the *Diomede*, of Salem.

Ship *Cod Hook*, with a cargo of 700 hhds. of salt, some dry-goods, crates, flour, bread, and iron; captured by the *Diomede*, and sent into Castine.

Schooner *Victoria*, captured by the letter-of-marque cutter sloop *Hero*, of New York, on her passage from France; she was manned and ordered for an American port, but was soon after retaken by a British vessel-of-war, and the American prize crew were all taken out but one man, and replaced by Englishmen. After being in possession of the British prize crew a few days, they agreed among themselves to bring her into the first American port. She was a fine, large schooner, laden with rum and molasses, and arrived safe at Charleston.

The very valuable cargo of the Russian ship *Joachim*, which was sent into a Southern port by the *Caroline*, was condemned as British property; vessel cleared.

Schooner *Robert Hartwell*, from Antigua for Bermuda, laden with sugar and molasses, valued at $20,000, was sent into Newbern by the cutter *Hero*, of New York.

Brig *Liddelle*, from Liverpool for Newfoundland, with salt, captured by the *Amelia*, of Baltimore, and made a cartel of, to dispose of her prisoners.

Brig *Jessie*, of 6 guns, from London for Newfoundland, laden with bread, porter, etc., captured by the same, and burnt.

Schooner *Ann*, with an assorted cargo of dry-goods, captured by the same, divested of her effects, and sent, as a cartel, to Halifax.

The *Diomede*, after making many prizes, was herself captured and sent into Halifax, June 25th.

Several valuable prizes made by the *Amelia*, were manned and ordered into port. She arrived at New York, after a cruise of 85 days, during which time she had taken 1,400 tons of shipping, with property valued at $1,000,000. She also made 80 prisoners.

Two vessels were captured by the *Hero*, of New York, on her voyage from France, and ransomed.

Schooner *Octavia*, sent into a southern port by the *Harrison*, of Baltimore.

Schooner *Funchall*, with rum and sugar, sent into Newbern, N. C, by the *Hero*, of New York.

The private armed schooner *Perry*, of Baltimore, was out ninety days on a cruise, during which time she captured twenty-two British vessels, eighteen of which she destroyed, and sent four to the United States. The editor here remarks, that if our government would employ fifteen or twenty such vessels to carry the war to the British coasts, it would terribly annoy our enemy. Twenty of these schooners properly fitted and manned, might dash across the Atlantic, and destroy two or three hundred vessels on the coast of England, before their presence would be suspected. If the enemy's ships of war were too thick for them, they might return home with very little loss, probably not more than two or three of them would be captured.

July 23rd.—The privateer *Surprise*, of Baltimore, arrived at Newport, R. I., from a cruise of 103 days, a part of which time she was in the British and Irish Channels, and near the Western Isles. She was chased sixteen times, and made in all thirteen prizes, some of which arrived safe, several others were burnt,

The *Zebec Ultor*, of Baltimore, in passing through Long Island Sound, was attacked by two British boats; she captured one with eight men, the other made her escape. The commander of the barge was killed; and buried at New London, where the prisoners were landed.

Charleston, July 21st.—The privateer schooner *Saucy Jack*, opened a rendezvous yesterday at 11 o'clock, for the enlistment of her crew. Before 5 p.m. one hundred and thirty able-bodied seamen were shipped in six hours, and ready to engage in the glories and dangers of an Atlantic cruise. Probably such a thing is unprecedented even in this country, so remarkable for maritime enterprise and dispatch.

The elegant ship *London packet*, 12 guns, laden with 400 pipes of brandy and wine, sent into an eastern port by the *Chasseur*, of Baltimore. The British brig *Astrea*, with 10 guns and twenty men, laden with fish, was taken by the *Midas*, and sent into Savannah.

On the return of the privateer *Midas*, from a cruise, when off Tybee light, she fell in with and captured a small English schooner privateer, called the *Dash*; she was armed with one long gun, and several small ones, with a crew of forty men.

Previous to her capture she had taken and manned three coasting vessels belonging to Savannah, laden with cotton; the cargoes of the three, inclusive, was 700 bales. The *Midas* immediately sailed in pursuit of them, and had the good fortune to return to Savannah with the three coasters, after an absence of five days.

Schooner *Union*, with fish, oil, etc., sent into port by the *Amelia*, of Baltimore.

Sloop *Friendship*, with dry-goods, and $7,000 in specie, captured by the *Revenge*, divested and destroyed.

Schooner *Alert*, captured by the same, and destroyed.

Schooner *Mary Ann*, taken by the same, divested, and given up to the prisoners.

Sloop *Active*, captured by the *Fairy*, of Baltimore, and burnt.

Brig *Lord Nelson*, of Belfast, from Rio Janeiro, with jerk beef, captured by the *Zebec Ultor*, and burnt.

Schooner *Nancy*, and two others whose names are not known, captured by the same, divested, and burnt.

Schooner ———, in ballast, taken by the same, and made a

cartel for prisoners.

Beside the before-mentioned vessels, two other small vessels were taken by the same, and burnt; the *Zebec* also made prizes of five or six other British vessels, which were permitted to proceed. A brig of 14 guns was manned, and ordered for France, and two others were sent to the United States.

Portuguese ship *St. Jose*, from Liverpool for Rio Janeiro, with dry-goods, hardware, etc., valued at $500,000 or $600,000, said to be British property, sent into Portland by the *Yankee* of Bristol.

Privateer schooner *Amnesty*, one gun, twenty-four men, captured by the *Zebec Ultor*, of Baltimore, and burnt.

Sloop *Tickler*, sent into Wilmington, N. C, by the same.

Schooner *Rambler*, with dry-goods, sent into Wilmington, N. C, by the *Perry*, of Baltimore,

Schooner *Fairy*, of Waterford, Ireland, two guns mounted, and six in the hold, laden with flour, sent into Wilmington, N. C, by the same.

His Britannic Majesty's schooner *Bulaboo*, of 6 guns and thirty men, captured by the same, after some resistance, and sent into Wilmington, N. C.

The ship *Friendship*, under Swedish colours, from London for Lisbon, with a cargo invoiced at £100,000, sterling, supposed to be British property, sent into Wilmington, N. C, by the *Herald*, of New York.

Ship *Hugh Jones*, from Belfast for Guadeloupe, with a full cargo of valuable goods, captured by the *Yankee*, divested, and ordered into port. This privateer had safely arrived from her fifth successful cruise.

Schooner *Fox*, captured off the Irish coast by the *Surprise*, was made a cartel of, to dispose of her prisoners.

Brig *James and David*, in ballast, captured by the same. She being of small value, was allowed to proceed on her voyage.

Brig *Fidelity*, taken by the same, and burnt.

Schooner *Ellen*, from Belfast, Ireland, for Lisbon, laden with beef, pork, and lard, sent into Beaufort, N. C, by the *Herald* of

New York.

Brig *Duke of York*, of Greenock, captured by the *General Armstrong*, of New York, and burnt.

Sloop *George*, taken in sight of Ireland, by the same, and sunk.

Brig *Swift*, in ballast, taken by the same, and made a cartel of, to dispose of her prisoners.

Brig *Defiance*, with whiskey, butter, and bread, for Lisbon, captured by the same, and burnt.

Brig *Friendship*, with a similar cargo, taken by the same and burnt.

Brig *Stag*, with a very full and very valuable cargo of dry-goods, captured by the same, divested of some articles, and burnt, a British frigate, brig and schooner, being in sight. The privateer had only time to take a few valuable articles.

Ship *Dorcas*, cut out of Anguilla, by the boats of the *General Armstrong*, and sunk.

During the last cruise of the *General Armstrong*, she made several prizes, three of which were very valuable. These she manned, and ordered to proceed to the first port in the United States. She arrived at New York, having on board a large amount of valuable merchandise, taken from the enemy.

Ship *Berry Castle*, 6 guns, with *barilla* and some wine, captured by the *Yankee*, who took out the wine, threw her armament overboard, and let her go.

Schooner *Linnet*, with fish and oil, captured by the *Snap-Dragon*, of Newbern, and sent into that port.

Schooner ———, captured by the same, divested of her valuable articles, and burnt.

Six vessels captured in the English channel, and sent into Havre de Grace, France, by the *Prince of Neufchâtel*.

By Loyd's List, the 3rd of June, there were thirty-seven British merchant vessels captured by American privateers, all within a few weeks; some of them were reported to be very valuable; many of these prizes were destroyed, others divested of their cargoes, while the most valuable portion of them were sent to the United States.

On the 18th of June, in Boston bay, the privateers *Grampus*, *Patapsco*, of Baltimore, and the schooner *Dash*, of Boston, were all chased by Captain Chapel, in the *La Hogue*, seventy-four. Although hard pushed for some time, they were fortunate enough to make their escape. Captain Chapel, during the pursuit, imagined he had one or more of them within his grasp, and when he found they had all made good their retreat, it is said, he was highly exasperated at their impudent audacity, and, of course, damned all the Yankees that infested the ocean without a British license.

DESPERATE BATTLE BETWEEN THE PRIVATEER *PRINCE DE NEUFCHÂTEL*, OF NEW YORK. COMMANDED BY CAPTAIN ORDRONAUX. AND A LARGE NUMBER OF BOATS, BELONGING TO A BRITISH MAN-OF-WAR. [4]

The *Prince de Neufchâtel* was a splendid vessel, of 310 tons burthen, hermaphrodite rigged, mounting 17 guns, with blunderbusses, muskets, boarding pikes, etc. Her full complement of men, including officers and marines, probably amounted to 150 souls, when she left New York.

She was a most fortunate vessel, and made several successful cruises during the war, causing great loss to the enemy. She was chased by seventeen men-of-war during her present cruise, and escaped them all.

The goods she brought to the United States were estimated to be worth from $250,000 to $300,000, besides having on board a considerable amount of specie.

At noon, on the 11th of October, off Nantucket, that island bearing north, distant about half a mile, Captain Ordronaux discovered a frigate off Gay Head, which gave chase to him, and while the privateer lay becalmed, the frigate took a fresh breeze and came up very fast.

At 3 p.m., the *Neufchâtel* got the breeze, and took her prize, the ship *Douglass*, in tow; the frigate, at the same time, about

---

4. See note at end of chapter.

twelve miles from the privateer.

At 7 in the evening, it fell calm, when the privateer and her prize came to anchor about a quarter of a mile from each other, as the current was sweeping them on shore.

At half-past 8 p.m., a signal was made from the prize that several boats were coming from the frigate to attack them. All hands were then called to quarters, and every preparation made to give them a warm reception.

As the boats drew near, the privateer commenced firing, which the enemy disregarded, and were soon alongside. The boats were five in number, one on each side, one on each bow, and one under the stern.

A warm action then took place, with muskets, pistols, cutlasses, etc. In every attempt the enemy made to board, he was promptly met and repulsed.

About twenty minutes from the commencement of the action, the enemy cried out for quarters, which were granted.

Of the five barges (which contained 111 men, including officers and marines), one was sunk, with forty-three men, of whom only two were saved; three drifted off from alongside, apparently with no living soul on board; one was taken possession of. She contained thirty-six men at the commencement of the action, of whom eight were killed, twenty wounded, and eight unhurt. It was then ascertained that they were from the British frigate *Endymion*. They were all armed with blunderbusses, pistols, muskets, boarding pikes and cutlasses.

The second lieutenant of the frigate (F. Ormond, who was unhurt), three midshipmen, two of whom were severely wounded, with one master's mate also wounded, were permitted to come on board. The remainder of the prisoners (fifteen seamen and marines), were kept astern all night in the launch; after taking out the arms, oars, etc., the commander being afraid to trust them on board, having only eight men fit for duty, while there were thirty-seven prisoners confined below.

The *Prince de Neufchâtel*, at the commencement of the action, had only thirty-three men, including officers at quarters. After the battle was over, it was found that six of the privateer's crew were killed; also Mr. Charles Hilburn, a Nantucket pilot, taken out of a fishing vessel. There were also fifteen severely wounded, nine slightly, and eight unhurt.

The next morning, the lieutenant, midshipman, and master's mate, signed an agreement in behalf of themselves, the seamen and marines pledging their honours not to serve against the United States during the war unless regularly exchanged, and were then towed on shore at Nantucket in the privateer's launch.

Shortly after, Captain Ordronaux sent fifteen of his other prisoners, and fifteen of his own men who were wounded, on shore.

All the prisoners were placed in charge of the United States Marshal. In his enfeebled situation. Captain Ordronaux got under way and proceeded to Boston, at which place he arrived on the 15th October.

It was subsequently ascertained by persons from Nantucket, that the British acknowledged a loss of thirty-three killed, thirty-seven wounded, and thirty made prisoners.

Among the killed were the first lieutenant, and a master's mate. The third lieutenant, two master's mates, and one midshipman were wounded.

The commander of the frigate said he had lost as many men as he should have done if engaged with a vessel equal in force to his own, and gave great credit to the officers and crew of the privateer, for their gallant defence.

He had 111 men in the attack. He said that a part of his men succeeded in gaining the deck of the *Prince de Neufchâtel*, but that the Americans then rallied and drove them overboard.

The foregoing was one of the hardest fought battles that occurred during the war, considering the number of men acting on the defensive.

Prizes Captured by Privateers

Brig ——, from Madeira, for Liverpool, captured by the

Rambler, of Boston, on her passage to Canton. She was divested of eighty or ninety casks of wine, and given up, not having men enough to send her to the United States.

Frig *Fortitude*, from Rio Janeiro, with a full cargo of hides, coffee, dye-wood, etc., sent into Union River, Maine, by the *Surprise*, of Baltimore.

Schooner *George Canning*, from Spain, for England, laden with merino, wool and fruit, captured by the *General Armstrong*, of New York, and sent into Thomastown.

Ship *Pizarro*, from Liverpool, for Amelia Island, with dry-goods, crates, copper and salt, sent into Savannah by the *Midas*, of Baltimore.

Brig *Espiranza*, from Amelia Island for Havana, with cotton, rice, and flour, sent into Savannah by the *Midas*, of Baltimore.

Brig *Elsinore*, from Turk's Island for Amelia Island, with salt, sent into the same port by the *Midas*.

The privateer *Harrison*, of Baltimore, captured the following British vessels: ship *Julia*, brig *Mary Ann*, schooner *John Duncan*, ——— *Louisa*. After removing from the prizes to the privateer, valuable goods to the amount of £18,000 or £20,000, sterling, she gave up two of them and destroyed the others.

Schooner ———, with a large amount of specie on board, captured by the same, and manned for the United States. The *Harrison* arrived safe at Savannah with her rich spoils.

Brig *Betsy*, with a cargo of fish, from Newfoundland for Barbadoes, sent into Boston by the *York*, of Baltimore.

Ship *Alfred*, in ballast, sent into a southern port by the *Harpy*, of Baltimore.

Ship *Antonia*, under Russian colours, from Lisbon for St. Michaels, laden with dry-goods, brandy, some hardware and crockery, sent to a southern port by the same.

Two brigs in ballast, captured by the same, and burnt.

CAPTURE OF THE BRITISH PACKET *PRINCESS ELIZABETH* BY THE PRIVATEER *HARPY*, OF BALTIMORE.

In September the *Harpy* fell in with the British packet *Prin-*

cess *Elizabeth,* and after a warm but short action, the packet surrendered. She had three men killed, and several wounded, and was much cut up in her sails and rigging. The privateer had one man killed.

The *Princess Elizabeth* was armed with 10 guns, and thirty-eight men, 8 twelve-pound carronades, and 2 long brass nine-pounders; she had on board as passengers, a Turkish Ambassador, for England, an English officer, Aid to a British general, and a second lieutenant of a 74. The privateer divested the packet of $10,000 in specie, and five pipes of Madeira wine, with two long brass, and two iron guns; the remainder of her armament she threw overboard, and ransomed the vessel for $2,000, and then allowed her to proceed on her course to England.

Ship *Hero,* from Newfoundland, with 4,333 quintals of codfish, sent into Hyannis by the *Ida,* of Boston.

East India Company's ship *Countess of Harcourt,* 520 tons, 6 heavy guns, and ninety men, outward bound, laden with dry-goods, brandy, rum, gin, etc., separated from the fleet in a gale, and captured in the British Channel by the *Sabine* of Baltimore, and sent into a southern port. This British East Indiaman was a very valuable prize to her captors.

His Majesty's packet , the cutter *Landraile,* —— guns, thirty-three men, captured after a hard battle, in the British Channel by the *Syren,* of Baltimore, divested, and the prisoners taken to New York.

Two brigs captured by the same; one burnt, the other released, after having first despoiled her of the most valuable part of her cargo.

Fourteen enemy's vessels, captured in the British Channel by the *Governor Tompkins,* of New York, divested them of their valuable articles, and destroyed them. The privateer had also taken six other prizes; some she burnt, and some of the most valuable she sent to the United States.

Brig *Betsey and Mary,* from Spain for London, with wool, etc., captured by the *Kemp,* of Baltimore, divested of 105 bales of merino wool, and burnt.

Ship *Calypso*, under Swedish colours, and with Swedish papers, captured by the same, divested of thirty bales of dry-goods, and $3,000 in specie, belonging to the paymaster of the 41st Regiment (who was paroled), and suffered to proceed.

Brig *New Frederick*, from Smyrna for Hull, captured by the *Kemp* (and out of humanity to an Italian lady), permitted to proceed, after divesting her of some articles. The *Kemp* arrived at North Carolina, from Nantes. She obtained her cargo, from the enemy which was exceedingly valuable. She was a letter-of-marque, belonging to Baltimore.

Schooner *Contract*, laden with salt, sent into North Carolina by the *Roger*, of Norfolk.

His Majesty's transport brig *Doris*, captured by the *Grampus*, of Baltimore, sent into Marblehead. The *Doris* was from Senegal, bound to Portsmouth, England, and had on board thirty or forty soldiers, also two elegant horses, one hyena, two jackals, etc., presents for the Prince Regent.

Ship *Hoppet*, and brig *Eliza*, from Amelia Island, bound to England, sent into Savannah by the *Saucy Jack*, of Charleston.

The *London Gazette* of June 21st, officially announced the capture of the American privateers *Hawk* and *Polly*, by two frigates.

The *David Porter*, privateer, arrived at New York; was chased nine hundred and forty miles, by a frigate and two sloops of war.

The *Mammoth*, privateer, of Baltimore, was dealing destruction to the enemy's commerce, off the coast of Newfoundland. She had an action with an English transport ship, with three or four hundred troops on board. The privateer had one man wounded, and finding the transport had too many men with muskets, she hauled off and continued on her cruise, for something more valuable.

The *York*, of Baltimore, arrived at Boston, filled with the richest spoils of several vessels, among them, the East India ship *Coromandel*, of 500 tons.

The privateer *Surprise*, of Baltimore, arrived at Salem, after a fortunate cruise of one month, during which time she captured twenty British vessels; some of them were valuable, these she ordered into port; the remainder, amounting to eight or ten, she destroyed: and after loading the privateer with valuable goods, she returned into port to discharge her cargo and refit for another cruise.

Schooner *Mary*, with dry-goods, valued at £3,000, sterling, from Jamaica for St. Domingo; sent into New Orleans by the *Shark*, of New York.

Brig *Maria Wirman*, from Havana for Scotland, with 1500 or 1600 boxes of sugar; sent into Hyannis by the *Yankee*, of Bristol. This vessel was called a Swede, but her cargo was found to be British property.

Cutter *Wasp*, captured by the *Rattlesnake*, privateer, off the English coast, and burnt.

Brig *Dover*, of London, captured by the same, and burnt.

British brig *Pike*, captured by the privateer *Pike*, of Baltimore, and burnt.

Schooner ———, from St. John's, N. B., divested of her valuable articles by the *Pike*, and made a cartel of, to dispose of her prisoners.

British schooner *Industrious Bee*, captured also by the *Pike*, and burnt.

Schooners *Venus*, *Lord Nelson*, and brig *Jane*, also taken by the *Pike*; the last, with provisions and dry-goods; divested of part of her cargo, and made a cartel of, to dispose of the prisoners. The other two ordered into a port in the United States.

Brig *Orient*, from Portsmouth, England, for Tenerife, with dry-goods, captured by the same privateer; divested of her valuable goods, and sunk.

Brig *John*, from London for Tenerife, taken by the same, and burnt, within long-gun-shot of a British man-of-war brig.

The *Pike* captured several other vessels, which were released or made cartels of. This privateer was subsequently chased ashore, on the southern coast, and taken possession of by some of the enemy's vessels. A part of the crew, however, escaped; the remainder, forty-three in number, were made prisoners. She paroled 250 prisoners during her cruise.

A British brig and a schooner sent into Ocracock, laden with fish; by the *Herald*, of New York.

Ship *Samuel Cummings*, 400 tons, laden with sugar and coffee; taken by the *Pike*, of Baltimore, but wrecked on the southern coast: part of the cargo was saved.

Ship *Five Sisters,* captured by the letter-of-marque schooner *Dash*; divested of 200 puncheons of Jamaica rum, and permitted to proceed on her voyage.

Schooner ——, taken by the *Leech*, of Salem, and ransomed.

Brig ——, 200 tons, an assorted cargo, estimated to be worth $30,000; sent into Newbern by the *Hero*, of that place.

Brig *Mars*, from Mogadore, captured by the *David Porter*, of Boston (the *Whig*, of Baltimore, in company); divested of a considerable part of her cargo, and ordered to a port in the United States.

Brig *Cornwallis*, taken by the same; divested, and made a cartel of.

Ship *Vester* from Rio Janeiro for England, 6 guns; captured by the *David Porter*; divested of her least bulky and most valuable articles, and ordered into port.

Brig *Horatio*, from Rio de Janeiro, for England, taken by the *David Porter,* and ransomed for a bill of exchange on England for $20,000; cargo of hides and tallow. During her cruise, the *David Porter* made several other prizes.

Brig *Endeavour*, a transport vessel, laden with sails, anchors, army stores and coal, captured by the *Surprise*, of Baltimore, and destroyed on Rockaway beach, near New York, by the British men-of-war. Cargo partially saved.

Cutter *Jubilee*, from Tenerife, with wine, captured by the *Whig*, divested of part of her cargo, and made a cartel of, to dispose of her prisoners.

Schooner *Alexandria*, in ballast, captured by the same and burnt.

British brig *Irish Minor*, captured by the *Whig*, and made a cartel of, to get rid of her prisoners.

Brig *Princess Mary*, from Ireland, for London, with government provisions; also captured by the *Whig*, and destroyed.

Brig *Eliza*, from the same place, to the same port, also captured by the *Whig*; cargo thrown overboard and vessel made a cartel of.

British Schooner *Espérance*, from ——, for Corunna, Spain, captured by the same and destroyed.

Ship *London*, from Merimachi, for Liverpool, with timber, also captured by the *Whig* and burnt

Ship *Postethwell*, from Cork, for Merimachi. in ballast, captured by the same and burnt.

The *Whig* made several other prizes on this cruise, and arrived at New York with some goods, and twenty-three prisoners. She also made some prizes in company with the *David Porter*.

Brig *Nancy*, from Liverpool, for Halifax, laden with dry-goods, captured by the *Portsmouth*, of Portsmouth, divested of 318 bales and packages of goods, invoiced at £27,000, sterling, and ordered into port. This was a great prize. The privateer, with her rich spoils, safely arrived. (See Appendix.)

A sloop, from Halifax, captured also by the *Portsmouth*, divested of her valuable goods, and given up to the prisoners.

Schooner *Columbia*, from Halifax, for Barbadoes, with fish and lumber, worth $4,000, captured and sent into Newburyport, by the *Portsmouth*.

Brig *Fire Fly*, from Smyrna, for London, with a full cargo of drugs, wines and silks, brought into Wilmington, North Carolina, by the *Sabine*, of Baltimore. The privateer safely arrived, and had on board the *optima spolia* of the enemy's vessels. She took goods to the amount of $100,000.

Brig *Mary and Eliza*, from Halifax, laden with lumber, etc., captured by the *Argo*, of Baltimore, and chased ashore near Barnegat, where she was burnt.

Schooner ——, with a cargo of provisions, sent into an eastern port by the same privateer *Portsmouth*, of Portsmouth, N. H.

Brig *Argo*, from Dublin, with 100 puncheons of Irish whiskey, a quantity of port wine and provisions, sent into Portland by the *Surprise*, of Baltimore.

Brig ——, laden with rum and molasses, sent into a southern port by the *Grampus*, of Baltimore.

Sloop *Farmer*, with provisions, captured by the *Mammoth*, of Baltimore, on the coast of Nova Scotia, and sunk.

The *Mammoth* also captured brig *Britannia*, from St. Andrews, for Liverpool, with lumber; she not being of much value, was destroyed by the captors.

Three other brigs, in ballast, bound to Pictou and Merimachi, were captured by the same privateer and burnt.

Brig *Ceres*, of Glasgow, with brandy, etc., divested and given up to release the prisoners, by the same.

The privateer *York*, of Baltimore, captured the following vessels, namely: The British brig *Harvest*, laden with furs, seal skins, oil and salmon, and manned her for the United States. British brig *William*. 10 guns, and fourteen men, from Rio de Janeiro, with 350 tons of sugar, with a large quantity of coffee, and sundry other articles; ordered her into an American port. The brig *Rover*, from Havana, for Guernsey, laden with sugar and coffee, sent her to a port in the United States. Sloop *Regulator*, of Nantucket, re-captured by the *York*; she had a valuable cargo, and arrived safe at Chatham, Cape Cod.

The well known and gallant Captain David Maffet, of Philadelphia, spoken of in this chapter, first commanded the privateer-schooner *Atlas*, and made many captures. He subsequently commanded the *Rattlesnake*, and made a great many prizes. He vanquished the enemy in several hard-fought battles.

The little *Saucy Jack*, of Charleston, also mentioned in this chapter, figured conspicuously throughout the war.

NOTE

Since the first edition of this work appeared, I have received a more particular account of the desperate battle fought between Captain John Ordronaux, of the privateer The *Prince of Neufchâ-*

tel, of New York, with five British barges belonging to the English frigate *Endymion*, off Nantucket, on the 11th of October, 1814; by which it will be seen that under all the circumstances, it was the hardest fought naval engagement and the most conspicuous victory achieved during the war.

It was a contest waged against a force more than three times superior numerically; advancing in separate divisions under the cover of night, and assisted by the presence of a heavy frigate, while at the same time, and as a most serious obstacle of a successful defence, Captain Ordronaux was encumbered with thirty-seven British prisoners, who were refractory and all ready for revolt.

He was therefore obliged to handcuff his prisoners, and confine them in the hold just before the action.

He had recently manned so many prizes that he had left only thirty-three men, including officers and marines at quarters, when simultaneously attacked by five British barges, manned with one hundred and eleven men, beside the before-mentioned thirty-seven prisoners confined below, who were striving to get loose from their manacles, and unite themselves to their fellow countrymen.

Fearing that the British frigate would attack the privateer with her boats, Captain Ordronaux made the following preparation for the contest, beside the usual number of muskets, pistols, boarding-pikes and sabres, belonging to his vessel: He had made a large augmentation of fire-arms taken from sundry British prizes during the cruise, so that his gun-room was literally filled with these implements of death and destruction. He accordingly took the precaution before night to have some two or three hundred muskets and pistols loaded and placed in a position to grasp at a moment's warning.

The loaded pistols were put into baskets and placed behind the bulwarks, so that when the strife should commence, it would not be necessary to reload these weapons. He had also his shot-lockers all filled with heavy shot, to throw into the enemy's boats, and stave in their bottoms, if brought to close quarters, when he could not use his carriage-gun.

Being thus prepared, the brave captain waited with the most intense anxiety for the approach of the enemy: it was about nine o'clock, the night being dark, they heard the sound of oars at a distance, silently approaching. In the obscurity they could not see the boats of the enemy; a few shot were fired from the *Neufchâtel* in the direction of the sound, to draw a shot from his adversary, with a view to ascertain his position, and how he meant to attack, but the ruse did not succeed.

Captain Ordronaux had no intention of running away from the fight, nor did he mean that the enemy should, when once engaged in the deadly strife, it being well understood by all on board that rather than surrender to the enemy the privateer should be blown up. Such was the condition of things at the commencement of the action.

The *Neufchâtel* lying at anchor, was now fully prepared to receive the enemy, who approached with five barges in the following order, namely, one on each side, one on each bow, and the other under the stem. A warm action then took place with muskets, pistols, sabres and boarding-pikes. The enemy were promptly met and repulsed, and in about twenty minutes many in the boats cried out for quarters, which were granted to those amidships.

The men in the two barges under the bows of the privateer, however, succeeded in gaining the forecastle, when Captain Ordronaux, with two or three of his faithful followers, discharged one of his main-deck guns, loaded with canister shot and bags of musket balls. This gun was trained upon the forecastle, which had the effect of killing and wounding great numbers of the enemy, and of driving the remainder overboard. In this discharge he unfortunately wounded several of his own men. The five barges which attacked the privateer contained at the commencement of the action one hundred and eleven men, including officers and marines.

One barge was sunk with forty-three men, of whom two only were saved. Three boats drifted off from alongside, apparently with no living soul on board ; one was taken possession of. She contained thirty-six men at the beginning of the action, of whom eight were killed and twenty wounded, and eight uninjured.

The second lieutenant of the frigate, (F. Ormond, who was not injured,) three midshipmen, two of whom were severely wounded, with one master's mate also wounded, were permitted to come on board. The remainder of the prisoners (fifteen seamen and marines) were kept astern all night in the launch—after taking out the arms, oars, etc., the commander being afraid to trust them on board, having only eight men fit for duty.

After the battle was over, it was found that six of the privateer's crew were killed, and nineteen wounded, beside Mr. Charles Hilburn, a Nantucket pilot who was stationed at the helm during the action; it is stated that he was several times wounded, and finally killed by the enemy. The British in this action acknowledge a loss of thirty-three killed, thirty-seven wounded, and thirty prisoners.

During the hottest part of the engagement the prisoners in the hold were loudly cheering their countrymen to continue the fight, and constantly striving to break loose, while Captain Ordronaux and his First Lieutenant, Mr. Millen, were obliged to watch their prisoners, and guard every point to prevent a recapture from the enemy.

The brave captain, though wounded, could not be attended by the surgeon, for this gentleman was also wounded in the fight, and unable to assist those who were suffering; so that through this long and dreary night, Captain Ordronaux and his First Lieutenant, Mr. Millen, were obliged to keep guard at each hatchway, with pistol in hand, to prevent the prisoners from breaking loose, while his own poor fellows were lying about the deck, suffering from their wounds, with no one to attend them, or even to give them a drink of cold water.

Thus passed this awful night of painful anxiety. I will leave the reader to imagine the anxious feelings of Captain Ordronaux, and his faithful followers, during the long and sleepless night, surrounded by the dead and wounded, with mingled sounds of groans and curses of those who were wallowing about the deck, while the frigate at a distance was seen burning port fires, and sending up signal rockets for her barges to return.

He also feared that at the break of day the frigate would bear down upon them, and thus defeat all that he had gained in this eventful struggle. At last the morning dawned upon these weary, battle-stained watchers, who had passed the dreary night without once leaving their posts. The colours of the *Neufchâtel* were still flying, though her decks were in an awful condition. Some thirty or forty men lay dead and wounded in every condition of mutilation, while the broken arms and implements of warfare scattered around told how desperate had been the struggle on that bloodstained deck; and now had arrived the most difficult part of Captain Ordronaux's duty.

As has been stated, he had but eight men fit for duty after the termination of the action; all his prisoners were to be paroled and landed under the eye of a numerous enemy. He was, therefore, obliged to employ five or six of his men in a large launch, and at the same time to keep up an appearance of strength to deceive his adversaries. He was, therefore, obliged to resort to stratagem to carry out his plan.

Accordingly, he had a sail hung up abaft the main hatches, to serve as a screen, wherewith to conceal the quarter-deck. After this was done, he kept two boys there, one beating the drum, the other blowing the fife, and tramping heavily about the deck, to make the enemy believe that a large number of men were stationed there at quarters, to enforce his orders. Thus while the attention of the enemy was drawn off from his enfeebled state, sixty-seven of the prisoners were passed over the side into the launch, and transported to the shore, where they were placed in the possession of the United States Marshal.

He also landed his own wounded men, that they might be better attended to, and receive more medical assistance than could be given them on board of the privateer. And thus after having landed all his prisoners, except some five or six, who had been paroled, these being young and active he retained on board to assist his crew in weighing the anchor, and navigating his vessel to Boston.

In this adroit management, Captain Ordronaux displayed a vast deal of cool, deliberate judgement, as well as uncommon tact in disposing of his numerous prisoners, and hiding his own weakness in point of numbers.

He showed himself a great tactician, and, like General Jackson, knew how to avail himself of every advantage for enabling a small force to compete successfully with a large one.

A near relative of Captain Ordronaux has furnished the writer of these pages with the brave captain's journal, the original parol given by the English in their own handwriting, and many other valuable papers and documents, which clearly establish the truth of this unparalleled victory.

I shall, therefore, make no apology for thus discharging my duty to the memory of a distinguished fellow-citizen, by communicating these facts in full.

I think it will be conceded on all hands that Captain Ordronaux evinced as much bravery and tact in disposing of his prisoners after the battle, as in defending his vessel against the enemy during the severe conflict. There are many men who can fight bravely, but few who can manage as well as he did, to profit by and secure the fruits of a glorious victory.

On his arrival at Boston, a large number of patriotic merchants and other citizens proposed presenting the brave captain with a sword and a vote of thanks for his gallantry, but the unaspiring modesty of the heroic Ordronaux begged, through his friends, that it should not be done.

For, so far from coveting applause, his unassuming, retiring disposition, led him to shun publicity of every kind, and often prevented him from receiving that just share of public approbation which his merit so richly deserved; so that the world knows but little of the gallant deeds of this distinguished nautical hero.

CHAPTER 8

Compelled to Leave the Channel

CRUISE AND CAPTURE OF THE *LEO*

The *Leo* was a fine Baltimore built vessel of 320 tons, a remarkably fast sailer, and in every respect a superior vessel. She was lying in the harbour of L'Orient on the 1st of November, 1814, and was then owned by Thomas Lewis, Esq., an American gentleman, residing in Bordeaux. On the 2nd of November, she was purchased by an association of American gentlemen (then in France) placed under my command, and her commission as a letter-of-marque endorsed over to me under the sanction of the Hon. William H. Crawford, who was at that time our minister at Paris. It was determined that I should make a short cruise for the purpose of capturing a few prizes from the enemy, and then proceed to Charleston for a cargo of cotton, and return to France as soon as possible.

As there were at this time quite a number of American seamen in Bordeaux, Nantes and L'Orient, supported by the government of the United States, through the consuls at those ports, it was desirable to take home as many of them as the schooner could conveniently accommodate. I took with me, as first officer, Mr. Pierre G. Depeyster, and left Bordeaux by diligence, for L'Orient. On our way we stopped a day or two at Nantes, where I engaged, with the consent of our consul at that port, forty seamen and two petty officers.

Mr. Azor O. Lewis, a fine young man, brother of the former owner of the *Leo*, was one of my prize masters, and to him I committed the charge of bringing about forty more seamen from Bordeaux to L'Orient. The residue of the officers and men were picked up at L'Orient, with the exception of four or five of my petty officers, who came up from Bordeaux to join the schooner at L'Orient.

Early in November we commenced fitting her for sea. We found her hull in pretty good order, but her sails and rigging were in a bad state. I, however, set everything in motion, as actively as possible, and put in requisition sailmakers, blockmakers, blacksmiths, etc., etc.; while others were employed taking in ballast and filling water casks, in fine, hurrying on as fast as possible, before we should be stopped.

The English had so much influence with the new government of Louis XVIII. that I felt extremely anxious to get out on the broad ocean without delay, and therefore drove on my preparations almost night and day.

After ballasting, I took on board three tons of bread, thirty barrels of beef, fifteen ditto of pork, and other stores to correspond, being enough for fifty days.

I got ready for sea on the 6th of November. My crew, including the officers and marines, numbered about one hundred souls, and a better set of officers and men never left the port of L'Orient. But we were miserably armed; we had, when I first took command of the schooner, one long brass 12-pounder, and four small 4-pounders, with some fifty or sixty poor muskets. Those concerned in the vessel seemed to think we ought, with so many men, to capture prizes enough, even without guns.

With this miserable armament, I was now ready for sea, and had dropped the schooner down near the mouth of the outer harbour, and was only waiting for my papers from Paris, to proceed on my intended voyage; when to my severe mortification, I was ordered by the public authorities to return into port, and disarm the vessel. The order was imperative, and I was of course compelled to obey. I accordingly waited on the commanding officer of the port, and told him it was a hard case not to allow me sufficient arms to defend my vessel against the boats of the enemy.

He politely told me he was sorry, but that he must obey the orders of his government, and that I must take out all the guns except one, and at the same time laughingly observed that one gun was enough to take a dozen English ships before I got to Charleston.

I, of course, kept the long 12-pounder, and in the night smuggled on board some twenty or thirty muskets. In this situation I left the port of L'Orient, on the 8th of November, 1814, and stood out to sea in the hope of capturing a few prizes. After getting to sea we rubbed up the muskets, and with this feeble armament steered for the chops of the British Channel. I soon found that when the weather was good and the sea smooth, I could take merchantmen enough by boarding; but in rough weather the travelling 12-pounder was but a poor reliance, and not to be depended upon like the long centre gun that I had on board the *David Porter*.

It is true, my officers and men were always ready to board an enemy of three times our force; but, in a high sea, if one of these delicately Baltimore built vessels should come in contact with a large, strong ship, the schooner would inevitably be crushed and sunk. For this reason, I was compelled to let one large English ship with twelve guns escape while in the English Channel, because the weather was too rough to board her.

November 13th.—At six p.m. sounded in sixty-five fathoms water, the Scilly Islands bearing N.W. fifteen leagues distant. Light winds and variable through the night. At 6 a.m. saw a brig to windward. At 7 *ditto* she set English colours; gave her a gun, when she struck her flag. She proved to be an English brig from Leghorn, bound up the Channel. It now commenced blowing a strong breeze-from the N.W., and soon there was a high sea running. Saw a large ship steering up the Channel; left the prize, made sail in chase of her. At 10 a.m. she set English colours, and fired a gun. Had the weather been smooth, I think we could have carried her by boarding in fifteen minutes, or had I met her at sea, I would have followed her until the weather was better, and the sea smooth: but being now in the English Channel with a high sea, it would have destroyed my schooner if she had come in contact with this wall-sided ship. She showed six long nines on each side. After exchanging a few shot, I hauled off, and returned to our prize.

Nov, 14th.—Fresh breezes and cloudy weather. At 2 p.m. the weather moderated, when I took out of the English prize brig the captain, mate, and crew, and put on board of her a prize-master and seven men, with orders to proceed to a port in the United States. At 4 p.m. saw a sale to windward, when we made sail in chase. At 8 *ditto* it became dark and squally; lost sight of the chase. At 8 a.m. saw our prize ahead; we soon came up with her, when I supplied her with two casks of water and a quantity of bread, and left her to proceed on her course to the United States.

Nov. 15th.—Fresh gales from the westward, with a rough sea running. Middle and latter part of these twenty-four hours, the wind continued to blow strong from the westward, with a high sea. As it was now the middle of November, and no prospect of much fine weather, and my schooner so badly armed, I concluded to leave this rough cruising ground and run to the southward, in hopes of finding better weather, where I could profit by a superior number of men in making prizes Lat, 47° 28' North.

Nov. 17th.—At 3 p.m. boarded the Spanish brig *Alonzo*, from Tenerife, bound to London. On board of this vessel I put the late captain of our prize brig.

Nov. 18th.—Light winds and fine weather; a man-of-war brig in chase of us, about two miles distant. At 8 p.m. light breezes from the southward; passed near a brig standing to the eastward; had not time to board her, as the man-of-war was still in chase. At midnight the wind became fresh from the W.S.W., with dark, rainy weather. Took in all the light sails, and hauled close upon the wind to the W.N.W. At 7 a.m. saw a small sail on our weather-bow; made sail in chase. At 10 *ditto* came up with and captured the chase; found it was an English cutter, from Tenerife, bound to London, with a cargo of wine.

Nov. 19th.—Strong gales from the northward, and a high sea running. At meridian took out of the prize twenty quarter casks of wine, together with her sails, cables, rigging, blocks, &c, and after removing the prisoners, scuttled her. At 1 p.m. she sank. At 7 a.m. saw a sail to windward; tacked ship to get the weather-gage. At 11 *ditto* got her on our lee beam, when I made her out to be an English brig-of-war of sixteen guns. I commenced firing my long twelve. At noon, after receiving about thirty or forty shot from the enemy, without any material damage, I hauled off. Some of his shot passed over us, some fell short; and only one hulled us: this shot passed through our bends amidships, and lodged in the hold. I could out-sail him with the greatest ease. and if I had had a long well-mounted centre gun, I could have annoyed him without receiving any injury by keeping just out of the reach of his carronades.

Nov. 21st.—Fresh winds from the N.N.E., and squally weather. At meridian saw a sail bearing W.S.W.; made sail in chase. At 4 p. m., she being directly to leeward, I ran down to discover the character of the chase; I soon made her out to be a frigate. When within three miles distance, I hoisted an English ensign. The frigate showed Portuguese colours, and resorted to every stratagem in his power to decoy us down within the range of his shot. Finding I could out-sail him with ease, I hauled down the English colours, set an American ensign, and hauled close upon the wind, and soon lost sight of her. During the night we had fresh gales at E.N.E., and squally weather. At 7 a.m. saw a small sail bearing S.S.W.; made sail in chase. I soon came up with and boarded an English schooner from Malaga, bound to Dublin, with a cargo of fruit. Took out the prisoners and a supply of fruit, and then manned her and gave orders to the prize master to make the best of his way to the United States. Lat. by account 45° 33' N.; long. 12° 0' W.

Nov. 22nd.—Light airs and fine pleasant weather. At 3 p.m.

ame up with and boarded a Danish galliot; at 12 o'clock, midnight, put ten English prisoners on board of her. I supplied them with provisions and a quarter cask of wine, and the galliot proceeded on her voyage.

Nov. 23rd—Fresh gales from the southward, with dark, rainy weather. At 1 p. m. wore ship to the S.E. in chase of a brig; at three came up with and spoke her. She proved to be a Prussian from Oporto, bound to Hamburg, with a cargo of wine and fruit. Middle part of the twenty-four hours, strong gales from the N.N.W. At noon discovered two frigates to leeward. They both made sail in chase of me. I plied to windward, tacking every hour, and beat them without difficulty; but, as there were two of them, I was not quite at ease until I had got out of their neighbourhood.

Nov. 24th.—Fresh gales from the N.W., and squally, with showers of rain and a high head-sea running; the two frigates still in chase of us. At 5 p.m. the weather-most frigate was about ten or twelve miles distant to leeward ; finding I could beat them with so much ease, I reefed the sails, and plied to windward. Towards morning the wind moderated, and at daylight there was nothing in sight. Lat. by obs. 44° 34' N., long. 15° 8' W.

Nov. 25th.—Moderate breezes from the westward, and fine weather. At 3 p. m. discovered a sail bearing about S.E.; made sail and bore away in chase. At half-past three made her out to be a frigate, when I hauled upon the wind. At four *ditto* she fired a gun, and showed American colours. I set an American ensign for a few minutes, and then hauled it down and hoisted a large English ensign. She fired three or four shot, but finding they fell short, stopped firing, and crowded all sail in chase of me. Night coming on, I soon lost sight of her.

Nov. 26th.—Strong gales from the W.N.W., and thick, squally weather. At 1 p.m. discovered a sail to the windward, bearing N.W.; made sail in chase, tacking every hour. At 5 *ditto*, made him out to be a ship standing upon the wind to the N.E. At half-past 9 o'clock, after getting on his weather quarter, ran up alongside, hailed him, and ordered him to heave to, which order was immediately obeyed. I sent my boat on board, and found him to be an English ship, burthen about 200 tons, from Palermo, bound to London, with a cargo of brimstone, rags, mats, etc. He mounted six guns, with a crew of about twenty men. We kept company through the night. The latter part of these twenty-four hours, light winds and fine weather. Lat. by obs. 42° 31' N., long. 15° 46' W.

Nov. 27th.—Light breezes from the N.W., and fine, pleasant weather. In the forenoon of this day removed the prisoners from the ship, and put on board a prize master and a crew of ten men; I also took out her guns, powder, shot, and some fruit, and then ordered her to proceed to the United States. At 2 p.m. made sail and steered to the S.W., and at 5 *ditto* lost sight of the prize. Lat. by obs. 41° 3' N., long. 15° 46' W.

At half-past 6 a.m., daylight, saw a small sail bearing S.E.; at 7 spoke her; she was a small schooner, one day from Lisbon, bound to Oporto. At this time made the Burling Rocks, bearing S.S.E. five leagues distant; several small sail in sight. At meridian, the Rock of Lisbon bore S. by E., seven leagues distant Fresh breezes from the N.E. and fine weather. Lat. by obs. 39° 1' N.

Dec. 1st.—These twenty-four hours commenced with fresh breezes at N.N.W., with open, cloudy weather.

At 1 p.m. saw a ship on our weather quarter, coming up with us very fast I made sail, steering to the westward, to get to windward of the ship, in order to ascertain her character. It was then blowing a strong breeze from the N.N.W., and the weather was somewhat squally; a head-sea was running. About half-past 2 p.m. the schooner gave a sudden pitch, when, to the astonishment of every person on board, the foremast broke, about one-third below its head, and in a moment after, it broke again, close to the deck. While in this situation, I had the mortification to see the ship pass us, within pistol-shot, without being able to pursue her.

I believe she was an English packet, just out of Lisbon, and bound for England; and, I doubt not, if this unfortunate accident had not occurred, we should have captured her in less than one hour from the time she was first seen. At this time the packets transported large quantities of specie to England, and this ship would, in all probability, have proved a rich prize to us. I have no doubt the mast was defective, and that it should have been renewed before leaving port. From this untoward circumstance resulted all the misfortunes attending the cruise.

I cannot express the disappointment and mortification I now felt, not so much on my own account, as for the loss incurred by the gentlemen who planned and fitted out the expedition. The Rock of Lisbon bore E.S.E. thirty miles distant, and my only hope was to get into Lisbon or St. Ubes before daylight the next morning, and thus escape capture. I accordingly cleared away the wreck, rigged a jury foremast, and bore away. At 4 p.m., an hour after the accident occurred, we were going at the rate of seven knots an hour, and had the breeze continued through the night, should have got into port by daylight next morning; but, unfortunately, the wind became light during the night, and we made little progress.

At 5 a. m., daylight, made Cape Espartel and the Rock of Lisbon, when it became almost calm. We then commenced sweeping and towing, with two boats ahead, until 1 p.m., when a light air sprung up from the westward, and I had strong hopes of being able to get in, or run the vessel on shore and destroy her, and thus escape capture.

At 2 p.m., being about four miles from the land, I deceived a Lisbon pilot on board. The ebb-tide now commenced running out of the Tagus, and I had the mortification to see a British frigate coming out with the first of it, with a light breeze from off the land. At 2 p.m. I was under her guns. She proved to be the *Granicus*, a 38 gun frigate, Captain W. F. Wise. We were all removed to the frigate, and the schooner taken in tow for Gibraltar.

Two days after our capture, *viz*., on the 3rd of December, we arrived at Gibraltar. Nearly all my officers and men were distributed and sent to England in different ships; the first and second lieutenants, with myself, were retained on board the *Granicus* to undergo an examination at the Admiralty Court.

The next day after our arrival, the frigate left port for Tetuan Bay, Morocco, opposite Gibraltar, to obtain water, and to be painted. We were taken on this little voyage, and had I not been a prisoner, I should have enjoyed very much the novelty of the excursion, which occupied three or four days. Captain Wise was a fine, gentlemanly man, and always treated me and my officers with respect and kindness. We messed in the ward-room. I had a state-room to myself, and was as comfortable and happy as I could be under the circumstances.

I used to dine with Captain Wise almost daily; he frequently said to me, "Don't feel depressed by captivity, but strive to forget that you are a prisoner, and imagine that you are only a passenger."

In the course of conversation, he said to me:

> Coggeshall, you Americans are a singular people as it respects seamanship and enterprise. In England, we cannot build such vessels as your Baltimore clippers; we have no such models, and even if we had them, they would be of no service to us, for we never could sail them as you do. We have now and then taken some of your schooners with our fast sailing frigates. They have sometimes caught one of them under their lee, in a heavy gale of wind, by out-carrying them. Then, again, we have taken a few with our boats in calm weather. We are afraid of their, long masts and heavy spars, and soon cut down and reduce them to our standard. We strengthen them, put up bulkheads, etc., after which they lose their sailing qualities, and are of no further service as cruising vessels.

He also remarked that the famous privateer *True Blooded Yankee,* which had done them so much mischief, once belonged to their navy; that they captured her from the French; that she was afterwards re-taken, and finally got into the hands of the Americans; that she then out-sailed everything, and that none of their cruisers could touch her, and concluded by adding that we were a most ingenious people.

I observed that perhaps he gave us too much credit for our skill in seamanship. He replied that he did not, but only stated the simple truth.

He soon afterward related a very amusing anecdote about one of our little schooners, near the mouth of the Garonne, in the Bay of Biscay. He said the *Superb*, seventy-four, was cruising off the mouth of that river, and that one morning, in a fog, they found one of our little schooners under her guns. They, of course, concluded she could not make her escape. The captain had his wife with him, who had the curiosity to watch the little schooner from the quarter deck, and on her return to England, related to her friends all the circumstances of her escape, which were as follows: "One morning we were quite near one of the American schooners, but could not catch her."

When asked the reason why, she replied: "Because we could not turn round soon enough."

Captain Wise then observed, that the lady related all the facts in the case in the few words, "Because we could not turn round soon enough." A nautical man, in describing it, would probably have said:

> The ship got into the wind and made a stern board, and before we could get sufficient steerage way upon her to tack after the schooner, the little craft had already made three or four tacks right in the wind's eye, and was soon out of reach of our shot, and thus made her escape, to our great surprise and mortification.

On another occasion, the conversation turned on the action between the *Constitution* and the *Guerriere*, when Captain Wise observed, that Captain Dacres was a cousin of his, and a personal friend. I remarked that Captain Hull was a relative of mine, and first cousin to my father; that I had personally known him for many years. He added, that it was a singular coincidence; and after discussing the subject good-naturedly for some time, a young midshipman, who was dining with us, expressed a wish that he could have an opportunity of being engaged with an American frigate, under like circumstances, when Captain Wise reprovingly replied: "Don't boast, youngster, perhaps if you should, you might get handsomely whipped."

In this way we often discussed the relative merits of our respective countries, with kindness and social courtesy. Captain Wise occasionally invited Mr. Depeyster, my first lieutenant, to dine with him, and in the characteristic goodness of his heart, said he would endeavour to get us paroled, and thus prevent our being sent to England. We stated to him, that we had voluntarily released more than thirty British prisoners, notwithstanding the American government gave a bounty (to letters-of-marque and privateers) of ten dollars per head for British prisoners brought into the United States. These facts Captain Wise represented to the governor, and also added, that the five English prisoners, found on board the *Leo*, said they had been very kindly treated, and he hoped his Excellency would release me and my two lieutenants upon our parole, and let us-return direct to the United States.

The governor refused to comply with the kind request of Captain Wise, and said he had positive orders from the British government to send every American prisoner, brought into that port, to England. When Captain Wise informed us that he was unable to obtain our liberty on parole, he gave me a letter of introduction to a friend in England, requesting him to use his best interest to get myself and my first and second lieutenants released on parole, and thus enable us to return forthwith to the United States. Mr. Daly, an Irish gentleman, second lieutenant of the *Granicus*, who was connected with several persons of distinction in England, also gave me a letter to a noble lady of great influence at court.

I regret I do not recollect her name, but I well remember the emphatic expression of the kind-hearted and generous Daly when he handed me the letter to his noble friend. "Cause this letter to be presented," said he, "and rely upon it, this lady will never allow you or your two friends to be sent to prison in England."

Mr. Depeyster was a high-spirited man, and when he learned that we could not obtain our liberty on parole, he became extremely vexed and excited, and told the ward-room officers that if it should ever please God to place him in a letter-of-marque or privateer, during the war, he would never again release an English prisoner, but would have a place built in the vessel to confine them until he should arrive in the United States; that the bounty given by the United States government rendered it an object to carry them into port, but from motives of humanity he had released many of their countrymen; and now they refused to parole three unfortunate men who were in their power. I said but little on the subject, but from that moment resolved to make my escape upon the first opportunity.

The next day after this conversation (December 8th), Captain Wise said,

> Captain Coggeshall, it is necessary that you and your officers should go on shore to the Admiralty Office, there to be examined with respect to the condemnation of your schooner, your late cruise, &c, and if you will pledge me your word and honour that you and your officers will not attempt to make your escape, I will permit you and the other two gentlemen to go on shore without a guard.

I told him at once that I would give the pledge not to attempt in any way to make my escape, and would also be answerable for Mr Depeyster and Mr. Allen. This ready compliance on my part resulted from a desire to gain an opportunity to reconnoitre the garrison, or in seaman's phrase, "to see how the land lay," in order to profit by the first chance to make my escape when not on parole.

We accordingly went on shore without a guard, and were conducted to the Admiralty Office. I was first examined, and was asked a great many questions, the greater part of which were from a printed copy; the answers were written down opposite the questions. It seemed to me to be more a matter of form, than for any special purpose. By-the-by, many of the inquiries appeared to me very unmeaning and unimportant. When they had finished with me, they commenced with Mr. Depeyster; and after asking him a few questions, the court of inquiry was adjourned until the next morning at 10 o'clock; and notifying us to be there precisely at the time appointed, we were dismissed. We then took a stroll about the town for an hour or two, returned on board, and reported ourselves to Captain Wise.

Thus far, not a shadow of suspicion had been visible on the countenances of Captain Wise, or his officers, that either of us would attempt to make our escape. In the evening, I consulted with Messrs. Depeyster and Allen on the subject of giving them the dodge upon the very first opportunity. I told them if the captain required my parole the next morning I would not give it, neither would I advise them to pledge their word and honour that they would not make their escape. I told them, furthermore, that I was resolved to slip away the first moment I saw a favourable opportunity, and would advise them to do the same, and not, from motives of delicacy, wait a moment for me.

The next morning, when dressing, I put all the money I had, say about one hundred gold twenty-*franc* pieces, in a belt that was around my person, and some fifteen or twenty Spanish dollars in my pocket, with some little relics and trifling keepsakes. Thus prepared, I went to breakfast in the ward-room. About 9 o'clock, Captain Wise sent for me, when the following dialogue ensued:

> Well, Coggeshall, I understand you and your officers are required at the Admiralty Office at 10 o'clock, and if you will again pledge your honour, as you did yesterday, that you will neither of you attempt to make your escape, you may go on shore without a guard, otherwise I shall be obliged to send one with you.

I watched his countenance closely, for a moment, to ascertain his real meaning, and whether he was determined to adhere strictly to the words he had just uttered, and then replied, "Captain Wise, I am surprised that you should think it possible for anyone to make his escape from Gibraltar."

He instantly saw I was sounding him, when he pleasantly but firmly said, "Come, come, it won't do, you must either pledge your word and honour that neither you nor your officers will attempt to make your escape, or I shall be compelled to send a guard with you."

I felt a little touched, and promptly replied, "you had better send a guard, sir."

Accordingly, he ordered the third lieutenant to take a sergeant and four marines with him and conduct us to the Admiralty Office.

At the hour appointed they recommenced the examination where they had left off the day before with Mr. Depeyster. I was sitting in the court-room, and Mr. Allen standing at the door, when he beckoned to me. I instantly went to the door, and found the lieutenant had left his post, and was not in sight. I then asked the sergeant whether he would go with us a short distance up the street to take a glass of wine. He readily complied with my request, leaving the marines at the door to watch Mr. Depeyster, and walked respectfully at a few paces behind us, up the street. (I had been once before at Gibraltar, and understood the town perfectly well). We soon came to a wine shop on a corner, with a door opening on each street.

While the soldier was standing at the door, Mr. A. and myself entered and called for a glass of wine, I drank a glass in haste, but unfortunately had no small change, and this circumstance alone, prevented my worthy friend from going with me. I hastily told him I would cross the little square in front, turn the first corner and there wait for him to join me. I then slipped out of the shop, passed quickly over the little park, and turned the corner agreed upon, without being seen by the sergeant, while he was watching at the opposite door. I waited some minutes on the corner for Mr. Allen, and was sadly disappointed that he did not make his appearance. I had now fairly committed myself, and found I had not a moment to spare. I therefore walked with a quick step towards the Land Port Gate, not that leading to the Peninsula, but the gate situated at the north-west extremity of the town.

My dress was a blue coat, black stock, and black cockade, with an eagle in the centre. The eagle I took care to remove, and then it was *tout-à-fait* an English cockade, and I had, on the whole, very much the appearance of an English naval officer. I said to myself when approaching the guard at the gate, "Now is the critical moment, and the most perfect composure and consummate impudence are necessary to a successful result."

I gave a stern look at the sentinel, when he returned me a respectful salute, and I was in another moment without the walls of Gibraltar.

I walked deliberately down the mole, or quay, where I was accosted by a great number of watermen offering to convey me on board my vessel. I employed one, and after getting off in the bay, he said, "Captain, which is your vessel?"

Here again I was at a loss to decide on an answer, but after gazing for a few moments on the different ships and the flags of different nations, my eye caught sight of a galliot with a Norwegian ensign flying, and I said to myself, "The Norwegians are a virtuous, honest people, and I am not afraid to trust them."

I had been in their country, and understood the character of these hardy, honest-hearted sons of the North. After a moment's hesitation, I replied to the boatman, "That is my vessel," pointing to the friendly galliot, and we were soon alongside. I jumped on board, and inquired for the captain, who soon made his appearance. I told him I had something to communicate to him. He told me to follow him into the cabin. I immediately asked him whether he was willing to befriend a man in distress.

He said, "Tell me your story, and I will try to serve you." I frankly told him I was captain of the American letter-of-marque schooner lately sent into port by the frigate *Granicus*, and that I had made my escape from the garrison, and desired to get over to Algeciras as soon as possible; that I had money enough, but still I wanted his friendship, confidence, and protection.

The good old gentleman had scarcely waited to hear my story to the end, before he grasped me by the hand and said, in a kind and feeling manner, "I will be your friend, I will protect you; I was once a prisoner in England, and I know what it is to be a prisoner; rest assured, my dear sir, I will do all I can to assist you." I offered him a dollar to pay and discharge the boatman, and remained myself below in the cabin.

He said, "Put up your money, I have small change, and I will pay him what is just and right."

After dispatching the boatman, he returned below and said, "Now take off your coat, and put on this large pea-jacket and fur cap."

In this costume, and with a large pipe in my mouth, I was, in less than two minutes, transformed into a regular Norwegian. Returning again on deck, I asked my good friend the captain whether I could rely on his mate and sailors not to betray me; he said, "They are honest, and perfectly trustworthy, and you need be under no apprehension on their account."

We took a social dinner together, when he observed; "I will now go on shore for an hour or two, and hear all I can about your escape, and will come back early in the evening and relate to you all I learn."

In the evening the old captain returned, pleased and delighted. He said he never saw such a hubbub as there was about town; that the whole garrison seemed to be on the look-out, that the Town Major, with the military and civil police, were searching every hole and corner in Gibraltar for the captain of the American privateer; that both of my officers were put in confinement, and that the lieutenant of the frigate who had the charge of us had been arrested; in short, there was "the devil to pay," because the captain of the privateer could not be found.

The next morning I stated to my worthy friend how extremely anxious I was to go over to Algeciras, and how mortified I should be to be taken again on board the *Granicus*. He answered,

> Leave that to me I am well acquainted with a gang of smugglers who belong to Algeciras, and often sell them gin, tobacco, and other articles of trade; they will be here on board my galliot at 9 o'clock this evening, and will probably start for Algeciras about midnight, after they have made all their purchases. When they come I will arrange with them to take you as a passenger.

About 9 o'clock that evening, a long, fast-rowing boat came silently alongside filled with men; and certainly a more desperate, villainous-looking set was never seen. Their leader and several of his men came on board the galliot. and after having purchased several articles and taken a glass of gin all around, the old captain inquired of the *patroon* of the boat what hour he intended to start for Algeciras, and said, that the reason of his asking the question was that his brother wanted to go to that place for a few days upon business, and he wished to engage a passage for him, and that he should be glad if his brother could lodge for a few days with his family.

He answered that he should return again about midnight, and would willingly take the captain's brother, and that if he could put up with rough fare, he was welcome to stay at his house as long as he pleased. I accordingly got ready my little bundle, which consisted of a few small articles, such as a shirt or two (for I did not forget to wear three at the time I left the *Granicus*), and stowed it away in my hat. I agreed with my friend, the Norwegian, to leave the cap and pea jacket with the American Consul at Algeciras, to be returned to him by some safe conveyance in the course of a few days. Agreeable to promise the boat came on board precisely at 12 o'clock, and after my friend, the captain, had again cautioned the *patroon* of the boat, to take good care of his brother, we started.

The water in the bay was smooth, though the night was dark and favourable to the safe prosecution of the passage. The distance is about eight or ten miles from Gibraltar; and after rowing two hours, we arrived near the harbour, when we showed a light in a lantern for a minute or two, and then covered it with a jacket. This signal was repeated two or three times, until it was answered in the same way from the shore. We approached the port cautiously, and landed in silence. The *patroon* took me by the arm, and lead me through many a dark winding passage. On our way we passed by several sentinels, and were frequently hailed with the shrill sound of "*Quien Viva?*" To these salutations some friendly answer was returned, and thus everything passed smoothly on, until at length we arrived at the humble dwelling of the smuggler.

In Spain, the *contrabandists* are a desperate class of men, and often spread dread and fear through a wide region of country. In many instances they are so numerous and strong that they often put the whole power of the government at defiance. The gang that brought me to Algeciras were about twenty in number, all armed to the teeth with long knives, pistols, swords, &c, and had no doubt made their arrangements during the day with the officers and sentinels who were to mount guard that night. Of course they made them a compensation in some way or other, in order that they should meet with nothing to interfere with, or obstruct their nocturnal enterprises.

Early in life I had made several voyages to Spain and its colonies in America, and had acquired a pretty good knowledge of the Spanish character. I had also picked up enough of the language to enable me to make my way among them without difficulty.

There is something about the Spaniard that immediately inspires confidence; so much so, that although surrounded by this desperate gang of smugglers, I had not the smallest fear for my safety. It was now near three o'clock in the morning, when we entered the small, low cabin of the *patroon*. The interior consisted of one room of moderate size, with a mat hung up, to serve as a partition, to separate the different members of the family, which consisted of the *patroon*, Antonio, his wife, and two children. The eldest, a girl, was about eight or nine years of age, and the boy, a fine little fellow, about six. Antonio was thirty-five or forty years old, and his wife, a good-looking woman, twenty-eight or thirty.

With this family I was soon placed upon the most friendly and intimate footing. A straw bed was prepared for me behind the mat screen. Before saying good-night Antonio told me he should leave the house very early in the morning to look after his boat and smuggled goods, and should not return until noon next day. He said his wife and little daughter would provide breakfast for me, and would purchase whatever I wished at any time. After these preliminaries were settled we all said, "*Buenas noches*," and dropped asleep.

About 7 o'clock the next morning I furnished the smuggler's wife with money to purchase bread, butter, eggs and coffee; and when breakfast was prepared, the mother, the two children, and myself, ate our social meal together. I then took a stroll about the town of Algeciras in my Norwegian costume, and silently observed what was going on, without conversing with any person; when I entered a coffee house I generally took a newspaper, and, as I said nothing, no one appeared to notice me. I had broken the quarantine laws, and therefore deemed it prudent to keep on my disguise for a few days, and continue to live in perfect seclusion. The next night, Antonio was to leave this place for Gibraltar, and by him I sent the following letter to my friend the good Norwegian.

"Algeciras, Dec. 13th, 1814.

"Captain of the Galliot:

"My dear, Good Friend: I am happy to inform you that I landed here last night, or rather at 2 o'clock in the morning, and have taken up my abode in the family of our friend, the *patroon* Antonio, and now consider myself in perfect safety—all which I owe to your kind and generous conduct. While I live my heart will ever beat with gratitude to you, my excellent friend, and if it should never be in my power to reward your disinterested kindness, I sincerely pray that God will reward and bless you and yours to the third and fourth generations. Although I live in an obscure cabin, and am here a stranger in a strange land, still I am happier than I could possibly be in a palace, deprived of my liberty.

"I shall remain here a few days in disguise, and shall be happy to receive a letter from you *per* Antonio. I am extremely anxious to hear what has become of my officers, and whether they have been sent prisoners to England. You said it was possible you might come over to Algeciras. I hope you will conclude to do so, and thin I shall have the pleasure of enjoying your society, while you remain in this place.

"*Adieu*, my dear Sir, and believe me always with esteem,
"Your grateful friend,
"George Coggeshall."

Antonio was absent almost all the time during the three days I remained in his family. I furnished money, and the good Maria purchased and prepared our frugal meals. When I returned from a stroll about the town, I always took care to provide cakes and *bonbons* for the children; so we soon became very good friends, and all lived very happily together, and upon terms of the most perfect equality.

After remaining here for a period of three days, I began to tire of this mode of life, and was determined to ascertain how I could get to Cadiz, where I knew I should find friends, and be further removed from the mortifying scenes through which I had so lately passed. Accordingly, on the morning of the fourth day of my landing at Algeciras, I repaired to a café, and inquired of one of the servants whether there was an American Consul residing in the city. The boy seemed intelligent, and instantly replied, that *Don* Horatio Sprague, the former Consul at Gibraltar, was residing here, and that he was, "*un hombre de bien*." I asked for his address, when he called a boy to show me the house; so that in fifteen minutes after, I was knocking at Mr. Sprague's door, and was soon admitted into his hospitable mansion.

He was, of course, surprised to see a man of my appearance walk boldly into his parlour. I soon, however, explained that I was not exactly what I appeared to be; that I was an American in distress, and throwing off my great fur cap and pea-jacket, looked somewhat more like an American. I told my story, and was received and treated like a brother. He was just going to take breakfast and said, "You will breakfast with us, and then I will send my nephew, Mr. Leach, with you for your bundle, and you will then return and take up your abode with me during your stay at Algeciras."

After a social breakfast, having doffed my cap and pea-jacket, and being supplied with a hat and other articles of dress to correspond, Mr. Leach kindly accompanied me to the humble dwelling of Maria. To my great surprise, on entering the cabin, the poor woman was very distant, curtsied with profound respect, and appeared altogether like another person, while the children were shy, and appeared to avoid me.

At first I felt hurt at the alteration, but a moment's reflection convinced me that it was quite natural, and I loved them not the less for their distant behaviour: while in my disguise, they looked upon me as one of the family; but now the circumstances were changed, they regarded me in quite another light; and I felt for a moment that the artificial rules of society were chilling to a generous heart. Maria told Mr. Leach that she always thought I was a gentleman, and that she was quite happy to serve me.

After making the family suitable presents, I took my leave, promising that they should frequently see me while I remained in Algeciras, which promise I took care rigidly to fulfil.

I was now quite at home with one of the best of men, whose greatest pleasure has ever been to make others happy. His excellent nephew, William Leach, Esq., was also a fine young gentleman, and as we were all Americans together, the most perfect confidence reigned throughout this delightful family. During my stay here, I was amused with a little incident that occurred while at dinner at Mr. Sprague's table.

A young English friend came over on Sunday to dine with Mr. Sprague. During dinner, Mr. Sprague asked the young man what was said in Gibraltar about the captain of the American letter-of-marque having made his escape from the garrison. He said that it caused a great deal of excitement and speculation; some said the lieutenant who had charge of him was very culpable, and even insinuated that there must have been bribery connected with the business; that it was altogether a very strange affair, that a man should be able, in open daylight, to make his escape from Gibraltar. After answering many other questions on the subject, he wound up by saying that the captain must be a clever man, and for his part he wished him God-speed.

The young man had no suspicion that I was an American, or had any connection with the business. During the conversation, whenever I caught the eye of Mr. Leach, it was with the greatest difficulty I could command my countenance. Everything, however, passed off very well, and we often joked on the subject of the honest simplicity of their young English friend.

I remained from day to day at Algeciras, anxiously waiting to hear from my two lieutenants, Messrs. Depeyster and Allen; in hopes that they would by some means be able to make their escape, and not be sent prisoners to England. During the daytime I used frequently to ride in the country with Mr. Sprague. In the evening we often made up an agreeable whist party, and, among other social enjoyments, my young friend Leach introduced me to two or three respectable and very agreeable Spanish families. In these families I spent many pleasant evenings, and had my officers and crew been at liberty, I should have been quite contented and happy.

At length, after waiting at Algeciras about ten days, I learned with pain and sincere regret that all my officers and men had been sent as prisoners to England. and I now began seriously to think of leaving this place for Cadiz.

There are only two ways of travelling with safety in Spain: one is genteel and expensive, *viz.*, with a strong guard of soldiers; the other is in simple disguise, so that no robber can feel any interest in molesting you on the road. This mode I determined to adopt.

Algeciras lies in lat. 36° 7' North, long. 5° 24' West, on the west side of Gibraltar Bay, and distant from that place by water about eight miles; while to go round the bay by land is about double the distance, say seventeen or eighteen miles. It contains a population of about 4,500 to 5.000 souls, has a good harbour and considerable traffic. It is a very old city, and in ancient times was strongly fortified.

Mr. Sprague [1] is a native of Massachusetts, and has long been the American Consul at Gibraltar. He is extensively known and universally beloved and respected. His house has been for many years the seat of a generous hospitality. Although he has resided so long abroad, he has not lost a particle of American feeling, or the ardour of a true patriot. His nephew, Mr. William Leach, as also a worthy, gentlemanly man, of superior abilities, and will ever be remembered by me with deep gratitude.

After remaining in Algeciras about a fortnight, I hired a mule and a guide to proceed with me to Cadiz. My kind friends furnished me with provisions and stores for a journey of two days. I procured a dress such as the peasants wear in this part of Andalusia, and thus prepared, on the morning of the 26th of December, 1814, bade *adieu* to my two excellent countrymen, from whom I had received so many disinterested favours.

After leaving the town, we travelled about a league on a tolerably smooth road, and then turned off into a winding footpath. I was on the mule, and my guide, a merry fellow, trudged along on foot, sometimes by my side, sometimes a few yards ahead, and when we came to a smooth path, I allowed him to ride on the beast behind me. The distance from Algeciras to Cadiz is about forty miles, and it was our intention to go to Medina and put up for the night. I soon found we had a very intricate and difficult journey to perform.

The whole country presented a most wild and desolate appearance; in fact it seemed to me that there could have been little or no change in this part of Spain, for the last five or six centuries. There were no public roads, a very thin and scattered

---

1. When this narrative was written, Mr. Sprague was alive, but I am sorry to say, he is now dead Without this explanation, there would be a discrepancy in the relation of this part of my history.

population, that lived in a wretched state of poverty.

Sometimes we travelled through deep and dark ravines, overgrown with trees and bushes: and after passing a deep and gloomy dell, where we lost sight of the sun at times for a space of half an hour, we would then commence ascending a high mountain. We generally found a time-worn foot-path running in a zigzag direction up these dreary mountains. This mode of ascending would, in seaman's phrase, be called "beating up."

The progress certainly is slow and fatiguing, but the traveller is richly rewarded for all his toil, when once on the top of one of these stupendous mountains. Here he has a splendid view of the Straits of Gibraltar and the broad Atlantic on the south and east, while the wild and unbroken scenery of the surrounding country is truly magnificent.

We continued to travel on in this manner until about 2 o'clock in the afternoon, when we came to a miserable *posada*. Here we stopped to feed the mule and rest and refresh ourselves for an hour, and found, to my great surprise, we had only made about ten miles from Algeciras, and were still about the same distance from Medina.

The people of the United States can scarcely believe that an old country like Spain is in such a wretched condition as I found this part of it; without roads, the land generally uncultivated, without hotels or taverns to accommodate strangers, and infested with robbers and *banditti*; even in the vicinity of cities and large towns, there is no safety in travelling without a military guard. This is certainly a gloomy picture of poor Spain— once so great and powerful, now distracted by factions and civil war, divested of the greatest part of her once rich colonies, her government weak, without money and without credit.

There are many causes for this sad downfall, but the principal are, ignorance, idleness, superstition, priest-craft, and bad government.

Oh, happy America! how glorious art thou among the nations of the earth! Long may an all-wise Being shower his blessings upon thee, and keep thee from the wiles of superstition and popery!

My guide Manuel said the mule was ready, and he only waited my pleasure to proceed. I said, "*Adios, Señor,*" to our ignorant *posadero*, and we were again wending our intricate way towards Medina. It is impossible for me to describe the windings and turnings, the uphill and down course of these villainous passageways. (I will not call them roads, for they deserve not the name,)

At length we caught sight of the desired city where we were to remain during the approaching night. On beholding Medina I was forcibly struck with the beautiful simile of the Saviour's, that "a city set on a hill cannot be hid."

This is literally true with respect to Medina; it stands on a high hill, its walls, churches and houses are all plastered and whitened, and it may be seen at a great distance in every direction. For about a league before we reached this elevated city, we came into a more pleasant country; we now and then met with patches of cultivated and pasture land, and saw also occasionally a small *hacienda*, with running brooks and marks of civilization. In the immediate neighbourhood of the town, I frequently saw small stone bridges, which appeared extremely ancient; they were evidently not built in modern days, but were probably erected either by the Romans or Moors, in the olden times, when Spain was subdued by these ancient and once powerful nations. For some distance around the foot of the hill or mountain on which Medina is located, the grounds are pleasantly diversified with olive fields, orange gardens and green meadows, on which herds of cattle were grazing.

When we passed through these rural scenes, the weather was soft and fine, and here we inhaled the light and exhilarating air from the orange groves. What a delightful country! God has done everything for this people, but they have done nothing for themselves. How lovely is nature when softened and cultivated by the hand of industry, and how happy is man when governed by just and righteous principles, for the benefit of himself and his fellow-man!

Fortunately we arrived at this singular city just before sundown, which enabled me to enjoy a beautiful view from its high walls, while the sun was gilding with its setting rays the towers of the churches, and the clouds and mountains beyond them. It certainly was not so grand and sublime as that which I saw in the morning from the top of the lofty mountains, but it was truly delightful to behold the peaceful scenery of pastoral life, contrasted with the wild and savage ravines in the background of the picture. Who can behold such scenes as these and not become a better man, while thus looking through nature up to nature's God?

"How wonderful are thy works, O God, in wisdom hast Thou made them all."

My guide led me to a miserable *posada* to put up for the night. When I asked for a room, I was shown into a dark, gloomy, prison-like place about ten feet square, with a stone floor and but one chair, without a bed or a table, and all I could get from the *posadero* was a few boiled eggs, with some sour wine. Fortunately, my kind friends in Algeciras had provided stores for myself and guide; so that with the eggs and wine we made a tolerable supper. Being fatigued with the day's ride, I asked for a bed, when a coarse one of straw was brought and spread upon the stone floor, without either blanket, sheet, or pillow. I threw myself upon this bed, and, with my cloak for a covering, was soon asleep, and scarcely awoke until roused at daylight, by my guide, to resume our journey.

Whether Manuel took me to this miserable stopping place from motives of policy—to avoid suspicion and observation—I know not. It is, however, more than probable that there are better lodging-houses for those better acquainted with the town. I had entire confidence in my guide, he being recommended by my kind friends Messrs. Sprague and Leach, and was therefore satisfied. After settling our bill, we were soon on the road descending from the lofty city. I regret I had not an opportunity of seeing more of the town, but as we had not made but half the journey, and Cadiz was still twenty-two miles distant, it was absolutely necessary to hasten our departure.

I saw it was a walled town, and was told it contained about eight or ten thousand inhabitants; with a fort, or castle, two or three churches, five or six monasteries and two hospitals, and that there were several manufactories of earthenware, which was principally sold in Cadiz and Seville.

After leaving Medina, we found the country less mountainous and the roads tolerably good. We passed through several small towns and villages, and as we drew near to Cadiz, were able to purchase the ordinary necessaries of life. Notwithstanding we had only a journey of twenty-two miles from Medina, we did not arrive in Cadiz until 5 o'clock in the afternoon, on the 28th of December, 1814. Here I put up at one of the principal hotels for the night. The next morning I settled with and dispatched my guide; we parted mutually satisfied. I then sallied out in pursuit of my own countrymen, and soon had the good fortune to meet with an old friend, James Haggarty, Esq., a native of Richmond, Virginia. I immediately took lodgings with that gentleman, in a private-family, which consisted of a widow lady and her four daughters.

Señora Quartini was a native of Cadiz, and a kind, excellent woman. The daughters were very amiable and obliging, and from their frequent intercourse with American gentlemen, two of them had acquired a pretty good knowledge of the English language. These benevolent people were full of sympathy and kindness. They were truly pious, without ostentation, and although Roman Catholics, were free from bigotry. Their goodness of heart and simple manners made even strangers feel perfectly at home, and I regarded myself as fortunate in becoming an inmate of this delightful family.

My friend Haggarty introduced me to our Consul, Joseph E. Bloomfield, Esq., and also to Richard W. Mead, Esq., and his amiable family. Mr. Mead, was from Philadelphia, and a resident merchant here at this time. During my stay, I experienced much hospitality both from our worthy Consul and Mr. Mead. The latter gentleman politely gave me a free ticker to his box in the theatre, and rendered me many little civilities, which are always gratifying to a stranger. My friend Haggarty was always ready to negotiate my drafts on Bordeaux or London, so that, as far as personal comfort was concerned, I had nothing to complain of.

A few days after my arrival here, I received a letter from my friend William Leach, Esq., informing me that the good old Norwegian, soon after I left Algeciras, came over from Gibraltar to see me, and that he had been unable to learn the fate of my officers. The letter also brought me glad tidings of the victory of General Brown over the British, at Port Erie, and of the prospect of an early treaty of peace being agreed upon by the ambassadors of the two nations, at Ghent.

On the first of January, 1815, I wrote to my first lieutenant, informing him of my movements since we parted at Gibraltar, and enclosed him a supply of money and the letters of introduction, so kindly given to me by Captain Wise, and Lieutenant Daly, hoping that they might be of use to him and the other officers if they were sent to England.

The Spaniards are a peculiar people, and their character can only be learned by a long residence in their country. An intelligent Spaniard prides himself more on what his country has been, than on what it is at present. He mourns over her fallen greatness, and shrugs his shoulders with a sigh.

The higher classes are extremely romantic, both in love and friendship, and they consider their word fully equal to a sealed bond. This high sense of honour sometimes descends even to the highway robber; for example, I once knew a gentleman who was robbed of $400 (all the money he had with him), on the highway from Seville to Cadiz. He observed that his was a hard case, that he had not sufficient means to defray his expenses back to Cadiz.

The robber observed, "*Amigo meo,*" (how much will be sufficient to pay expenses on the road?)

The gentleman replied, "I think about fifteen or twenty dollars."

The robber handed him twenty dollars, with a pompous air, and drawing himself up to his full height, said: "Take it, and don't say, on your return to Cadiz, that you met with a robber, who was incapable of a generous action."

The ladies also partake of the same characteristic traits; they are very effeminate and interesting, with soft and pleasing manners, and though so gentle and fascinating, are, when roused, perfect, heroines in courageous action. At the time of which I am writing there was a large circus or amphitheatre in the vicinity of Cadiz, spacious enough to accommodate 10,000 people. I have seen the edifice filled to overflowing with all classes of the community, from the Governor and the public authorities of the town with their families, down to the common boatmen and labourers, collected together to see three or four men, on foot and on horseback, fight and kill eight or ten wild bulls.

When a bull has shown uncommon fury, and a corresponding degree of coolness and courage was displayed on the part of the matadors, I have seen this vast assemblage thrown into perfect ecstasies, and the fine ladies in the boxes wave their white handkerchiefs with enthusiastic cries of "*Viva, Viva,*" and throw down garlands of flowers to the matadors in the arena.

After relating these apparent contradictions in the Spanish character, I think it will readily be conceded that it requires a long residence among them fully to understand their peculiarities. I have been for many years in communication with Spain and her colonies, and have arrived at the conclusion that there is less medium in the Spanish character than among other nations, and that there, the best and the worst people in the world are to be found.

I was living here perfectly at leisure, and, what with the social intercourse of the friendly family with whom I lodged, the theatre and other public amusements, I found the time passed away pleasantly and rapidly.

On the 14th of January I received a warm-hearted letter from my kind and ever obliging friend Horatio Sprague, in which he mentioned that my escape had been the wonder of Gibraltar, that an unremitted search was made for me during three days, both in the city and among the vessels in the bay, and that the noble old Norwegian was fairly infested with midshipmen and others searching after me. Although I was agreeably located in Cadiz, and found many kind friends from whom I had received much hospitality and friendly favours, still I was an idler, and began to tire of such an inactive, useless life; and as there was no prospect of obtaining a passage home from this place, I decided to take passage in a small Portuguese schooner for Lisbon.

This was a coasting vessel, manned with a captain, mate, and ten men, just double the number of men that would be employed to navigate an American vessel of the same size. In this schooner I agreed for a berth in the cabin, and was to furnish my own stores, with the proviso, that the cook should likewise do all the cooking I might require. With this understanding, I purchased a few hams, a bag of bread, a demijohn of wine, tea, sugar, coffee, and other stores, sufficient for fifteen days.

The schooner being ready, I bade *adieu* to all my friends in Cadiz on the 15th of February, having been there just forty-nine days. I sailed out of the bay with a heavy heart at parting with so many who were true and faithful. I had a few choice books with me to read on the passage, and had become so much accustomed to all kinds of life, that I felt I should be able to accommodate myself to almost any condition. I soon found that the captain was a good disciplinarian, and managed his vessel very well. Although he had never made a foreign voyage, he knew the coast, and understood his business, and I felt myself fortunate in having fallen into such good hands.

This was the first time I had ever sailed under the Portuguese flag, and many of their customs were quite new to me. One peculiarity I never witnessed before.

Three times a day the captain summoned everybody on board to the quarter-deck; then they all knelt down, morning, noon, and evening, and repeated their prayers, the captain always taking the lead. The schooner was a dull sailer, and as we had generally light winds. we did not reach Cape St, Vincent until the fifth day after leaving Cadiz. This is a high, bold cape, lying in lat. 37° 3' North, long. 9° 2' West, We passed close to this conspicuous headland, I should think not more than half a mile distant, on the 20th of February at 4 o'clock in the afternoon, when the captain called all hands to the quarter-deck, and addressed them as follows:

> Officers and men, it has pleased God to bring us in safety thus far on our voyage; now let us all kneel down and thank him for his goodness and mercy to us poor sinners, and beseech him to conduct us in safety to our destined port.

They were, I should think, some fifteen or twenty minutes occupied in prayer and then returned to their ordinary avocations.

We crept slowly along the shore, and on the 23rd of February got safe into Lisbon, after a passage of eight days. I regret that I recollect neither the captain name nor that of his vessel. I had made so many voyages to this place, that upon landing I felt quite a home, and was soon in the society of many of my own countrymen. I met in Lisbon a New York friend James L. Kennedy, Esq., who came out to that place supercargo of an American vessel, and was, like myself very desirous of returning to New York. Mr. Kennedy, during his stay in Lisbon, became acquainted with a Portuguese house in the wine trade.

These gentlemen owned a nice little brig of about one hundred and eighty tons burthen, called the *Tres Hermanos*. They loaded her with a cargo of wine, oil, etc., and agreed with him to proceed in her to New York as supercargo, with liberty to return again to Lisbon in the brig, or remain in New York, whichever should suit his interest. She was commanded by a very young man, with but little experience, and had a miserable set of Portuguese sailors.

In this brig one of the owners offered me a passage, free from charge, upon condition that I would assist the young captain with my experience and advice. He had never been to the

United States, and said he should be very happy to profit by my experience. My friend Kennedy was also very desirous that I should go, and said we should enjoy each other's society, and that would shorten the passage. I must confess I had some serious misgivings on the subject of sailing under the Portuguese flag with an inefficient captain and a filthy crew; but as there was no American vessel to sail for several weeks, and the treaty of peace with Great Britain was not ratified, I concluded to take passage in this neutral vessel.

Before sailing, the principal owner told the captain to attend to the comfort of Mr. Kennedy and myself, and to treat us with respect, and consult me always on the most judicious course to steer, etc., etc. He promised to comply with the request of the owner, and with much complacency said he had no doubt we should be very happy together. All these promises he most shamefully broke a few days after we got to sea. I remained in Lisbon just eighteen days, and, on the 13th of March, sailed in the good brig *Tres Hermanos* for New York.

After getting to sea, I was determined not to interfere with the course of the vessel, nor to proffer my advice, unless it was called for, and then with the greatest delicacy; and never, in the slightest degree, made any remark to offend the mates or sailors during the long and tedious passage. The little, narrow-minded captain did not consult me at all on the course of the vessel, and absolutely appeared so jealous of me, that my position was almost insupportable; and had not my friend Kennedy been on board, and the brig bound to New York, I should probably have been worse treated by these wretches.

Although I scarcely exchanged a word with one of his men during the passage, I once overheard them say they should like to knock me in the head and throw me overboard. In lieu of steering a judicious course, and keeping a fair distance to the northward of the Western Islands, the poor devil steered down among the islands, where we were becalmed for several days, and made miserable progress getting to the westward.

The brig was in such a filthy condition, that Mr. Kennedy

and myself suffered out of measure with one of the plagues of Egypt. The probability is, that before leaving Lisbon the sailors were allowed to sleep in the berths in the cabin, and thus every part of the vessel was overrun with vermin.

By contrary winds and bad management, our passage was prolonged to fifty-eight days, On the 9th of May we took a Sandy Hook pilot, and the same day arrived in New York. I was rejoiced to land once more in the United States, after an absence of sixteen months and twenty-one days.

I cannot leave this brig without warning my friends and countrymen never to take passage across the Atlantic in a Portuguese-vessel of any description.

On my return home, I found all my family and friends well. Peace was again restored to the United States.

Seven and a half months after this date, I received a letter from Mr. Henry Allen, the worthy young man, who was second lieutenant with me in the *Leo*, from which I make the following extracts:—

Salem, December 24th.

Captain George Coggeshall:

Dear Sir: If you have seen Mr. Depeyster, he has probably informed you of my unfortunate attempt to escape from Gibraltar.

After waiting about ten minutes, (time I thought sufficient for you to reach the mole), I left the wine shop in the same manner as yourself, and had already passed the two gates, and was on the mole, when I was arrested by the sergeant under whose charge we were, who demanded, in the most severe manner, where you were. Sensible that you must have been on the mole at the time, I told him that when you left me, you were going to Messrs. Turnbull & Co.'s.

He immediately turned back, and with myself proceeded to the house. After gaining it, and passing away about forty-five minutes, he suspected I was deceiving him, consequently returned with me to the mole to make all inquiries, but in vain. He left your description with the officer of the mole. He then dragged me to the town major, who went immediately on horseback to every passage in the garrison with your description.

Fortune and my best wishes, however, favoured your escape.

We were carried to England, and remained till the 29th of April, then released, and I came home as an agent for one of the cartels.

CHAPTER 9

Great Meeting of Merchants

The privateer *York*, of Baltimore, having returned safe home from a successful cruise on the coast of Brazil, and among the Islands in the West Indies, we find in connection with this fortunate vessel the following remarks, published in a weekly journal at that time:

> The successful cruises of our privateers, speak in a voice of thunder, and tell Congress how the enemy should be assailed. The prizes of the *York*, privateer, are worth at least, a million and a half dollars.
>
> It is true that the two richest prizes recently captured by the *York*, may be recaptured by the enemy, still the privateer will reap a plentiful harvest from the spoils with which she is laden.
>
> We hope and trust the Navy department will be directed to fit out fifty such vessels as the *York*, to cruise during the coming winter, with orders to burn, sink and destroy the enemy's property, which we hope may amount to some fifteen or twenty millions of dollars. Perhaps this is the best way to fight England at sea, after all. We have already reaped a full harvest of naval glory, and we should now attack the foe in the way that we can do him the most essential injury.
>
> The *York* did not lose a single man during her cruise of thirteen weeks

Prizes Captured by Privateers

The following prizes were taken by the *Surprise*, and burnt: brig *Queen Charlotte*, ship *Milnes*, brig *Lively*, schooner *Prince Regent*, brig *Wilting Maid*, brig *Polly*, schooner *Sally*. The English privateer *Lively*, 1 gun, seventeen men, brought into Salem. Ship *Caledonia*, from Cork for Quebec, with dry-goods rum, etc., worth , $250,000, divested her of goods to the value of $50,000. Brigs *Eagle*, *Traveller*, *Wellington* (4 guns and fifteen men), and *Eliza*, were made cartels of, to release the prisoners. The *Surprise* also captured the brig *Albion*, schooner *Charlotte Ann*, and recaptured the boat *Ann*.

The privateer *Surprise*, belonged to Baltimore, and was a very fortunate vessel. During her last cruise, which only occupied one month, she captured twenty sail of British merchantmen, including one small privateer. She made 197 prisoners, released 160, and brought into port thirty-seven. She divested the ship *Caledonia*, and other prizes, of British goods to the amount of $60,000, and arrived safe at Salem, laden with rich spoils taken from the enemy. Soon after she captured the *Caledonia*, the English sailors left on board recaptured her, but fortunately the privateer fell in with her again, took out all the Englishmen, and sent her into Salem.

A St. Johns, Newfoundland paper of Sept. 8th. mentions the capture of several vessels by the *Surprise*, and adds, Captain Sexton, of the *Endeavour*, McFarlane, of the *Caledonia*, Captain Reid, of the *Milnes*, with their crews, were landed this morning from the brig *Traveller*. They speak in the handsomest terms of the politeness and attention they experienced from Captain Barnes and his officers, during the time they were on board the privateer.

Three vessels, captured by the *Shark*, of New York, off the coast of Portugal, and being of little value, were given up. Two others were manned, and ordered for the United States.

Ketch Expedition, with 75 pipes of wine, and 1,150 quintals of *barilla*, sent into New York by the *Grampus*, of Baltimore.

Schooner ———, with dry-goods, sent into Salem by the *Vi-*

per, of that port.

Brig *Catherine and William*, of London, with dry-goods, prize to the *Grampus*, lost near Beaufort, S. C, on the 20th of Sept.

Cutter *Flying Fish*, with sweet oil, captured by the *Sabine*, of Baltimore, and sent into a southern port.

Brig *Aaron*, with wine and codfish, captured by the same, and sent into an eastern port.

Two ships taken by the *Syren*, off the British coast, and. destroyed.

The *Steady*, from Bordeaux for Newfoundland, and the *James*, from St. Jean de Luce, taken and burnt, by the *Prince of Neufchâtel*.

Brig *Colier*, from Cork for Quebec, with a full cargo of provisions, captured by the *Amelia*, of Baltimore, and burnt.

Brig *Harmony*, from Alicant, for Newfoundland, with salt and wine, captured by the same, divested of the latter, and made a cartel of, to relieve her of prisoners.

Brig *Elizabeth*, from Cork for Newfoundland, captured by the same and burnt.

Ship ———, of 8 guns, from Greenock for Newfoundland, with dry-goods and wine, captured by the same, divested of her cargo, and sent into port.

The *Amelia* also captured, and ordered into port the brig *Ann*, with a valuable cargo. She had a short combat with the *Neptune*, but no person was hurt on either side. When last heard of, she had thirty-two prisoners onboard, who were very troublesome. After manning all her prizes, she had only fifty-eight of her crew left.

British schooner ———, captured by the *Leach*, of Salem, divested and given up to the prisoners.

Sloop *Jane*, 70 tons, from St. Jean de Luce, for Falmouth, captured by the *Prince of Neufchâtel,* privateer, of New York, and burnt.

Brig *Triton*, 187 tons, two guns, from Cadiz for London, with an assorted cargo, captured by the same, part of the cargo taken out and the vessel sunk.

Transport brig *Aaron*, 142 tons, 4 guns, from Gibraltar for Lisbon, in ballast, taken by the same, and burnt.

Brig *Apollo*, 135 tons, from St. Ubes for Riga, with a cargo of salt, captured by the same and burnt.

Cutter *General Doyle*, 87 tons, coppered, from Leghorn for Bristol, with a cargo of oil, captured by the same, and burnt.

Sloop *George*, 50 tons, from Milford Haven for Plymouth, with coals, taken by the same, and sunk.

Brig *Barewick Packet*, from Cork for Bristol, in ballast, with fifty passengers, taken by the same, and made a cartel of.

Brig *Sibron*, 200 tons 4 guns, from Greenock for Cork, in ballast, captured by the same, and sunk.

Brig *Nymph*, 150 tons, from St. Jean de Luce for Cork, with dry-goods, etc., captured by the same, divested of the dry-goods; the rest of the cargo was thrown overboard. The *Nymph* was then given up to the prisoners.

Brig *Albion*, 155 tons, 4 guns, from Greenock for Cork, with dry-goods and other valuable articles, captured by the same, divested of her valuable articles, and burnt.

Ship *Harmony*, 290 tons, 4 guns, from Greenock for Cork, with dry-goods and other valuable articles, captured by the same, divested, and ordered into port. She was retaken by the English a few days after.

Brig *Charlotte*, 190 tons, 8 guns, from Rio Janeiro, with a cargo of hides, captured by the same, and burnt.

Brig *Mary Ann*, 103 tons, from St. Johns for Barbadoes, with a cargo of lumber, captured by the same, and burnt.

Ship *Neptune*, from Greenock for Newfoundland 450 tons burthen, 8 guns, captured by the *Amelia*, and sent into New York, with an assorted cargo of valuable goods.

Schooner *Ann*, with sugar and molasses, from Halifax for the new British port of Castine, captured in the following manner: When she sailed, she had on board four American seamen, who shipped in Halifax, and when off the mouth of the Penobscot river, they rose upon the captain and the remainder of the crew (six in number), confined them below, secured all the fire-arms on board, and arrived in safety at Thomastown.

Ship *James*, from London for Quebec, with dry-goods, etc., captured by the *Portsmouth*, of Portsmouth, and divested of 260 bales and cases of goods, valued at from $200,000 to $300,000, and then ordered into port. The privateer, with her rich spoils safely arrived. The cargo of the *James* was invoiced at £100,000, sterling. She safely arrived at Portsmouth, N. H.

Brig ——, captured by the *Dash*, of Portland, and divested of 150 hhds. of rum, and given up. The *Dash* arrived at Wiscasset.

Schooner ——, from Halifax, laden with salmon and herrings, sent into Wilmington, N. C, by a letter-of-marque schooner from that port.

State of Affairs at this Period of the War

A great many additional large privateers were now out during this month, and sailed from and returned to most of our Atlantic ports, when it best suited their convenience.

The Chesapeake Bay was, at this time, unfortunately in the power of the enemy, but still the spirit of enterprise, and skill of the people residing on its shores and rivers did not relax in energy. And though their privateers were prevented, for a time, from entering the ports of the Chesapeake, they were cruising in almost every sea, and sending their prizes into the different Atlantic ports. Fine large schooners were built at many other places besides Baltimore—that is to say, after their construction.

Their beautiful models were imitated and adopted all over the United States. The capital of our wealthy merchants in the Atlantic cities was liberally employed in building and fitting out privateers against our common enemy; for, thank God, we had many harbours and places that they could not blockade, notwithstanding their declaration that our ports were blockaded from Maine to Georgia.

Among the privateers fitted out, were some stout vessels, one with 22 long heavy guns, and two others carrying from 20 to 30 guns. In a newspaper of this day, we notice the sailing of five privateers, and the building of three in the neighbourhood of

Boston—one called the *Reindeer*, pierced for 22 guns—a noble vessel, coppered, built of the best material, and completed in thirty-five working days. On her cradle, the *Avon*, of the same rate, was laid down to be finished in eighteen working days. They were also building the *Blakely*, of like size and dimensions, to be finished with the same dispatch. In New York they were exceedingly busy with vessels of this kind. And the exertions of individuals, aided by the project lately adopted by Congress, to fit out twenty vessels, which was to be carried into immediate execution, in order to make the enemy feel the war much more sensibly than he had done; giving a "demonstration" of his inability to defend his own coasts, much less to blockade all the ports of the world.

But some measure must be provided to bring in a part of the prisoners they took. The enemy did not acknowledge paroles made at sea, except in some few isolated cases, and held many of our gallant seamen in captivity. These brave fellows should be released to repay favours received. The balance of prisoners of this class would have been greatly in our favour, if one half of those taken had been brought into port. There was a real difficulty in doing it, but it should have been done, one way or another.

Public Opinion in Great Britain.

The English papers teem with articles about our privateers. Their fears and sufferings magnified their numbers prodigiously! The master of a vessel who was captured three times, and as often recaptured, reported in London, that he had seen no less than ten of these terrible things during his voyage! The *Wasp* had created a wonderful sensation; and the United States brig *Syren* was playing a frightful tune; she had burnt many valuable vessels. The schooners were poking themselves into their very ports, and John Bull, while he grumbled most lustily, was sorely mortified, and not a little surprised at their impudence! Meetings of merchants were held at several places to remonstrate against their depredations! We notice the proceedings at Liverpool and Glasgow as samples:

"At Halifax, insurance has been absolutely refused on most vessels; on others, 33 *per cent,* has been added to the former premiums!"

We do not hear of the capture of but one privateer for several weeks; that was the *Harlequin,* a new vessel, elegantly fitted from an eastern port. She was taken by the *Bulwark,* 74, by stratagem. The depredations of the American privateers on the coasts of Ireland and Scotland had produced so strong a sensation at Lloyd's, that it was difficult to get policies underwritten, except at enormous rates of premiums. Thirteen guineas for £100 was paid to insure vessels across the Irish Channel! Such a thing never happened, we believe, before.

London, September 9th.—At a meeting of merchants, shipowners, etc., at Liverpool, to consider of a representation to government on the subject of the numerous captures made by American cruisers. Mr. Gladstone proposed an address to the lords of the Admiralty, but after many severe observations that representations had been made to that department without redress, Mr. Clear proposed an address to the Prince Regent, which, after warm opposition on the part of Mr. Gladstone, was carried.

The address conveys a censure upon the Admiralty. Subsequently, a counter address to the Admiralty was voted at another meeting, to which Mr. Crocker replied, on the 3rd inst., that an ample force had been under the orders of the admirals commanding the western stations; and that, during the time when the enemy's depredations are stated to have taken place, not fewer than three frigates and fourteen sloops were actually at sea, for the immediate protection of St. George's channel, and the western and northern parts of the United Kingdom.

In the memorials of the merchants, etc., of Liverpool, to the Admiralty, complaining of a want of sufficient naval protection against American captures, they speak of privateers destroying vessels as a novel and extraordinary practice, which they Bay they are informed is promoted by pecuniary rewards from the American government, and they wish measures adopted to prevent, as much as possible, the ruinous effects of this "new system of warfare."

At a very numerous meeting of the merchants, manufacturers, ship-owners, and underwriters, of the city of Glasgow, called by a public advertisement, and held by special requisition to the Lord Provost, on Wednesday, the 7th of September, 1814, the Lord Provost in the Chair, it was:

"Unanimously resolved, that the number of American privateers with which our channels have been infested, the audacity with which they have approached our coasts, and the success with which their enterprise has been attended, have proved injurious to our commerce, humbling to our pride, and discreditable to the directors of the naval power of the British nation, whose flag, till of late, waved over every sea, and triumphed over every rival. That there is reason to believe, that in the short space of less than twenty-four months, above eight hundred vessels have been captured by that power, whose maritime strength we have hitherto impolitically held in contempt.

"That, at a time when we were at peace with all the rest of the world, when the maintenance of our marine costs so large a sum to the country, when the mercantile and shipping interests pay a tax for protection, under the form of convoy duty, and when, in the plenitude of our power, we have declared the whole American coast under blockade, it is equally distressing and mortifying that our ships cannot, with safety, traverse our own channels; that insurance cannot be effected but at an excessive premium; and that a horde of American cruisers should be allowed, unheeded, unresisted and unmolested, to take, burn or sink, our own vessels, in our own inlets, and almost in sight of our own harbours.

"That the ports of the Clyde have sustained severe loss from the depredations already committed, and there is reason to apprehend still more serious suffering, not only from the extent of the coasting trade and the number of vessels yet to arrive from abroad, but as the time is fast approaching when the outward-bound ships must proceed to Cork for convoys, and when, during the winter season, the opportunities of the enemy will be increased, both to capture with ease and escape with impunity.

"That the system of burning and destroying every article which there is fear of losing—a system pursued by all the cruisers, and encouraged by their own government—diminishes the chances of recapture, and renders the necessity of prevention more urgent.

"That from the coldness and neglect with which previous remonstrances from other quarters have been received by the Admiralty, this meeting reluctantly feels it an imperious duty at once to address the Throne, and that therefore a petition be forwarded to his Royal Highness, the Prince Regent, acting in the name and on behalf of His Majesty, representing the above grievances, and humbly praying that his Royal Highness will be graciously pleased to direct such measures to be adopted, as shall promptly and effectually protect the trade on the coast of this kingdom, from the numerous insulting and destructive depredations of the enemy; and that the Lord Provost be requested to transmit the third petition accordingly.

"That the thanks of this meeting be given to Mr. Ewing, for the ability with which he prepared and introduced the business of this day.

"That the thanks of this meeting be given to the gentlemen who signed this requisition.

"R. Finlay, Provost."

The *True Blooded Yankee,* American privateer, has been completely refitted for sea, manned with a crew of 200 men, and sailed from Brest on the 21st of November, supposed for the purpose of cruising in the British Channel. Her orders were to sink, burn and destroy, and not to capture with the intention of sending into port; but to divest all prizes of their valuable articles. Respecting this vessel, see appendix.

POLITICAL DIVINITY—ANECDOTE TO SHOW THE SPIRIT OF THE TIMES

"War is a national punishment for national sins." Good.

"The English nation is more at war than any other in Christendom." True.

Then "the bulwark of our holy religion is the greatest sinner in Christendom." Undeniable logic.

"An American officer who carried a flag over to the British lines, after having dispatched the business of his mission, was invited by the commanding British officer to dine. As usual, the wine was circulated, and a British officer being called upon for a toast, gave, "Mr. Madison, dead or alive;" which the Yankee drank without appearing to notice it.

When it came to the American's turn to give a toast, he gave, "the Prince Regent, drunk or sober."

"Sir," said the British officer, bristling up and colouring with anger, "that is an insult."

"No, sir," answered the American very coolly, "it is only a reply to one."

Prizes Captured by Privateers

Brig *Concord*, captured by a letter-of-marque of Wilmington, N. C, and made a cartel of.

Brig *Sir John Sherbrook*, 12 guns, from Halifax for Alicant, laden with fish and oil, captured by the *Syren* of Baltimore, and driven on shore at Rockaway, N. J., to avoid a recapture by the blockading squadron off New Jersey. On abandoning her, the prize-crew set her on fire. She was burnt, but her armament, etc., was saved.

Ann and Eliza from Newfoundland for Merimachi, captured by the *Mammoth* and destroyed.

Ships *Urania* and *Anisby*, captured by the same, and also destroyed.

Eliza, from Newfoundland for Prince Edward's Island, captured by the same, and given up.

Ship *Dobson* from Cork for Quebec, captured by the same and burnt.

Sallust, from England for Quebec, captured by the same, divested, and made a cartel of. The *Sallust* arrived at Liverpool,

England.

The *Mammoth*, when last heard of, namely by prisoners, from Liverpool, had been out seven weeks, and made sixteen prizes. She cruised seventeen days off Cape Clear, Ireland, where several valuable vessels were manned by her for the United States.

English privateer, *Thinks-I-to-Myself*, two guns, twenty men, captured by the *Dash*, of Portland, and taken into that port.

Schooner *Britannia*, in ballast, commanded by Captain Freeman, late of the privateer *Liverpool Packet*, captured by the *Harpy*, of Baltimore, and burnt.

Brig *Halifax Packet*, from Aberdeen for Halifax, with a valuable cargo of dry-goods, hardware, and sundries, captured by the same, and divested of her richest articles. She arrived at Portsmouth. N. H.

The *Harpy* sailed from Portsmouth, N. H., and returned there after a cruise of twenty days, laden with the choicest spoils of the foe, and sixty prisoners. She also captured the transport ship *Amazon*, 6 guns, eighteen men, an elegant vessel, from London for Halifax, with a cargo of provisions. Also, the transport ship *Budges*, 440 tons, six 18-pound carronades, with a large cargo of rum, brandy, beef, pork, flour and bread—both of which were manned and ordered into port. Among the prisoners brought in, are two majors, and several other officers. These two vessels belonged to the fleet that lately sailed from Portsmouth, England. The prizes of the *Harpy*, may be moderately valued at $400,000 to $500,000

Schooner *Prince Regent*, 380 bbls. alewives and a quantity of salmon, sent into Portland by the privateer *Dash*, of that place.

English privateer *Retaliation*, 5 guns, twenty men, captured near Barnstable, Massachusetts, by the sloop *Two Friends,* fitted out for the occasion, and manned by volunteers. By good management she was taken by complete surprise, and carried by boarding, without resistance.

Schooner *Two Brothers*, laden with fish, captured by the *Mammoth*, and burnt.

Brig *Uniza*, for Merimachi, in ballast, captured by the *Mam-*

moth, and burnt.

Brig *Sarah*, from Cork for Merimachi, with 600 bbls. of flour, captured by the same, and burnt.

Brig *Sir Home Popham*, with fruit, captured by the same and burnt.

Schooner *Rapid*, from Newfoundland for Lisbon, with fish, captured by the same and burnt.

Ship *Champion*, from London for Quebec, captured by the same, divested of her cargo, worth from $80,000 to $100,000, and made a cartel of, to disembarrass the privateer of her prisoners.

Two other small vessels, taken by the same, and destroyed, names not recorded.

The *Mammoth* also captured and ordered into port, the barque *Mary*, brigs *Alexander* and *Charlotte*, and the ship *Mentor*, with valuable cargoes, and gave up the schooners *Thomas* and *Good Intent*, and brigs *Joseph* and *Eliza*. She made in all twenty-one prizes, and paroled about 300 prisoners. The privateer arrived at Portsmouth, N. H., full of rich spoils from the enemy.

The valuable brig *Europa*, armed with 8 eighteen-pound carronades, 2 long-nines, and twenty-two men, with 175 tons of sweet oil, etc., sent into a southern port by the *Patapsco*, of Baltimore. She was from Malta for London, before she was captured.

Brig *Canada*, 10 guns, from Bermuda, laden with puncheons of rum, sent into Wilmington, N. C, by the *Lawrence*, of Baltimore.

The English brig *William* from the Coast of Africa, laden with 194,087 pounds of gum. estimated to be worth fifty or sixty thousand dollars, was captured and sent into Newbern, N. C, by a Baltimore privateer, whose name is not given.

Ship *Ann Dorothy*, cargo of hides and tallow, sent into Boston by the *Saratoga* of New York. A valuable prize. This vessel was captured by the *Saratoga*, recaptured by the *Maidstone* frigate, recaptured by the *David Porter*, and is now satisfactorily accounted for. Her cargo afforded a clear profit to the captors of from $100,000 to $120,000. A very clever affair.

The *Saratoga* privateer returned, after a cruise of 110 days, during which she captured: schooner. *Mary*, brig *Swiftsure*, schooner. *James*, ship *Ann Dorothy*, and ship *Enterprise*, all of which were manned and ordered for the United States. The privateer also brought into port a quantity of indigo, ivory, and furs—all valuable goods taken from the enemy.

The privateer *Syren*, of Baltimore, returning from a cruise, was chased off New York, and was lost on making the Delaware, November 16th, being run ashore by the pilot; where she was attacked by three barges, from a *razee* at anchor, which were kept at bay for two hours; but finding no chance of escape, the privateer was set on fire, and her crew (only twenty in number, with six prisoners in charge), reached the New Jersey shore in safety. One of the enemy's barges is said to have sunk. The *Syren* captured and manned several valuable vessels.

Brig *Hiram*, from Liverpool, last from Cork, with a convoy from which she separated in a gale, bound for St. Johns, with a cargo of dry-goods, crockery, cordage, etc., captured by the *David Porter*, of Boston, divested of goods to the value of $100,000, and given up.

The *David Porter* arrived at Boston, with her rich spoils, after a cruise of only fifteen days, during which she captured the *Hiram* and two brigs, which she ordered into port.

Brigs *Susan* and *James*, and schooner *Retrieve*, captured by the *Fox* of Portsmouth, and burnt.

Brig *Concord*, captured by the same, and made a cartel of, to disembarrass her of her prisoners.

Brig *Cossack*, laden with wine, sent into Boston, by the *Surprise* of Baltimore. This vessel had been captured by the *Grand Turk* of Salem, recaptured by the *Bulwark* 74, and retaken by the *Surprise*.

Schooner *Pink*, captured by the *Grand Turk*, and sunk.

Brig *Brothers*, from St. Johns for Liverpool, with lumber, captured by the same, and sunk.

Brig *Belgrade* from Malta, for Falmouth, captured by the same, divested of some guns, etc. and permitted to proceed.

Brig *Robert Stewart*, with lumber, taken by the same and burnt.

Schooner *Commerce*, laden with fish, captured and destroyed by the same.

The *Grand Turk* arrived at Salem, after a cruise of 103 days, with forty-four of her original crew (the rest being on board her prizes), and fifty prisoners.

Beside the above, she captured seven or eight other vessels, one with an invoice of £30,000, sterling, all of which were manned and ordered for United States. The *Grand Turk* had on board goods to the value of $20,000.

Schooner *Mary*, from Halifax, with mackerel, captured by the *Surprise* and sunk.

Schooner *Bird*, from Newfoundland for the West Indies, with fish, captured by the *Grand Turk,* and sent into Salem.

Ship *Ocean*, 380 tons, of and for London, laden with a cargo of masts, thirty-five bowsprits for men-of-war, and a quantity of timber and lumber, sent into Salem by the *General Putnam*, of Salem, This privateer was subsequently captured by the English.

Schooner *Georgiana*, from Martinico, for Newfoundland, with rum and sugar, sent into port by the *Grand Turk*.

Sloop ——, captured by the *Scorpion* of Salem, mounting one gun, and sent into that port.

Schooner ——, taken by the same and destroyed.

Schooners *Eugene* and *Stinger*, captured by the *Midas*, of Baltimore, divested and destroyed.

Schooner *Betsey and Jane*, from St. Johns, for Castine, with one hundred and nineteen packages of dry-goods, valued at $150,000, brought into Thomastown by the *Cadet*, of Salem.

Brig ——, laden with fish, sent into port by the letter-of-marque, *Jonquilla*, of New York.

Sloop ——, from St. Lucia, captured by the *Saucy Jack*, divested and given up to the prisoners.

Schooner ——, taken by the same, divested and given up; being of little value.

Schooner *Kingston*, packet, captured by the same, and made a tender of.

Sloop *Cyrus*, captured by said tender, and burnt.

Sloop *Jane*, with provisions, captured by the *Saucy Jack*, divested and given up to the prisoners.

Ship *Amelia*, four long guns, and eight 12 pound carronades, with a rich cargo of dry-goods, captured by the *Saucy Jack*, after a severe engagement of an hour. The privateer had one killed and one wounded; the *Amelia*, four killed and five wounded.

The *Saucy Jack* also captured on this cruise the British schooner *Weasel*, laden with provisions, and sent her into St. Mary's.

Schooner *Jane*, from Jamaica, bound for St. Johns, Newfoundland, laden with rum and sugar, was also captured by the *Saucy Jack*, and sent into Savannah. The privateer had arrived with a full cargo of British goods valued at $15,000, taken out of her prize—the *Amelia*.

A Bold Dash, but Without Success

The little privateer *Saucy Jack*, of Charleston, while cruising off Cape Tiberon (west end of St Domingo), on the 31st of October, with her little tender called the *Packet* in company, at 1 a.m. saw two ships standing to the westward, gave chase, and at 2 a.m., being within gun-shot, fired three shots at them from our long gun, on which one of the ships returned the fire, and both immediately shortened sail. At 6 a.m., being within half gun-shot of them, we found that one mounted 16 and the other 18 guns, but did not appear to be well manned. At 7 a.m. hoisted the colours, and began the engagement with the nearest ship; at ten minutes past 7 boarded her on the larboard beam, and then found her to be full of soldiers.

The *Saucy Jack*, on perceiving this, immediately sheered off, when the two ships continued to chase her until a quarter before 8 o'clock, pouring in at the time a constant fire of grape and musketry; it was 8 o'clock before the schooner got out of reach of the enemy's guns. In this engagement the *Saucy Jack* had eight men killed, and fifteen wounded; received two balls in her hull, and her spars and rigging were very much cut up.

English Account of the Same Action

"*Kingston, Jamaica, Nov. 2nd.*—Yesterday morning, the *Volcano*, bomb-ship, Captain Price, and transport ship *Golden Fleece*, from the Chesapeake, having on board 250 troops, appeared in the offing, but from the baffling winds were not enabled to reach Port Royal, at the time this paper was put to press.

"On Sunday night, about 12 o'clock, off Navassa Island, the *Volcano* perceived a schooner standing towards her, which fired several shot, which were returned. The *Volcano* shortened sail, in order that the schooner might approach her. At about eight o'clock the following morning, she was ascertained to be a large black vessel, with white streaks; she ran alongside, and attempted to board, but finding the *Volcano* was not a merchantman, she endeavoured to sheer off, at which time several volleys of musketry and great guns were discharged at her, that swept her deck, and killed most of those who endeavoured to board, when the remainder were seen to run below.

"The *Volcano* then chased her for three miles, but perceiving no probability of coming up with her, relinquished the pursuit. During the contest a very enterprising officer of the marine-artillery, Lieutenant W. P. Futzen, and two seamen were killed, and two men wounded. The privateer had in company a Balahoo schooner, which did not attempt to afford her any assistance; she mounted six carriage guns, and one on a pivot, and was full of men."

Prizes Captured by Privateers.

Brig *Louisa*, laden with salt and tin, captured by the *Macedonian* of Portsmouth, divested of the tin, and burnt.

English brig *Britannia*, from St. Johns, N. B., for Liverpool, laden with 195 tons of ship timber, and sundry other articles was captured by the *Macedonian*, and burnt.

The *Macedonian* also captured the British ship *Sir Edward Pellew*, burthen 307 tons, 2 guns, and nineteen men. She was in ballast, and not worth sending into port, the privateer destroyed her.

The *Macedonian* also captured three other British vessels on this cruise, two of them she manned and ordered into the United States. The other, the schooner *Mariner*, laden with fish, being of little value, was made a cartel of, to disembarrass her of her prisoners.

The *Macedonian* was at sea only twenty days; having carried away her bowsprit in a severe gale of wind, she was obliged to return home to Portsmouth to refit; she however made several prizes, and brought into port twenty-two prisoners.

The British schooner ——, laden with codfish, was captured by the Baltimore privateer *Resolution*, and sent into Charleston, S. C.

A Schooner, laden with salt, name not reported, was captured by the *Young Wasp*, of Philadelphia, and sent into Ocracock, N. C.

The British schooner *Hazard*, from Halifax, bound for Annapolis, Nova Scotia, laden with West India produce, and a quantity of English goods of considerable value, was captured by the *Surprise*, of Baltimore, and after divesting her of the most valuable part of her cargo, destroyed her.

A Short and Very Successful Cruise, Made by the Privateer Schooner *Kemp*, of Baltimore, Under the Command of Captain Jacobs.

The *Kemp* sailed from Wilmington, N. C, on a cruise to the West Indies, November 29th, 1814.

On the 1st of December, at 8 p. m., two days after leaving port, while in the Gulf Stream, she descried a small fleet of merchant ships, and made sail in chase. At 12 meridian, got near enough to ascertain they were eight in number, and under convoy of a frigate. They were then in lat. 32° 32' N., long, 77° 0' W.

Soon after noon, the frigate gave chase to the schooner and drove her away from the fleet. Captain Jacobs made short tacks to windward, and drew the frigate away from his convoy, in pursuit of the *Kemp*.

During the night, the privateer dodged the frigate, and saw

no more of her.

Early next morning, she steered to the eastward, in pursuit of the fleet.

She soon discovered them again, bearing N.N.E. on the weather beam, the wind being north.

On the 3rd of December, at 11 o'clock in the forenoon, the *Kemp* drew near the fleet, which consisted of three ships, three brigs and two schooners—all drawn up in a line prepared for action.

At 2 p.m. they bore away for the privateer, and, as they respectively passed, commenced firing upon her in rotation. She reserved her fire, and tacked. While passing through their line, she opened her whole armament upon the enemy, which soon threw them into confusion.

At half-past 2 p.m., she boarded one of the brigs and captured her without loss, except one seaman being wounded.

The whole of the enemy's vessels continued to fire upon the *Kemp* with considerably spirit, which was as warmly returned.

At 3 p.m., fell on board the ship *Rosabella*, when Mr. Myers, first lieutenant, with Mr. Sellers, sailing-master, and eight seamen, succeeded in capturing her, without loss on the part of the privateer. Three men were wounded on board the *Rosabella*.[1]

When in the act of boarding one of the schooners, she struck, and cried out for quarters.

The privateer then attacked the largest of the brigs, and, after a contest of fifteen or twenty minutes, she also surrendered; thus augmenting the number of prizes to four out of the eight vessels which, at the commencement of the action comprised the fleet.

As the privateer could not conveniently spare from her crew a sufficient number to man any more prizes, she was obliged to let the residue of the enemy's vessels proceed on their voyage.

---

1. The ship *Rosabella*, prize to the *Kemp*, was an excellent vessel, of 261 tons burthen, with a full cargo of sugar and coffee. She was ordered to proceed to Charleston, but unfortunately on entering the port, she grounded on the bar, and was totally lost This vessel and her cargo were estimated at $300,000. The wreck of this vessel was finally burnt by a British man-of-war brig.

On this cruise the *Kemp* made seventy-one prisoners, fifty-three of whom she brought into port. The remainder were left on board the prizes.

The aggregate force of the enemy was 46 guns and 134 men.

The *Kemp* had one man (John Irwin) killed. Four who were wounded soon recovered.

The prizes were valuable vessels, laden mostly with sugar and coffee.

They were all sent into Charleston, Wilmington, and other southern ports.

This cruise only lasted six days, but was a very profitable one for the captors, and all others concerned in the fortunate schooner *Kemp* and her gallant captain, officers and crew.

Prizes Captured by Privateers

Brig *Courtney*, 200 tons, with an assorted cargo, sent into Fairhaven, by the *Yankee*, of Bristol, R. I. The invoice of this vessel amounted to $200,000.

Schooner *Polly*, from Halifax, for Martinique, with fish, sent into Boston by the *Dash*, of Portland.

Schooner *Swift*, laden with fish and lumber, from St. Johns, for Granada, captured by the *Expedition*, of Baltimore, and sent into ———. The *Expedition* had taken three other prizes.

Ship *L'Aimable*, from Havana, under Spanish colours. sent into Wilmington, N. C, by the *Roger*, of Norfolk; cargo, sugar.

Schooner ———, with a valuable cargo, sent into Beaufort, by the *Hero*, of Newbern.

Schooner *Mary*, from St. Johns, for Castine, with a rich cargo of dry-goods, captured by the *Cadet*, of Salem; divested, manned, and arrived in port. The privateer safely arrived, with her rich spoils, at Thomastown. This prize was under convoy of an armed schooner with whom the privateer *Charles Stewart* had a fight, but seeing the *Cumberland* privateer coming up, and supposing she might be a British vessel, the *Charles Stewart* sheered off. The *Cumberland* engaged the Englishman, and was beaten off, with the loss of one killed and one wounded; but the convoyed schooner (the *Mary*) was afterwards taken, and served as above stated, by the *Cadet*.

American Privateers in the East Indies

London, November 26th.—The East India Company's ship *Adele*, has been captured by an American privateer off Pontana. Other privateers were cruising off the coast of Sumatra.

We learn by the news from Batavia, July 27th, 1815, that an embargo was laid by the government, to prevent merchant ships from falling into the hands of American privateers, who had captured many vessels in that neighbourhood, and also on the coast of Sumatra.

Prizes Captured by Privateers

The *Harpy* privateer had recently arrived at Salem, after a very successful cruise. She reports that the United States ship *Wasp* was off the Canaries, doing a great business among the English merchant ships.

Schooner *St. John*, with coffee, captured by the letter-of-marque *Jonquil*, of New York, and sent into Jacquemel. where she was ransomed.

Schooner ——, captured by the same, divested, and made a cartel of.

Brig *General Maitland,* from Martinique, for Bermuda, with rum and sugar, captured by the *Dash*, divested of part of her cargo and ordered into port; arrived at Portsmouth, N. H.

Sloop *Mary*, for Bermuda, with a variety of British goods, captured by the same, and made a cartel of.

The *Dash* safely reached Portland, laden with various articles, worth from $40,000 to $50,000.

Schooner ——, with an assorted cargo, from Halifax, for Castine, taken by the *Fame*, of Thomastown, and sent into that port.

Sloop *Eliza*, captured by the *Caroline*, and burnt.

Schooner *Mariner*, dry-goods, captured by the same, divested and made a cartel of.

The privateer schooner *Caroline*, of Baltimore, captured the British brig *Stephen*, 14 guns and thirty men, from St. Thomas, bound for Curacoa, laden with fine English goods. After taking out all the valuable part of the cargo, the privateer gave her up to the prisoners. The *Caroline* subsequently arrived safe at Wilmington, N. C, with a full cargo of valuable British goods.

Sloop *Trinidad*, with coffee, hides and log-wood, captured by the letter-of-marque, *Jonquil*, divested and burnt.

The *Jonquil* arrived at Beaufort, with a valuable cargo, nine days from Port-au-Prince.

Brig *Equity*, from Greenock, for Quebec, laden with an assorted cargo, taken by the *Orlando*, of Gloucester, and sent into Boston.

Brig *Lord Wellington*, from Halifax, for Havana, captured by the letter-of-marque *Diamond*, of Baltimore, on her voyage from Havana to New York. The *Diamond* gave up her prize to the crew and some Spanish passengers, and let her proceed on her voyage.

Brig *Margaret*, from Lisbon, for England, with a full cargo of Lisbon wine, captured off the British coast, by the *Young Wasp*, of Philadelphia, and sent into that port.

Ship *Hero*, of 610 tons, 14 guns and twenty-seven men, from Halifax, for Jamaica, laden with fish and lumber, captured by the *Ino*, of Boston, and sent into that port. The *Hero* struck without firing a gun.

Schooner *Nancy*, from Poole, for Newfoundland, 250 tons, with an assorted cargo of bale goods, provisions, etc., captured by the same, partially divested of her richest goods, and ordered into port.

Ketch *Caroline*, under Danish colours, from London to Lisbon, taken by the same, divested of a quantity of dry-goods, as British property, and allowed to proceed on her voyage.

Brig *Susannah*, from St. Andrews for Barbadoes, with lumber, captured by the *Amelia*, and made a cartel of.

British schooner *Mary*, formerly the Climax, of Baltimore, 16 guns and twelve men, captured by the same, after a long chase, and sent into Philadelphia.

British brig *Pallas*, formerly the French privateer Sans Souci, 8 guns, twenty-one men, with a cargo of fish, captured by the same privateer, after an action of twenty minutes, and sent into Philadelphia.

The privateer *Amelia* of Baltimore, arrived safe at Philadelphia, in April, 1815, with a full cargo of valuable goods, taken from the enemy. During her cruise she captured ten British vessels; some she destroyed, some she ordered into port, and one she gave up as a cartel for her prisoners. During the cruise she put into L'Orient, where her captain and officers were well received, and treated politely by the public authorities of that place.

On her return home she touched at St. Barts, for a supply of water. The governor would not allow her any supplies, but, on the contrary, ordered her captain to leave the island forthwith. The *Amelia* carried but 6 guns, and seventy five men. The captured vessels amounted to 2,270 tons, 112 prisoners, and 32 carriage guns. She was frequently chased by the enemy, and once for fifty-three hours, but was fortunate enough to evade all her pursuers, and finally made an excellent cruise.

The East India ship *General Wellesley*, 16 guns, 86 men, 500 tons, coppered, and found in the best manner, with a valuable cargo of 18,000 bars of iron, etc., etc., outward bound, namely, for Calcutta, separated from her convoy, and was captured by the privateer *Yankee*, after a running fight. She was manned and ordered to proceed to Charleston, but unfortunately, while entering that port, she was lost on the bar. Her original crew consisted of thirty-six Englishmen, fifty lascars, all of whom were drowned, but seven. Two of the prize crew were also lost; the *Yankee* was left in pursuit of a fleet of twenty sail. This valuable ship being wrecked on the bar, was doubtless a great disappointment to her captors.

British brig ——, 170 tons, a valuable vessel, from Castine for Jamaica, laden with fish and lumber, brought into ——, by the *Paul Jones*.

Cutter *Eliza and Peggy*, from Malaga for London, with fruit, captured by the *Lawrence* of Baltimore, divested of part of her cargo, and made a cartel of, to get rid of prisoners.

Cutter *Dart*, with a cargo of wine, raisins, etc., from Malaga, captured by the same, divested of a portion of her cargo, and burnt.

Ship *Christian*, from Faro for London, with a full cargo, taken by the same privateer, and burnt.

Schooner *Atalanta*, from Halifax for Martinique, with fish, taken by the same, and burnt.

The privateer *Lawrence*, arrived at New York on the 25th of January. During her cruise, she took thirteen prizes, eight of which were manned; some of them very valuable. One vessel she gave up to the prisoners as a cartel. She made 106 prisoners, but brought in only fifteen. Her prizes in the aggregate amounted to more than 3,000 tons. She also brought in a quantity of English goods.

British brig *Lord Wellington*, with fish and lumber, captured by the *Expedition*, of Baltimore, and burnt.

English schooner *Goldfinder* (formerly belonged to New York), with salt, captured by the *Young Wasp*, of Philadelphia, and sent into Elizabeth City, N. C.

A transport, with 250 troops, from Halifax for Castine, chased ashore near the latter place by three privateers, and lost. The troops, however, got safely to land, and marched to Castine.

Sloop *Governor Hodgdon*, with a few cases of English goods and hats, some cordage, white lead, etc., captured by the *Dash*, of Portland, divested, and given up to the prisoners.

Brig *Only Son*, from Barbadoes for St. Johns, with rum, sugar and shrub, captured by the same, and given up.

English brig ———, laden with provisions for the English army, captured near the mouth of the Mississippi, where she had grounded. She was then captured by a privateer and burnt.

Ship *Jane*, from Merimachi, laden with lumber, captured and burnt by the *Harpy*, of Baltimore.

Brig *William Neilson*, of Liverpool, from Quebec, with a number of passengers, and a cargo of lumber, captured by the same, and made a cartel of, to disembarrass her of her prisoners.

English schooner *Nine Sisters*, from Lisbon for Liverpool, with a cargo of fruit, captured by the same and burnt.

British brig *Louisa*, from Gibraltar for Greenock, with a cargo of wine, figs, raisins, etc., was also captured by the *Harpy*, divested of part of her goods, and manned for the United States.

LOSS OF THE PRIVATEER-BRIG *ARROW*, CAPTAIN CONKLIN, OF NEW YORK

It is with sincere regret that I herewith record the total loss of the beautiful privateer-brig *Arrow*. She sailed from New York the 14th January, 1815, on a cruise to the West Indies. She mounted 14 guns, and had a complement of 150 men. She was well equipped and supplied with everything necessary for a long cruise, but, sad to relate, no tidings were ever received from this vessel after she left port. She being heavily sparred, it was conjectured that she was capsized at sea, or run under while chased by an enemy.

SUCCESS OF THE PRIVATEER HARPY

English ship *William and Alfred*, from London, for Antigua, with dry-goods and plantation utensils, was captured by the *Harpy*, divested of her dry-goods, manned, and ordered for the United States.

Ship *Jane*, from London, for Antigua, laden with provisions for government account, captured by the same. After taking out a portion of her cargo, and destroying the remainder, gave her up to the prisoners to proceed to a British port as a cartel.

The *Harpy* also captured the valuable ship *Garland*, with a full cargo of rum and sugar, which ship arrived at Salem.

The *Harpy* arrived at Salem in April, 1815. She had on board a valuable cargo of rich merchandise of every description, taken from several of her prizes, made while cruising on the coast of England, in the Bay of Biscay, and along the coasts of Spain and Portugal. Here follows a memorandum of the goods, namely, 118 boxes and trunks, and 116 hhds. and casks of dry-goods, jewellery, plate, ladies' rich dresses, navy trimmings, rich clothing, etc., 330 boxes fresh Malaga raisins, 66 frails fresh Turkey figs, 158 pieces British manufactured goods, 29 bolts of canvas, a quantity of cordage, ten pipes of sherry wine, three bbls. of powder, carronades, muskets. pistols, cutlasses, sails, signal flags, lamp and paint oil, white and patent sheet lead, nautical instruments, cut and other glass, medicines, and sundry other articles; also, upward of £100,000, sterling, in British Treasury notes and bills of exchange.

She was frequently chased, but escaped with ease. She was at sea 85 days, and cruised off the coast of Ireland, in the British Channel, Bay of Biscay, etc. She was a noble vessel of 349 tons, carrying 14 heavy guns, and about 100 men. The following honourable acknowledgements of the kind treatment of Captain Nichols, of the *Harpy*, to his prisoners, deserves record:

"Captain William Drysdale, late of the ship *William and Alfred,* captured the 2nd January, 1815, by the brig *Harpy*, returns his grateful acknowledgement to William Nichols, Esq., commander of the said brig, and all his officers, for their great civility, indulgent lenity, and humane usage, while on board, and generously delivering up all his private property. And should, at any future time, Captain Nichols or any of his officers come to London, Captain Drysdale will be happy to see them at his house, Stepney Green, near London. Given under my hand on board the *Harpy*, at sea, this day, 6th of January, 1815.

"William Drysdale,
"Late captain of the ship *William and Alfred.*"

"We, the undersigned, feeling congenial sentiment with Captain Drysdale, toward Captain Nichols, Lieutenant Place and the officers on board the *Harpy*; and desirous that such humanity and goodness may be made public, as well in the United States as in England, declare that our treatment is worthy of every praise and encomium; and that all our private property has been held sacred to us, and a cartel fitted for us as early as circumstances would permit.

"Geo. Harrison,
"W. Newell,
"J. W. Hall
"Andrew McCarthy.
"Late Masters of Vessels taken by the Harpy."

PRIZES CAPTURED BY PRIVATEERS

Brig *Courtney*, from London, for Rio Janeiro, with dry-goods, copper, etc., captured by the *Yankee*, divested of her richest articles and manned for the United States.

Ship *St. Andrew*, 8 guns, from London for Tenerife, captured by the same, and sent to the United States.

Brig *Speculator*, captured by the Yankee, and made a cartel of, to disembarrass her of her prisoners.

Brig *Patriot*, from Prince Edward's Island, with timber, sent into Charleston by the *Brutus* of Boston.

Brig *Dantzic*, sent into an eastern port, by the *Paul Jones*, of New York.

Brig *Peter*, from Messina, for London, a very valuable vessel, sent into North Carolina by the *Lawrence*, of Baltimore; she had a full cargo of valuable merchandise.

Brig *John*, from Liverpool for Leghorn, with a cargo of dry-goods and hardware, captured by the *Perry* of Baltimore, divested of many valuable articles; manned. and ordered into any port in the United States:

Brig *Nancy*, from Malaga, for London, with fruit, captured by the same and made a cartel of.

The *Perry* arrived in the Delaware about the 1st of Feb., with a full cargo of chosen spoils, after having made a capital cruise. She was chased some eight or ten times by brigs, sloops-of-war, frigates, and *razees,* but laughed at them all; except once, when close in on the coast, she had to receive the fire of a *razee*, from which she escaped, though much cut up in her hull and sails. She was so close that the shot from the ship frequently reached her, but though so hardly pressed, she finally escaped.

The three masted schooner ——, captured by the *Warrior*,

of New York, was subsequently lost on New Inlet bar, North Carolina.

British ship *William*, captured by the *Charles Stewart*, of Boston, and sent into Bath, cargo of lumber.

British brig ——, captured by the *Harrison*, of Baltimore, divested of a quantity of English goods and ransomed.

Schooner ——, under Spanish colours, captured by the same, and divested of a quantity of goods, belonging to British merchants in Jamaica, and given up.

The captain of the *Harrison* was afterwards killed in a battle with a British sloop-of-war.

The privateer arrived at Wilmington, N C, with a full cargo of goods taken from the enemy.

The *York*, of Baltimore, arrived at Boston in April, 1815, after a very unsuccessful cruise, having captured only one vessel, which was immediately retaken. She suffered exceedingly by gales of wind; in one of which she lost overboard four seamen, with several guns, anchors, etc., etc.

Ship *Mary*, 246 tons, 6 guns, from Newfoundland, for Lisbon, laden with fish, captured by the *Little George* of Boston, and sent into Marblehead. The *Mary* was a very fine vessel.

English brig ——, with liquor and dry-goods, sent into Ocracock, by the *Kemp*, of Baltimore.

Sloop *Enterprise*, from Guernsey, for Madeira, with dry-goods and flour, captured by the *Whig* of Baltimore, divested of her cargo, and given up to the prisoners.

Brigs *Brunswick* and *Race Horse*, and schooner Britannia, captured by the same and burnt.

British schooner *Lucy Ann*, captured by the *Surprise,* and made a cartel of, to get rid of prisoners.

Brig *Forth*, from Halifax, for Pictou, in ballast, captured by the same, and burnt.

Two vessels laden with fish, oil and coal, captured by the *Ranger*, and burnt.

English ship ——, a collier, captured off the coast of England by the *Ranger*, of Boston, and burnt.

English brig *Athill*, 8 guns, from the Mediterranean, bound to England, with a valuable cargo, was captured by the *Lawrence* of Baltimore, and sent into Brest, France.

I find it stated, that on the 24th of December, 1814, the Baltimore privateer *Surprise* was at Brest, and there fired a salute, which was answered by the French admiral with 11 guns.

On the 9th of January, 1815, the *Surprise* sailed from that port, bound on a cruise.

Five days after leaving port, *viz.*, on the 14th of January, the privateer was chased for several hours by a British ship-of-war, who fired fifty guns at her, but without effect. She was fortunate enough to make her escape during the night, and proceeded on her cruise.

Battle Between the *Surprise* and the British Ship Star— Capture of the *Star*.

While cruising in lat. 24° 10' North, long. 35° 50' West, on the 28th of January, the *Surprise*, at 11 o'clock in the forenoon, saw a sail on her lee quarter. The wind being light, the privateer manned her sweeps and kept away for the strange sail.

At half-past 12 meridian, being within gunshot, the stranger set English colours. The privateer hoisted American colours, when the action commenced on both sides, and was kept up with spirit and energy by the contending parties until a quarter-past 2 o'clock. At that time, the privateer, with the aid of her sweeps, managed to gain a raking position under the stern of the enemy, who then struck his colours.

She proved to be the English ship *Star*, mounting 8 twelve-pounders, with twenty-six men, from Batavia, bound for London, laden with coffee and other valuable East India produce.

The *Star* had one man killed and one wounded. She received several shots in her hull, and was considerably damaged in her sails and rigging.

The *Surprise* did not lose a man, nor have one wounded. She received several shots through her sails, and had her fore-mast and fore-top-mast wounded by round shot.

The privateer removed from the *Star* a considerable portion of her cargo, and then put a prize-master and mate, with eighteen seamen on board, and proceeded in company with her towards New York.

On the 26th of February, while drawing near the coast, the *Surprise* separated from her prize in a snowstorm. They both subsequently arrived safe at New York with the whole of this valuable cargo.

The portion brought in by the privateer was valued at $150,000.

The entire cargo of the *Star* was estimated at $300,000.

It consisted of the following articles: 1,180 bags of sugar, 5,021 bags of coffee, 45 tubs of camphor, 297 bags of sago, 224 cwt. of sapan-wood, 22 bales of nankeens, 83 cases of cinnamon, and 45 cases of tortoise-shell.

The English three-masted schooner *George*, from Rio Grande, Africa, to Goree, with timber, captured by the *David Porter*, and made a cartel of, to get rid of prisoners.

British brig ———, with fish and oil, sent into Portsmouth, by the *Champlain*, privateer.

Brig *Susanna*, of Liverpool, 200 tons burthen, coppered, with a full cargo, captured on her voyage from Havana, for England, by the *Sine-qua-non* privateer, of Boston, and sent into Portsmouth, N. H. The *Susanna* was under Spanish colours, and was called the *Antonia*, but her true name and character were afterward discovered; and both vessel and cargo proved to be English.

Brig *Flying Fish*, 240 tons, coppered, with a rich cargo, captured on her voyage from London to Trieste, by the *David Porter*, and sent into New Bedford; cargo valued at from $150,000 to $200,000. The Flying Fish was a brig 110 feet on deck, and in every way a fine vessel.

The English packet brig *Lady Mary Pelham*, mounting 10 guns and twenty-six men, was captured by the *Kemp*, of Baltimore, and sent into Wilmington, N. C. The packet opposed the privateer with a manly spirit, until she had one man killed, and eight wounded, when she surrendered to the *Kemp*, which vessel had one man killed and three wounded.

SUBSTANCE OF AN AMUSING CHASE BY AN ENGLISH FRIGATE AND THE PRIVATEER WARRIOR, CAPTAIN CHAMPLIN, OF NEW YORK.

On the 15th of December, Captain Champlin made the island of Fayal, and at 8 o'clock in the morning, while about entering the harbour, he saw an English frigate lying there at anchor.

As soon as the frigate discovered the privateer, she slipped her cable and made sail in pursuit of her. The *Warrior*, of course, carried all the sail she could bear, to avoid the enemy, and after a chase of some forty or fifty miles, with, a strong breeze and squally weather, the frigate approached within long-gun-shot of the privateer, and commenced firing upon her from her two bow guns.

At this moment, Captain Champlin brought his long-torn to bear, and luffed-to a little, to show his starboard battery, which indicated a disposition to fight (as the enemy supposed), which induced the frigate to shorten sail, and give battle in due form.

Under these favourable circumstances, Captain Champlin threw overboard all his lee guns with shot and other heavy articles.

After having lightened his vessel, he made sail and dodged the enemy during the night, and thus made his escape.

TRUE MAGNANIMITY

The following statement was extracted from a London paper, called the *Aurora*, dated December 1st, 1814:

"Mr. Editor: You will please a great number of your readers in Great Britain, who are zealous in spreading the Divine Gospel all over the earth, by showing them that there are some American citizens who are willing to unite with us in sending Missionaries to all parts of the globe.

"The Rev. Mr. Benson read the following note, which was transmitted to him by one of his brethren in Wales:

"A few weeks since, a trading vessel, laden with corn, from

Cardigan, in Wales, was taken in the channel by an American privateer. When the captain of the latter entered the cabin to survey his prize, he espied a small box with a hole in the top, similar to that which tradesmen have in their counters, through which they drop their money, on which the words 'Missionary box' were inscribed. On seeing this, the American captain seemed not a little astonished, and addressed the Welsh captain nearly as follows: 'Captain, what is this?' pointing to the box with his stick.

"'Oh!' replied the honest Cambrian, heaving a sigh, 'tis all over now!'

"'What?' said the American captain.

"'Why, the truth is,' said the Welshman, 'that I, and my poor fellows, have been accustomed, every Monday morning, to drop a penny each into that box, for the purpose of sending out missionaries to preach the gospel to the heathen; but it is all over now.'

"'Indeed!' answered the American captain, 'that is very good.' After pausing a few minutes, he said: "'Captain, I'll not hurt a hair of your head, nor touch your vessel,' and immediately departed, leaving the owner to pursue his course to his destined port."

The privateer *Portsmouth*, of Portsmouth, was a conspicuous cruising vessel. She was commanded by John Sinclair, and made a great many valuable prizes. His widow, a very respectable lady is still living, and resided in Brooklyn, New York.

The celebrated privateer-brig *Yankee*, also alluded to in this chapter, was owned by James De Wolf, Esq. of Bristol, R. I. In several of her first cruises, she was commanded by —— Wilson, and subsequently by —— Smith. She was a most fortunate vessel, and made a great many captures. She took the *Royal Bounty*, a British letter-of-marque-ship, after a severe engagement. She ran all the war, and was never captured.

The privateer-schooner *Jack's Favourite,* belonged to New York. On several of her first cruises, she was commanded by —— Johnson, and made several prizes. She was subsequently commanded by —— Miller.

CHAPTER 10

Captain Boyle's Cruise

REMARKS ON THE BATTLE BETWEEN THE UNITED STATES SHIP *HORNET*, J. BIDDLE, COMMANDER, AND THE BRITISH SLOOP-OF-WAR *PENGUIN*, CAPTAIN DICKENSON, ON THE 25TH OF MARCH, 1816, NEAR THE ISLAND OF TRISTAN D'ACUNHA.

I have selected this action from among many others, because I believed the two vessels as nearly equal, both in men and guns, as could possibly be chosen from the navies of their respective countries. Consequently, I think this action a very fair test between Young America and Old England, in point of seamanship, skill, and bravery. I consider this one of the fairest and best fought battles, on both sides, that occurred during the war.

In some of the other naval battles fought between single American and British ships, it so happened that the force of the American vessels was slightly superior in men and guns to the English; but in this instance, I trust, the English will not raise that objection, but on the contrary, acknowledge it without a cavil, to have been a fair-fought action, and a decided victory in favour of the American ship.

These two sloops-of-war had, previous to their meeting, been wishing and seeking for an opportunity to distinguish themselves by gaining a decisive battle over the enemies of their respective countries, in an honourable combat on the broad ocean.

When the *Penguin* hove in sight, and the two belligerent parties understood the character of each other, their hearts beat high with hope for a glorious victory.

The *Penguin* bore up, and ran off a little, to get clear of the land. At the same time, the *Hornet*, being a little to leeward, backed her main-top-sail, and waited for her opponent to come down, that they might commence the action.

As the two ships neared each other, the *Penguin* hoisted English colours, and fired a gun, which said, as plain as a gun could speak, I am ready for the fight.

Captain Biddle set his colours, and here follows his official account of the action:

"Hon. Secretary of the Navy.

"Sir,—I have the honour to inform you, that on the morning of the 23rd instant, at half-past ten o'clock when about to anchor off the north end of the Island of Tristan d'Acunha, a sail was seen to the southward and eastward, steering to the westward, the wind fresh from the S.S.W. In a few minutes she had passed on to the westward, so that we could not see her for the land. I immediately made sail for the westward, and shortly after getting in sight of her again, perceived her to bear up before the wind. I hove-to for him to come down to us. When she had approached near, I filled the main-top-sail, and continued to yaw the ship, while she continued to come down, wearing occasionally to prevent her passing under our stern.

"At forty minutes past one p.m., being nearly within musket-shot distance, she hauled her wind on the starboard tack, hoisted English colours, and fired a gun. We immediately luffed-to, hoisted our ensign, and gave the enemy a broadside. The action being thus commenced a quick and well-directed fire was kept up from this ship, the enemy gradually drifting nearer to us, when at five minutes to 2 o'clock he bore up apparently to run us on board. As soon as I perceived he would certainly fall on board, I called the boarders, so as to be ready to repel the attempt. At the instant every officer and man repaired to the quarterdeck, where the two vessels were coming in contact, and eagerly pressed me to permit them to board the enemy; but this I would not permit, as it was evident, from the commencement of the action, that our fire was greatly superior both in quickness and in effect.

"The enemy's bowsprit came in between our main and mizzen rigging, on our starboard side, affording him an opportunity to board us, if such was his design, but no attempt was made. There was a considerable swell on, and as the sea lifted us ahead, the enemy's bowsprit carried away our mizzen-shrouds, stern davits and spanker-boom, and he hung upon our larboard quarter. At this moment an officer, who was afterwards recognized to be Mr. McDonald, the first lieutenant, and the then commanding officer, called out that they had surrendered.

"I directed the marines and musketry-men to cease firing, and while on the taffrail asking if they had surrendered, I received a wound in the neck. The enemy just then got clear of us, and his fore-mast and bowsprit being both gone, and, perceiving us wearing to give him a fresh broadside, he again called out that he had surrendered. It was with difficulty I could restrain my crew from firing into him again, as he had certainly fired into us after having surrendered. From the firing of the first gun, to the last time the enemy cried out he had surrendered, was exactly twenty-two minutes by the watch.

"She proved to be his Britannic Majesty's brig *Penguin*, mounting 16 thirty-two-pound carronades, two long-twelves, a twelve-pound carronade on the top-gallant forecastle, with swivels on the capstan and in the tops. She had a spare port forward, so as to fight both her long guns of a side. She sailed from England in September. She was shorter upon deck than this ship, by two feet, but she had a greater length of keel, greater breadth of beam, thicker sides, and higher bulwarks than this ship, and was in all respects a remarkably fine vessel of her class. The enemy acknowledged a complement of 132 men, twelve of them supernumerary marines, from the *Medway* 74, received on board in consequence of their being ordered to cruise for the American privateer *Young Wasp*. They acknowledge also a loss of fourteen killed, and twenty-eight wounded; but Mr. Mayo, who was in charge of the prize, assures me that the number of killed was certainly greater.

"Among the killed is Captain Dickenson, who fell at the close of the action, and the boatswain; among the wounded are the second lieutenant, purser, and two midshipmen. Each of the midshipmen lost a leg. We received on board in all, 118 prisoners, four of whom have since died of their wounds. Having removed the prisoners, and taken on board such provisions and stores as would be useful to us, I scuttled the *Penguin* this morning, before daylight, and she went down. As she was completely riddled by our shot, her foremast and bowsprit both gone, and her mainmast so crippled as to be incapable of being secured, it seemed unadvisable, at this distance from home, to attempt sending her to the United States.

"This ship did not receive a single round shot in her hull, nor any material wound in her spars; the rigging and sails were very much cut, but having bent a new suit of sails, and knotted and secured our rigging, we are now completely ready in all respects, for any service. We were eight men short of complement, and had nine upon the sick list the morning of the action.

"Enclosed is a list of the killed and wounded. I lament to state that Lieutenant Conner is dangerously wounded. I feel great solicitude on his account, as he is an officer of so much promise, and his loss would be a serious loss to the service.

"It is a most pleasing part of my duty to acquaint you, that the conduct of Lieutenants Conner and Newton, Mr. Mayo, acting Lieutenant Brownlow of the marines, Sailing-Master Romney, and the other officers, seamen, and marines I have the honour to command, was in the highest degree creditable to them, and calls for my warmest recommendation. I cannot, indeed, do justice to their merits. The satisfaction which was diffused throughout the ship when it was ascertained that the stranger was an enemy's sloop-of-war, and the alacrity with which every one repaired to quarters, fully assured me that their conduct in the action would be marked with coolness and intrepidity.

"I have the honour to be, etc.,

"J. Biddle."

The loss on board the *Hornet*, was one killed and eleven

wounded.

Remarks on the Action, Continued

The question has been often asked by intelligent men of every civilized country—how is it that a young nation, like the United States, with but a small navy, and that unaccustomed to naval battles, should be able to cope successfully, upon equal terms, with British ships-of-war! A thousand reasons have been alleged and as many times contradicted.

The English have always asserted that in these conflicts our ships were larger, carried heavier guns, and that we had so small a navy that we were enabled to man our ships of war with picked seamen from the merchant marine. This assertion has been again and again repeated, and when by us refuted, some other subterfuge has been raised, to evade the simple facts of the case.

Mr. Fenimore Cooper, in a charitable spirit, attributed our successes to our having got the start of the English in the modern improvement of gunnery. There may be some truth in this, but I think the true reason has not yet been touched upon, or brought forward, by any writer on this subject.

I will therefore proceed to give what I believe to be the true cause of our gaining so many victories over our experienced rival.

In my opinion, it grows out of the different formation and practical workings of a monarchical government on the one hand, and a free republic on the other.

In England, during the period of our last war, if their seamen were unwilling to enter on board of their men-of-war, they were impressed for an indefinite time, forced to fight against their wills, and except they belonged to respectable families, and could make interest at court, stood no chance of promotion.

They felt they were fighting for the King and the nobility, for a country in whose affairs they had no voice or vote, and when at home, were of no consideration, and only expected to obey their superiors. In fine, they knew they were only instruments in the hands of the aristocracy, and not a constituent part of the nation.

On the other hand, the American seamen were shipped for a term of two or three years, and knew when their time expired, they were free; and could not be forced on board against their wills. Another reason for their willingness to fight, was that the English for many years, had been in the habit of impressing them into their men-of-war, where they were compelled to fight against nations with whom they had no quarrel.

Another strong inducement for the American seamen to enter into the war with spirit was, that the government of the United States had declared war principally on their account. This fact inspired them with courage and enthusiasm, and led to their favourite motto;

"Free trade and sailor's rights, and no impressment."

An American seaman also feels that he is a man, and when he performs his duty like a man, that he is entitled to the respect due to a free citizen of a great republic, and is therefore bound to sustain its honour and its glory. He also feels that if capable, he can rise to fame and fortune, irrespective of birth or family influence.

In the estimation of character, an American appreciates a man according to his talents and virtue, and not by his artificial rank. Witness in this action the feeling I have attempted to describe: though Captain Biddle was said to be a strict disciplinarian, still, by reading the account of the battle, it is easy to see how much he was beloved by his crew, and how ready they were to resent the outrage committed upon him after the enemy had surrendered.

In these remarks, I do not mean to say that the captains and superior officers in the British navy are not brave and gallant men, and that they are not willing to fight for their king and country, whenever called upon; on the contrary, I believe them to be ever ready to shed the last drop of their blood in defence of their country's honour and glory. But. in my opinion, this does not apply to the petty officers and seamen on board their ships-of-war.

If this assertion be not true, how then, can any one account for the many English and Irish seamen found on board of our men-of-war and privateers, fighting against their own nation, when not one American, to my knowledge, voluntarily fought against his country?

I have questioned several English seamen on the subject of their fighting against their country, and the reply, in all cases, was about the same. They said, it is true I was born in England, but never had any concern in its social or political institutions, for everybody knows that in that country a poor man has no part or lot in its government. And as for the nobility and privileged classes, I hate them worse than poison.

These facts are not generally known in England, when they are seeking for reasons to account for their many defeats in their naval engagements with the United States.

The British soldiers (called marines) on board of their men-of-war, are brave enough, it is true, but are mere tools in the hands of the aristocracy. The great portion of their duty is to protect the officers and watch the seamen, to prevent desertion; consequently they are generally despised and hated by the sailors.[1]

I am aware that I am writing on a very delicate subject, but as I have attempted to prove that our successes were not owing to employing picked seamen to man our ships, or to their superior weight of metal, but almost entirely to the peculiar nature of our government, contrasted with a monarchical one; and in carrying out my argument, I have been obliged to bring out several facts which I suppose will not be very agreeable to an English ear.

As a corroborating fact of what I have stated, I ask the reader to call to mind the many glorious victories gained by the French republic during its great struggle against combined Europe. With an army of a hundred thousand men, singing the *Marseilles Hymn*, by whole battalions, accompanied by eighty

---

[1] After the above remarks on the marine corps, candour prompts me to say that they are a very important arm to every navy, not only to support discipline, but to add a martial appearance to a man-of-war.

pieces of artillery playing the chorus, they swept entire armies before them. Yes, it is such exciting scenes that fully develop the power of republican enthusiasm, and lead men to face death at the cannon's mouth.

During our war with England, in 1812, the proneness of the people of that country to credit every statement in disparagement of their adversaries, was eagerly seconded by the government.

The government papers at that period abounded with falsehoods so gross, and with perversions so reckless, that the people might well suppose the Americans to be an uncivilized race, between whom and the Indians, little difference existed.

The official reports of battles at that epoch, whether on sea or land, were studiously deceptive.

No account by any British naval or army officer, of his defeat or disaster could be published until "revised and corrected" by the Admiralty or the Horse Guards.

Every success was magnified and exaggerated, while every defeat was qualified and attributed to any other cause than American valour, seamanship, or generalship.

The victories of Hull, Perry, McDonough, and Jackson, were ascribed to monstrous disparity of force on our side, aided by those untoward accidents which bravery and skill can neither avert nor overcome.

I need not say to any American reader, that the frigate *President* was captured after one of the most gallant and well conducted battles in naval annals.

She encountered a British squadron, consisting of the frigate *Endymion*, the majestic *razee*, and the frigates *Pomone* and *Tennydos*.

She had a severe running fight with the *Endymion* for two hours and a half, and had so completely beaten that ship, that she was silenced, and dropped far astern, waiting for the other three ships to come up; and yet the government papers announced, in their usual inflated language of triumph; the capture of the American frigate *President*, by His Majesty's ship *Endymion*.

They have now in England and its colonies, beautiful engravings in rich frames, representing a most gallant victory by the *Endymion* over the *President*, the two ships lying side by side, and no other vessel in the picture, nor any indication by note or comment, that it was any other than a single battle between the two ships.

If we measure the degree of civilization of a people by their humanity in war, we adopt a just standard. The savage and the Christian differ in few respects, more strikingly, than in their bearing towards their enemies. Cruelty, plunder, and slaughter are inseparable from the idea of bravery and glory in the estimation of the former, while the elevating spirit of our religion and of the civilization, of which that religion is the fountain, impel the latter to mercy and humanity.

With civilized powers, the triumph of the victor is not complete until he has manifested, not only forbearance but kindness towards the vanquished. Prisoners of war cease to stand as enemies, and are thenceforth but fellow-men, entitled to those humanities which man owes to his fellow-man. Civilized nations, in waging war, are ever bound to respect and shelter private persons, and in passing through an enemy's country, to protect private property, defenceless age, women and children. The brutal passions of depraved soldiers must be restrained and unnecessary bloodshed avoided.

The British lay high claim to such civilization and to such humanity. It would be unjust to deny that their humane and gallant officers have, in very many instances, justified such claim. Such men, for instance, as Sir Thomas Hardy and Captain W. F. Wise, are an honour to any nation. From the latter, the writer acknowledges for himself and his officers, with warm friendship and gratitude, the reception of the most delicate and generous attention, while prisoners on board the frigate *Granicus*.

But such was not the customary treatment received by American prisoners in the war of 1812. As a general thing, when an American merchant ship or private armed vessel was captured, all charts, books and nautical instruments were seized and taken away; and the only answer to remonstrances was, that this conduct was under orders from the Admiralty. Nor did plunder always stop here, it was often extended, under the same plea, to the immediate personal effects of the captives.

The treatment of prisoners was generally most unjustifiable, and in many cases, such as to outrage decency and humanity. Captains, mates and supercargoes, as well as crews, were sent to prison, or stowed away in filthy prison-ships. They were not allowed their personal liberty on parole of honour, except in a few cases, where powerful interest could be brought to bear in behalf of individuals.

I believe that I may say for the credit of our flag, that whenever one of our national or private armed ships captured a British vessel, all private property of the officers and crew was held sacred, and when the prisoners reached the United States, captains, mates, and supercargoes were allowed social liberty on their parole of honour, with the full range of the city or town where they were quartered. Whenever their personal qualities were such as to entitle them to it, they enjoyed the social hospitality of our citizens. The seamen were so well fed and amply provided for, that in very many instances they left the country with great reluctance, when exchanged for American prisoners.

The writer of these pages has no wish or willingness to take a narrow view of so broad a subject as the characteristics of a great, powerful, enlightened, Christian, and brave nation. Such undoubtedly, our former enemy was and is, but still it is impossible in seeking for truth, to shut our eyes to the wide space which lies between her claims and her merits in these respects. The shocking and long-continued barbarities practised toward her prisoners in the war of our revolution, are recorded in the history of the *Old Sugar House*, *The Jail*, *The Jersey Prison Ship*, at the Wallabout, and other abodes of cruelty and wretchedness. The war which followed in 1812, witnessed her incomplete civilization in the miseries inflicted at Dartmoor prison.

With how much pride can we point, not only to our action toward the enemy on the sea, but to the conduct of our officers and soldiers in battle and after battle on the land. Such an act as the recent demolition by the British troops of the choice treasures of ancient art and learning, which the studies and toils of scholars and antiquarians had garnered up in the National Museum of Kertch, fixes an indelible blot on the escutcheon of England.

In blazing contrast to such shocking acts as this, and the sack of Badajoz, to which reference will presently be made, was the recent campaign by our troops under General Scott, from Vera Cruz to Mexico. Almost every mile of that long journey was rendered memorable by some sanguinary battle, and victory terminating in the surrender of the great city itself. Plunder, sack, and rapine were unknown. The very supplies taken from the inhabitants for our troops, were fully paid for; private property and houses were respected, and outrage upon age or sex was unknown.

It is not easy to say whether our troops, and their illustrious commander (General Winfield Scott), achieved more glory for their country by their intrepid and invincible valour, or in illustrating the civilization of America by their humanity and morality.

What more striking contrast can be presented than that between the conduct of the triumphant Americans under Scott, at Mexico, and that of the triumphant British under the Duke of Wellington, at Badajoz.

That I may avoid the charge of exaggeration in describing the conduct of the latter on that occasion, I will subjoin the narration of it, by the author of a recent English work, devoted to the eulogy of the great Duke.

The most of my readers will probably recollect, that during the siege of Badajoz, Lord Wellington promised his soldiers that if they would capture the place, they should be allowed to sack and plunder it.

After a sanguinary conflict, it was finally taken by storm, on the 6th of April, 1812; and, agreeable to promise, the ill-fated city was given up to rapine and outrage for a period of one day and two nights.

Here follows the recital of the savage brutality of the British soldiers, as given by Colonel Maxwell, of the British army, in his own words:

"No language can depict the horrors which succeed a storm. The following vivid, but faithful picture of Badajoz, as it appeared on the evening after it had been carried, will convey some idea of the dreadful outrages that ensued.

"It was nearly dusk, and the few hours while I slept had made a frightful change in the condition and temper of the soldiery. In the morning they were obedient to their officers, and preserved the semblance of subordination; now they were in a state of furious intoxication; discipline was forgotten, and the splendid troops of yesterday had become a fierce and sanguinary rabble, dead to every touch of human feeling, and filled with every demoniac passion that can brutalize the man. The town was in terrible confusion, and on every side frightful tokens of military license met the eye.

"One street, as I approached the castle, was almost choked up with broken furniture, for the houses had been gutted from the cellar to the garret, the partitions torn down, and even the beds ripped and scattered to the winds, in the hope that gold might be found concealed.

"A convent [2] at the end of the *strada* of St. John was in flames, and I saw more than one wretched nun in the arms of a drunken soldier.

"Further on, the confusion seemed greater. Brandy and wine casks were rolled out before the stores; some were full, some half-drunk, but more staved in mere wantonness, and the liquors running through the kennel.

"Many a harrowing scream saluted the ear of the passer-by; many a female supplication was heard asking in vain for mercy.

---

2. A general officer, having received secret information that a soldier's wife had been robbing, had her stripped by the provost, who found on her person an under garment of red velvet, bordered with gold lace, six inches deep. This article had evidently been the covering of a communion table.

How could it be otherwise, when it is remembered that twenty thousand furious and licentious madmen were loosed upon an immense population, among which many of the loveliest women upon earth might be found?

"All within that devoted city was at the disposal of an infuriated army, over whom for a time control was lost, aided by an infamous collection of camp-followers, who were, if possible, more sanguinary and pitiless even than those who had survived the storm!

"It is useless to dwell upon a scene from which the heart revolts. Few females in this beautiful town were saved that night from insult. The noble and the beggar—the nun, the wife and daughter of the artisan—youth and age—all were involved in general ruin. None were respected, and few consequently escaped.

"The madness of those desperate brigands was variously exhibited; some fired through doors and windows; others at the church bells; many at the wretched inhabitants as they fled into the streets to escape the bayonets of the savages, who were demolishing their property within doors; while some wretches, as if blood had not flowed in sufficient torrents already, shot from the windows their own companions as they staggered on below.

"What chances had the miserable inhabitants of escaping death, when more than one officer perished by the bullets and bayonets of the very men whom a few hours before he had led to the assault?

"Strict measures were taken on the second day by Lord Wellington to repress these desperate excesses, and save the infuriated soldiery from the fatal consequences their own debauchery produced.[3]

"A Portuguese brigade was brought from the rear, and sent

---

3. "On entering the cathedral, I saw three British soldiers literally drowned in brandy. A spacious vault had been converted into a spirit depôt for the garrison; the casks had been perforated by musket balls, and their contents escaping, formed a pool of some depth. These men, becoming intoxicated, had fallen head-foremost into the liquor, and were suffocated, as I found them."

into the town, accompanied by the provost marshal and the gallows.

"This demonstration had its due effect, and one rope carried terror to rioters, whom the bayonets of a whole regiment could not appal."[4]

In presenting this fearful picture, I am actuated by no desire to foment ill-feeling between the people of the two great nations.

War is a sore calamity and a curse, and that nation achieves the greatest victory which mitigates its cruelties and wrongs. But while history records such fiendish deeds as I have cited, and the history of British India is one of unchristian oppression and cruelty by the great Christian nation of Europe, we may well claim for our country that her page, thus far, is brighter, purer, clearer than that of our mother country.

The writer of these pages arrived at Lisbon a few weeks after the fall of Badajoz, and saw great numbers of wounded British officers, who came down from that place to Lisbon for a change of air, and relaxation from military duty to recover from their wounds.

A few days previous to the capture of Badajoz, several American gentlemen left Lisbon from motives of curiosity to witness the siege of the unfortunate city, and if it fell, they intended to visit it, while given up to plunder and rapine. They accordingly saw the assault and surrender of the place, and the next day visited the town.

The most of these gentlemen have since died, there is, however, one of them still living in New York City, Alexander Hamilton, Esq. This gentleman not only confirms all the revolting scenes related by Colonel Maxwell, but adds, as an eye witness, many other heart-rending sights, which are enough to freeze the blood with horror.

After my severe remarks on the English, some of my readers

---

4. These extracts are from Maxwell's *Victories of Wellington and the British Armies*, (page 268) author of *Stories of Waterloo, The Bivouac, The Life of Wellington* etc., etc. London: Henry G. Bonn, 1852.

may accuse me of being prejudiced against them. It is true that my father, in the revolutionary war, was a prisoner for several months on board the *Jersey* Prison Ship, in New York, and that I had a brother who was a prisoner in 1812, at Dartmoor, during the massacre; still I think I can do the English justice, and herewith challenge the world to name a single instance in this history, where I have deviated from the truth in the smallest degree.

Prizes Captured by Privateers

Brig Lady *Trowbridge*, 8 guns, 208 tons, with a cargo of live stock, from the Cape de Verds for Barbadoes, captured by the brig *Ino*, of Boston, and burnt. This vessel was captured and destroyed within two miles of the Island of Barbadoes, and within view of the British vessels-of-war, lying at Bridgetown. The *Ino* was lost off Charleston, the particulars are interesting, and are as follows:

Extracted from a Charleston Paper

"*Charleston, March 7th.*—The officers of the *Ino* reached town yesterday morning, from Bull's Bay, and politely furnished the editor of the *City Gazette*, with the subjoined particulars of the cruise, and subsequent destruction of said vessel. The name of the reef on which the *Ino* struck, is Racoon Key. Her crew, 82 in number, arrived here yesterday, having come from the scene of their shipwreck on foot. The *Ino* belonged to Boston, and was owned by the Hon. William Gray.

"It is to be observed, that on Friday last, the 3rd instant, twelve days had elapsed since the date of the President's proclamation, and thirteen since the ratification of the treaty of peace, which by one of its articles, allows twelve days to put an end to hostilities on our coast, of which circumstance the captain of the *Severn* could not but be informed; and yet he drove the *Ino* on shore, and made prisoners of two of her crew. This may be peaceable and friendly conduct in the vocabulary of John Bull, but it is very different in that of Americans. We hope it is the last act of the kind we shall hear of."

"*March 7th.*—Early in the morning in ten fathoms water, off Charleston, standing in, discovered a large ship at anchor off the bar, wind light at N.N.E., hauled close on the wind, starboard-tacks aboard. The ship, which we soon discovered to be a frigate, weighed and stood for us, and by the shifting of the wind, hemmed us in between her and the shore; after making every exertion with sweeps, etc., to get clear, found that the frigate, by the help of her boats, and a breeze, which sprung up from the offing, came so fast upon us, that we could neither get into Charleston, nor weather away Cape Romain, so that we were obliged to bear up, and endeavour to get into Bull's Bay, in which attempt the *Ino* unfortunately struck upon a reef.

"On this being perceived, the frigate immediately sent her boats to attack us, but by a few well-directed rounds of grape and canister, they were forced to retire. In the night the *Ino* bilged, and threatening to go to pieces, we (having lost our boats some days before) proceeded to construct rafts, to transport ourselves on shore. At 4 a.m. cut away our masts, she being in a very dangerous condition, and laying on her beam ends. At daylight discovered the frigate at anchor, and her boats pulling for us—prepared to receive them, when within grape range, hoisted our flag on a pike-staff, and gave them a broadside of grape and canister; on which they precipitately hauled off. We then manned our rafts, and set fire to the *Ino*. At 2 p.m. she blew up.

"While at the most imminent hazard of our lives, our rafts torn to pieces by the breakers, and part off us swimming, they again came in with their boats, and valiantly took two poor fellows, who were swimming for their lives, and carried them off. We finally succeeded in getting on a sand bar, from which unpleasant situation we were relieved by the humanity of Captain John Phillips, of Charleston, commanding a small schooner lying in the bay. The officers of the *Ino*, for the present, forbear making any comments on this extraordinary transaction, but merely observe that they had no idea of peace having taken place, but have ascertained that the captain of the frigate *Severn* had known it for many days."

British ship *Mary and Susan*, 470 tons, with an immense cargo of dry-goods, etc., from London for Jamaica, captured by the *Chasseur*, and sent into Savannah. The *Mary and Susan* was a fine vessel, and her cargo very valuable.

The schooner *Arrow*, from Catalonia for London, with 100 casks of almonds, 1650 casks of hazel-nuts, sent into Salem, by the *America* of that port. The *Arrow* was captured January 22nd and the *America* had previously made several valuable prizes on the same cruise.

Ship *Adventure* for Havana, with a valuable assorted cargo, captured by the *Chasseur*, and ordered for Charleston, but she was unfortunately recaptured by the *Severn* frigate. We call her a good prize, however, because her most valuable effects were taken out by the *Chasseur*, and in this way secured.

Schooner *Robert*, from Portsmouth, England, for St. Michael's, captured by the *America*, of Salem, and destroyed.

Sloop *Jubilee*, from Tenerife, for Jersey, with wine and *barilla*, captured by the same, divested of a few pipes of wine, and destroyed.

Ship *Emulation*, captured by the *Syren* privateer, and put into Gracioso, Western Isles, where, it is said, she was abandoned by her prize-crew.

British ship ——, captured by the *McDonough*, of Rhode Island, and burnt.

EXTRACT FROM THE LOG-BOOK OF THE *McDONOUGH*

"*Jan. 31st.*—At 12 m. discovered a large ship under our lea, making signals, about two leagues distant, showing two tiers of ports. At 1 o'clock, p.m., edged down for her, and discovered her lower battery to be false; immediately prepared for action. At 2 o'clock, bore up for his weather quarter, and hoisted our colours; the enemy at the same time hauling up his courses, and lying by for us. At half past two commenced the action within musket shot, observing the enemy to fire seven guns from his broadside, besides swivels, with a tremendous shower of musketry, which led us to suppose her to be a troop ship, in which we were not mistaken. At half past three, passed close under her bows to rake her, when we discovered her decks full of soldiers, who gave us a tremendous volley.

"At three quarters past three, our braces, bowlines and haulyards, being all shot away, our sails literally cut to pieces, rigging much damaged, and two guns dismounted, eleven men wounded, seven severely, seven shot in our hull, our fore and main masts badly wounded, our stern boat had two 18 pound shot through her, the enemy being far superior to us in point of metal, having eighteen nine pounders, and at least 300 soldiers, besides her crew, thought it prudent to haul off.

"Our enemy having suffered, to appearance, bore away for Tenerife, with some of her people slung over the sides, stopping shot holes. At 3 a.m. tacked ship to the S.W., all hands employed repairing sails, rigging, gun carriages, and other damages."

The *McDonough* arrived at Savannah, March 7th.

Schooner *Ceres*, from Newfoundland for Dublin, cargo 15,000 gallons of oil, captured by the *Reindeer*, of Boston, and destroyed.

Schooner *William*, of London, from White-Haven for St. Michaels, in ballast, captured by the same, and burnt.

Sloop *Unity*, from Lisbon for Brook-Haven, with oranges, captured by the same, and made a cartel of, to get rid of prisoners.

Brig *Daphne*, 2 guns, 200 tons, with a full cargo, for London, captured by the same, divested of a quantity of cloves, etc., manned and ordered to a port in the United States.

The *Reindeer* also captured another valuable brig, name not given, which she manned and ordered to a port in the United States.

The privateer *Young Wasp* returned to Philadelphia, laden with valuable goods, from a successful cruise off the coasts of England and Spain, and from thence off the Cape of Good Hope and around the island of St. Helena. She was one hundred and seventy days absent, and made eight prizes; the most of them valuable. She had three engagements with the enemy. The first with a well armed and manned letter-of-marque ship, which she mistook for a sloop-of-war, and hauled off. The second with a man-of-war brig; they soon separated. The third with the ship *Clarendon*, of 14 guns and fifty men, from Batavia, bound for London, with a valuable cargo. With this ship the privateer had a battle for a short time, when the enemy surrendered. In this affair the *Wasp* had one man killed and two wounded.

She manned the *Clarendon* and ordered her to proceed to the first port in the United States, and then continued on her cruise. She also captured the English brig *Plutus*, from London for Tenerife, with an assorted cargo. The privateer divested her prize of a considerable portion of her cargo, when an English frigate hove in sight, which obliged her to abandon her prize and make her escape. Subsequently she captured the ship *Mary Ann*, from the Cape of Good Hope, bound for Malacca, and after divesting her of sundry articles, allowed her to proceed on her voyage.

During this cruise, the *Wasp* traversed a space of 30,000 miles, and with but little loss.

Brig *Lord Duncan*, from Liverpool for Bermuda, captured by the *Morgiana*, of New York, and burnt.

Brig *Cossack*, 6 guns, from Cork, for Jamaica, captured by the same, divested, and made a cartel of, to get rid of her prisoners.

Schooner *Resolution*, with sugar, molasses, etc., sent into a southern port by the *Kemp*, of Baltimore.

Sloop ———, captured by the same, in the West. Indies, divested, and given up to the prisoners.

Ship *Otway*, 3 guns, from Liverpool for Jamaica, with a rich cargo of British goods and sundries, captured by the same, divested of as many goods as the privateer could stow away, manned and ordered her into port.

The *Kemp* arrived safe at Baltimore with 200 bales and packages of British goods, 1,800 stand of arms, and sundry other articles of merchandise.

The *Kemp* captured a British brig (name not given), mounting 14 guns, with forty men, after a warm action of forty minutes, when the enemy struck his colours. Divested the prize of sundry articles, and manned her for the United States.

In this action the *Kemp* had one man killed and two wounded.

On board of the brig there were two killed and eight wounded.

Soon after the capture of this vessel, the prize crew-were obliged to abandon her, being closely pursued by a British ship-of-war. They were obliged to take to their boats and return to the privateer.

Brig *Alexander*, captured by the *Leo*, of Baltimore, and cast away near Ferrol, while entering that port in a heavy gale of wind.

Brig *Eagle*, captured by the *Lawrence*, of Baltimore; afterwards re-captured and wrecked. She was chiefly laden with dry-goods.

The British ship *Arabella*, of Calcutta, was captured by the letter-of-marque ship *Rambler*, of Boston, on her passage to Canton, and carried into Macao. A letter from Captain Edes, of the *Rambler*, dated at Canton, December 6th, says:—

"Our prize (the ship *Arabella*) arrived at Macao the same day we arrived at Canton, and was taken possession of by the Portuguese government, and given up to the British Admiral on this station. I have protested against this proceeding, and hope a proper representation will be made to the Portuguese government, who ought, in justice, to pay us the amount she was insured for, at Calcutta (60,000 *rupees*), eighteen days out. I also captured the British brig *Madeira*, took out 75 casks of wine, and gave her up."

Ship *Anne*, 417 tons, — guns, 25 men, with a great cargo of mahogany, log-wood and fustic; coppered, and in fine order, captured by the *Zebec Ultor*, of Baltimore, after a slight resistance, and sent into New York.

English brig *Crown Prince*, with a cargo of merino wool, sent into Sedgewick, by the *Portsmouth*, of Portsmouth. The value of this prize was supposed to be $300,000.

British brig *Juno*, a transport, captured by the same, divested, and made a cartel of, to get rid of prisoners.

Brig *Ocean*, from Merimachi for Glasgow, laden with timber, captured by the same, and burnt.

Brig *Langton*, from Richiebucto, N. S., for Scotland, captured by the same, and ransomed.

Brig *Adeona*, with 450 bales and packages of broadcloths, etc., captured by the *America*, of Salem, and sent into that port, this was a very valuable prize.

Schooner *Sultan*, laden with cocoa, captured by the *Morgiana*, of New York, and sent into Wilmington, N. C.

Brig *Sarah*, for Alicant, with codfish, captured by the *Warrior* of New York, and burnt.

Brig *Legal Tender*, with a valuable cargo, captured by the *David Porter*, and recaptured by the *Spencer* 74, on the 7th of March.

Ship *Antigua*, 320 tons, with a full cargo of West India produce, was captured off the Western Islands by the *Fox*, of Portsmouth, and sent into that port.

Ship *City of Limerick,* with a very valuable cargo, from London for Jamaica, captured by the *Morgiana*, of New York, and ordered into port, after having been divested of the most valuable part of her cargo.

Brig *Helen*, from London for Jamaica, laden with dry-goods and iron, captured by the same, and ordered into port.

We accounted these good prizes, for the *Morgiana* arrived with property valued at $230,000, which she took out of her prizes.

Schooner *Perseverance*, from Granada for Demarara, captured by the same, and burnt.

Brig *John*, from Martinique for Antigua, captured by the same, and burnt.

Brig *Maria Annabella*, from Dublin for St. Kitts, captured by the *Zebec Ultor*, divested of a few Irish linens, and burnt. Her cargo consisted chiefly of provisions.

Sloops *Twins* and *L"Espirance*, captured by the same, divested, and given up.

Sloop *Constitution*, from St. Barts for Dominica, captured by the same, and burnt.

Brig *Mohawk*, of Jamaica, captured by the *Zebec Ultor*. We account this a fortunate circumstance, being a good prize by the terms of the treaty; she safely arrived in port.

Ship ——, captured by the letter-of-marque ship *Jacob Jones*, of Boston, on her passage to Canton, and divested of $60,000 worth of opium, etc., and then sent her to a port in the United States.

Brig *Baltic*, captured by the *Grand Turk*, of Salem; recaptured by the British, and since lost. She had a cargo of sweet oil.

Cutter *Sloop Busy*, of Guernsey, from Plymouth for St. Michaels, with potatoes, captured by the *America* of Salem, and burnt.

Schooner *Black Joke*, of London, for Terceira, with coal, porter, etc., captured by the same, and burnt.

Packet ship *Elizabeth*, in ballast, 8 guns, thirty-one men, captured by the same, after a short battle, in which the *Elizabeth* had two men killed, and thirteen wounded, and was literally cut to pieces, her masts, spars, hull, and sails being penetrated by more than 700 shot, while the America received no injury, either in men, rigging, or hull. The *Elizabeth* was divested of her armament, and given up to her original crew. She was bound from Rio Janeiro to Falmouth, England. Beside the foregoing and two others, the *America* captured and manned a very valuable ship, from Rio Janeiro, and a brig laden with sugar, from Antigua for Glasgow. The *America* had on board more than $10,000 worth of valuable goods, taken out of her prizes at sea. This fortunate ship safely arrived at Salem on the 10th of April, after a cruise of 134 days, without losing a single man either by sickness or casualty. It is stated that she had, during the war, cleared more than $600,000 for her owners.

The privateer *Avon*, of 14 guns, was captured by the British brig *Barbadoes*, of 17 guns, after a warm action of an hour and a half, the British brig-of-war *Columbine* being within three miles in chase, and coming up. The *Avon* had one man killed, and four wounded, the *Barbadoes* one killed, and three wounded. Twenty-two of the best men belonging to the former were absent at the time of the fight, in a small sloop, for the purpose of cutting vessels out from St. Kitts. The sloop was also captured by the British the next day.

The privateer *Hyder Ali,* Captain Thorndike, of Boston, was captured in the East Indies, by the British frigate *Owen Glendower.* She had been chased for three days by the *Salsetta,* frigate, from which ship she escaped, but in so doing, the privateer was driven within gun-shot of the *Owen Glendower,* which ship soon brought her within the reach of her musketry, when she was obliged to surrender. She had, previous to her capture, made nine prizes, which vessels were unfortunately recaptured.

The famous privateer *Prince of Neufchâtel,* was captured and sent into England.

An American letter-of-marque schooner, a fast sailing vessel, arrived at Canton in December, 1814, with a cargo of seal skins, valued at $300,000. These skins were taken from the Fejee, and other islands in the Pacific.

She was out of the influence of the war, and made a very successful voyage.

British schooner, name not given, captured by the *Fox* privateer of Portsmouth, N. H.; after divesting the prize of the valuable part of her cargo, destroyed her. This privateer annoyed the enemy during the whole of the war, and arrived safe at Portsmouth, after having made seven successful cruises.

Schooner *John and Ann,* from Halifax for the West Indies, captured by the *Young Wasp,* of Philadelphia, manned, but lost on Ocracock bar, N. C.

SKETCH OF THE GALLANT ACHIEVEMENTS OF THE HEROIC CAPT. T. BOYLE, OF THE PRIVATEER BRIG *CHASSEUR*, OF BALTIMORE, ON HIS LAST CRUISE IN THE BRITISH CHANNEL, AND AMONG THE W. INDIA ISLANDS, IN THE WINTERS OF 1814 AND 1815.

The *Chasseur* was a very formidable vessel, carrying sixteen long twelve pounders, and at the commencement of a cruise her crew probably amounted to one hundred men, including officers, seamen, and marines.

Here follows a list of prizes made by this distinguished commander. This list is a portion (by no means all) of his captures, during a period of three months.

Sloop *Christiana*, of Kilkadee, Scotland, made a cartel of her, to disembarrass him from prisoners

Brig *Reindeer*, of Aberdeen, from the Island of Lanzarote for London, with a cargo of wine and *barrilla*; manned her for the United States.

Schooner *Favourite*, also from Lanzarote, bound for London, with a similar cargo.

Brig *Marquis of Cornwallis*, from the same island, bound also for London. This vessel, being of small value, was made a cartel of, to get rid of prisoners.

English brig *Alert*, of Poole, from Newfoundland with a cargo of timber, taken and destroyed.

Brig *Harmony*, of Aberdeen, from Newfoundland bound for London, made a cartel of her, to be relieved from prisoners.

Ship *Carlbury*, of London, from Jamaica, with a very valuable cargo of cotton, cocoa, hides, indigo, etc. divested her of two hundred and thirty-seven *ceroons* of indigo, and manned her for the United States. The goods taken from this prize were estimated at fifty thousand dollars.

Brig *Eclipse*, a valuable vessel of fourteen guns, sent to New York, at which place she arrived safe.

Brig *Commerce*, also a valuable vessel, laden with fish, ordered her to proceed to the United States.

Brig *Antelope*, carrying eight eighteen pound carronades, with a long torn, from Havana, laden with nine hundred boxes of sugar; she made no resistance, and was also sent to the United States.

British schooner *Fox* from Newfoundland, laden with fish for the Mediterranean, sent her to the United States.

Ship *James*, of London, with twelve guns and twenty men

from the river La Plata, with hides, tallow, bark, furs, etc.

Brig *Atlantic*, also of London, with eight guns and fifteen men, from the river La Plata, loaded with a similar cargo. The *James* and the *Atlantic* were in company, and were both captured and manned for the United States.

Ship *Theodore*, of Liverpool, with eight guns, from Marenham, with 1,600 bales of cotton, etc., etc.

Brig *Amicus* of Liverpool, from Lisbon, with wool fruit, and two bales of woollen goods.

Besides the vessels already enumerated there were others, whose names are not noticed in this list. The whole number of vessels captured by Captain Boyle, on this cruise, was eighteen, and many of them very valuable. Captain B. brought into port forty-three prisoners, and paroled one hundred and fifty. Had the *Chasseur* been a United States vessel, acting under orders to burn, sink, and destroy all prizes, the loss to the enemy by this brig alone, would have exceeded a million and a half of dollars. Although many of these prizes were probably recaptured, still the *Chasseur* must have made a very profitable cruise, for all who were concerned in this very fortunate privateer.

During Captain Boyle's cruise in the British Channel and around the coast of Great Britain, he had many hairbreadth escapes. He was once so near a frigate as partially to exchange broadsides with her. At another time he was nearly surrounded by two frigates and two brigs-of-war, and, in hauling off to avoid them, one of the frigates threw a shot on board of his brig, and wounded three men; he, however, at length made his escape, and out-manoeuvred and out-sailed them all.

At this period, it was the general custom for the British admirals on our coast to issue what the Americans called paper-blockades, declaring nearly the whole coast of North America in a strict state of blockade, which, to have done effectually, would have required all the ships in the. world. Several of these blockade-proclamations had recently been issued by Admiral Sir John Borlaise Warren and Sir Alexander Cochrane.

As a *burlesque* on these paper-blockades, Captain Boyle, while in the British Channel, issued the following proclamation, and sent it by a cartel to London with a request to have it posted up at Loyd's Coffee House:

By Thomas Boyle, Esquire. Commander of the private armed brig *Chasseur*, etc., etc.

PROCLAMATION

Whereas it has become customary with the Admirals of Great Britain, commanding small forces on the coast of the United States, particularly with Sir John Borlaise Warren and Sir Alexander Cochrane, to declare all the coast of the said United States in a state of strict and rigorous blockade, without possessing the power to justify such a declaration, or stationing an adequate force to maintain said blockade.

I do, therefore, by virtue of the power and authority in me vested (possessing sufficient force), declare all the ports, harbours, bays, creeks, rivers, inlets, outlets, islands and sea coast of the United Kingdom of Great Britain and Ireland in a state of strict and rigorous blockade.

And I do further declare, that I consider the force under my command adequate to maintain strictly, rigorously and effectually, the said blockade.

And I do hereby require the respective officers, whether captains, commanders, or commanding officers, under my command, employed or to be employed, on the coasts of England, Ireland and Scotland, to pay strict attention to the execution of this my proclamation.

And I do hereby caution and forbid the ships and vessels of all and every nation, in amity and peace with the United States, from entering or attempting to enter, or from coming or attempting to come out of any of the said ports, harbours, bays, creeks, rivers, inlets, outlets, islands, or sea coast, under any pretence whatsoever.

And that no person may plead ignorance of this, my proclamation, I have ordered the same to be made public in England.

Given under my hand on board the *Chasseur*, day and date

as above.

Thomas Boyle.

(By command of the commanding officer.)
J. J. Stanbury, Secretary,

LETTER FROM CAPTAIN BOYLE, TO MR. GEORGE P. STEPHENSON, ONE OF THE OWNERS OF THE *CHASSEUR*.

"At Sea, March 2nd, 1815.

"Dear Sir: I have the donor to inform you, that on the 26th of February, being about six leagues to windward of Havana, and two leagues from the land, at 11 a.m. discovered a schooner bearing N.E. of us, apparently running before the wind; made every possible sail in chase, the convoy in sight from the mast head, to leeward, laying-to off Havana. At meridian, gaining fast on the chase, which appeared to be a large, long, low pilot boat built schooner, with yellow sides; she hauled up more to the northward, and apparently was endeavouring to escape us. At half-past 12 meridian, I fired a gun, and hoisted the American flag, to ascertain, if possible, to what nation the schooner belonged; but she showed no colours, was carrying a press of sail, and in a few minutes carried away her fore-top-mast. She was at this time about three miles from us.

"They cut away the wreck of the top-mast immediately, and trimmed her sails sharp by the wind. At 1 p.m. drawing up with her very fast; she fired a stern chase gun at us, and hoisted English colours, showing at the same time only three ports on the side next us.

"Under the impression that she was a running vessel, bound to Havana, and weakly armed and manned, I tried every effort to close with her as quick as possible. I saw very few men on her deck, and hastily made some preparation for action, though neither my officers nor myself expected any fighting; of course we were not completely prepared for battle. At 1.26 p.m. we were within pistol shot of the enemy, when he opened a tier of ten ports on a side, and gave us his whole broadside of round, grape, and musket balls. I then opened the *Chasseur's* fire from the great

Battle between the Brig Chasseur and the Schooner St. Lawrence off Havanna on the 26th February, 1815

guns and musketry, and endeavoured to close with him, for the purpose of boarding; we having quick way at the time, shot ahead of him under his lea, he put his helm up, for the purpose of wearing across our stern, to give us a raking fire, which I prevented by timely noticing his intention, and putting our helm hard up also. He shot quickly ahead, and I closed within ten yards' of him. At this time both fires were heavy, severe, and destructive. I now found that his men had been concealed under his bulwark, and that I had a powerful enemy to contend with, and at 1:40 p.m., gave the order for boarding, which my brave officers and men cheerfully obeyed with unexampled quickness; I instantly put the helm to starboard to lay him on board, and when in the act of boarding she surrendered.

"Mr. W. M. Christie, prize-master, from his courage and activity, got first on board of her—she proved to be his Britannic Majesty's schooner *St. Lawrence*, commanded by Lieutenant J. C. Gordon, formerly the famous privateer *Atlas*, of Philadelphia, built on the Chesapeake,-mounting 15 guns, 14 twelve pound carronades, upon an improved construction, and a long nine pounder, with a complement of 75 men, and had on board a number of soldiers, marines, and some gentlemen of the navy, passengers, bound express to the squadron off New Orleans.

"She had, by the report of her commander, six men killed and seventeen wounded, most of them badly, and several of them mortally. She was a perfect wreck, cut to pieces in the hull, and scarcely a rope left standing, and by report of her commander, he had not an officer onboard, that was not either killed or wounded, himself among the latter. The *Chasseur's* sails and rigging suffered much, and from the zeal and anxiety of my brave crew to do their duty, and thereby exposing themselves, I had five men killed, and eight wounded, myself among the latter, though very slightly. Thus ended the action, in fifteen minutes after its commencement, and about, eight minutes close quarters, with a force, in every respect, equal to our own.

"The *Chasseur* mounted six twelve pounders, and eight short nine pound carronades (the latter taken from one of our prizes), ten of our twelve pound carronades having been thrown overboard, while hard chased by the Barosa frigate. The *St. Lawrence* had on board 89 men, beside several boys.

"From the number of hammocks, bedding, etc., etc., found on board of the enemy, it led us to believe that many more were killed than were reported. The *St. Lawrence* fired double the weight of shot that we did, from her twelves, at close quarters she fired a stand of grape and two bags, containing two hundred and twenty musket balls each, when, from the *Chasseur's* nines, were fired six and four pound shot, having no other, except some few grape. Were I to close this letter without mentioning the determined bravery of my first lieutenant, Mr. John Dieter, I should be acting very unjustly to my own feelings. My other lieutenants, Mr. Moran and Mr. Hammond N. Stansbury, as well as every other officer, behaved with a firmness, seldom, if ever equalled, and I believe never surpassed,

"Yours, with respect,

"Thomas Boyle.

"Mr. G. P. Stephenson, Baltimore."

"P. S.—On the night of the 26th the main-top-mast of the *St. Lawrence* went by the board; such was her wretched condition, and from motives of humanity, and the solicitation of her commander, I made a flag or cartel of her to carry the wounded to Havana, for their better comfort and convenience, as I know you would wish that I should mitigate the sufferings of the unfortunate wounded. I hope you will not be displeased at what I have done, there was no other alternative but to make a cartel of her, or destroy her. I should not willingly perhaps, have sought a contest with a king's vessel, knowing it was not our object; but my expectations were at first a valuable vessel and a valuable cargo, also.

"When I found myself deceived, the honour of the flag entrusted to my charge, was not to be disgraced by flight. I sent to the wounded a parcel of shirts, and two bales of purser's slops, to be distributed among them, and the other prisoners. A copy of the correspondence between the captain of the *St. Lawrence* and myself you have herewith enclosed, as well as my letter to your friends in Havana.

"Very respectfully yours,

"T. B."

Copy of a Certificate to Captain Thomas Boyle, from the Commander of his Britannic Majesty's Schooner St. Lawrence; Dated at Sea, February 27th, 1815, on Board the United States Private-Armed-Brig Chasseur.

In the event of Captain Boyle's becoming a prisoner of war to any British cruiser, I consider it a tribute justly due to his humane and generous treatment of myself, the surviving officers and crew of His Majesty's late schooner *St. Lawrence*, to state that his obliging attention and watchful solicitude to preserve our effects, and render us comfortable, during the short time we were in his possession, were such as justly entitle him to the indulgence and respect of every British subject.

I also certify that his endeavours to render us comfortable, and to secure our property, were carefully seconded by all his officers, who did their utmost to that effect.

J. C. Gordon,
Lieut. and Com. of His Majesty's
late Schooner *St Lawrence*.

Britannia needs no bulwark,
No towers along the steep;
Her march is o'er the mountain waves,
Her home is on the deep.

Arrival of the Privateer Chasseur.

Captain Boyle arrived in Baltimore on the 15th of April, 1815, in the brig *Chasseur*, full of rich goods. spoils from the enemy, after a successful cruise among the Islands in the West Indies.

On entering the port, the *Chasseur* saluted Fort McHenry in a handsome style. Her brave captain and crew were welcomed by all classes of the community.

The *Chasseur* was a fine, large brig, and familiarly called *The Pride of Baltimore*. She was indeed a fine specimen of naval architecture, and perhaps the most beautiful vessel that ever floated on the ocean. She sat as light and buoyant on the water as a graceful swan, and it required but very little help of the imagination to feel that she was about to leave her watery element, and fly into the clear, blue sky.

Although this gallant vessel was so elegant and attractive to her friends, she carried dismay and terror to her enemies. During her last cruise, only seventeen days previous to her arrival in port, her heroic commander captured His Britannic Majesty's schooner *St. Lawrence*, mounting 15 carriage guns, with a crew of 75 men.

This action lasted but fifteen minutes, when the Englishman surrendered his vessel, having been completely cut to pieces. Fifteen of his crew were killed, and twenty-five wounded; the *Chasseur* had but five men killed, and eight wounded, and received little or no damage in her hull.

Her sails and rigging were somewhat injured, but were soon repaired, so that in a few hours she was ready for another action.

The *Chasseur* made several other prizes on this cruise, which have been recorded in their proper places.

On Captain Boyle's return home to Baltimore, he heard that a treaty of peace had been signed at Ghent, by the Ambassadors of the American and English governments. He then returned to the peaceful avocations of private life, to enjoy the esteem and applause of all those who had the honour of his acquaintance.

I cannot conclude my remarks on Captain Boyle's services to his State and country, without expressing a wish that his name may be honoured and cherished by every American heart, and I think he is richly entitled to a national monument, to perpetuate his memory to the latest generations.

The writer regrets that he never had the pleasure of a personal acquaintance with Captain Boyle; but from all he can learn of his character, to say that he was a dashing, brave man, would, in his case, be but common-place eulogy, for he was infinitely more than that idea expresses. He evidently possessed many of the elements of a great man, for in him were blended the impetuous bravery of a Murat, with the prudence of a Wellington. He wisely judged when to attack the enemy, and when to retreat, with honour to himself, and to the flag under which he sailed.

The reader will please observe his daring bravery in cruising in the British Channel; and call to mind his many gallant victories, particularly when in command of the schooner *Comet*, in an action off Pernambuco, with a large Portuguese man-of-war-brig and three English merchantmen.

They were all well-armed and manned, notwithstanding which, Captain Boyle captured the three British vessels, and beat off the man-of-war.

The details of this battle may be found in the fourth chapter of this work.

In his last cruise in the *Chasseur* he also captured his Britannic Majesty's schooner *St. Lawrence*, of at least equal force with himself.

And then, reflect on his prudence in the management of his prizes.

He destroyed the dullest and poorest of them, and sent into port the best and most valuable, after having removed the specie, and all the most valuable articles into his own vessel, so as to secure a successful cruise to his owners, and to all others concerned in the enterprise,

As far as I can judge, he displayed in all his acts a sound judgement, beautifully blended with patriotic bravery.

Had this gentleman been a commander in the United States Navy, his fame and deeds of valour would have been lauded throughout our great republic; but as he only commanded a privateer, who speaks of him? Or of such men as Diron, Champlin, Murphy, Stafford, Wooster, Ordronaux, and a host of others, who fought and bled in their country's cause.

Is it not then narrow-minded prejudice not to award a just appreciation of the services of the gallant men who commanded privateers and letters-of-marque during our severe struggle with England for an equal right to navigate the ocean, the great highway of nations. For it must certainly be conceded, that while contending with the enemy at that period, the privateers and private armed vessels formed in fact a large portion of our navy, and were an indispensable auxiliary to it, as the militia and volunteers were to the United States army.

The privateer-ship *America*, alluded to in this chapter, was a well-armed and well-manned vessel. She was very conspicuous and very fortunate during the whole war. She belonged to Salem, and was commanded by I. W. Chever. Perhaps this vessel made more money for her owners, captain, officers and crew, than any other privateer, cruising out of the United States.

The heroic Captain Boyle commanded two privateers during the war, *viz.*, the *Comet*, and afterwards the *Chasseur*. She captured a great many prizes, and vanquished the enemy in several hard-fought battles.

CHAPTER 11

Arrival at Fayal

CAPTAIN REID'S FAMOUS DEFENCE OF THE PRIVATEER-SCHOONER
GENERAL ARMSTRONG, AT FAYAL

Captain Reid sailed from Sandy Hook on the 9th of September, 1814, bound on a cruise. On the same night after leaving port, Captain Reid was chased by a British frigate, and a ship of the line. He out-sailed them both, when at noon the next day, they thought proper to give up the chase. On the 11th, two days after leaving port, he boarded the private armed-schooner *Perry*, six days from Philadelphia. The *Perry* had thrown all her guns overboard, being hard pressed by the enemy.

The next day, on the 12th, Captain Reid exchanged a few shots with a British man-of-war brig, and then proceeded on his course. On the 24th, boarded a Spanish brig and a schooner, and also a Portuguese ship, all from Havana. He allowed them all to proceed on their respective courses. On the 26th of September, Captain Reid came to anchor in the Fayal Roads, for the purpose of filling up water, and obtaining refreshments. From this date I shall leave the brave captain to tell his own story; here follows the relation of that gentleman:—

"I called on the American Consul, who very politely ordered our water immediately sent off, it being our intention to proceed to sea early the next day. At 5 p.m. I went on board, the Consul and some other gentlemen in company. I asked some questions concerning the enemy's cruisers, and was told there had been none at these islands for several weeks, when about dusk, while we were conversing, the British brig *Carnation*, suddenly hove in sight, close under the N.E. head of the harbour, within gun-shot. When first discovered, the idea of getting under way was instantly suggested, but finding the enemy's brig had the advantage of a breeze, and but little wind with us, it was thought doubtful if we should be able to get to sea without hazarding an action.

"I questioned the Consul to know, if in his opinion the enemy would regard the neutrality of the port? He gave me to understand I might make myself perfectly easy, assuring me at the same time, they would never molest us while at anchor. But no sooner did the enemy's brig understand from the pilot-boat who we were, than she immediately hauled close in, and let go her anchor within pistol-shot of us. At the same moment the *Plantagenet* and frigate *Rota*, hove in sight, to whom the *Carnation* instantly made signals, and a constant interchange, took place for some time.

"The result was, the *Carnation* proceeded to throw out all her boats; dispatched on board the Commodore, and appeared otherwise to be making unusual exertions. From these circumstances, we began to suspect their real intentions. The moon was near its full, which enabled us to observe them very minutely, and I now determined to haul in nearer the shore.

"Accordingly, after clearing for action, we got under way, and began to sweep in. The moment this was observed by the enemy's brig, she instantly cut her cable, made sail, and dispatched four boats in pursuit of us. Being now about 8 p.m., as soon as we saw the boats approaching, we let go our anchor, got springs on our cable, and prepared to receive them. I hailed, them repeatedly as they drew near, but they felt no inclination to reply. Sure of their game, they only pulled up with the greater speed.

"I observed the boats were well manned, and apparently as well armed; and as soon as they had cleverly got alongside, we opened our fire, which was as soon returned ; but meeting with rather a warmer reception than they had probably been aware of, they very soon cried out for quarters, and hauled off. In this skirmish I had one man killed, and my first lieutenant wounded. The enemy's loss must have been upward of twenty killed and wounded.

"They had now repaired to their ships to prepare for a more formidable attack. We, in the interim, having taken the hint, prepared to haul close into the beach, where we moored head and stern, within half pistol-shot of the castle. This done, we again prepared, in the best possible manner, for their second reception.

"About 9 p.m. we observed the enemy's brig towing in a large fleet of boats. They soon after left the brig, and took their station in three divisions, under cover of a small reef of rocks, within about musket shot of us. Here they continued manoeuvring for some time, the brig still keeping under way to act with the boats, should we at any time attempt our escape.

"The shores were lined with the inhabitants, waiting the expected attack; and from the brightness of the moon, they had a most favourable view of the scene. The Governor, with most of the first people of the place, stood by and saw the whole affair. At length, about midnight, we observed the boats in motion (our crew having laid at quarters during the whole of this interval). They came on in one direct line, keeping in close order, and we plainly counted twelve boats.

"As soon as they came within proper distance we opened our fire, which was warmly returned from the enemy's carronades, and small arms. The discharge from our long-tom rather staggered them; but soon reconnoitring, they gave three cheers and came on most spiritedly. In a moment they succeeded in gaining our bow and starboard quarter, and the word was board. Our great guns now becoming useless, we attacked them sword in hand, together with our pikes, pistols and musketry, from which our lads poured on them a most destructive fire.

"The enemy made frequent and repeated attempts to gain our decks, but were repulsed at all times, and at all points, with the greatest slaughter. About the middle of the action, I received intelligence of the death of my second lieutenant; and soon after of the third lieutenant, badly wounded. From this and other causes, I found our fire had much slackened on the forecastle, and fearful of the event, I instantly rallied the whole of our after-division, who had been bravely defending, and now had succeeded in beating the boats off the quarters.

"They gave a shout, rushed forward, opened a fresh fire, and soon after decided the conflict, which terminated in the total defeat of the enemy, and the loss of many of their boats; two of which belonged to the *Rota*, we took possession of them, literally loaded with their own dead. Seventeen only escaped from them both, who swam to the shore. In another boat, under our quarter, commanded by one of the lieutenants of the *Plantagenet*, all were killed saving four. This I have from the lieutenant himself, who further, told me that he jumped overboard to save his own life.

"The duration of the action was about forty minutes. Our decks were now found in much confusion, our long-torn dismounted, and several of our gun-carriages broken; many of our crew having left the vessel, and others disabled. Under these circumstances, however, we succeeded in getting long-tom in his berth, and the decks cleared, in order for a fresh action, should the enemy attack us again before daylight.

"About 3 a.m. I received a message from the American Consul, requesting to see me on shore, where he informed me the Governor had sent a note to Captain Lloyd, begging him to desist from further hostilities. To which Captain Lloyd sent for answer, that he was now determined to have the privateer at the risk of knocking down the whole town; and that if the Governor suffered the Americans to injure the privateer in any manner, he should consider the place an enemy's port, and treat it accordingly. Finding this to be the case, I considered all hope of saving our vessel to be at an end.

"I therefore went on board, and ordered all our wounded and dead to be taken on shore, and the crew to save their effects as fast as possible. Soon after this it became daylight, when the enemy's brig stood close in, and commenced a heavy fire on us with all her force. After several broadsides she hauled off, having received a shot in her hull, her rigging much cut, and her fore-top-mast wounded (of this I was informed by the British Consul). She soon after came in again, and anchored close to the privateer. I then ordered the *General Armstrong* to be scuttled, to prevent the enemy from cutting her off. She was soon afterwards boarded by the enemy's boats, and set on fire, which soon completed her destruction. They also destroyed a number of houses in the town, and wounded some of the inhabitants.

"By what I have been able to learn from the British Consul and officers of the fleet, it appears there were about 400 officers and men in the last attack by the boats, of which 120 were killed, and about 130 wounded. Captain Lloyd, I am told by the British Consul, is badly wounded in the leg; a jury of surgeons had been held, who gave it as their opinion that amputation would be necessary to insure his life. 'Tis said, however, that the wound was occasioned by an ox treading on him.

"The fleet has remained here about a week, during which time they have been principally Employed in burying the dead, and taking care of the wounded. Three days after the action, they were joined by the ship *Thais*, and brig *Calypso* (two sloops of war), they were immediately taken into requisition by Captain Lloyd, to take home the wounded men. The *Calypso* sailed for England with part of the wounded on the 2nd instant, among whom was the first lieutenant of the *Plantagenet*. The *Thais* sails this evening with the remainder, Captain Lloyd's fleet sailed today, supposed for the West Indies.

"The loss on our part, I am happy to say, is comparatively trifling; two killed and seven wounded. With regard to my officers in general, I feel the greatest satisfaction in saying, they one and all fought with the most determined bravery, and to them I feel highly indebted for their officer-like conduct, during the short period we were together; their exertions and bravery deserved a better fate.

"I here insert, for your inspection, a list of the killed and wounded.

"Killed—Mr. Alexander O. Williams, second-lieutenant, by a musket ball in the forehead, died instantly; Burton Lloyd, seaman, wounded by a musket ball through the heart, died instantly.

"Wounded—Frederick A. Worth, first lieutenant, in the right side; Robert Johnson, third lieutenant, in the left knee; Razilla Hammond, quarter-master, left arm; John Piner, seaman, wounded in the knee; William Castle, in the arm; Nicholas Scalsan, in the arm and leg; John Harrison, in the arm and face, by the explosion of a gun.

"It gives me much pleasure to announce to you. that our wounded are all in a fair way of recovery, through the unremitting care and attention of our worthy surgeon.

"Mr. Dabney, our Consul, is a gentleman possessing every feeling of humanity, and to whom the utmost gratitude is due from us for his great care of the sick and wounded, and his polite attention to my officers and myself.

"Mr. Williams was a most deserving and promising officer. His country, in him, has lost one of her brightest ornaments, and his death must be sadly lamented by all who knew his worth.

"Accompanied with this, you will find a copy of my protest, together with copies of letters, written by Mr. Dabney, to the Governor of Fayal; our Minister at Rio Janeiro, and our Secretary of State. These letters will develop more fully, the circumstances of this unfortunate affair. We expect to sail tomorrow in a Portuguese brig for Amelia Island, which takes the whole of our crew, till when,

"I remain, gentlemen,
"Your very obedient, humble servant,
"Samuel C. Reid."

Destruction of the *General Armstrong*

The details that follow, though they regard only a private armed vessel, will be read with great interest. We are called as much to admire the gallantry and perseverance of our seamen, as the impudence of the enemy in violating a neutral territory.

But they paid dearly for this irruption on the sovereignty of Portugal and the rights of hospitality. The vessels that attacked the *General Armstrong*, arrived at Jamaica on the 5th *ult.*, and acknowledged a loss of 63 killed, and 110 wounded, having three lieutenants killed, and three wounded, total 173. This is not the whole by a great deal. They lost about 300, as the captain of the *Rota* acknowledged to our Consul that they had 120 men killed, or dead of their wounds, the day after the battle, and according to the general scale of such things, there must have been at least double that number remaining wounded.

Some of the most splendid victories the British have ever gained, were less dearly purchased. Sir Richard Strachan, with four ships of the line, and four frigates, fought a French fleet for several hours, on the 3rd of November, 1805, and captured four ships of 74 and 80 guns, with a loss of only 135 killed and wounded—less according to his account than by the British accounts of the attack on the Armstrong, they lost in capturing a privateer, hemmed up in a port. A few such victories as this, would teach them better manners.

The Court of Portugal is bound to pay for the privateer, and receive satisfaction for the outrage from that of Great Britain.

COPY OF A LETTER FROM OUR CONSUL AT FAYAL TO THE SECRETARY OF STATE

"Fayal, 5th October, 1814.

"Sir: I have the honour to state to you, that a most outrageous violation of the neutrality of this port, in utter contempt of the laws of civilized nations, has recently been committed here by the commanders of His Britannic Majesty's ships, *Plantagenet*, *Rota* and *Carnation*, against the private armed brig *General Armstrong*, Samuel C. Reid commander; but I have great satisfaction in being able to add that this occurrence terminated in one of the most brilliant actions on the part of Captain Reid, his brave officers and crew, that can be found on naval record.

"The American brig came to anchor in this port in the afternoon of the 26th of September, and at sunset of the same day, the above named ships suddenly appeared in these roads; it being nearly calm in this port, it was rather doubtful if the privateer could escape, if she got under way, and relying on the justice and good faith of the British captains, it was deemed most prudent to remain at anchor.

"A little after dusk, Captain Reid, seeing some suspicious movements on the part of the British, began to warp his vessel close under the guns of the castle, and while doing so, he was, at about 8 o'clock p.m., approached by four boats from the ships, filled with armed men. After hailing them repeatedly, and warning them to keep off, he ordered his men to fire on them, and killed and wounded several men. The boats returned the fire, killed one man, and wounded the first lieutenant of the privateer, and returned to their ships; and, as it was now bright moonlight, it was plainly perceived from the brig, as well as from the shore, that a formidable attack was premeditating.

"Soon after midnight, twelve or more large boats, crowded with men from the ships, and armed with carronades, swivels, blunderbusses, small arms, etc., attacked the brig. A severe contest ensued, which lasted about forty minutes, and ended in the total defeat, and partial destruction of the boats, with a most unparalleled carnage on the part of the British.

"It is estimated, by good judges, that near four hundred men were in the boats when the attack commenced, and no doubt exists in the minds of the numerous spectators of the scene, that more than one half of them were killed or wounded. Several boats were destroyed; two of them remained along side of the brig, literally loaded with their own dead. From these two boats, only seventeen men reached the shore alive; most of them were severely wounded.

"The whole of the following day, the British were occupied in burying their dead; among them were two lieutenants and one midshipman, of the *Rota*; the first lieutenant of the *Plantagenet*, it is said, cannot survive his wounds, and many of the seamen who reached the ships were mortally wounded, and have been dying daily.

"The British, mortified at this signal and unexpected defeat, endeavoured to conceal the extent of their loss. They admit, however, that they have lost in killed, and who have died since the engagement, upward of one hundred and twenty of the flower of their officers and men. The captain of the *Rota* told me he lost seventy men from his ship.

"Two days after this affair took place, two British sloops-of-war, *Thais* and *Calypso*, came into port, which Captain Lloyd immediately took into requisition to carry home the wounded officers and seamen. They have sailed for England—one on the 2nd, and the other on the 4th instant; each carried twenty-five men, badly wounded. Those who were slightly wounded, to the number, as I am informed, of about thirty, remained on board their respective ships; and sailed last evening for Jamaica.

"Strict orders were given that the sloops-of-war should take no letters whatever to England, and those orders were rigidly adhered to. In face of the testimony of all Fayal, and a number of respectable strangers who happened to be in this place at the moment, the British commander endeavours to throw the odium of this transaction on the American Captain Reid, alleging that he sent the boats merely to reconnoitre the brig, and without any hostile intentions; the pilots of the port did inform them of the privateer the moment they entered the port.

"To reconnoitre an enemy's vessel, in a friendly port, at night, with four boats carrying, by the best accounts, one hundred and twenty men, is certainly a strange proceeding! The fact is, they expected, as the brig was warping in, that the Americans would not be prepared to receive them, and they had hopes of carrying her by a *coup de main*. If anything could add to the baseness of this transaction, on the part of the British commander, it is the want of candour, openly and boldly to avow the facts. In vain can he expect, by such subterfuge, to shield himself from the indignation of the world, and the merited resentment of his own government and nation, for thus trampling on the sovereignty of their most ancient and faithful ally, and for the wanton sacrifice of British lives.

"On the part of the Americans, the loss was comparatively nothing; two killed and seven slightly wounded, Of the slain, we have to lament the loss of the second lieutenant, Mr. Alexander O. Williams, of New York; a brave and meritorious officer.

"Among the wounded, are Messrs. Worth and Johnson, first and third lieutenants. Captain Reid was thus deprived, early in the action, of the services of all his lieutenants; but his cool and intrepid conduct secured him the victory.

"On the morning of the 27th *ult.*, one of the British ships placed herself near the shore, and commenced a heavy cannonade on the privateer. Finding further resistance unavailing, Captain Reid ordered her to be abandoned, after being partially destroyed, to prevent her from falling into the hands of the enemy, who soon after sent their boats and set her on fire.

"At nine o'clock in the evening (soon after the first attack), I applied to the Governor, requesting his Excellency to protect the privateer, either by force, or by such remonstrance to the commander of the squadron, as would cause him to desist from any further attempt.

"The Governor, feeling indignant at what had passed, but feeling himself totally unable, with the slender means he possessed, to resist such a force, took the part of remonstrating, which he did in forcible, but respectful terms.

"His letter to Captain Lloyd had no other effect than to produce a menacing reply, insulting in the highest degree. Nothing could exceed the indignation of the public authorities, as well as of all ranks and descriptions of persons here, at this unprovoked enormity. Such was the rage of the British to destroy this vessel, that no regard was paid to the safety of the town. Some of the inhabitants were wounded, and a number of the houses were much damaged. The strongest representations on this subject were prepared by the Governor for his court Since this affair, the commander, Lloyd, threatened to send on shore an armed force, and arrest the privateer's crew, saying there were many Englishmen among them, and our poor fellows, afraid of his vengeance, have fled into the mountains several times, and have been harassed extremely.

"At length, Captain Lloyd, fearful of losing more men, if he put his threats in execution, adopted this stratagem: He addressed an official letter to the Governor. stating that in the American crew were two men who deserted from his squadron in America, and as they were guilty of high treason, he required them to be found and given up. Accordingly, a force was sent into the country, and the American seamen were arrested and brought to town, and as they could not designate the said pretended deserters, all the seamen here passed an examination of the British officers, but no such persons could be found among them.

"I was requested by the Governor and British Consul to attend this humiliating examination, as was also Captain Reid, but we declined to sanction by our presence any such proceedings.

"Captain Reid has protested against the British commanders of the squadron, for the unwarrantable destruction of his vessel in a neutral and friendly port, as also against the government of Portugal, for their inability to protect him.

"No doubt this Government will feel themselves bound to make ample indemnification to the owners, officers and crew of this vessel, for the great loss they have severally sustained.

"I shall, as early as possible, transmit a statement this transaction to our Minister at Rio Janeiro for government.

"I have the honour to be, with great respect,
"Sir, your most obedient servant,
"John B. Dabney.

HONOUR TO THE BRAVE

On Captain Reid's arrival at Savannah from Fayal, he was treated with great respect and kindness by classes of people.

On his way home to New York, he was invited, and partook of a splendid public entertainment at Richmond, Virginia. The company was very numerous, and among them, the Governor, and others of the first character in Virginia. The Speaker of the House of Delegates (Mr. Stevenson), President, and the members of the Legislature constituted a large portion of the entertainers.

The toasts were highly characteristic of generous Virginia. We select the following:

"The navy—whose lightning has struck down the 'meteor flag of England.' They have conquered those who had conquered the world."

"The private cruisers of the United States—whose intrepidity has pierced the enemy's channels, and bearded the lion in his den."

"The army of the Niagara, the rivals of our seamen—their gallant deeds will live to endless ages, in the records of time."

"Brown, Scott, Gaines and Porter—Chippewa, Bridgewater, Plattsburg and Erie, are the deathless monuments of their fame."

"Barney, Boyle, and their compatriots—who have ploughed the seas in search of the enemy, and hurled retaliation upon his head."

"Our Ministers at Ghent—who breathe the spirit of their country, war in preference to the slightest sacrifice of honour."

"Foreign Nations—let us hold them as did our fathers, 'enemies in war; in peace friends.'"

"Legislators—may the people abandon 'those who sacrifice the safety of their country to the shadow of popularity.'"

"Volunteers"—by the Vice-President, Mr. Wirt—"the memory of the *General Armstrong*; she has 'graced her fall, and made her ruin glorious.'"

"By Judge Cabell—The Spirit of our fore-fathers, displayed in concert and energy of action; not wasted in endless and fruitless discussion."

"By Judge Brockenborough—Neutral Ports—whenever the tyrants of the ocean dare to invade these sanctuaries, may they meet with an *Essex* and an *Armstrong*."

"By General Cocke—American seamen—their achievements form an era in the naval annals of the world; may their brother soldiers emulate their deeds of everlasting renown."

On Captain Reid's retiring: "By the President—Captain Reid—his valour has shed a blaze of renown upon the character of our seamen, and won for himself a laurel of eternal bloom."

CONTINUATION OF PRIZES CAPTURED BY PRIVATEERS AND LETTERS-OF-MARQUE, AFTER THE TREATY OF PEACE WAS SIGNED THOUGH UNKNOWN AT THAT TIME, TO EITHER OF THE BELLIGERENT PARTIES

The privateer *Warrior*, of New York, captured the following British vessels:

Brig *Hope*, from Glasgow for Buenos Ayres, divested of a large quantity of English goods, and manned for the United States.

Ship *Francis and Eliza*, burthen 377 tons with ten guns and thirty-five men, from London bound for New South Wales. This ship had on board 124 male and female convicts. After divesting her of sundry articles of merchandise, the privateer allowed her to proceed on her voyage.

The British ship *Neptune*, 259 tons burthen, 8 guns and fifteen men, from Liverpool for St. Salvador, with a cargo of British goods. The *Warrior* removed from her the most valuable portion of her cargo, and sent her to the United States.

Brig *Dundee*, of Dundee, from London also for St. Salvador, with British goods to a large amount. After removing to the privateer a large quantity of valuable goods, manned her for New York.

After the *Warrior* had taken out of her prizes 323 bales and packages of English goods, and fifteen thousand dollars in specie, she made sail for New York, at which port she safely arrived.

During the cruise, she was often chased by frigates, and received several shot from one of them. She was at another time so hotly pursued by an English 74, that in passing she received several of her shot, but finally made her escape with but little injury. The *Warrior* was a beautiful brig of 430 tons burthen, built on the pilot boat construction, mounted 21 guns, and carried 150 men.

The privateer *Mammoth*, of Baltimore, returned to New York after a long and unprofitable cruise, without making any captures. She was several times chased by British frigates, but fortunately escaped. During her cruise, in a calm, she was attacked by several of the enemy's boats, but beat them off without loss to herself.

The privateer *Ludlow* returned to Portsmouth, after a cruise of fifty-six days, without making a single capture.

It would appear by this that British ships and vessels had become somewhat scarce on the ocean, as our privateers returned with but very few prizes.

The letter-of-marque *Brutus*, of Boston, made the following captures:

Ship *Adventure*, with an assorted cargo of British merchandise; divested her of the most valuable portion of it, and destroyed the vessel.

Schooner *Margaretta*, with a small assorted cargo of not much value. Removed the same to the privateer, and made a cartel of her, to get rid of prisoners.

Transport brig *Guardiana*, from Halifax for Plymouth, English 4 guns and fifteen men. Divested her of all her cargo worth removing, and made a cartel of her, to dispose of the prisoners.

Brig *Phoebe*, from Malta for London, with an assorted cargo. Divested her of a portion of her valuable goods, and manned her for the United States.

Brig *Tagus*, from Smyrna for London, mounting four guns, with fifteen men. This was a very valuable prize, said to be worth $400,000. The *Brutus* removed from this vessel 143 bales of silk, and then manned and ordered her to proceed to Boston, at which port she fortunately arrived.

Beside the before enumerated prizes, the *Brutus* also captured on this cruise, the British ship *Albion*, from London bound for Bermuda. This ship was 365 tons burthen, with eight guns and fifteen men. Her cargo was valued at $200,000. She was manned and ordered to proceed to a port in the United States.

British schooner *Victoria*, laden with crates, oil, and sundry British goods, was also captured by the *Brutus*, and ordered to proceed to Charleston.

After the *Brutus* had taken and manned all the before named prizes, she made sail for Boston, at which port she arrived, laden with a very valuable cargo of silks and other rich goods, taken from the enemy.

British schooner, name not given, from Halifax for Barbadoes, with a cargo of fish, was captured by the *Avon*, of Boston, and sent into Port Royal, Martinique, and was there ransomed for her former owners.

British Brig *Success*, from Cadiz for Newfoundland, laden with salt, and fruit, etc., was captured by the *Blakely*, of Boston, and sent into that port.

British brig *Jubilee*, from St. Ubes for Ireland, with salt, etc., was also captured by the *Blakely*. Divested the prize of a portion of her cargo, and then destroyed her.

The British schooner *Thistle*, from the Mediterranean, with a valuable cargo, was captured by the *America* of Salem, on her last cruise. This prize was recaptured by the British sloop of war *Cossack*, off Cape Sable, on the 19th of March, and sent to Halifax, but was subsequently restored to the American captors, according to the treaty regulations, between the two governments on that subject.

English Brig *Ocean*, with 8 guns, and fifteen men, from Sicily for St. Petersburg, with an assorted cargo, was captured by the Macedonian, of Boston, and sent into Portsmouth, N. H.

British packet *Windsor Castle*, armed with eight carronades, and two long brass nine pounders, with thirty-two men, and nine passengers from Falmouth, England, for Halifax, with five mails, was captured by the privateer *Roger*, of Norfolk and sent into that port.

British schooner *Fanny*, with nine guns from Laguira, for London, was captured by the *Lawrence* of Baltimore, and ordered into a port in the United States, but in consequence of bad weather, she put into Cuba to refit, being in distress.

British schooner, name not given, from Fayal for St. Michael, captured by the *Macedonian* of Boston; divested of her cargo, and permitted to proceed on her voyage.

Galliot ———, under Swedish colours, captured also by the

Macedonian; divested of her English property, and permitted to proceed on her voyage.

The *Macedonian* also captured and burnt the sloop ——, from Forway for Naples, with a cargo of fish.

The English ship ——, from Newfoundland, for the Mediterranean, was also captured by the *Macedonian* and burnt.

British brig *Acorn*, 14 guns 12-pounders, from Liverpool for Rio Janeiro, with a full cargo; captured by the *Grand Turk*: divested of a large portion of her most valuable articles, then manned and ordered into a port in the United States.

The privateer *Grand Turk*, arrived at Salem, with $17,500 in specie, and 180 bales of English goods, taken from sundry British vessels, during her last cruise.

A small English schooner, a tender to the English 74, *Dragon*, commanded by a lieutenant, was captured by the *Saranac*, of Baltimore, and sunk.

A British packet, name not given, was also captured by the *Saranac*, in the West Indies and sunk. The *Saranac* had returned to port after an unsuccessful cruise. She spoke many neutral vessels, but saw nothing worth taking from the enemy.

Galliot *Ann*, with a cargo of British goods, was captured by the *James Monroe*, and sent into L'Orient, France, and from thence was sent to New York, at which port she subsequently arrived.

British ship *Agenoria*, from Waterford for London, laden with provisions, was captured by the *McDonough*, and sent into Bricaux, France."

British ship *Ashburton*, from Lisbon for England, was captured by the *James Monroe*, divested of her cargo, and given up to the prisoners, and allowed to proceed on her voyage.

The British ship *Nancy*, from Liverpool for Sicily, was captured by the *Abaellino*, of Boston; while cruising in the Mediterranean, and sent into Tunis.

The English cutter *Joanna*, was captured by the *Macedonian*, of Portsmouth, and burnt.

British ship *Triumvirate*, from St. Johns Newfoundland, for the Mediterranean, with fish and oil, was also captured by the

Macedonian, and burnt.

Schooner *Recovery*, captured by the *Macedonian*, and after having taken sundry articles of merchandise, gave her up to the prisoners as a cartel.

The privateer *George Little*, of Boston, was captured by the English frigate *Granicus*. The privateer carried 14 guns, and eighty men, and had taken no prizes.

The British ship *Amity*, from Waterford for London, was captured by the *McDonough*, and sent into Morlaix, France.

The British schooner *Swift*, of London, from St. Michael, laden with fruit, was captured by the *America*, and ordered to proceed to Salem. The prize being in want of provisions, subsequently put into Terceira, where she was demanded by the British Consul. It was said the Governor of the Island ordered her to be restored to her former owners.

Brig *Staff-of-Life*, from Liverpool for Havre-de-Grace, with a valuable assorted cargo, captured by the *McDonough*, and sent into France.

Brig *Endeavour*, from Falmouth for Liverpool, with barley, etc., captured by the same, and sent to France.

Brig *Ceres*, from Cork for London, with a full cargo, captured by the same and sent to France.

Brig *Unity*, from Waterford for London, with a full cargo, captured by the *McDonough*, and sent into France.

Sloop *Eliza*, from Dublin for London, with beef and butter, captured by the same, and sent to France.

EXTRACT FROM THE LOG-BOOK OF THE *McDONOUGH*

"Having put out all our men, was obliged to bear up for France, and arrived at Morlaix, on the 7th of February, 1815. February 16th, an English man-of-war schooner arrived there, and anchored within pistol-shot of our vessel, and demanded of us to give up our prizes; we refused and being all ready to engage her, she did not see fit to urge the demand."

PRIZES CAPTURED BY PRIVATEERS

British brig *Nicholson*, of 300 tons burthen, mounting 10

guns, and twenty men, from Liverpool for Rio Janeiro, with a valuable cargo of British goods, was captured by the privateer-brig *Warrior*, of New York, and sent to that port, where she subsequently arrived safe.

The British transport-ship *Mosely*, 16 eighteen-pound carronades, with some twenty or thirty men, from Algoa Bay for the Cape of Good Hope, in ballast; was captured by the letter-of-marque *Rambler*, of Boston, and after divesting her of sundry articles of not much value, allowed her to proceed on her voyage. The *Rambler* was from Canton, with a rich China cargo, and was fortunate enough to arrive safe at Boston.

The British ship *Adele*, of Penang, laden with a valuable cargo of India goods, with a considerable amount of gold dust, was captured by the letter-of-marque ship *Jacob Jones*, of Boston, on her passage out to Canton. After divesting the prize of the most valuable part of her cargo, allowed her to proceed on her voyage. The *Jacob Jones* also captured, on the same passage, the English brig *Bourwan*, of Penang, laden with opium and other valuable goods. After removing from the prize the most valuable portion of her cargo, allowed her to proceed on her voyage. The amount of property taken from these two vessels was worth $90,000. The *Jacob Jones* was a fine ship of 554 tons, carrying 16 guns, and sixty-seven men. She returned to Boston with a full cargo of China goods. The profits on her voyage, together with the choice spoils taken from the enemy was, probably in the result, one of the greatest voyages ever made from the United States.

The privateer *Macedonian* arrived at Portsmouth May the 2nd, 1815. During her cruise she captured and manned three vessels, besides what have been before recorded, namely: brig *Margaret and Trevis*, with British goods; ship *Somerset*, 260 tons burthen, mounting 4 guns and fifteen men, laden with wine and brandy; and the brig *Mercury*, with 160 pipes of Oporto wine, and other articles of merchandise.

British brig *Polly*, was captured, and sent into Cadiz. by the privateer *Amelia*, of Baltimore.

British brig *Elizabeth* (cargo not mentioned), was captured by the *Leo*, of Boston, and burnt.

British brig *George*, from Prince Edward's Island, was also captured by the *Leo*, and destroyed.

Cutter *Jane*, from St. Michael, for London, with a cargo of fruit, was also captured by the same privateer, and sent to France.

The American privateer *Sine-qua-non*, of Boston, with seven guns and eighty-one men, was captured by the English, in the neighbourhood of Madeira, early in February, 1815.

British schooner *Dunsten Castle*, from Alicant for Marseilles, with fruit, was also captured by the same privateer, and sent into Tunis.

Three small Maltese vessels (British), with full cargoes, were also captured by the *Abaellino*, and sent into Tripoli.

British brig *Mary and Gilbert*, from Naples for Palermo, was captured by the *Abaellino*, and ransomed.

British brig *Bernadotte*, a Maltese vessel, was captured by the same privateer, divested of her cargo, and given up to the prisoners.

The *Abaellino* permitted several small Maltese vessels to escape without capture.

At the time peace was concluded at Ghent, but not known in the United States, there were several large privateers fitting out of the different ports along the Atlantic board. Among others, there was fitted, at Boston, at that time, and ready for sea, a fast-sailing ship, called the *Charles Morris*, mounting two long-nines, and eight six-pound carronades, with swords, musketry, etc., and a complement of 100 men, all told. This efficient ship was commanded by a personal friend of the author, Captain Henry Russell, a native citizen of Boston.

I have no doubt, had the war lasted a few months longer, and Captain Russell been permitted to go to sea, that he would have inflicted a severe blow upon the commerce of the enemy.

The British brig *Enterprise*, from Buenos Ayres, bound to England, laden with hides and tallow, was captured by the ship *America*, of Salem. The prize being leaky, put into Fayal in distress, where she was condemned as unseaworthy. The cargo was green in charge of the American Consul, at that port. The British ship *Charles*, of London, partly loaded with oil, from San Salvador, was captured off that port by the *Blakely*, of Boston. She was ordered to proceed to the United States, and subsequently arrived safe at Boston.

British brig *Sailor's Friend* was captured by the privateer *Prince de Neufchâtel*, and sent into Havre de Grace, and after the peace, she left that place, and arrived safe at Boston.

The British Brig *Ann Elizabeth*, from Amsterdam, was captured by the *Rattlesnake*, privateer, and ordered to Philadelphia, at which port she safely arrived.

The British brig (name not given), from the Mediterranean, bound to London, with fruit, was captured by the *Brutus*, sent into Brest, and subsequently arrived safe at Boston.

The British schooner *Commercial Packet,* from Trieste for London, laden with fruit, was captured by the *Abaellino*, of Boston, and sent into Tunis.

British brig *Hope*, from Pattras for London, with fruit, was captured by the same privateer, and sent into Tunis.

CONCLUDING REMARKS ON THE HISTORY OF THE AMERICAN PRIVATEERS AND LETTERS-OF-MARQUE; ALSO ON THE LATE WAR AND ITS CONSEQUENCES.

In the introduction to my work, I observed, that a war between two commercial nations was simply a trial which could do the other the greatest harm; and now, the war being ended, my readers will naturally expect to hear how the account stands at the winding up of the severe conflict.

This I will endeavour to give; but before I proceed to record the losses on both sides, it may be well to give a slight sketch of the great disparity of force employed at the commencement of the war by the belligerent parties.

The English entered the contest with a navy of one thousand and sixty men-of-war, eight hundred of which were in commission, and were effective, cruising ships or vessels.

To oppose this immense force, the United States had but seven effective frigates, with some twelve or fifteen sloops-of-war. Of the latter, the greater part were lying in the dock-yards repairing.

The war lasted about three years, and the result was. as near as I have been able to ascertain, a loss to Great Britain of about two thousand ships and vessels of every description, including men-of-war and merchantmen.

Eighteen hundred sail are recorded as having been taken, burnt, sunk, or destroyed.

To this number may be added two hundred more, which were either destroyed or considered too insignificant to be reported; making an aggregate of two thousand sail of British shipping captured by our little navy, with the aid of privateers and letters-of-marque.

This statement does not include captures made on our great lakes, which would swell the number to a much larger figure.

I have not had sufficient time in giving this summary to ascertain, precisely, what proportion of these two thousand vessels were captured by the United States government ships, but at a rough estimate, should judge one-third part of the whole number, leaving two-thirds, or, say thirteen hundred and thirty sail, to have been taken by American privateers and private-armed vessels.

I have found it difficult to ascertain the exact number of our own vessels taken and destroyed by the English; but, from the best information I can obtain, I should judge they would not amount to more than five hundred sail. It must be recollected that the most of our losses occurred during the first six months of the war. After that period, we had very few vessels afloat, except privateers and letters-of-marque.

A large portion of our merchant-ships fortunately returned home within the first two or three months after the commencement of the war, and were laid up out of reach of the enemy. Some of them were taken up our navigable rivers, and others dismantled in secure places.

A few of our East Indiamen and whaling ships, the commanders of which had no knowledge of the war, were captured on their return home, and not unfrequently at the mouths of our own harbours; but, thank God, they were not many.

On the other hand our men-of-war and privateers continued to harass and prey upon British trade and commerce, during the whole period of the contest, and even after the treaty of peace was signed.

In those times there were no ocean steamers, to cross. the Atlantic in ten or twelve days, nor any magnetic telegraphs to communicate news between distant cities. For this reason, it not unfrequently occurred that we were without news from Europe for a period of fifty or sixty days.

The great battle of New Orleans was fought and won by General Jackson, fifteen days after the treaty of peace was signed at Ghent. So also the sloop-of-war *Penguin* was captured, by Captain Biddle, in the *Hornet*, three months after.

I have recorded a long list of prizes made by our privateers and letters-of-marque, that were cruising in distant seas, and had not heard of the peace.

In this estimate of losses by the belligerent parties, it must be borne in mind, that I am not writing a history of the war, but simply of the privateers, and private-armed vessels, with the addition of a few naval victories on the broad ocean, by the United States ships-of-war.

I have but slightly alluded to the splendid victories gained by the United States vessels over entire fleets of the enemy on our great Lakes.

Neither does it come within the province of this history to record the barbarous transactions of the English at Washington, in their wanton destruction of that city, and many other acts of a kindred nature.

Nor shall I enter into a detailed account of the gallant destruction of Havre-de-Grace, Hampton, and many other small defenceless villages, by these modern Goths, led by the redoubtable Sir George Cockburn, of famous memory. All these illustrious acts and deeds have become matters of history, and been recorded by more able pens than mine. I only allude *en passant*, to these memorable instances of English humanity, as evidences of their vaunted boast of superior civilization.

Contrast these acts with those of the French. Bonaparte, in his successful career, over-ran the greater part of continental Europe, and took most of its capital cities, but in no instance did he ever destroy one of them.

The English landed from their men-of-war, made a forced march upon Washington burnt it, and then hurried back to their ships.

I deem it unnecessary to enlarge upon this subject, as it is familiar to every intelligent American.

My object in referring to these by-gone scenes is, to warn the present generation, not to sleep at their posts, nor to rely on British magnanimity for security.

More than forty-one years have elapsed since the ambassadors of the United States and Great Britain signed the treaty of peace, at Ghent, and the most of those who bore a conspicuous part in the war have passed away. The few surviving leaders, and those who distinguished themselves in those exciting times, are rapidly disappearing from among their brethren, and will soon only live on the pages of their country's history.

Having now brought my account of the privateers and letters-of-marque to a close, I hope every dispassionate American will agree with me, that it was beyond all doubt, owing to the good seamanship and gallant bravery of our little navy, in combination with the indefatigable annoyance of the privateers and letters-of-marque, that an honourable peace was so soon restored to our beloved country.

And here I would respectfully ask my readers to reflect for a moment, on the immense advantages this war has conferred upon the United States.

In my opinion, it has advanced the nation more than half a century in wealth and prosperity. It has given us a navy in which the whole nation has the most entire confidence, has been the cause of fortifying our seaports, has built up our manufactories, and enriched the country in a thousand other ways by developing its resources.

It has given us a home feeling of self-reliance on our own strength, and power to protect ourselves against foreign aggression. And what is far above every other consideration, it has given us a national character, and caused our flag to be respected in every part of the world. It has inspired every individual American with a feeling of self-respect, and a stronger and deeper love for his country's honour and glory; and it continues to cherish a growing feeling of patriotism, which, after all, is a nation's surest and best protection.

Since our war with England, an American citizen, whether at home or abroad, is not ashamed to hold up his head, to defend and sustain the honour of his native land.

After the dastardly attack on the frigate *Chesapeake*, by the British, we were often made to blush for the honour of our country. But, since the war, what American is there that does not feel his heart warm with gratitude, and his pulse beat quicker when reading our numerous naval victories.

My book is written in a spirit of truth and justice, and though I have enumerated many wrongs and insults inflicted upon us in our national infancy, still I would counsel the young men of the present generation, not to indulge in a revengeful spirit. I hope and trust they will ever cherish a vigilant watchfulness over the liberties of their country. They must "remember to ask from other nations nothing that is not clearly right, nor submit to anything that is palpably wrong."

This is the road all great nations have travelled, and the only sure one that leads to greatness and undying glory.

Notwithstanding what I have said respecting our late war with England, I would not be understood as being in favour of another war with that nation, at present. On the contrary, I see no sufficient cause of war between the two countries, and there are a thousand reasons why we should cultivate the most friendly relations for our mutual benefit.

Our country having become strong and powerful, I hope we shall not hereafter enter into war with any power weaker than ourselves, on account of slight or imaginary wrongs. But should any great nation offer us insult, or invade one foot of our territory, I hope every man capable of bearing arms will rush to the rescue, and that the young men will march in a solid phalanx to meet the foe. Should they fall in the conflict, they will fall with the glorious consolation, that their memories will be forever embalmed in the hearts of their countrymen.

In conclusion, I have only to express the regret that I did not commence my book a year sooner. I am now nearly seventy-two years of age, and being fearful that I might drop off before I could see it published, I have not been able to devote as much time and care to its composition, as the subject deserves.

But should it please God to prolong my life a few years, I hope to be enabled to correct some errors and omissions that may be observed in this history. Such as it is, however, whether for good or for evil, with all its faults and deficiencies, I now present it to the American public, to sink or swim on its own merits.

The Author.

Brooklyn, New York, May, 1856.

During the several years of the war, the number of privateers and letters-of-marque belonging to New York, amounted to fifty-five. Of all the captains who commanded these vessels, but two are living at the present time, —Captain Reid, and the author of these pages.

Historical Facts and Reminiscences

CONNECTED WITH OUR WAR WITH ENGLAND, IN 1812, '13, AND '14, AND ITS GLORIOUS TERMINATION IN THE EARLY PART OF 1815

In March, 1814, the allied armies entered Paris, when a general peace was concluded between the European nations for a short period. Louis XVIII. was placed on the throne of France, and the Emperor Napoleon Bonaparte sent, by mutual agreement, to the Island of Elba; so that after a general and sanguinary war had convulsed Europe from its centre to its utmost boundaries, for a period of twenty-four years, a general peace was suddenly proclaimed, and the old Bourbon dynasty again restored to power.

In consequence of these arrangements, the United States of America were left alone and single-handed to wage war against England, with her immense fleets and armies to assail us on every side, both by sea and land. It was presumed by the nations of Europe that the United States would fall an easy prey to her powerful enemy.

At this period, the writer of these pages was at La Rochelle, where many a worthy Frenchman, friendly to the United States and her institutions, said to him: "What now will become of your unfortunate country, thus left without the aid of any other friendly nation to fight England? Will she not with her immense power crush and destroy you without mercy?"

I replied that I had no fear for the final result; and it was my opinion. that if England sent an army to invade the United States, very few of those composing it would ever live to return home again; that notwithstanding her immense navy, covering almost every sea, our little navy and privateers would so harass and annoy her trade and commerce that she would very soon be glad to make peace with us for her own interest. I was persuaded that the merchants of Great Britain, if compelled to pay such enormous rates of premium on their ships, while at war with the United States, could not carry on trade to any advantage and compete with the rest of Europe.

They dreaded the policy of the American Government to burn, sink, and destroy every capture made from the enemy, and her instructions to every national vessel not to attempt to send a single British captured vessel into port for fear of recapture.

To carry out this plan of destruction, the American Government had determined to send to sea twenty swift vessels. This fleet was to be called the Flying Squadron. The Government had also decided to augment the bounty allowed to privateers, to act upon the same principle. This system enraged the English almost to madness, which evinced itself against the Americans in the massacre perpetrated on unarmed seamen at Dartmoor prison.

As the general peace in Europe was supposed to be permanently established, it was obvious that the British Government had no further use for its fleets and armies in that quarter of the globe. It, therefore, resolved to send a large fleet and army to the United States, to humble the Americans, and make them sue for peace, by laying waste the cities along the Atlantic board. For this purpose, the British formed a grand plan of concentrating all their disposable force at Jamaica, after the battle of Toulouse. Lord Wellington's veteran troops had been, for several years, campaigning in Spain and Portugal, under the immediate eye of him whom the English familiarly called the Grand Duke.

These soldiers had been trained and drilled by Marshal Beresford, Lord Hill, General Packenham, and other veteran chiefs, and often boasted of having gained numerous victories over the French in almost every part of the Peninsula. These troops came from Toulouse to Bordeaux, where the writer of these pages saw them reposing on their laurels previous to their departure for Jamaica. Here they quietly remained until ordered to resume their wonted occupation of war and bloodshed. After a few months' relaxation, they were embarked on board men-of-war and transports for Jamaica. In combination with this fleet, a small squadron of men-of-war with two thousand troops, sailed from Portsmouth, Spithead, on or about the 1st of October, 1814. In the frigate *Statira*, belonging to this fleet, the Commander-in-Chief, Sir Edward Packenham. took passage.

On their way out they touched at Barbadoes, took a few more soldiers from that garrison, and then proceeded down to Jamaica, where they were joined by another fleet with troops from the Chesapeake Bay, after their defeat at Baltimore. On their arrival at Jamaica, they all landed, and were reorganized and drilled, to accomplish their grand plan of capturing New Orleans. To make success doubly sure, and sweep everything before them, they augmented their numbers by taking with them two regiments of black soldiers, making together about fifteen or sixteen hundred men.

This army consisted of seven thousand soldiers, exclusive of seamen and marines, which probably swelled their numbers to nine or ten thousand men. There were in this army four generals, *viz*.: Lambert, Gibbs, Keane and Sir Edward Packenham. The last-named was brother-in-law to the Iron Duke, and with him a great favourite. The whole of this army being placed under the command of Sir Edward Packenham, embarked on board forty ships and vessels of various sizes, and sailed from Jamaica, about the 1st of December, 1814, on their destined expedition to capture New Orleans.

They proceeded to Ship Island, in St. Louis Bay. This island is situated at the entrance of sundry lakes, lying North and East of New Orleans. The design of the invaders was to attack that city in the rear. Besides the fleet containing the troops, which entered the lakes, the British Admiral sent into the Mississippi a small squadron, composed of two bomb-vessels, one sloop, one brig and a schooner, to co-operate with the land forces in the destruction of New Orleans, and subjugation of Louisiana. This marine force proceeded up the river to their anchorage, near Fort St. Philip, or Plaquemine, which fortification is located about forty-three miles below New Orleans, on the left bank of the river. At this place the channel is narrow while the forts are strong and efficient, having more than thirty-five pieces of heavy cannon, and a garrison of five hundred men.

On the 9th of January, 1815, the enemy commenced firing from their heavy sea mortars, prudently keeping out of the range of the shot from the fort, which they dared not attempt to pass, and thus contented themselves with cannonading the fort with bombshells. They continued their fire from the 9th to the 18th of January, a period of nine days, without doing the Americans any material damage, considering the length of the siege. The enemy threw in and about the fort more than a thousand heavy shells, besides shot and shells from howitzers, with round and grape. These they discharged from their boats under cover of night, when the Americans could not see them from the fort, and return their fire to much advantage.

The gallant commanding officer of the fort, W. H. Overton, says,

> The enemy was too timid to approach near enough to give us an opportunity of destroying him. He always kept at a respectful distance, except in the darkness of the night, when he stealthily fired from his boats, and then made a precipitate retreat. The total loss of the Americans in the fort was only two killed and seven wounded.

The whole of the American naval force was about as follows: The Ship *Louisiana*, the Schooner *Caroline*, and a few other small vessels, stationed at New Orleans. On the Lakes, about forty or fifty miles to the eastward of New Orleans, was a small flotilla of gun-boats. The whole of the naval force belonging to the United States on this station was placed under the command of the gallant Commodore Daniel T. Patterson, who himself remained at New Orleans, to assist in defending that city from the ravages of the enemy. He delegated the command of the flotilla on the Lakes to the young but gallant Lieutenant Commandant Thomas Ap. Catesby Jones, with orders to defend the lakes and passes leading to New Orleans, to the best of his abilities.

The whole force of Lieutenant Jones was as follows: Five gun-boats, four of which carried five guns each; the fifth had but three, making together twenty-three carriage-guns. The boats were manned with from thirty to forty men each, including officers and marines, making an aggregate of one hundred and eighty-two men all told, armed with swords, muskets, pistols, boarding-pikes, tomahawks, sabres, cutlasses, etc.

Besides the above flotilla, there was a schooner called the *Sea Horse* with one six-pounder and fourteen men; also the small sloop *Alligator*, (tender to the flotilla,) with one four-pounder and eight men. The schooner being at a considerable distance from the fleet in the Bay of St. Louis, was destroyed to prevent her falling into the hands of the enemy. The little tender, being detached from the flotilla, was soon captured by the British.

Lieutenant Jones states, in his official account of the action, that on the 12th of December, 1814, the enemy's fleet off Ship Island had so increased in numbers he deemed it imprudent to remain in his present position with his small fleet. He therefore concluded to steer as soon as possible to the westward, and gain a station near the Malheureux Islands, and place his little squadron in a position to oppose the further progress of the enemy up the lakes.

At the same time he wished to give himself an opportunity of retreating, if necessary, to the fort at the Petite Coquilles. At 10 a.m., on the 13th, he discovered that a large flotilla of barges had left the fleet, and were shaping their course towards the Pass Christian. At 2 p.m., the enemy's flotilla having gained the Pass, continued their course to the westward, which convinced him that an attack on the gun-boats was meditated. At 3 p.m., he got under weigh, and proceeded, the best way he could, on his passage towards the Petite Coquilles.

He says:

> About 1 o'clock a.m., on the 14th, it became quite calm, and our vessels, for want of wind, became unmanageable, when we came to anchor at the west end of Malheureux

Islands near the isle of St. Joseph.

At daylight the next morning, December the 15th, it being perfectly calm, the enemy's flotilla was lying at anchor about nine miles distance from us.

They soon, however, were put in motion, and were seen rapidly advancing towards us. We, therefore, had but one alternative, and that was to place our vessels in the best possible position to give the enemy a 'warm reception.'

The commanders of all the gun-boats were called on board of Lieutenant Jones' vessel, and made acquainted with his plan of defence.

It was decided to anchor the little squadron in close line athwart the channel, put springs upon their cables, and await the attack of the enemy.

Commander Jones adds:

At 9 a.m. I clearly saw the foe advance with forty-two heavy launches and gun-barges, besides three light gigs.
"At half-past 9 the enemy's flotilla came to anchor a little out of the reach of our shot, apparently preparing for the attack. At half-past 10 the enemy got under way, and formed a line abreast of our fleet in open order, steering directly for our line.
As soon as he came within the reach of our shot, we opened a fire upon him, but without much effect, his boats being comparatively but small objects. A few minutes before 11 o'clock our adversaries opened their fire from their whole line, when the action became general and destructive on both sides.
At 11.49 the advance boats of the foe, three in number, attempted to board one of our squadron, but were repulsed with the loss of every officer killed or wounded, and two of their boats sunk. A second attempt to board was made by four other boats, who shared an almost similar fate.

At this moment Commander Jones received a wound from a musket ball in his left shoulder. The wound was so severe, and the loss of blood so great, that he was compelled to go below, and resign the command of the deck to Mr. George Parker, masters mate, with orders to continue the action. Mr. Parker bravely defended the vessel until he was severely wounded, when the enemy, by superior numbers, succeeded in getting possession of the deck, and was enabled to turn the guns of the captured vessel upon the American gunboats. After they had nobly sustained the honour of the flag against overwhelming numbers, at close quarters, for more than two hours, they were reluctantly obliged to surrender to a superior force, and were all made prisoners of war.

Commodore Jones, Lieutenants Spedden and McKeever, together with all the other officers and seamen engaged in the gallant defence of their flag and little fleet, are richly entitled to the gratitude of their country; and as their names are enrolled on the pages of its history, their memories will ever be embalmed in the heart of every true American.

The writer of these pages begs leave of the reader to digress for a few moments from narrating the further acts of the British flotilla, while he proceeds to pay a just tribute to the gallant Lieutenant Jones. While at Lima, and at other ports on the western coast of South America in the years 1825 and 1826, the writer became acquainted with Captain Thomas Ap. Catesby Jones, who was then in command of the United States Sloop-of-war *Peacock*, which ship was cruising on that coast I take this occasion to acknowledge Captain Jones as one of my personal friends.

I think it would be difficult to find a more worthy man, or a braver and more efficient commander. Independently of these warlike qualities, I take pleasure in adding that Commodore Jones is a perfect gentleman in all the moral and social relations of private life, and a good model for the young officers in our navy. In a word, I think him an honour to his country. Although eleven years had elapsed since Captain Jones received the wound in his shoulder while defending the flotilla against the English, he could not, at this date, 1826, put on his coat or take it off without assistance.

In the defence of the five gun-boats against the English flotilla, the American loss, as furnished me by Commodore Jones on the 27th June, 1856, was as follows: Six killed and thirty-six wounded. Total number of killed and wounded, forty-two. On board of gun-boat No. 156, commanded by Lieutenant Jones himself, there were at the commencement of the action thirty-six souls, including officers, seamen, and marines. Out of this number four men were killed and fifteen wounded, making nineteen out of thirty-six. Further comment on this hand-to-hand fight is unnecessary.

This summary is copied from au official document made up immediately after the action; and as the name of every individual is given that was killed or wounded who belonged to the American flotilla, there can be no possible mistake in this detailed report of the American loss in their gallant defence of the flotilla, and in their nobly sustaining the honour of the American flag.

The force of the British in this action was as follows: Forty launches and barges, mounting one carronade, each of 12, 19, and 24-pound calibre, one launch mounting one long brass 12-pounder, and another launch of the same description, carrying one long brass 9-pounder, three gig-boats with small arms only.

Total number of boats,	45
Total number of cannon,	42

The above flotilla was manned with twelve hundred men and officers, commanded by Captain Locker, who received three severe wounds in the action.

The enemy, as usual on such occasions, would not acknowledge his loss in men and boats; but from the nature of the combat, and from the observations overheard by our officers while prisoners on board of the English fleet, their loss in killed and wounded may be fairly estimated at three hundred, among whom were an unusual proportion of officers.

After the capture of the American flotilla by the British fleet, on the 15th of December, there was nothing to obstruct their progress into Lake Borgne. The distance from the Island of St. Joseph (where the battle was fought between the flotillas), to New Orleans, is about forty miles. From Lake Borgne the English proceeded with their shallops and flat-bottomed boats through a small creek called Bayou Bienvenu, and then through a small plantation canal, which, with much labour and difficulty, they succeeded in widening and deepening so as to pass through it with their boats loaded with a considerable portion of their army, artillery, and military stores, with provisions for their troops. This canal brought them within a short distance of the Mississippi; so that on the 23rd of December, a considerable portion of the enemy's troops encamped on the left bank of the river, seven or eight miles below New Orleans, on the same side on which that city is located.

It is necessary for those unacquainted with this region to understand that the whole country around New Orleans is extremely low ground, pierced with creeks or small bayous, with wide-spread, dreary cypress swamps, interwoven with underwood and bushes, generally submerged with stagnant water. Except near the banks of the Mississippi and on the borders of the lakes where the ground is banked up, drained and cultivated, it is only a fit habitation for serpents and loathsome alligators.

This region, the lower part of Louisiana, is beyond all doubt one of the worst countries on earth for European troops to invade. Had the English army landed here in the summer, it would all have been swept away with the ordinary diseases of the country, arising from the climate and poisonous swamps, As it was, even in the winter season they could scarcely find dry ground enough to form a comfortable encampment. On their arrival in the afternoon of the 23rd, they spread themselves about half a mile along the bank of the river, with a cypress swamp in their rear. As they had already about three thousand men in camp, they doubtless felt themselves too strong to be attacked by any force the Americans could send against them, and were probably anticipating a good night's rest after a fatiguing day passed in removing from their boats to their camp grounds.

But that same evening about 8 o'clock, scarcely had they commenced lighting up their camp fires before they were attacked by Generals Jackson, Carroll, and Coffee. Besides these brave men with their several divisions, there was a detachment of artillery under the direction of Colonel McRea; there were also two 6-pounders under the command of Lieutenant Spots. The whole of the American land forces in this battle did not exceed seventeen hundred men.

Commodore Patterson soon dropped the U. S. Schooner *Caroline* down the river, opposite the British camp. The *Caroline* was directed at a given hour to open her fire upon the British troops. This was to be the signal for a general attack on the enemy's camp. General Coffee was ordered to turn the enemy's forces on the right near the swamp, while General Jackson and the other divisions attacked the enemy's strongest position on the left, near the river.

At the same time the *Caroline* kept up a constant cannonading from her battery on the invader's camp, without receiving the least injury, as the English had at that time no cannon mounted to return the compliment. General Jackson says, in his official dispatches, that General Coffee's men, with their usual impetuosity, rushed on the enemy's right, and entered his camp, while his men advanced with equal ardour. He further adds, that had not a thick fog set in, his troops would probably have destroyed or captured the greatest portion of the enemy.

Under all the circumstances of the case, after continuing the fight for about an hour, General Jackson contented himself with lying on the field the remainder of the night; and at 4 o'clock in the morning he withdrew to a stronger position, about two miles nearer the city. At this position General Jackson encamped, and there waited the arrival of the Kentucky militia, and other reinforcements.

General Jackson further remarks on his night assault upon the English camp, that all his officers and men performed their duty manfully, that they fought like veteran soldiers, that they merited his warmest approbation, and well deserve the gratitude of their country.

This night battle on the 23rd of December was the first meeting between the belligerent parties, and was a gratifying proof that the invaders were not invincible, as they here met with a severe check in their own camp, soon after placing their feet upon the American soil. Although the extent of their loss was not known at that time, it was subsequently ascertained to be as follows:

Killed,	100
Wounded,	230
Prisoners taken by the Americans:	
One major, two lieutenants, one midshipman, with sixty-six non-commissioned officers and privates, inclusive	70
Total,	400

Making a grand total of the enemy put *hors de combat* at the commencement of the campaign, which must be acknowledged a very gratifying prelude to future events.

The Americans lost about one hundred and seventy-five in killed, wounded, And missing. Among the officers, Colonel Lauderdale was killed, Colonels Dyer and Gibson of the same corps wounded.

From the time of the battle on the night of the 23rd, the Americans and British frequently exchanged shot from their artillery, and there was often brisk skirmishing between the outposts of the belligerent parties. The schooner *Caroline*, from her anchorage in the river, continued to harass and annoy the enemy's camp until the night of the 26th, when the British, under cover of darkness, succeeded in erecting a small battery from which they fired hot shot, and from this battery on the 27th succeeded in setting her on fire. The brave Captain John D. Henley, in his dispatches to Commodore Patterson, says:

> On the 27th of December, at daylight in the morning, the enemy opened a fire upon my vessel with shells and hot shot, and soon succeeded in setting her on fire. We

were, therefore, obliged to abandon her in our boats, as we could make no further resistance. Our loss was one man killed and six wounded. All my officers and men in this affair behaved with great gallantry, and merit my entire approbation.

Soon after leaving the *Caroline* we had the mortification of seeing her blow up, not, however, without the consolation of our having inflicted much damage to the enemy.

I will here digress from a continuation of my narrative of the invaders of our soil, collected from official documents, and insert an account of the burning of the *Caroline*, given me about two years after the peace was concluded between the United States and Great Britain, by Lieutenant S——, a gentleman belonging to the British Navy.

Lieutenant S——was a brave, worthy man, and a sincere lover of truth. This gentleman said in his statement of the affair, that he was employed in superintending the transportation of the artillery from their boats to the banks of the Mississippi; that on the, night of the 23rd of December the schooner *Caroline* harassed and annoyed them almost incessantly; that they had no guns to return her fire during two nights and one day ; that himself and his men were obliged to lie low, and shelter themselves the best way they could behind a small bank or *levée* along the river side, and that many of his countrymen had frequently to retreat into the cypress swamp to screen themselves from the grape and canister shot discharged from the battery of this destructive vessel.

At length, however, they collected from the neighbouring swamp a large quantity of bushes and brushwood. With these materials, and bags of earth to fill in among the bushes, they succeeded on the night of the 26th in constructing a redoubt sufficiently strong and solid to protect them from the galling fire of the *Caroline*. Behind this breastwork, he said, they soon mounted five pieces of cannon, and that at daylight in the morning on the 27th, they commenced a severe discharge of shot and shells upon the schooner, and soon succeeded in setting her on fire, to the great joy of all the British army.

General Jackson in his official account, states:

> On the morning of the 27th of December, the enemy succeeded in blowing up the *Caroline* by means of hot shot thrown from a land battery, which he had erected the previous night.
>
> Emboldened by this event, he marched his whole force along the *levée*, in hopes of driving us from our position, and with this view opened his fire upon us at a distance of about half a mile with bombs and rockets. He was, however, repulsed with considerable loss, not less, it is believed, than one hundred and twenty men killed.
>
> Our own loss was inconsiderable, not more than six men killed and twelve wounded. Since this attack, he has not ventured to repeat the attempt, though lying close together. There has, however, been frequent skirmishing between our pickets.

General Jackson here laments that he had not sufficient means to carry on offensive, operations against his adversaries.

On the 28th of December, the brave Colonel Henderson and several private soldiers were killed by the advance of the enemy on the left wing of the army. Colonel Henderson was a brave, meritorious officer, and a great loss to our army.

The Kentucky troops had not yet arrived, and General Jackson's effective force at this point did not exceed three thousand men, while the British army were more than double that number. Prisoners and deserters both agreed that more than seven thousand British troops had landed from their boats.

While General Jackson pursued the undeviating policy of harassing the enemy along his advance posts with the United States troops and drilled volunteer regiments, his main line of defence was daily being strengthened by recruits from the interior of Kentucky and Tennessee. It is to be presumed that a large portion of these men were farmers, who, from their childhood, had been accustomed to the use of the axe and the spade, and therefore were extremely useful in erecting temporary fortifications.

These men, under the direction of Colonel La Tour, the chief engineer, were constantly employed in collecting and placing logs of forest trees along the whole line, while numerous citizens from New Orleans were occupied in collecting bags of cotton and placing them in a position to form embrasures for the artillery. These logs, with cotton bags and other materials filled in with mud and earth, soon formed, as it were, a wall of defence about six feet high. In front of these works was a broad wet ditch, and although these fortifications were rudely constructed, they were nevertheless sufficiently strong and thick to protect the Americans from the fire of their assailants.

In our Western States, almost every farmer is trained from his boyhood to the use of the rifle; consequently a large proportion of these troops were good marksmen, and very efficient in defending fortifications.

General Jackson's main defence, according to a draft or plan by Colonel La Tour, was between 1,800 and 1,900 yards, that is a little over a mile in length. The right commenced at the river side and ran across the plain to the extreme left, extending to a large wet cypress swamp.

The writer of these pages visited the battle ground where these thrilling scenes transpired, some eighteen months after their occurrence, and within a few years has again passed over the same memorable fields, so that he is still familiar with all the important locations within a circle of fifty miles from New Orleans.

After this little digression, I will proceed to follow up the historical narration connected with these important events. On the right bank of the river, opposite General Jackson's strong defence, General Morgan had an entrenched camp protected by two marine batteries on the bank, erected and superintended by Commodore Patterson. Within this camp General Morgan had under his command the New Orleans Contingent, the Louisiana Militia, and a detachment of Kentucky troops. Commodore

Patterson had placed his vessel, the United States Ship *Louisiana*, in the river near the fort to protect General Morgan's camp, and also to protect General Jackson's flank on the opposite side of the river, and to repel the invaders whenever they should come within the reach of his guns. By all accounts, the heroic Patterson was in every place where he could do the enemy the most harm.

In Commodore Patterson's dispatches to the Secretary of the Navy, dated December the 29th, he says

> Yesterday morning our advanced guards retreated towards our lines. The enemy pursued throwing rockets, firing shot and shells from field artillery while they advanced on the road behind the *levée*. I got springs on the cables of the Louisiana, and soon brought her broadside to bear on the invaders.
>
> At half-past eight the enemy opened their fire upon the ship, with shells, hot shot, and rockets. We instantly returned their fire, which was continued without intermission till 1 p.m., when the enemy slackened their fire, and retreated with a part of their artillery, evidently with great loss.
>
> At 3 p.m. the enemy were silenced; at 4 we ceased firing from the ship, the invaders having retired beyond the reach of our guns. Many of their shot passed over the ship, and their shells burst over our decks, which were strewed with their fragments; and yet after an incessant cannonading of upwards of seven hours, during which time eight hundred shot were fired from the ship, one man only was slightly wounded by a piece of shell, and one shot passed between the bowsprit and the heel of the jib-boom.

General Jackson having applied for officers and seamen to work the heavy cannon on his lines, Lieutenants Norris and Crawley, late of the schooner *Caroline*, with the greater part of her crew, instantly volunteered, They behaved with great gallantry, under the immediate eye of the commander-in-chief.

EXTRACT OF A LETTER FROM AN OFFICER UNDER GENERAL JACKSON'S COMMAND, TO HIS FRIEND IN BALTIMORE, DATED: CAMP, FOUR MILES BELOW NEW ORLEANS, JANUARY 6TH.

The enemy have made several attempts to carry our works, but up to this date have been uniformly repulsed and driven back. It is now fourteen days since the first battle took place between our troops and the British, and for the whole of the last two weeks we have been almost constantly employed in cannonading the invaders.
"We have battered down their advanced works as fast as they could erect them. I am sorry to say we have lost from a hundred and fifty to two hundred men, among whom were some of our most respectable citizens. General Jackson is a perfect hero. I think, however, he exposes himself too much, for should a chance shot take him off, it is impossible to say what would be the consequence to our army. His head-quarters are so near the British lines, that at least thirty cannon balls have passed through the plantation house which he occupies.
The opposing lines are so near each other, that the picket-guards skirmish daily.

While the cannonading and skirmishing were kept up without much cessation by both the belligerent parties, it was evident to General Jackson, from some uncommon movements he discovered in the British camp, that the enemy was preparing to make a general assault upon his lines, and if possible, carry his defences by storm. He therefore kept up a show of resistance opposite the British out-posts, while he ordered the main army to fall back and retire to the rear of his strong defence.

He arranged the different corps of his army as follows: the regular troops and part of the militia of Louisiana occupied and defended six hundred yards on the right, next to the river; General Carroll's division, twelve hundred strong, eight hundred yards in the centre; General Coffee's Corps of riflemen, seven hundred strong, the remainder of the ground on the extreme left near the swamp.

Besides the foregoing, there were about six or eight hundred of the Kentucky militia in the rear of the line, to act as a reserve corps, to assist at any point where their services should be most required,

General Jackson says in his official report, that the whole number of his men, on this side of the river, did not exceed three thousand five hundred and ninety.

All along this extended line were placed parks of artillery, fusiliers, and riflemen, so that the Americans were all ready, and anxiously awaiting the assault of the invaders.

Having brought my readers to the eve of the great and decisive battle between the Americans and the invading army, I will observe that this region of country, for many miles below New Orleans, is an entire dead level, so that the enemy had neither hill nor hollow to protect him from the destructive fire of the Americans.

The commander-in-chief being satisfied that his own defences were sufficiently strong to repel any force the enemy could send against him, had leisure to turn his attention to the right bank of the river. With his usual activity and quick-sightedness to watch and guard every weak point, he forthwith resolved to strengthen Commodore Patterson and General Morgan's force, to protect their batteries, which were located opposite his own camp and stronghold. He accordingly ordered a detachment of four hundred Kentucky militia, under the command of Colonel Davis, to leave the camp at 7 o'clock in the evening, on the 7th of Jan., to proceed forthwith to New Orleans, and from thence cross over the river in boats, join General Morgan's camp, and assist in repelling the English, should they make an assault upon his camp or marine batteries.

Having made these preliminary arrangements on both sides of the river, the Americans anxiously awaited the enemy, being prepared to give him a warm reception whenever it should suit his pleasure to commence the deadly conflict. What may have been the feelings of the belligerent parties, while reposing that night on the battle-field, I will not attempt to portray, but will leave each one of my readers to conjecture for himself. They all expected the deadly strife to commence the next morning. In all human probability a large portion of friends and foes would soon mingle in the dust, and thus pass from time to eternity.

It will not do, however, for soldiers at such times to be very sentimental, or indulge in much reflection, when there is no alternative but to kill or be killed.

But after all, there was a glorious consolation on the part of the Americans, "that they, had their quarrel just;" were fighting to defend their wives and children from the foul pollution of the hireling and the spoiler, who came from a foreign land to defile their soil, and by brute force to trample under foot their cherished liberty and sacred rights.

These feelings, mingled with a patriotic faith in a just God, inspired their hearts to believe that an All-wise Being would reward the just and innocent, and punish the guilty oppressor.

Suffice then to say, that the next day before daylight on the morning of the 8th of January, the enemy silently prepared a large and strong force to storm General Jackson's line of defence. Their columns, in the obscurity of the morning, advanced unperceived until within about half a mile of the American camp, where they met and drove in the picket guard. At half-past 6 o'clock, soon after daylight, they advanced with great vivacity in two strong and deep columns, one on the right next to the river, the other on the extreme left, next to the swamp. The column on General Jackson's right was composed of two thousand five hundred picked grenadiers, supposed to be the very flower of the British army. The division on the left was said to number three thousand five hundred, composed of artillery-men and fusiliers. Against the centre of the line were directed mortars, bombs, and *obusiers*, or small mortars. A considerable portion of the men were provided with fascines to fill up the ditch, and with scaling ladders to ascend and storm our works at the point of the bayonet.

They commenced the assault with a furious discharge of

Congreve rockets, artillery, and bombshells. The soldiers were gallantly led on by their officers; and when they approached to within about half musket shot distance, General Jackson opened a tremendous fire from his whole line of artillery, muskets and rifles. As the enemy was so near our works, and the ground level, the infliction upon the foe was terrible in the extreme. The artillery being well directed, made as it were entire lanes through the dense columns of the English, while the incessant fire of musketry covered the field and ditch with their killed and wounded. In fine, the enemy were swept down like grass before the reaper. Notwithstanding they fell by hundreds, still they continued to advance, even to the edge of the ditch, and almost to the very muzzle of the guns of the American defences.

Though the whole line was attacked, yet the most severe assault was made on the extreme left next to the swamp, where General Coffee's brigade of Tennessee riflemen were stationed. Although a portion of these brave men next to the swamp were up to their knees in mud and water, they defended that point with deadly effect. There the carnage was prodigious. The men being sheltered by the breast-works took steady and deliberate aim, so that almost every shot took effect.

The ditch near the swamp was nearly filled with killed and wounded, and the whole field in that vicinity almost literally covered with the dead and dying. The roar of the artillery and the sharp sound of the musketry from our lines kept up a continuous roar, resembling a vivid thunder storm. The incessant sheets of fire, poured forth from every quarter, so filled the atmosphere with smoke and vapour, that it was difficult at times to distinguish near objects in the American camp for several moments.

During the whole of this memorable battle, which continued for an hour and a quarter, the brave Jackson was rapidly passing along his whole line of defence, encouraging and cheering the soldiers with such animating words as "Give it to them, my boys;" "Let us finish the business today, and teach our enemies such a lesson that they will not soon forget the 8th of January."

The British columns were headed by their principal Generals, Packenham, Gibbs, and Keane. The first two were killed, bravely fighting at the head of their troops. The latter, General Keane, was severely wounded, and carried off the field. Twice their columns were repulsed and broken, and obliged to retreat and form anew. A third attempt was made to rally the men for another assault, but their principal generals being either killed or wounded it was found impossible to rally them. Being disorganized and cut to pieces they soon fled in confusion from the field, leaving the ditch and the adjacent ground literally covered with their dead and wounded.

The total loss of the British in this action, as stated in General Jackson's official report, was, in killed, wounded, and prisoners, as follows:

Killed,	700
Wounded,	1,400
Prisoners taken: One major, four captains, eleven lieutenants, one ensign, with four hundred and eighty-three camp officers and privates,	500
Making together a grand total of	2,600

Besides the numerous English prisoners taken by the Americans in this battle, they also took from the enemy about one thousand stand of arms of various descriptions.

General Jackson stated his own loss to be but ten killed and as many wounded. In the history of wars and battles, either in ancient or modern times, I believe there is no instance on record where there was so much suffering on one side, and so little on the other, as in this memorable battle of New Orleans on the 8th of January, 1815.

Simultaneously with the attack of the British on General Jackson's lines at daylight on the 8th of January, the British threw over the river in boats six hundred men under the command of Colonel Thornton. They had already on that side of the river four hundred, which augmented their numbers on the right bank of the Mississippi to one thousand efficient artillery-men and fusiliers. This force made a bold dash upon General Morgan's marine batteries, which, after a short resistance, were captured by the enemy. These batteries, however, were not taken until after the guns had been spiked and the powder destroyed by Commodore Patterson, assisted by his brave officers and seamen.

After the severe repulse of the British on the morning of the 8th, their principal generals being either killed or wounded, the command of the army devolved upon Major-General Lambert, who had been in command of a reserve corps stationed in the rear. This officer now came forward to direct the movement and operations of the scattered British forces, and if possible to retrieve the misfortunes of the day. He found the soldiers retreating in disorder and confusion; but from the habit of strict discipline and obedience, they were soon restored to order.

After General Lambert had examined the situation of affairs, he saw the utter hopelessness of attempting to force General Jackson's strong defence. He prudently withdrew his troops out of the reach of the fire of the Americans, and finally from the battle-field. At this time the Americans kept up an incessant fire upon the flying foe until out of the reach of their artillery. After the firing had ceased on both sides, General Lambert, about noon, sent a flag of truce to General Jackson, asking for a cessation of hostilities for two days to bury the dead and take care of the wounded.

The sagacious and quick-sighted commander-in-chief of the American forces answered General Lambert that he would agree to the cessation of hostilities for twenty-four hours for the purpose required, upon condition that neither party should send reinforcements to the opposite or right bank of the river, and that both parties should be at liberty to continue offensive operations there. The British general required a short time to consider these propositions. In the meantime he ordered Colonel Thornton to leave the right bank, cross the river, and join the remnant of the British army a few miles below the American camp. This, of course, was joyful news to the Americans, who immediately retook possession of their marine batteries.

The next morning, January 9th, General Lambert, after making some frivolous excuse for the delayed answer, agreed to General Jackson's terms of a cessation of arms for twenty-four hours to bury the dead and take care of the wounded.

General Morgan soon replaced the four long 24-pounders in position to protect General Jackson's lines on the left bank of the river. Beside his own defences, he had the assistance of the brave Commodore Patterson, with his ship *Louisiana*.

In addition to these four long 24's, he had several twelve pounders, and was now fully prepared to renew the conflict, should the enemy conclude to make another assault upon his works.

Although the enemy's mortars were so long directed against General Jackson's centre, and many bombs sent into his works, it is surprising how little harm was effected to his troops by the bursting of these missiles. As the firing had now ceased for a brief space, both parties were employed in burying the dead, and taking care of the sick and wounded. While the British were occupied in burying their dead, and removing the wounded within their own lines, the Americans were busy in securing their numerous prisoners. Such of them as were in a condition to be removed, to the amount of several hundred, were sent up to Natchez.

The English sick and wounded were taken to the hospitals and barracks in New Orleans, where everything was done on the part of the Americans to make them comfortable, and in every way to relieve their sufferings as much as possible.

A call was made on the citizens of New Orleans for mattresses for the wounded English, when four hundred and forty were voluntarily furnished, and many other necessary articles given to the sufferers by the humane and philanthropic inhabitants of that city.

After the time had expired for the cessation of hostilities

between the belligerent parties, General Jackson sent from his camp a detachment of troops to strengthen General Morgan's force on the right bank of the river, and with his usual zeal and activity, again reopened a hot fire from his artillery on the enemy's camp and outposts. He, also, by scouts and every other means in his power, continued to harass and annoy the invaders, until their final retreat within their old camping grounds, where they took the precaution to entrench themselves.

And here I will leave them for the present, and proceed to narrate an account of the transactions of General Morgan and Commodore Patterson, Who were located on the right bank of the Mississippi, nearly opposite General Jackson's camp and strong line of defence.

It will be recollected by my readers, that General Jackson, on the evening of the 7th of Jan., ordered Colonel Davis, with a detachment of Kentucky militia, four hundred strong, to leave his camp, proceed to New Orleans, cross the river, and join General Morgan's forces, to defend their camp and batteries. By a subsequent account it appears that these four hundred men proceeded to New Orleans, as they were ordered, but on their arrival at that city, there was a great lack of muskets, and only sufficient fire-arms to supply two hundred of them. The remaining two hundred therefore returned to General Jackson's camp early on the morning of the 8th.

The two hundred that crossed the river state that they had hardly entered into the lines before they were attacked by a strong British force, and obliged to retreat to the rear before superior numbers, or be cut to pieces and annihilated without rendering any service to their country. In direct contradiction to this statement, General Morgan and Com. Patterson avow that the Kentucky militia ignobly fled from the enemy, and by their act created a panic among the other troops, which enabled the English to assault and capture the two marine batteries which had been so long and bravely defended.

General Jackson also adds in his official report to the Secretary of War of the defence of the Americans on the right bank of the Mississippi, that the Kentucky militia ingloriously fled before the enemy, and by their example drew after them the remainder of General Morgan's troops. In another account of the battle, he said:

> Had not the militia on the right bank of the river ignominiously fled, the entire destruction of the British army would have been inevitable.[1]

These official accounts relating to the conduct of the Kentucky militia were of course very mortifying to the principal officers connected with the army from that State, and caused much controversy, and some recrimination. They naturally felt a deep interest for the zeal and honour of their troops, and were extremely mortified that their courage should be impeached.

The account; of their sudden retreat, given by so many reliable witnesses, cannot be doubted, but how far they were justified in the act, must be left with experienced military men to decide.

I think that cool and deliberate firmness in battle cannot be expected from raw troops unaccustomed to war.

All experience proves that raw militia will generally fight pretty well behind breast-works, or when supported and encouraged by regular experienced soldiers; but in the open field they can rarely be made to stand a furious charge of the bayonet from regularly bred infantry. A raw militiaman flies from his enemy for safety, the veteran faces the foe upon the same principle. The latter believes there is less risk in confronting the enemy than in flight; besides, an old regular feels that it is highly disgraceful to be shot in the back.

As a general principle, all men have an instinctive fear of death, and it is only by training and habit that they overcome that fear; hence it follows that one hundred veterans in the open field, are more reliable than double their number of raw recruits, who have never been in action.

---

1. A court of inquiry was subsequently held on Colonel Davis. After strict investigation of all the transactions, he was honourably acquitted.

Military men accustomed to war say, that numbers do not necessarily constitute success, for when a panic ensues, the greater the number the more the confusion in a general rout.

General Washington, in our Revolutionary War, understood by experience, how little reliance could be placed upon raw troops, unaccustomed to war in the open field, and was therefore obliged to place them by the side of veteran troops, or provide them with the pick-axe and shovel, to throw up breast-works.

General Jackson wisely acted upon the same principle in this successful campaign. It is true that in his first battle with the English on the 23rd of December, he attacked the invaders with about 1,700 men, having, it is presumed, only about half their number, but still he knew his men. They were mostly regular troops, and were aided by reliable, high-minded volunteers.

He also knew he had a safe retreat higher up the banks of the Mississippi, should retreat become necessary.

After the signal defeat of the English on the 8th, they uniformly acted on the defensive, entrenching and fortifying their camp, while diligently preparing to leave a country where they had met with nothing but defeat and disappointment from the first attack upon the American flotilla, until their final evacuation of the soil they had so ruthlessly invaded.

The only advantage they can boast of was the capturing of General Morgan's marine batteries, which they could not retain, and were obliged to abandon to the Americans the same day on which they were taken. The whole army, from the 8th, was broken down, disorganized and dispirited. Two of their principal generals, Packenham and Gibbs, were killed. [2] General Keane was severely wounded; and of the four generals who led the invading host, but one, General Lambert, survived to take command of the retreating remnant of a once powerful army.

In Europe, a large portion of these troops had gained the

---

2. A London newspaper, dated March 14th, 1815, states: "Yesterday the remains of Generals Packenham and Gibbs arrived at Portsmouth, in the *Plantagenet*. 74. The bodies of these two distinguished generals were placed in leaden coffins and shells, and taken to London for interment."

appellation of "Wellington's Invincibles", who vainly boasted that they had conquered the flower of the French army, when commanded by Soult and other leading French marshals, while campaigning in Spain and Portugal, during the protracted Peninsula wars.

Farther comment on this subject is unnecessary: suffice it to say that the English had met a new enemy in a nation of freemen. In writing accounts of some of our naval engagements with the English, I have remarked that they had found a new enemy in the Americans on the sea, so that I trust I may add without vanity, that they had also found a new enemy in the Americans on the land.

After the repulse of the British on the 8th, they kept up a menacing attitude, and made frequent indications as if they intended to attack the American lines, while the rear of their army was constantly retiring. Though they made a great display of men during the day, and kept up large fires at night, they were secretly embarking on board of their boats all their sick and wounded, together with as much as they could spare of their heavy baggage and munitions of war.

From their boats everything was transferred to the shipping on the lakes. They protected themselves with batteries to cover their retreat, while they strove to impress upon the Americans a belief that they were waiting for a reinforcement to commence a new campaign.

The Americans had no fears on account of this beaten and dispirited army. Their only cause for fear was that a British fleet might be able to pass Fort St Phillip, ascend the Mississippi, and attack New Orleans from their ships. But the great Ruler of the Universe had ordered it otherwise. The gallant defender of this fort had withstood a siege of nine days. After receiving in and about the fort more than one thousand large bombshells, exclusive of small ones and shot, with the loss of only two killed and seven wounded, the enemy retired from the siege, and sailed out of the Mississippi about the last of January.

On the 18th Jan. all the American prisoners on shore were

delivered up, an exchange having been previously agreed upon. Those Americans prisoners on board of the British fleet were delivered to their countrymen at the fort at Petite Coquilles. After all these exchanges had been made, the Americans had an excess of several hundred English prisoners.

From the most authentic and reliable sources I can obtain, I have arrived at the following conclusion, grounded upon the opinions of General Jackson and his principal officers. They estimated the loss of the British from their first attack on the American flotilla until the day they left the soil of Louisiana, on the 27th of Jan., comprising a space of forty-two days, by battle, sickness and other casualties, to be at least four thousand men. The loss of the Americans in all the various battles, did not amount to more than four hundred and eighty.

On the night of the 18th of January, all that remained of the British army precipitately retreated to their boats, leaving behind about twenty pieces of artillery, which were spiked, and one hundred and twenty to one hundred and thirty prisoners, including the wounded, who could not be conveniently removed.

On the 19th, General Jackson ordered Major Hind with a body of cavalry to pursue after the enemy, and make prisoners of such as could be overtaken, and also to ascertain whether the enemy had actually embarked his whole force to evacuate the country. This valuable officer, with his usual zeal and activity, pushed forward and made about ninety more prisoners. The most of these being wounded had been left behind with a surgeon to attend them. They were left by a British officer, recommended to the humanity of General Jackson. They were, accordingly, conveyed to his head-quarters and treated with the utmost kindness and humanity.

On the night of the 20th of January the gallant Mr. Shield, purser in the U. S. Navy, succeeded, with a party of seamen, in capturing several British boats on Lake Borgne, and made fifty-four prisoners, among whom were four officers.

Had General Jackson indulged in a selfish ambition for his

own personal aggrandizement, he doubtless could have taken or destroyed a large portion of this retreating army; but patriotism and humanity forbade it. He had already harassed and killed enough of the invaders to teach them a salutary lesson which I hope may descend to several generations, and admonish them not to tyrannize over nations less powerful than themselves, nor to hold their enemies too cheap in the scale of equality.

It was of course joyful and very gratifying news throughout the United States to hear that our soil was relieved of the sacrilegious feet of the spoiler, and to know that the American arms had triumphed so gloriously at the winding up of the war. The picket guard, whose duty it was to watch and report the movements of the retreating army, stated that at eleven o'clock on the morning of the 27th of January, 1815, the last British vessel conveying troops disappeared from the shores of Lake Borgne, steering towards Ship Island in the Bay of St. Louis, to secure the same anchorage ground they had left on the 10th of December, with the sanguine hope of invading and conquering the rich and important State of Louisiana.

In my estimation this was a just retribution for offensive war. Long may an All-wise Being punish invaders with a similar fate, and now, methinks, I hear a thousand American voices repeat, Amen!

This powerful British army had attempted to invade a foreign State. They had fought bravely, had endured every kind of hardship, and suffered more than it is possible to relate. A large portion of them had been either killed or wounded; they had gained no honour or renown; had been beaten in almost every attack upon the enemy.

Broken down, dispirited, sick, suffering, disappointed and dejected, they were now returning home to be treated with coldness and neglect by their own countrymen. As they had gained no laurels they could expect no sympathy.

Yet such is war and its vain glory; and when unsuccessful, those engaged in it become contemptible even in the eyes of their own friends.

Remarks on the Memorable Battle of the 8th of January, 1816, with Reflections on the Terrible Consequences that Would Have Ensued had the British Succeeded in Storming General Jackson's Defences and Capturing New Orleans.

It is now more than forty-one years since the occurrence of this ever memorable event, and the most of those who took part in the conflict have passed away; still there are enough remaining, as well as the faithful pages of history, to establish the truth of every sentence I have written on the subject of the assault and defeat of the English in their last effort to triumph over a finer people.

Sufficient time has now elapsed for the passions of men to have cooled down, so that they can take a dispassionate view of all the facts in the case. First, it is well known to every intelligent American that the British officers promised their soldiers forty-eight hours of indiscriminate license and plunder if they would take New Orleans. Notwithstanding this statement is contradicted by Mr. Stewart, an English traveller, and several British generals, they can never make the intelligent portion of the American nation believe their statement, after the diabolical acts practised by them at Badajoz, Hampton, and Havre de Grace.

That fact, I trust, will not be denied, even by the honest part of the English themselves. It is also well known that both officers and men had for their watchword, "Beauty and booty." The meaning of that motto requires no explanation; it speaks for itself. Again, it must be recollected that a large portion of these same men, only two years prior to this event, had despoiled and sacked Badajoz, in Spain; an account of which may be found recorded in the tenth chapter of this work.

My readers must here bear in mind that the British army, under the command of Lord Wellington, was sent to Spain and Portugal as friends and protectors, to assist them against the invasion of the French, and prevent that nation from overrunning their country.

And now I ask, in the name of common sense, if these ruthless men treated their friends in the manner described by one of their own officers, what would have been the shocking scenes enacted by these hell-hounds, these devils incarnate, if let loose to prey upon their avowed enemies, the inhabitants of New Orleans?

The heart shudders and sickens at the very idea of such scenes of horror; and now methinks I hear some of the English partisans here inquire: Are you not mistaken? are they not a civilized, Christian nation, and would they indeed be guilty of such dreadful deeds as you have anticipated?

I again answer, did they not perform these worse than savage acts at Hampton, Badajoz, and other places under similar circumstances? How then can anyone imagine that New Orleans would have escaped a similar fate.

Suffice then to say, that a just God did not permit them to succeed in their diabolical intentions.

Is it then a wonder that the female portion of New Orleans should erect triumphal arches of evergreen bowers for these patriotic heroes to pass through, and that they should crown General Jackson and his officers with wreaths and garlands of flowers, while their hearts overflowed with kindness and gratitude to their deliverers who had saved them from pollution and ruin, from the very dregs of hell.

Were I an Englishman, while reading the outrages committal at Badajoz and Hampton, I should blush for the honour of my country, and would never boast of its Christianity or civilization so long as the military portion of the kingdom were allowed to commit such horrid acts against other nations.

On the 6th of March an express arrived from Washington, at General Jackson's head-quarters, Camp Henderson, bringing the pleasing intelligence that peace was made and ratified between the United States and Great Britain.

After the general peace was established in Europe, the British Government planned and organized this great expedition for the invasion and subjugation of Louisiana, and sent their most experienced generals and the very flower of their army to carry out their unjust project.

And now, after their experiment proved a total failure, and the foul invaders have been beaten and driven from our soil, I ask, what American can read the account of this expedition, and follow up the chain of its proceedings, link by link, until its final defeat, and not see the finger of God aiding those who were fighting to defend their homes and the honour of their beloved country?

Commencing with the commander-in-chief and his brave coadjutors, who, I repeat, can read of the various battles gained in defence of their country, and not feel a profound veneration for their gallant and patriotic deeds of daring, in leading on the citizen, the yeoman, the artisan—in fine, every description of freeman?

Yes, our admiration and gratitude should extend to every individual who took the smallest part in the defence and consequent honour of our country,

For the commander-in-chief, the heroic Jackson, one feels his heart warm up with admiration and gratitude. amounting almost to idolatry; for under God he was the Saviour of New Orleans, and the great defender of his country's honour and lasting glory.

This brave chief was always in the midst of the fire, exposed on every side, but still shielded and protected by Divine power to fulfil his mission and duty to his country, and second only to Washington as a lasting monument to perpetuate the American name.

When the petty jealousies of the present day shall have passed into oblivion, the names of these great and good men will live fresh in every American heart, and millions yet unborn will live to bless, their memory, and will teach their children's children to lisp and sing their praise.

In giving this sketch, I cannot particularize all the gallant leaders who took a prominent part in repelling the invaders. Their names are already recorded in the pages of our national history, and their eulogies have been written by abler pens than mine. Such names as Coffee, Carroll, Henderson, Lauderdale, Morgan, Patterson, Adair, and a host of other brave, patriotic defenders of their country, will ever be revered by the wise and good of all nations.

Yes, their names will be perpetuated as a countersign and watchword for future generations to rally round, when their country and its institutions shall be in danger of foreign aggression.

It would be a pleasing duty for the writer of these pages to notice a greater number of the gallant officers and men who distinguished themselves in these various battles, did time and space admit of it.

Suffice then to say, that they are one and all entitled to their country's everlasting gratitude.

An American officer who fought in these various battles said to the writer, about two years after this memorable event, while warming up with enthusiasm:

> I trust we all did our duty, but the heroic Jackson is indeed a glorious fellow; he was always in the midst of the enemy's fire, and exposed on every side, but was miraculously preserved to save New Orleans from the sacrilegious pollution of the enemy.
> Our gallant chief was almost adored by the soldiers of the whole army, and no one can behold him without feelings of admiration.

Treaty of Peace

JAMES MADISON,
PRESIDENT OF THE UNITED STATES OF AMERICA,

To all and singular to whom these presents shall come, Greeting:

Whereas a treaty of peace and amity between the United States of America, and his Britannic Majesty was signed at Ghent, on the twenty-fourth day of December, one thousand eight hundred and fourteen, by the plenipotentiaries respectively appointed for that purpose; and the said treaty having been, by and with the advice and consent of the Senate of the United States, duly accepted, ratified, and confirmed, on the seventeenth day of February, one thousand eight hundred and fifteen; and ratified copies thereof having been exchanged agreeably to the tenor of the said treaty, which is in the words following, to wit:

TREATY OF PEACE AND AMITY BETWEEN HIS BRITANNIC MAJESTY AND THE UNITED STATES OF AMERICA

His Britannic Majesty and the United States of America, desirous of terminating the war which has unhappily subsisted between the two countries, and of restoring, upon principles of perfect reciprocity, peace, friendship, and good understanding between them, have, for that purpose, appointed their respective plenipotentiaries, that is to say: his Britannic Majesty, on his part, has appointed the Right Honourable James, Lord Gambier, late Admiral of the white, now Admiral of the red squadron of his Majesty's fleet, Henry Goulburn, Esq., a member of the

Imperial Parliament, and Under Secretary of State, and William Adams, Esq., doctor of civil laws:—And the President of the United States, by and with the advice and consent of the Senate thereof, has appointed John Quincy Adams, James A. Bayard, Henry Clay, Jonathan Russell and Albert Gallatin, citizens of the United States, who after a reciprocal communication of their respective full powers, have agreed upon the following articles:

Article the First

There shall be a firm and universal peace between his Britannic Majesty and the United States, and between their respective countries, territories, cities, towns, and people, of every degree, without exception of places or persons. All hostilities, both by sea and land, shall cease as soon as this treaty shall have been ratified by both parties, as hereinafter mentioned. All territory, places, and possessions whatsoever, taken from either party by the other, during the war, or which may be taken after the signing of this treaty, excepting only the islands hereinafter mentioned, shall be restored without delay, and without causing any destruction, or carrying away any of the artillery or other public property originally captured in the said forts or places, and which shall remain therein upon the exchange of the ratifications of this treaty, or any slaves or other private property.

And all archives, records, deeds, and papers, either of a public nature, or belonging to private persons which, in the course of the war, may have the hands of the officers of either party, shall be as far as may be practicable, forthwith restored and delivered to the proper authorities and persons to whom they respectively belong. Such of the Islands in the Bay of Passamaquoddy as are claimed by both parties, shall remain in the possession of the party in whose occupation they may be at the time of the exchange of the ratifications of this treaty, until the decision respecting the title to the said islands shall have been made in conformity with the fourth article of this treat position made by this treaty, as to such possession of the islands and territories claimed by both parties, shall in any manner whatever, be construed to affect the right of either.

Article the Second

Immediately after the ratifications of this treaty by both parties, as hereinafter mentioned, orders shall be sent to the armies, squadrons, officers, subjects and citizens, of the two powers to cease from all hostilities: And to prevent all causes of complaint which might arise on account of the prizes which might be taken at sea after the said ratifications of this treaty, it is reciprocally agreed, that all vessels and effects which may be taken after the space of twelve days from the said ratifications, upon all parts of the coast of North America, from the latitude of twenty-three degrees north, to the latitude of fifty degrees north, and as far eastward in the Atlantic Ocean, as the thirty-sixth degree of west longitude from the meridian of Greenwich, shall be restored to each side: That the time shall be thirty days in all other parts of the Atlantic Ocean, north of the equinoctial line or equator, and the same time for the British and Irish Channels, for the Gulf of Mexico and all parts of the West Indies: forty days for the North Seas, for the Baltic, and for all parts of the Mediterranean: sixty days for the Atlantic Ocean, south of the equator as far as the latitude of the Cape of Good Hope: ninety days for every part of the world south of the equator: and one hundred and twenty days for all other parts of the world, without exception.

Article the Third

All prisoners of war taken on either side, as well by land as by sea, shall be restored as soon as practicable after the ratification of this treaty, as hereinafter mentioned, on their paying the debts which they may have contracted during their captivity. The two contracting parties respectively engage to discharge in specie, the advances which may have been made by the other for the sustenance and maintenance of such prisoners.

Article the Fourth

Whereas it was stipulated by the second article in the treaty of peace, of one thousand seven hundred and eighty-three, between his Britannic Majesty and the United States of America, that the boundary of the United States should comprehend all islands within twenty leagues of any part of the shores of the United States, and lying between lines to be drawn due east from the points where the aforesaid boundaries, between Nova Scotia, on the one part, and East Florida on the other, shall respectively touch the Bay of Fundy, and the Atlantic Ocean, excepting such Islands as now are, or heretofore have been, within the limits of Nova Scotia; and whereas the several Islands in the Bay of Passamaquoddy, which is part of the Bay of Fundy, and the Island of Grand Menan in the said Bay of Fundy, are claimed by the United States as being comprehended within their aforesaid boundaries, which said Islands are claimed as belonging to his Britannic Majesty, as having been at the time of, and previous to, the aforesaid treaty of one thousand seven hundred and eighty-three within the limits of the province of Nova Scotia: In order, therefore, finally to decide upon these claims, it is agreed that they shall be referred to two commissioners, to be appointed in the following manner, *viz.*, one commissioner shall be appointed by his Britannic Majesty, and one by the President of the United States, by and with the advice and consent of the Senate thereof, and the said two commissioners so appointed shall be sworn impartially to examine and decide upon the said claims according to such evidence as shall be laid before them on the part of his Britannic Majesty and of the United States respectively.

The said commissioners shall meet at St. Andrews, in the province of New Brunswick, and shall have power to adjourn to such other place or places as they shall think fit. The said commissioners shall, by a declaration or report under their hands and seals, decide to which of the two contracting parties the several islands aforesaid do respectively belong, in conformity, with the true intent of the said treaty of peace of one thousand seven hundred and eighty-three.

And if the said commissioners shall agree in their decision, both parties shall consider such decision as final and conclusive. It is further agreed, that in the event of the two commissioners differing upon all or any of the matters so referred to them, or in the event of both or either of the said commissioners refusing, or declining or wilfully omitting, to act as such, they shall make, jointly or separately, a report or reports, as well to the government of his Britannic Majesty as to that of the United States, stating in detail the points on which they differ, and the grounds upon which their respective opinions have been formed, or the grounds upon which they, or either of them, have so refused, declined, or omitted to act.

And his Britannic Majesty, and the government of the United States hereby agree to refer the report or reports of the said commissioners, to some friendly sovereign or state, to be then named for that purpose, and who shall be requested to decide on the differences which may be stated in the said report or reports, or upon the report of one commissioner, together with the grounds upon which the other commissioner shall have refused, declined, or omitted to act, as the case may be.

And if the commissioner so refusing, declining, or omitting to act, shall also wilfully omit to state the grounds upon which he has so done, in such manner that the said statement may be referred to such friendly sovereign or state, together with the report of such other commissioner, then such sovereign or state shall decide *ex parte* upon the said report alone. And his Britannic Majesty and the government of. the United States engage to consider the decision of some friendly sovereign or state to be such and conclusive on all the matters so referred.

Article the Fifth

Whereas neither that point of the high lands lying due north from the source of the river St. Croix, and designated in the former treaty of peace between the two powers as the north-west angle of Nova Scotia, now the north-westernmost head of Connecticut river, has yet been ascertained; and whereas that part of the boundary line between the dominion of the two powers which extends from the source of the river St. Croix directly north to the above-mentioned north-west angle of Nova

Scotia, thence along the said highlands which divide those rivers that empty themselves into the river St. Lawrence from those which fall into the Atlantic Ocean to the north-westernmost head of Connecticut river, thence down along the middle of the river to the forty-fifth degree of north latitude; thence by a line due west on said latitude until it strikes the river Iroquois or Cataraguy has not been surveyed:—It is agreed that for these several purposes two commissioners shall be appointed, sworn, and authorized, to act exactly in the manner directed with respect to those mentioned in the next preceding article, unless otherwise specified in the present article.

The said commissioners shall meet at St. Andrews, in the province of New Brunswick, and shall have power to adjourn to such other place or places as they shall think fit. The said commissioners shall have power to ascertain and determine the points above-mentioned, in conformity with the provisions of the said treaty of peace of one thousand seven hundred and eighty-three, and shall cause the boundary aforesaid, from the source of the river St. Croix to the river Iroquois or Cataraguy, to be surveyed and marked according to the said provisions. The said commissioners shall make a map of the said boundary, and annex to it a declaration under their hands and seals, certifying it to be the true map of the said boundary, and particularizing the latitude and longitude of the north-west angle of Nova Scotia, of the north-westernmost head of Connecticut river, and of such other points of the same boundary as they may deem proper.

And both parties agree to consider such map and declaration as finally and conclusively fixing the said boundary. And in the event of the said two commissioners differing, or both, or either of them, refusing, or declining, or wilfully omitting to act, such reports, declarations, or statements, shall be made by them, or either of them, and such reference to a friendly sovereign or state, shall be made, in all respects as in the latter part of the fourth article is contained, and in as full a manner as if the same was herein repeated.

Article the Sixth

Whereas, by the former treaty of peace that portion of the boundary of the United States from the point where the forty-fifth degree of north latitude strikes the river Iroquois or Cataraguy to the Lake Superior, was declared to be "along the middle of said river into Lake Ontario, through the middle of said lake until it strikes the communication by water, between that Lake and Lake Erie, thence along the middle of said communication into Lake Erie, through the middle of said lake until it arrives at the water communication into the Lake Huron, thence through the middle of said lake to the water communication between that lake and Lake Superior."

And whereas doubts have arisen what was the middle of said river, lakes and water communications, and whether certain Islands lying in the same were within the dominions of his Britannic Majesty or of the United States: In order, therefore, finally to decide these doubts, they shall be referred to two commissioners, to be appointed, sworn, and authorised to act exactly in the manner directed with respect to those mentioned in the next preceding article, unless otherwise specified in this present article.

The said commissioners shall meet, in the first instance, at Albany, in the State of New York, and shall have power to adjourn to such other place or places as they shall think fit: The said commissioners shall, by a report or declaration, under their hands and seals, designate the boundary through the said river, lakes, and water communications, and decide to which of the two contracting parties the several Islands lying within the said river, lakes, and water communications, do respectively belong, in conformity with the true intent of the said treaty of one thousand seven hundred and eighty-three. And both parties agree to consider such designation and decision as final and conclusive. And in the event of the said two commissioners differing, or both, or either of them, refusing, declining, or wilfully omitting to act, such reports, declarations or statements, shall be made by them, or either of them, and such reference to a friendly sovereign or state shall be made in all respects as in the latter part of the fourth article is contained, and in as full a manner as if the same was herein repeated.

Article the Seventh

It is further agreed that the said two last mentioned commissioners, after they shall have executed the duties assigned to them in the preceding article, shall be and they are hereby authorized, upon their oaths impartially to fix and determine, according to the true intent of the said treaty of peace, of one thousand seven hundred and eighty-three, that part of the boundary between the dominions of the two powers, which extends from the water communication between Lake Huron and Lake Superior, to the most north-western point of the lake of the woods, to decide to which of the two parties the several islands lying in the lakes, water communications, and rivers, forming the said boundary, do respectively belong, in conformity with the true intent of the said treaty of peace, of one thousand seven hundred and eighty-three; and to cause such parts of the said boundary, as require it, to be surveyed and marked.

The said commissioners shall, by a report or declaration under their hands and seals, designate the boundary aforesaid, state their decision on the points thus referred to them, and particularize the latitude and longitude of the most north-western point of the lake of the woods, and of such other parts of the said boundary as they may deem proper. And both parties agree to consider such designation and decision as final and conclusive. And, in the event of the said two commissioners differing, or both, or either of them refusing, declining, or wilfully omitting to act, such reports, declarations, or statements, shall be made by them, or either of them, and such reference to a friendly sovereign or state, shall be made in all respects, as in the latter part of the fourth article is contained, and in as full a manner as if the same was herein repeated.

Article the Eighth

The several boards of two commissioners mentioned in the

four preceding articles, shall respectively have power to appoint a secretary, and to employ such surveyors or other persons as they shall judge necessary. Duplicates of all their respective reports, declarations, statements and decisions, and of their accounts, and of the journal of their proceedings, shall be delivered by them to the agents of his Britannic Majesty, and to the agents of the United States, who may be respectively appointed and authorized to manage the business on behalf of their respective governments.

The said commissioners shall be respectively paid in such manner as shall be agreed between the two contracting parties, such agreement being to be settled at the time of the exchange of the ratifications of this treaty. And all other expenses attending the said commissioners shall be defrayed equally by the two parties. And in the case of death, sickness, resignation, or necessary absence, the place of every such commissioner respectively shall be supplied in the same manner as such commissioner was first appointed, and the new commissioner shall take the same oath or affirmation, and do the same duties.

It is further agreed between the two contracting parties, that in case any of the islands mentioned in any of the preceding articles, which were in the possession of one of the parties prior to the commencement of the present war between the two countries, should, by the decision of any of the boards of commissioners aforesaid, or of the sovereign or state so referred to, as in the four next preceding articles contained, fall within the dominions of the other party, all grants of land made previous to the commencement of the war by the party having had such possession, shall be as valid as if such island or islands, had by such decision or decisions, been adjudged to be within the dominions of the party having had such possession.

Article the Ninth

The United States of America engage to put an end immediately after the ratification of the present treaty, to hostilities with all the tribes or nations of Indians, with whom they may be at war at the time of such ratification; and forthwith to restore to such tribes or nations, respectively, all the possessions, rights and privileges, which they may have enjoyed or been entitled to in one thousand eight hundred and eleven, previous to such hostilities: Provided always, that such tribes or nations shall agree to desist from all hostilities, against the United States of America, their citizens and subjects, upon the ratification of the present treaty being notified to such tribes or nations, and shall so desist accordingly.

And his Britannic Majesty engages, on his part, to put an end immediately after the ratification of the present treaty, to hostilities with all the tribes or nations of Indians with whom he may be at war at the time of such ratification, and forthwith to restore to such tribes or nations, respectively all the possessions, rights, and privileges, which they may have enjoyed or been entitled to, in one thousand eight hundred and eleven, previous to such hostilities: Provided always, that such tribes or nations shall agree to desist from all hostilities against his Britannic Majesty, and his subjects, upon the ratification of the present treaty being notified to such tribes or nations, and shall so desist accordingly.

Article the Tenth

Whereas the traffic in slaves is irreconcilable with the principles of humanity and justice, and whereas both his Majesty and the United States are desirous of continuing their efforts to promote its entire abolition, it is hereby agreed that both the contracting parties shall use their best endeavours to accomplish so desirable an object.

Article the Eleventh

This treaty when the same shall have been ratified on both sides, without alteration by either of the contracting parties, and the ratifications mutually exchanged, shall be binding on both parties, and the ratifications shall be exchanged at Washington, in the space of four months from this day, or sooner if practicable.

In faith whereof, we the respective plenipotentiaries have signed this treaty, and have thereunto affixed our seals.

Done in triplicate, at Ghent, the twenty-fourth day of December, one thousand eight hundred and fourteen.

(L.S.)	Gambier,
(L.S.)	Henry Goulburn,
(L.S.)	William Adams,
(L.S.)	John Quincy Adams,
(L.S.)	J. A. Bayard,
(L.S.)	H. Clay,
(L.S.)	Jona. Russell,
(L.S.)	Albert Gallatin,

Now therefore, to the end that the said treaty of peace and amity may be observed with good faith, on the part of the United States, I, James Madison, president as aforesaid, have caused the premises to be made public and I do hereby enjoin all persons bearing office, civil or military, within the United States, and all others, citizens or inhabitants thereof, or being within the same, faithfully to observe and fulfil the said treaty and every clause and article thereof.

In testimony whereof, I have caused the seal of the United States to be affixed to these (L. S.) presents, and signed the same with my hand.

Done at the City of Washington, this eighteenth day of February, in the year of our Lord one thousand eight hundred and fifteen, and of the sovereignty and independence of the United States the thirty-ninth.

James Madison.

By the President,
James Monroe, Acting Secretary of State.

Appendix

An Alphabetical List of Privateers and Letters-of-Marque, with the Names of the Captains, and Where Belonging, in the Years 1812, '13, and '14.

Denomination.	Names.	Commanders.	Where Belonging.
Privateer,	America,	Chever,	Salem.
Letter-of-Marque,	America,	Richardson,	Baltimore.
Letter-of-Marque,	Argus,	Snow,	Boston.
Privateer,	Atlas,	Maffet,	Philadelphia.
Privateer,	Alfred,	Williams,	Salem.
Privateer,	Alexander,	Crowningshield,	Salem.
Privateer,	Antelope,		Newburyport.
Letter-of-Marque,	Adeline,	Craycroft,	Philadelphia.
Privateer,	Anaconda,	Shaler,	New York.
Privateer,	Amelia,		Baltimore.
Privateer,	Active,	Patterson,	Salem.
Privateer,	Arrow,	Conklin,	New York.
Privateer,	Argo,		Baltimore.
Privateer,	Avon,	Snow & Nye,	Boston.
Privateer,	Abaellino,	Wyer,	Boston.
Privateer,	Buckskin,	Bray,	Salem.
Privateer,	Bona,	Dameron,	Baltimore.
Privateer,	Bunker Hill,	Lewis,	New York.
Privateer,	Benj. Franklin,	Ingersol,	New York.
Privateer,	Black-Joke,	Brown,	New York.
Letter-of-Marque,	Baltimore,		Baltimore.
Letter-of-Marque,	Bellona,		Philadelphia.
Letter-of-Marque,	Brutus,	Austin,	Boston.
Privateer,	Blakely,	Uran,	Boston.
Privateer,	Blockade,		Bristol.
Privateer,	Catherine,	Burnham,	Boston.
Letter-of-Marque,	Criterion,	Waterman,	New York.
Privateer,	Comet,	Boyle,	Baltimore.
Privateer,	China,		New York.

Denomination.	Names.	Commanders.	Where Belonging.
Letter-of-Marque,	Clara,		Baltimore.
Privateer,	Caroline,	Almeda,	Baltimore.
Letter-of-Marque,	Com. Decatur,	Brown,	Philadelphia.
Privateer,	Chasseur,	Boyle,	Baltimore.
Privateer,	Cossack,	Upton,	Salem.
Privateer,	Cadet,		Salem.
Privateer,	Curlew,	Wm. Wyer,	Boston.
Privateer,	Charles Morris,	Russell,	Boston.
Letter-of-Marque,	Cossack,		Baltimore.
Privateer,	Chas. Stewart,	Purcell,	Boston.
Privateer,	Cumberland,		Salem.
Privateer,	Champlain,		Boston.
Privateer,	Castigator,		Salem.
Privateer,	Dolphin,	Stafford,	Baltimore.
Privateer,	Dolphin,	Endicot,	Salem.
Privateer,	Dromo,		Boston.
Privateer,	Decatur,	Nickols,	Newburyport.
Privateer,	Decatur,	Diron,	Charleston.
Privateer,	Dart,	Davis,	Salem.
Privateer,	Divided we fall	Cropsey,	New York.
Privateer,	Diomede,	Briggs,	Salem.
Letter-of-Marque,	Delila,		Baltimore.
Privateer,	Delisle,		Baltimore.
Privateer,	Dash,		Portland.
Privateer,	Dash,	Carroway,	Baltimore.
Letter-of-Marque,	Dash,		Philadelphia.
Letter-of-Marque,	David Porter,	Coggeshall,	New York.
Letter-of-Marque,	Diamond,		Baltimore.
Privateer,	Eagle,		Charleston.
Privateer,	Eagle,	Beaufon,	New York.
Privateer,	Eldridge Gerry,		Portland.
Privateer,	Expedition,		Baltimore.
Letter-of-Marque,	Eliza,		Charleston.
Privateer,	Enterprize,	Morgan,	Salem.
Privateer,	Fame,	Webb,	Salem.
Privateer,	Fame,	Green,	Boston.
Privateer,	Fair-Trader,	Morgan,	Salem.
Privateer,	Fox,	Jack,	Baltimore.
Privateer,	Fox,	Handy and Brown,	Portsmouth.
Privateer,	Fly,		Salem.

Denomination.	Names.	Commanders.	Where Belonging.
Privateer,	Frolic,	Odiorne,	Salem.
Letter-of-Marque,	Flirt,	Storer,	New York.
Privateer,	Fairy,		Baltimore.
Letter-of-Marque,	Falcon,	George Wilson,	Baltimore.
Privateer,	Gov. McKean,		Philadelphia.
Privateer,	Globe,	Murphy,	Baltimore.
Privateer,	G.Washington,		Norfolk.
Privateer,	Gen. Armstrong.	Reid,	New York.
Privateer,	Gen. Putnam,	Evans,	Salem.
Privateer,	Growler,	Lindsey,	Salem.
Letter-of-Marque,	Gossamer,	Goodrich,	Boston.
Privateer,	Gallinipper,	Wellman,	Salem.
Privateer,	Gov.Tompkins	Shaler,	New York.
Privateer,	Grand Turk,	Breed & Green,	Salem.
Privateer,	Gov. Gerry,		Fair Haven.
Letter-of-Marque,	Gypsey,		New York.
Privateer,	Gov. Plumer,	Mudge,	Portsmouth.
Privateer,	Guerriere,	Barnham,	Portsmouth.
Letter-of-Marque,	Grampus,	Murphy,	Baltimore.
Privateer,	Gen. Stark,		Salem.
Letter-of-Marque,	Galloway,		New York.
Privateer,	George Little,	Spooner,	Boston.
Privateer,	High Flyer,	Gavet,	Baltimore.
Privateer,	Hunter,	Upton,	Boston.
Privateer,	Holkar,	Rowland,	New York.
Privateer,	Hyder Ali,	Thorndike,	Boston.
Letter-of-Marque,	Hero,	Waterman,	New York.
Privateer,	Hornet,	Frost,	Baltimore.
Privateer,	Hero,		Newbern.
Privateer,	Hawk,		Washington.
Privateer,	Hazard,	Le Chantier,	New York.
Letter-of-Marque,	Henry Guilder,		New York.
Privateer,	Harrison,		Baltimore.
Privateer,	Harlequin,	E. D. Brown,	Portsmouth.
Letter-of-Marque,	Herald,		New York.
Privateer,	Harpy,	Nichols,	Baltimore.
Letter-of-Marque,	Hope,		Philadelphia.
Privateer,	Industry,		Marblehead.
Privateer,	Isaac Hull,		New York.
Privateer,	Invincible,		New York.

Denomination	Names	Commanders	Where Belonging
Privateer,	Ino,	White,	Boston.
Letter-of-Marque,	Ida,	Mantor,	Boston.
Privateer,	Jefferson,	Kehew,	Salem.
Privateer,	John,	Crowningshield and Fairfield.	Salem.
Privateer,	John & George,		Salem.
Privateer,	Joel Barlow,		Boston.
Privateer,	Jacks Favorite,	Johnson & Miller,	New York.
Letter-of-Marque,	Jonquill,	Carman,	New York.
Letter-of-Marque,	James Monroe,	Skinner,	New York.
Privateer,	Joseph & Mary	Wescott,	Baltimore.
Letter-of-Marque,	Jacob Jones,	Roberts,	Boston.
Privateer,	Kemp,	Jacobs,	Baltimore.
Privateer,	Leo,		Boston.
Privateer,	Lion,		Marblehead.
Privateer,	Leander,		Baltimore.
Privateer,	Leader,		Providence.
Letter-of-Marque,	Leo,	Coggeshall,	Baltimore.
Privateer,	Liberty,	Pratt,	Baltimore.
Privateer,	Lady Madison,		Charleston.
Privateer,	Lovely Lass,		Wilmington.
Privateer,	Lovely Cordelia,		Charleston.
Privateer,	Lark,	Banker,	New York.
Letter-of-Marque,	Lottery,	Southcomb,	Baltimore.
Privateer,	Ludlow,		Portsmouth.
Privateer,	Lawrence,	Veasy,	Baltimore.
Privateer,	Leach,		Salem.
Letter-of-Marque,	Little George,		Boston.
Privateer,	Madison,	Elwell,	Salem.
Privateer,	Marengo,	Redois,	New York.
Privateer,	Matilda,		Philadelphia.
Privateer,	Mars,		Portsmouth.
Privateer,	Mars,		New London.
Privateer,	Mars,		Portland.
Privateer,	Mars,		New York.
Privateer,	Mary Ann,		Charleston.
Privateer,	Montgomery,	Stout,	Salem.
Privateer,	Macedonian,	P. Townsend,	Portsmouth.
Privateer,	Macedonian,		Boston.
Letter-of-Marque,	Midas,	Thompson,	Baltimore.

Denomination.	Names.	Commanders.	Where Belonging.
Privateer,	Mammoth,		Baltimore.
Privateer,	Macdonough,		Rhode Isla
Privateer,	Macdonough,		Boston.
Privateer,	Morgianna,		New York.
Privateer,	Nonsuch,	Lovely,	Baltimore.
Privateer,	Nonpareil,		Charleston.
Privateer,	Nancy,	Smart,	Salem.
Letter-of-Marque,	Ned,	Dawson,	Baltimore.
Letter-of-Marque,	Orlando,	Babson,	Gloucester.
Privateer,	Owl,	Duncan,	Salem.
Privateer,	Orders in Council,	Howard,	New York.
Privateer,	Polly,	Handy,	Salem.
Privateer,	Paul Jones,	Hazzard,	New York.
Privateer,	Patriot,	Merihew,	New York.
Privateer,	Poor Sailor,		Charleston.
Letter-of-Marque,	Pilot,		Baltimore.
Privateer,	Patapsco,	Mortimer,	Baltimore.
Privateer,	Prince de Neufchâtel,	Ordronaux,	New York.
Privateer,	Providence,	Hopkins,	Newport.
Privateer,	Perry,	Coleman,	Baltimore.
Privateer,	Pike,		Baltimore.
Privateer,	Portsmouth,	John Sinclair & T. M. Shaw,	Portsmouth.
Privateer,	Rapid,		Charleston.
Privateer,	Rossie,	Barney,	Baltimore.
Privateer,	Rosamond,	Campan,	New York.
Privateer,	Revenge,	Sinclair,	Salem.
Privateer,	Revenge,	Miller,	Baltimore.
Privateer,	Revenge,		Philadelphia.
Privateer,	Regulator,	Mansfield,	Salem.
Privateer,	Rover,	Ferris,	New York.
Privateer,	Right of Search,		New York.
Privateer,	Retaliation,	Newton,	New York.
Privateer,	Rolla,	Dooley,	Baltimore.
Letter-of-Marque,	Rambler,	Edes,	Boston.
Privateer,	Rattlesnake,	Maffet,	Philadelphia.
Privateer,	Roger,	Quarles,	Norfolk.
Privateer,	Resolution.		Baltimore.

Denomination.	Names.	Commanders.	Where Belonging.
Privateer,	Reindeer,	Snow,	Boston.
Privateer,	Ranger,		Boston.
Privateer,	Snow-bird,		Marblehead.
Privateer,	Sword-fish,		Salem.
Privateer,	Spencer,		Philadelphia.
Letter-of-Marque,	Siro,		Baltimore.
Privateer,	Sarah Ann,	Moon,	Baltimore.
Privateer,	Saratoga,	Champlin,	New York.
Privateer,	Saucy Jack,	Chazel,	Charleston.
Privateer,	Sparrow,	Burch,	Baltimore.
Privateer,	Shadow,	Taylor,	Philadelphia.
Privateer,	Swallow,		New York.
Privateer,	Spy,		New Orleans.
Privateer,	Snap Dragon,		Newbern.
Letter-of-Marque,	Sabine,		Baltimore.
Privateer,	Swiftsure,		
Privateer,	Surprise,	Barnes,	Baltimore.
Privateer,	Surprise,		Salem.
Privateer,	Scourge,	Nicoll,	New York.
Privateer,	Shark,		New York.
Privateer,	Syren,		Baltimore.
Privateer,	Scorpion,	Osborn,	Salem.
Letter-of-Marque,	Sphynx,		Boston.
Letter-of-Marque,	Sine-qua-non,	Pond,	New York.
Privateer,	Sine-qua-non,	Luce,	Boston.
Privateer,	Saranac,		Baltimore.
Privateer,	Science,	Fernald,	Portsmouth.
Privateer,	Spit Fire,	Miller,	New York.
Privateer,	Squando,	W. Watson,	Portsmouth.
Privateer,	Teazer,	Dobson,	New York.
Privateer,	Tom,	Wilson,	Baltimore.
Privateer,	Turn-over,	Southmead,	New York.
Privateer,	Trasher,		Salem.
Letter-of-Marque,	Transit,	Richardson,	Baltimore.
Privateer,	Two Brothers,		New Orleans.
Privateer,	Thorn,	Hooper,	Marblehead.
Privateer,	Thomas,	Shaw,	Portsmouth.
Privateer,	Tartar,	King,	New York.
Privateer,	True blooded Yankee,	Hailey & Oxnard,	

Denomination.	Names.	Commanders.	Where Belonging.
Privateer,	Terrible,		Salem.
Privateer,	Timothy Pickering,		Salem.
Letter-of-Marque,	Tuckahoe,		Baltimore.
Privateer,	Tomahawk,	Besom.	
Privateer,	Two Friends,		Barnstable.
Privateer,	Unit'd we stand	Story,	New York.
Privateer,	Union,	Hicks,	New York.
Privateer,	Viper,		Salem.
Privateer,	Volunteer,		New York.
Letter-of-Marque,	Viper,	Dithurbide,	New York.
Letter-of-Marque,	Volant,	Perley,	Boston.
Privateer,	Wily Reynard,	Riggs,	Boston.
Privateer,	Wasp,		Philadelphia.
Privateer,	Wasp,	Taylor,	Baltimore.
Privateer,	Wasp,	Erving,	Salem.
Letter-of-Marque,	Water Witch,		New York.
Privateer,	Water Witch,		Bristol.
Privateer,	Whig,		Baltimore.
Privateer,	Warrior,	Champlin,	New York.
Privateer,	Xebec Ultor,		Baltimore.
Privateer,	Yankee,	Wilson & Smith,	Bristol.
Privateer,	Young Eagle,		New York.
Privateer,	Yorktown,	Story,	New York.
Privateer	Young Teazer,	Dobson,	New York.
Privateer,	Young Wasp,		Philadelphia.
Privateer,	York,	Staples,	Baltimore.
Privateer.	Yankee Lass,	Churchill,	

Captain Jasper Cropsey, after commanding the privateer *Divided We Fall*, took command of the letter-of-marque schooner *Brothers*, and sailed from New York on the 3rd of June, 1813, for Bordeaux, and was never after heard from. He is supposed to have been lost at sea. The letter-of-marque schooner *Sine-quanon*, of New York, commanded by Captain Adam Pond, a native of Milford, Conn., arrived at New York on the 26th of April, 1815, twenty-five days from La Rochelle, bringing the following intelligence, that Bonaparte had landed at Frejus, from Elba, with six hundred followers, where he was immediately joined by General Berthier, with twenty thousand men. With these he marched to Paris, where he arrived on the 20th of March, at the head of eighty thousand soldiers. He immediately resumed the throne. Louis XVIII. and his family fled in great haste to England.

The whole number of privateers and private-armed ships that were commissioned as cruising vessels, and all others actively engaged in commerce during our war with Great Britain, in the years 1812, 1813 and 1814, were two hundred and fifty sail. They belonged to the different ports in the United States, as follows:

From Baltimore		58
"	New York	55
"	Salem	40
"	Boston	31
The True-blooded Yankee was owned in Boston, but fitted out of France,		1
From Philadelphia,		14
"	Portsmouth, N. H.,	11
"	Charleston,	10
"	Marblehead,	4
"	Bristol, R. I,	4
"	Portland,	3
"	Newburyport,	2
"	Norfolk,	2
"	Newbern, N. C.,	2

From New Orleans,		2
" New London,		1
" Newport, R. I.,		1
" Providence, R. I.,		1
" Barnstable, Mass.,		1
" Fair Haven, Mass.,		1
" Gloucester, Mass.,		1
" Washington City,		1
" Wilmington, N. C.,		1
From places not designated, probably small vessels belonging to eastern ports,		3
Total		250

Since the first edition of this work was published, I find that in lieu of four privateers belonging to Marblehead, there were seven carrying together 45 carriage-guns, and about four hundred men. The whole number of seamen belonging to this port who served during the war of 1812 in public and private armed vessels, amounted to seven hundred and fifty men. This information was communicated to the Hon. James Guthrie, Secretary of the Treasury, by William Bartoll, Esq. Collector of that port on the 7th of July, 1856.

ALSO FROM LEONAUR
AVAILABLE IN SOFTCOVER OR HARDCOVER WITH DUST JACKET

CAPTAIN OF THE 95th (Rifles) by *Jonathan Leach*—An officer of Wellington's Sharpshooters during the Peninsular, South of France and Waterloo Campaigns of the Napoleonic Wars.

BUGLER AND OFFICER OF THE RIFLES by *William Green & Harry Smith* With the 95th (Rifles) during the Peninsular & Waterloo Campaigns of the Napoleonic Wars

BAYONETS, BUGLES AND BONNETS by *James 'Thomas' Todd*—Experiences of hard soldiering with the 71st Foot - the Highland Light Infantry - through many battles of the Napoleonic wars including the Peninsular & Waterloo Campaigns

THE ADVENTURES OF A LIGHT DRAGOON by *George Farmer & G.R. Gleig*—A cavalryman during the Peninsular & Waterloo Campaigns, in captivity & at the siege of Bhurtpore, India

THE COMPLEAT RIFLEMAN HARRIS by *Benjamin Harris as told to & transcribed by Captain Henry Curling*—The adventures of a soldier of the 95th (Rifles) during the Peninsular Campaign of the Napoleonic Wars

WITH WELLINGTON'S LIGHT CAVALRY by *William Tomkinson*—The Experiences of an officer of the 16th Light Dragoons in the Peninsular and Waterloo campaigns of the Napoleonic Wars.

SURTEES OF THE RIFLES by *William Surtees*—A Soldier of the 95th (Rifles) in the Peninsular campaign of the Napoleonic Wars.

ENSIGN BELL IN THE PENINSULAR WAR by *George Bell*—The Experiences of a young British Soldier of the 34th Regiment 'The Cumberland Gentlemen' in the Napoleonic wars.

WITH THE LIGHT DIVISION by *John H. Cooke*—The Experiences of an Officer of the 43rd Light Infantry in the Peninsula and South of France During the Napoleonic Wars

NAPOLEON'S IMPERIAL GUARD: FROM MARENGO TO WATERLOO by *J. T. Headley*—This is the story of Napoleon's Imperial Guard from the bearskin caps of the grenadiers to the flamboyance of their mounted chasseurs, their principal characters and the men who commanded them.

BATTLES & SIEGES OF THE PENINSULAR WAR by *W. H. Fitchett*—Corunna, Busaco, Albuera, Ciudad Rodrigo, Badajos, Salamanca, San Sebastian & Others

AVAILABLE ONLINE AT **www.leonaur.com**
AND OTHER GOOD BOOK STORES

www.ingramcontent.com/pod-product-compliance
Lightning Source LLC
Chambersburg PA
CBHW031306150426
43191CB00005B/102